THE MAVERICK
AND HIS MACHINE

THE MAVERICK
AND HIS MACHINE

THOMAS WATSON, SR.
AND THE MAKING OF IBM

Kevin Maney

WILEY

John Wiley & Sons, Inc.

Published by John Wiley & Sons, Inc., Hoboken, New Jersey.
Published simultaneously in Canada.

For general information on our other products and services please contact our Customer
Care Department within the U.S. at (800) 762-2974, outside the United States at (317)
572-3993 or fax (317) 572-4002.

Wiley also publishes its books in a variety of electronic formats. Some content that
appears in print may not be available in electronic books.

Library of Congress Cataloging-in-Publication Data:
Maney, Kevin, 1960–
    Thomas Watson, Sr., IBM, and the building of an American dynasty / Kevin Maney.
        p. cm.
    ISBN 0-471-41463-8 (cloth : alk. paper)
    1. Computer industry—United States—History.   2. International Business Machines
Corporation—History.   3. Businessmen—United States—Biography.   4. Watson,
Thomas John, 1874–1956.   5. Watson, Thomas J., 1914–   6. Waston, Arthur
Kittredge, 1919–1974.   I. Title.
    HD9696.2.U62 W386 2003
    338.7'61004'092—dc21
                                                                                    2002014047

Printed in the United States of America

10 9 8 7 6 5 4 3 2 1

For Alison and Sam

ACKNOWLEDGMENTS

 OWE A HUGE DEBT TO ROB WILSON FOR BULLDOZ-
ing through IBM's traditional policy of not
helping authors. My long tenure of fairly and
accurately covering IBM helped immensely—
well, that's what Rob told me, anyway. The decision went
up the chain to CEO Lou Gerstner. I owe him a thank you
for saying yes.

My good fortune continued. Members of Watson's family agreed to help, for which I am grateful. Watson-era IBM
executives and employees—most of them in their late 80s or
90s—readily agreed to be interviewed, some on the record
and some off. I was thrilled when Peter Drucker, the great
management writer, invited me to his home to talk about his
encounters with Watson and Watson's place in business history. He helped make everything make sense.

I'm also lucky to know Jim Collins. Over the years, he
and I have engaged in many conversations about leadership
and greatness, and about life in general. Jim had a tremendous influence on the way I thought about Watson. I can't
thank him enough for being such a good friend, mentor,
and colleague.

I have others I want to thank:

~ Everyone at *USA Today* for being so understanding,
particularly Tom Curley, Karen Jurgensen, Julie Schmit,
Geri Tucker, and John Hillkirk. Also, the staff in the
USA Today library, who came to my rescue on a number
of research problems.
~ The wonderful, professional, and helpful staff of the
IBM Archives: Paul C. Lasewicz, Dawn Stanford, Ken
W. Sayers, Ellen Pierce, Robert Godfrey, and Jennifer

Halloran. Also, in Kingston, working with IBM, John W. Roberts and Kay Zaharis of History Associates.

~ Lucinda Watson and Dave McKinney for being my links to the Watson family.

~ Robert Schumann for opening up his family collection, and for being so nice to my mom for so many years.

~ Ed Pears, director of the Watson Homestead. Watson's childhood home is now both a retreat and a guardian of Watson family history.

~ The *Binghamton Press,* for allowing me to rummage through its immense library of original newspaper clippings. Also in the Binghamton area: The Broome County Historical Society, Binghamton University, and the management and public relations staff at IBM's Endicott facilities. Thank you, Christine Dlugokencky, for helping with research as an intern for a semester.

~ In Dayton, Ohio: The Montgomery County Historical Society, the Dayton Public Library's Local History Research Room, and the NCR Archives and public relations staff.

~ The Elm's Inn in Ridgefield, Connecticut—my warm home away from home, where I could come back to life after a day spent digging through Watson boxes in a windowless room at IBM. Also: The City Square Café in Manassas, Virginia, for the perfect office on the second floor; Java Jack's in Manassas, for the friendly breaks when I came by for the necessary jolts of coffee; Eric and Beth Sullivan, for loaning me hundreds of postcards from the early days of IBM and Endicott-Johnson; Danny Shader and Larry Downes for early reads and suggestions; my friends Deb Perkins and Paul Kobrin, for always being ready to listen when I needed them most; and my brothers Dave and Scott, for their ideas, insights, and love.

~ In the world of books, my agent, Sandy Dijkstra, for convincing me I should do this project and then finding a way to make it happen; my editor, Airie Stuart, for believing in the book from the beginning and for her thoughtful suggestions throughout; Michelle Patterson, for her enthusiastic marketing and for putting up with Airié and me endlessly obsessing over the cover; Lori Sayde-Mehrtens, for getting the word out; I would like to offer special thanks to the managing editor for this book, the late Mark MacDonald, whose careful shepherding of this book and special energy through the production and copyediting process will be remembered; and Tom Laughman for his good work at North Market Street Graphics.

Finally, I thank my family for hanging in there through a couple of tortuous years, during which it seemed like I spent every waking hour working. My wife, Janet, held the house and kids together, cheered me on constantly, and acted as first reader as the chapters came out of the computer printer. I'm grateful that she's given me her love and support even in the darkest moments. Alison and Sam provided plenty of reason to keep going, because I knew that once I'd finished the book, I'd again have time for soccer on the side yard, day trips to the Smithsonian, wrestling on the floor, and all those other things that I like to do with the best daughter and son in the universe.

KEVIN MANEY
Clifton, Virginia
2002

CONTENTS

FOREWORD

RECALL THE DAY IN 1999 WHEN KEVIN MANEY called to describe his idea for this book. "IBM has told me that I can have access to all of Thomas J. Watson Sr.'s documents and files," he said. "Do you realize that there are boxes of letters and verbatim transcripts that haven't been opened in decades? A biography of Watson just begs to be done."

At first, the biography seemed like a right-angle turn for Kevin. His *USA Today* column had become de rigueur reading for anyone interested in the intersection of technology and business, and he was perfectly positioned to write the definitive work on the new economy at the very height of the Internet boom. Instead, he burbled over with excitement about unpacking crates and boxes of documents from a man who died four decades before most people had even heard of the Internet. He sounded like an archeologist who had stumbled upon a treasure trove of artifacts in the lair of a mythic hero, and he just had to bring his discoveries to the world.

We are fortunate that he did.

Kevin Maney has a peculiar genius. He is not first and foremost a business writer. Nor is he primarily a technology writer. He is a *people* writer. He has the ability to filter a cacophony of noise and sift through mountains of information to capture the inner essence of the people about whom he writes. Maney sees what people really are and then captures the truth in words. And just when we most need it, he has brought us a penetrating picture of one of the most important figures of the twentieth century, a man whose life teaches us about resiliency—individual and institutional—and much about what we need to recreate greatness in the future.

Five days after his 38th birthday, Thomas J. Watson Sr. awoke to read a banner headline, "NCR men indicted by Federal Grand Jury." There, in the second paragraph, in a long list of names, jumped out the horrific sight of the name *Watson*. Along with 30 other executives, Watson had been nailed for criminal antitrust violations, part of a scheme conceived and orchestrated by his mentor John Patterson. Two years later, at middle age when most successful people hit full stride in their work, Watson found his career shattered. Out of work and carrying the stigma of the NCR scandal, he had to start with less than zero.

There are three types of people, in terms of how they respond to crushing setbacks in life. First, there are those who never fully recover; they remain weakened and dispirited. Second, there are those who get their lives back to normal. And third, there are those, like Thomas J. Watson Sr., who turn calamity into a defining event of their lives, from which they emerge even stronger than before.

Watson set forth a mission for himself to not just get his career back on track, but to create a great company that would become a role model not only for its success, but equally, for its values. He would attain personal fame by building a successful, values-driven company and making himself known as its creator and leader. International Business Machines, the company he built brick by brick from an agglomeration of small enterprises with the innocuous name The Computing-Tabulating-Recording Company, became more than just a successful business. It became one of the most influential corporations in the world. Watson did for the concept of corporate culture what the founders of the United States did for the concept of capitalist democracy— he invented its modern model and proved that it could work in practice.

The great irony of Mr. Watson is that his own self-centric leadership style laid the seeds of IBM's later difficulties, yet his genius for building a culture transferred his personal trait of resiliency into an institutional trait that transcended him. The story of IBM's return to greatness in the 1990s is as much the story of Thomas J. Watson Sr. as it is the story of Lou Gerstner. I recall delivering a seminar in the early 1990s to a group of executives, where I shared the results of research done at Stanford on enduring great companies, which included IBM. A person in the front row thrust his hand in the air, leaned forward in his chair, and challenged: "How can we take this seriously with IBM in the study set? They're going the way of the dinosaurs." Not only had IBM just lost $5 billion in one year, but for the first time in its history, IBM found itself the subject of widespread derision. "Can John Akers save IBM?" ran a cover story in *Fortune*. "Giant Missteps" blared the front page of the *Wall Street Journal*. And as yet, no one had heard of Lou Gerstner, at least not in connection with IBM.

Even so, I explained, the research team believed that IBM would return to greatness and that its troubles would later be seen as simply a time of crisis and renewal, just as its previous episodes of struggle had come and gone in the long turbulent history of IBM. It's not that we had any special prescience, but that our research had uncovered a deep truth about IBM: It had the genetics of resilience built into its very DNA. We did not know how, we did not know when, we did not know who would be leading it—but this strain of resiliency gave us deep confidence *that* it would come back, perhaps even stronger than before.

Like other leaders who become larger than life during their lives, Watson Sr. had gigantic flaws to go with his towering strengths. He was clearly a genius with a thousand helpers, yet he managed to build an institution that could transcend the genius. He made mistakes, tons of mistakes, but on the really big points he had a 100 percent hit rate. He could be petty, mean, vain—the world's first truly modern celebrity CEO. More than once while reading this book, I found myself thinking, "Why on earth would anyone work for this man?" However, his people not only worked for him, they loved him. They loved him because, when it came right down to it, he cared about the company and its people at least as much as he cared about himself.

I found myself challenged by Maney's work, because it is so truthful. Watson, a great company builder, was not a likable man, but that does not diminish his importance. Leaders like Watson are like forces of nature—almost terrifying in their release of energy and unpredictable volatility, but underneath they still adhere to certain patterns and principles. The patterns and principles might be hard to see amid the melee, but they are there nonetheless. It takes a gifted person of insight to highlight those patterns, and that is exactly what Kevin Maney does in this book. Good or bad, inspiring or maddening, we see laid bare the raw truth of a great builder in action, and the consequences of his work.

JIM COLLINS
Boulder, Colorado
July 16, 2002

INTRODUCTION

HOMAS WATSON SR. APPEARED IN A DREAM AND told me, in his powerful voice, clearing his throat as usual every couple of words, "It is your fate that you should write about me."

Well, okay, maybe not. But a series of actual events stopped just short of a phantom visit from one of the greatest business leaders of the twentieth century. At times, it seemed like some force steered me to this book, much the way an invisible hand always guided Wile E. Coyote to stand precisely under the falling anvil.

It all began during my childhood. I grew up in Binghamton, New York, a few miles down Route 17 from Endicott. In Watson's day, Endicott was IBM's hometown—its heart and soul. Watson loved spending time there, and the locals considered him a hero, or perhaps a god. I grew up hearing about Watson, sometimes riding down Watson Boulevard, and a few times swimming in the IBM Country Club pool that Watson built in the 1930s for employees.

I went off to college to get a journalism degree, and afterward was offered a job at the *Binghamton Evening Press*. The editor, Dave Mack, told me that I had my choice: I could be a night cops reporter, or a business reporter. In those days, a lot of journalists would have taken the night cops beat. But since that beat probably entailed seeing blood, I took the business reporter job.

If you covered business in the Binghamton-Endicott area, you covered IBM. So I started learning about the company, its culture, and its products. IBM made mainframe computers the size of refrigerators, and had just introduced its first personal computer. It was perhaps the most powerful, most admired corporation on the planet. This was well before IBM's fall from grace.

A couple of years later, I moved to the Westchester Rockland Newspapers, a Gannett-owned operation based down the road from IBM's world headquarters in Armonk, New York. Again, much of my job was covering IBM. A year later, I joined *USA Today,* and continued covering IBM as part of a broader technology beat. For the next 15-plus years, I wrote about technology for *USA Today,* dipping in and out of a journalistic relationship with IBM. When Louis Gerstner took over as IBM's chief executive in 1993, I wrote *USA Today*'s cover story. When he announced his retirement in 2002, I wrote that cover story, too.

All the while, my mother had been working as a personal assistant to Robert Schumann, a grandson of A. Ward Ford. In 1914, Ford was a major shareholder in the Computing-Tabulating-Recording Company (C-T-R), the forerunner to IBM. Ford helped bring Watson to C-T-R, and then became a Watson friend and a supporter on the company's board of directors. Schumann had scrapbooks to show me and family stories to tell.

In 1990, Thomas Watson Jr., Watson's son and successor as IBM's chief executive, published his autobiography, *Father, Son & Co.,* cowritten by *Fortune*'s Peter Petre. I devoured the book. Watson Jr. wrote about his father in the first part of the book, providing a snapshot of the tempestuous, driven, charismatic man who built IBM. I wanted to read more, though, and yet the only full-blown biography focused on Watson was *The Lengthening Shadow*— published in 1962, commissioned by the company, and (as I later discovered) terrifically slanted in Watson's favor.

In early 2000, I started thinking about writing a book on Watson. I figured I could find retired IBMers in Endicott who'd known Watson. Bob Schumann could open some doors. But to bring Watson to life, I knew I'd need access to his personal papers.

So I called Rob Wilson, then IBM's vice president of

media relations, with whom I'd worked on stories for years. We'd had many lunches together. We both owned beagles.

I asked Rob if there might be a closet in IBM somewhere that might house some of Watson's letters or memos. He said five words that I will always remember: "Funny you should ask that."

In a warehouse in Kingston, New York, sat 340 dusty boxes of Watson papers. Most of the tens of thousands of documents had been untouched for decades. Hardly anyone knew they existed. However, only a month or so before I called Rob, IBM decided to start cracking the boxes open and cataloging what was inside. Few people outside of IBM had ever seen the papers.

My timing seemed fateful. I was early enough to be first to get at all the boxes, but late enough so that I could draft behind the catalogers, using their indexes to help me find what I needed. It was as if the hand of Watson dropped me down into the situation at exactly the right moment.

The last straw, as they say, was my first peek inside the boxes. Watson's papers were not just random letters or dry reports. I found word-for-word notes from business meetings, including the jokes made when someone arrived late. There were letters from Watson to his children, telegrams from presidents, lists of belongings in his house, and scathing internal memos to IBM vice presidents and engineers. The boxes contained the scattered essence of Watson.

Add everything together—the accident of my hometown, my choice to cover business, the coincidence of my mom's employer, and the discovery of Watson's papers—and I knew I had to write this book. I'm glad I did. The adventure has been fascinating.

KEVIN MANEY
Clifton, Virginia
2002

PROLOGUE

IERRE BONTECOU STOOD IN THE OPEN DOORWAY OF an office on the 17th floor of International Business Machines' headquarters in the heart of New York, and waited for his eyes to adjust to the dusky light. Large windows lined the office's back wall, but throughout the day the heavy red curtains remained all but closed, lending the room a funeral parlor eeriness. After a couple of seconds, Bontecou could clearly see the tall, square-jawed man sitting erect behind his desk, which was angled in a corner at the far end of the long room and piled untidily with papers. Bontecou knew better than to step inside until IBM's chief executive, Thomas J. Watson Sr., looked up at him. Only then did Bontecou enter and cross the dark blue carpet.

Watson had called together Bontecou and a small group of engineers on July 19, 1943. They all took places around a long, heavily varnished conference table. Fred Nichol, the trumpet-voiced, sparky Watson deputy, scurried into the room and found an empty chair. A magnificent grandfather clock ticktocked in a corner. On the walnut-paneled walls were elaborate colonial sconces, a portrait of President Franklin D. Roosevelt, two mounted abacuses, and one of the ubiquitous plaques that said THINK.

Bontecou—a lanky man with a long, angular face, high forehead, and intense eyes—anticipated praise for a detailed report that Bethlehem Steel had delivered to Watson days before. Bontecou managed IBM's steel industry accounts, and he had initiated the report and worked on it with Bethlehem's executives. As IBM's second-biggest customer, Bethlehem paid $1.5 million a year—$16 million in 2002 dollars—to rent IBM tabulating and accounting machines.

The report laid out 32 explicit recommendations—some about small improvements, others about major strategic directions. The previous Thursday, in a meeting with Bontecou and these same IBM engineers, Watson saw the report for the first time and read every one of the recommendations aloud, agreeing with most of them. He praised Bethlehem Steel for being candid and thorough. Therefore, at this follow-up meeting, Bontecou never expected Watson to rip into him.

"This is the most terrible thing that ever happened in this business," Watson barked.[1]

"Why did you let this develop?" Watson said, turning to Bontecou. "You know, that man Schick, he just kicked me and the IBM all over the place. And you fellows set up the pins for him to knock down, and I happened to be the center pin."

F. A. Schick was Bethlehem's comptroller. He'd been comptroller since the 1910s and always seemed to have it in for IBM. Schick personally handed Watson the report in question and sharply told Watson to fix those 32 items or Bethlehem would dump IBM.

"What that man Schick said to me—don't you realize what a position I was in?" Watson seethed. "I had to be nice to him. I didn't know what was in the book, *fortunately,* because if I had, I couldn't have held myself down. I would have blown it out of the window that night."

Watson was at the height of his power and fame. He'd built IBM into an international phenomenon. IBM had beaten the Great Depression, growing like mad while most companies shriveled. Watson was the highest-paid American through the 1930s, getting a bigger salary than the more glamorous contenders, Hollywood mogul Samuel Goldwyn and comedian Will Rogers. Watson had made himself into a celebrity businessman—the *first* celebrity businessman—in an era when company presidents weren't much admired. He got great gobs of coverage in the media.

"THINK"—the slogan that he'd invented—was so well known it was the subject of jokes and cartoons. Watson's progressive policies toward his workers, his ban on alcohol, his bizarre company songs, his revival-like conventions where attendees slept in tents—it all fed the fascination with Watson.

At the same time, IBM's products tickled the imagination of the public. Nobody but back-office workers buried deep inside big companies ever touched IBM machines—clacking, noisy electromechanical contraptions that sorted, counted, and manipulated data stored on rectangular cards punched with holes. However, to an average person on a street in Boston or a farm in Iowa, IBM made what the press called "electric brains." Such a machine was both scary and wonderful at the same time.

The fame coupled with IBM's startling growth made Watson certain that he was a man of destiny, and a man of destiny would not suffer a threat from an annoying mosquito like Schick. Watson wanted a showdown with Bethlehem Steel.

In his office that day, Watson understood what Bontecou and the others around the table just couldn't. Schick was playing a serious game. He had sent 55 Bethlehem men into IBM's engineering departments, on an invitation from Bontecou, to compile a report on the tabulating needs of the steel industry. The Bethlehem men researched all of IBM's plans, inventions, and pending fixes to problems. Then Bethlehem massaged the information, put it in a report full of suggestions for plans, inventions, and fixes, and presented the whole thing back to IBM, as if all the ideas had come from Bethlehem.

Schick made 150 copies of the report.

"Why did they want 150 copies?" Watson asked his men.

Silence. Then Nichol answered. "I could not say, Mr. Watson."

"I could say!" Watson stormed. "They wanted to be on record that Bethlehem Steel is running the development end of IBM. That's what they wanted it for. Why would they want 150 copies? They have distributed every one of them somewhere."

The report could allow Schick to claim that IBM's successes for years to come were the result of Bethlehem's ideas. Bethlehem might then be able to make IBM share patents or force IBM to give Bethlehem better deals on the dozens of tabulating machines that helped run the steelmaker's factories, tally its inventories, and account for workers' salaries.

Watson turned to Bontecou and told him to write a letter to Bethlehem saying that because Schick was so unhappy with IBM's current products, Watson would pull all IBM machines out of the steelmaker's factories and offices. Since the machines were rented, Watson could yank them from a customer. "If they aren't satisfied with our stuff and we are doing such a terrible job, I would like to take it all out," Watson told his men.

"I don't know what they would do if we did," Bontecou said.

"I don't care two hoots what they would do," Watson said. "They would welcome it right now."

"They couldn't run that yard without the equipment, Mr. Watson."

"He said they can, and I am going to let them have a chance to do it."

Watson knew that Bethlehem would grind to a halt, but IBM would barely feel any hurt. As World War II raged, Allied armies and war-related industries soaked up so many of IBM's machines, many potential customers had to be turned away. Watson could refurbish the machines pulled from Schick and install them at some desperate bank or manufacturer.

Nichol reminded Watson that Bethlehem was making steel for ships and tanks, structural steel for defense plants, and forgings for guns, shells, and aircraft engines. The federal government might come down on IBM for interfering with a war contract. Watson blew off Nichol's concern.

"What difference does it make?" Watson said. IBM could place the machines pulled from Bethlehem at another company that had war contracts. Just about every company had war contracts.

Watson sent Bontecou to deliver the message: Pull back the report, or we'll pull your machines.

Schick had no choice. He destroyed the report and acknowledged that its ideas were IBM's, not Bethlehem's. The contents never surfaced again.

As a last flourish, Watson made lucrative job offers to Schick's key underlings who did such a good job preparing the report.

1

MAVERICK KINDLING

HOMAS JOHN WATSON BEGAN HIS LIFE AT AGE 40, after Dayton, Ohio, nearly ruined him.

He'd lived his first 29 years in Upstate New York, most of it as an affable, determined, but lost young man. Over the next 11 years in Dayton, Watson learned how to win at all costs, deceive others, and gain power. The city showed him how to get to the top and enjoy wealth. It brought him a woman's love, and soon after ripped nearly everything from him except that love. In Dayton, Watson experienced fantastic success and near destruction. All of it had to happen for IBM to exist at all, and for Watson to take his place among history's great business figures.

Watson rode into Dayton by train in 1903, summoned to the city for a clandestine meeting. A gangly young man, he stood six feet, two inches tall, weighed about 175 pounds, and had to duck as he stepped through the railroad car door onto the station platform. His dark hair had thinned slightly in front, and the rest he combed tightly to his head. His face was almost rectangular when seen straight on. Watson's chin dominated his features, jutting out like the cowcatcher on a locomotive. His deep-set brown eyes looked intense but could turn warm when he unleashed his natural charm. Watson hadn't yet acquired the overpowering glare that would rattle subordinates in later years. He dressed neatly but not in any sophisticated way—he'd recently sat for a portrait wearing a checked jacket with a clashing checked shirt and a bow tie. Apparently, he considered it to be his most natty outfit. He didn't like jewelry, and he was unmarried, claiming he wanted to take his time finding exactly the right woman. That was quite a scandal for a man of 29.

Watson bounded away from the station and turned onto Dayton's streets, walking energetically, like it was a waste of time to stop moving. The city at the turn of the century buzzed. Dayton had money. Its factories turned out railroad cars, paint, and butcher scales. The people had things to talk about, like Orville and Wilbur Wright tinkering in their bicycle shop with a flying machine. Watson turned down Main Street, walking past storefront after storefront: Reed's Shoes, A. Hewsalt Jeweler, dry goods shops, piano stores, haberdasheries, and hotels. Men wearing derbies and wool suits barreled down the sidewalks. The women wore long, full skirts and broad-brimmed hats. Trolleys clattered down the center of the wide road, past horses and rigs haphazardly parked along the curb. An occasional automobile sputtered past and backfired, startling the pedestrians and horses.

Watson made his way through Dayton's center, climbed a slight rise at the edge of downtown, and first saw the headquarters and factories of the National Cash Register Company. One of the nation's most successful and innovative businesses, NCR looked nothing like any industrial company at the time. Beige brick buildings stood in a campus-style layout, overlooking a pond and lush gardens. Shrubs around all of the structures hid the foundations. Second-story walkways topped with bursting flower boxes stretched between buildings. In a company-owned field nearby, local boys sowed plots of land for vegetables for their families.

The whole place was built on the cash register, a relatively new phenomenon that had taken hold among merchants and saloonkeepers who liked the idea of being able to keep track of sales at the push of some keys. NCR, known to locals as "the Cash," monopolized the business.

At NCR's main building, behind the grand entrance framed by six gleaming white pillars, were the offices of the company's visionary, hard-driving, tyrannical founder, John H. Patterson. He and his second in command, Hugh Chalmers, had asked Watson to come see them in Dayton. As Watson approached the building, he didn't know why he'd been invited there. In the NCR organization, he was nobody special. So far, he'd been a good cash register sales-man, and after a promotion showed he could effectively manage an NCR branch office in Rochester, New York. Chalmers only told Watson to get on the train, and not tell anyone where he was going. The visit was to be kept secret.

Inside the main building, Watson found NCR's execu-tive offices to be small and spare. Dark wood lined the doors and windows and set them off against plain white walls. Patterson's office had a blackboard, a stand that held a large pad of paper for writing and drawing during pre-sentations, and a framed black-and-white drawing of an aerial view of the NCR factories. On the floor was a stand-up folding display that could be flipped to different lists that had been professionally printed in large, bold letters. One list laid out major things to do for NCR. One other docu-mented the people who were going to rent a cabin in an NCR-owned park for $100 for the summer. On Patterson's mahogany desk was a candlestick telephone and a rect-angular box with five buttons on top, each for buzzing a different secretary or subordinate.[1]

Chalmers and Patterson invited Watson to sit down, and the executives told Watson their plan. Watson was to set up an NCR-subsidized used–cash register operation. The purpose, Chalmers and Patterson explained, was to try to undercut and "knock out" the entire used–cash register industry, which was slicing into NCR's sales of new cash registers, damaging the company, and interfering with its right to control the cash register market. Watson should go back to Rochester, where he'd been living, pack, and immediately return to Dayton.

It's not clear whether Watson learned at that meeting everything that he was going to be required to do, but he certainly felt good about his assignment. On that trip back to Rochester, Watson stopped at his family home, outside of Painted Post, a town of 600 in New York State near the Pennsylvania border, to visit his seriously ill father. Watson described the mission for NCR and how important Patterson and Chalmers made it sound. He told his father that he'd have a budget of $1 million, an amount that was unfathomable to both father and son. "Well, I'm very pleased about that because what you have been doing hundreds of men can do, but now you're doing something different—something new," Watson recalled his father telling him. "It's a great opportunity."[2]

It was Watson's big break. Patterson and Chalmers had liked the way Watson handled himself in Rochester, where he showed he could be aggressive and competitive. Now Patterson and Chalmers were giving him a chance to make a major impact on the company. He would've celebrated, except that his father died that night. The timing left Watson determined to live up to his father's faith in him.

❧

In 1903, Watson disappeared from NCR records, not to reappear until 1907. He went undercover while creating The Watson Second-Hand Cash Register Company, a phony entity set up and funded by NCR, but disguised so well that it even had its own stock certificates. NCR wanted the secrecy so it could slip into the used business quietly and ruin it from within. One scrap of paper in Watson's scrawled handwriting adds up 572 shares in Watson's name. The company later was renamed American Second-Hand Cash Register Company, based in Chicago, and identified Watson as president. It advertised using fliers and postcards, and grew into a successful, profit-generating company, and it was all a ruse. The profits were an unintended consequence. The business's real purpose was to destroy the competition.[3]

Patterson was vicious when it came to competition. He believed, as did many of that era, that a monopolized industry worked better than an industry that had heated competition. Monopolies could provide uniform quality, gain economies of scale, and, of course, set prices so the monopoly business could thrive. The formula would work for companies ranging from Standard Oil in the early 1900s to Microsoft at the end of the century. Patterson also believed he had a God-given right to the cash register business. He regarded competition as a personal affront. He would not tolerate it.

In the late 1890s, Patterson realized that NCR was creating its own competition problem. NCR was so good at making cash registers that the machines tended to last for years. Independent dealers started buying used cash registers from establishments that either went out of business or bought newer models. The dealers buffed them up and sold them, more often than not to someone who otherwise would have bought a new NCR machine. It was maddening enough to Patterson when a competitor emerged to try to make a better product than NCR's. But these dealers were beating NCR with its own products. Patterson wanted it stopped.

As Watson ran it, the business worked like this: He would move into a new city and find a commercial neighborhood where one or more used–cash register businesses had storefronts. Watson would set up his storefront nearby and, for all anyone knew, open a legitimate used–cash register business. However, because Watson was backed by NCR and had no need to make a profit, he could pay more to get used cash registers and then sell them for less, both starving and undercutting all the competing stores. Watson's affable style then came into play. He or someone he'd trained would make friends with the guys running those competing storefronts. When the competing businesses started to crumble because of Watson's pricing, Watson's company, as a friendly gesture, would offer a deal. He'd buy the business out, usually for more than was necessary, which would help to prevent the competing owners from feeling railroaded. Watson would get the owners to sign a contract saying they wouldn't again get into the cash register business, except in some desolate state like Montana or Nevada. Watson would be left with the only used–cash register business in town, which he'd continue operating, eventually raising prices, making profits, and funneling the money back to NCR.

Watson aligned his operation with the wishes of NCR. In one letter dated September 7, 1907, NCR executive T. L. Ditzler ordered Watson to make sure that he shut down Messrs. Urban & Son, a second-hand dealer in Quincy, Illinois. Ditzler thought Watson had bought out all of the dealer's inventory and that the Urbans had agreed to get out of the business. But apparently they hadn't. "It would be well for you to get after them," Ditzler wrote to Watson.[4]

For nearly five years, Watson ran the used operation and ran it well. It was an extraordinary success. In city after city, used–cash register businesses were devastated. Watson did everything Patterson had hoped and more.

Of course, the whole operation stank. It was Watson's beginning and, six years later, nearly his end. The courts would rule that the operation was illegal. It was also morally wrong-headed. It involved deceit and intentionally hurt people whose only sin was opening a business that NCR didn't like.

Why did Watson take the assignment and then do it with such vigor? Watson was young and eager. He was plucked out of nowhere to come before the legendary founder of the company. Watson was in awe of Patterson, who no doubt passionately described to Watson an assignment that was extremely important to NCR. Watson had probably been told that success would bring him a promotion to NCR headquarters. Turning down the assignment would have hurt or ruined his career with the company. If someone of Patterson's stature was ordering this, Watson saw no reason to question it. If Patterson sermonized that it was right— that NCR had an obligation to rid the business of interlopers, at whatever cost—Watson would have seen no reason to argue. Watson had grown up poor and had failed in his early attempts at business. He wanted to escape his past. Add it all up, and Watson probably never considered saying no. There also is no evidence that he thought he *should* say no. He apparently had no crisis of conscience over his role in the used business. Right or wrong, Watson put everything into his new job, and had to atone for it for the rest of his life.

⁓

The used–cash register business remade Watson. First, it brought Watson to Dayton. Then his success gave him confidence that he could run his own business. In 1908, it won him a position as an assistant sales manager, a high-profile job at NCR headquarters. The promotion put Watson in constant contact with Patterson, who would be the most influential man in Watson's life for the next 30 years.

John Patterson was one of the meanest, most dynamic managers at the turn of the century. He didn't invent the cash register. He first saw one in a store in 1881. At the time, he and his brother Robert owned a Dayton coal business. The cash register was invented and sold by a 13-employee company called National Manufacturing. Intrigued, Patterson bought one of the machines for his retail coal office. Two years later, the Patterson brothers bought National Manufacturing, eventually renaming it National Cash

Register. In 1890, NCR sold 9,091 cash registers; in 1902, it sold 42,403 in the first 10 months.[5]

The brass-and-metal NCR cash registers could barely be carried by hand. Some models were decorated with so many ornate design flourishes, they looked like they should have been cash registers at Versailles. The machines were entirely mechanical—the keys pushed levers to add up sales, and a crank and gears rolled out the drawers that held the cash. Retail proprietors discovered that the contraptions could save them money. Clerks couldn't steal as easily, because the cash registers kept tabs on sales. The information from the receipts—information almost never before available—helped owners control inventory and operate more efficiently.

Patterson ran NCR like a Napoleonic dictator. He was short—no more than five feet, seven inches tall—and had a bushy white mustache, a high-pitched grating voice, and a seemingly permanent scowl. He was a tyrant. He wanted total control of NCR and of the lives of everyone who worked there. He fired men without reason and promoted them equally without reason. He was a master of manipulation.

When Watson ascended into the executive ranks, he found that Patterson regulated the details of his workers' existence. There were rules about when and how often to bathe. Posted in a shower room built for workers on the NCR campus, a sign stated: "Employees may bathe twice a week in summer and once a week in winter on the company's time." Other rules governed how much to tip hotel waiters, and what to pay for neckties, and where to buy them. The NCR sales manual, called the *Primer*, told salesmen exactly what to say, word for word. The salesmen were not to deviate from it.

Patterson manipulated his employees like a maestro in front of an orchestra. He would send rising executives overseas and tell them to spend lavishly. That way, as Patterson freely admitted, they would get a taste of the rich life and return to Dayton, hungry to make more money and ready to please Patterson to get it. During a physical fitness fad that swept up the nation, Patterson set up recreation facilities for his employees. He then ordered them to play. Executives wearing white shirts, vests, and ties would stand in unison behind their desks with arms outstretched, then touch their toes.[6] Patterson didn't promote recreation out of concern for his employees. He thought it would make them work more energetically. A contemporary biographer of Patterson wrote: "He really did not know what pleasure was. He did not know the meaning of the word recreation. He thought of pleasure and recreation not as things of themselves but as aids to efficiency."[7]

Whatever Patterson's motives, he turned NCR into an inventive and luxurious place to work. Officers each day got hot meals, which they ate together at a single circular table that sat 350. The grounds had baseball fields, tennis courts, and walking paths. Classes in a colonial-style NCR Hall of Industrial Education trained foremen and salesmen. A country club, with golf and horseback riding, was open to all employees, as was a 1,100-acre park of woods and campgrounds called Hills and Dales.

Patterson developed a system for motivating his sales force. He set up a quota system and each year welcomed those who met their quotas into what he called the Hundred Point Club. The members would go each year to a convention, where they would be wined and pampered at NCR's expense.

Watson sopped up Patterson's methods and believed in many of them. Later, at IBM, Watson would rule his company like a dictator, start an IBM school, and build an employee country club. He would create a quota system and a Hundred Percent Club.

Watson was in his 30s; Patterson, his 50s. Patterson

made Watson his protégé, and in 1910 elevated Watson from assistant sales manager to sales manager, putting Watson in charge of more than 900 salesmen in 200-plus branch offices.

Watson brought energy to the job. Though never athletic, he was slim and coiled, and seemed incapable of tiring. You can see it in a photograph of NCR's top 11 officers. Patterson sits in the middle on a bench with Watson to his immediate right. The others sit or stand around them. All look relaxed and patient, except Watson. He has a hand on one thigh and is leaning forward, ramrod stiff, as if he's ready to jump up and get going the second the flash pops.

As sales manager, Watson proved he wasn't simply a Patterson puppet. Open-minded and curious, Watson was willing to try new ideas at NCR. That's how he fatefully encountered inventor Herman Hollerith's tabulating machines.

He first saw one in Rochester, New York. Watson's mother had moved to Rochester after his father's death, and Watson still had friends in the city on the shore of Lake Ontario. On one visit, Watson stopped at Eastman Kodak, the film and camera company based in Rochester, to see Bill Ames. Watson had known Ames for years, and Ames had the same kind of job as Watson—sales manager—at Kodak. Ames told Watson that he had a new system that could monitor the performance of each salesman.

"He had a chart on the wall," Watson recalled. "He said, 'Here is Hambley in Kansas City, and he did so and so, and on such and such a day he was in St. Louis,' and he went through this and my head began to swim around because I thought—in fact, to tell you the truth, I thought I was just about as good a sales manager as Bill Ames. I said, 'Bill, by gracious, I would like to find out how to do that.' "

Ames walked Watson to the accounting department and showed him the Hollerith machines, which tabulated information using holes punched in stiff, rectangular cards. Ames asked a colleague, Jack Gorham, to pull out some cards on Kodak's salesmen. Ames would name a salesman, and Gorham would find the corresponding card and recite the salesman's numbers.

"That just opened my eyes," Watson said. When he got back to NCR, Watson contacted Hollerith's Tabulating Machine Company in Washington, D.C. Some time after the machines were installed and running, Watson called his district managers together. Without telling them about the machines, he started rattling off statistics about each district—numbers that headquarters never before could compile.

"I can see Walter Cool and Meyer Jacobs and Fred Hyde," Watson said, "because they were the three men that just always knew everything about their territories and what their men were doing, and they always got their heads together and exchanged ideas, and all three of them were writing in their notebooks. Finally . . . Mr. Hyde stood up, a great tall man, with great dignity and charm and everything else, and said, 'I want to take off my hat to you and your organization. I have always thought I was keeping track of my men. I have come out here . . . and you have told me a lot of things that I didn't know when we left home.' "

Watson let the men stay baffled all through lunch. Finally, he took them to the accounting room, showed them the machine, and let them in on his secret.[8]

∽

Watson's openness helped him win the loyalty of his salesmen. In 20 years, no one inside NCR had challenged the sales *Primer.* The *Primer,* however, stifled creativity. It told salesmen exactly what to say, and even when to point. An asterisk in the text signaled the moment to point. An example from the *Primer:*

This, * Mr. Merchant, is a National Cash Register of the most approved pattern. Now, sir, this register * makes the entries. The indication * of the transaction shows through this glass. *

As sales manager, Watson convinced Patterson that the *Primer* was too rigid. Watson and one of his most reliable staffers, Joe Rogers, wrote a new *Primer* that gave a salesman leeway to react to a situation, be creative, and develop a style that suited his personality.

NCR salesmen liked the more lenient approach. They became loyal to Watson, who, unlike Patterson, could be one of them. At a Hundred Point Club convention, Watson and a group of salesmen staged a raucous photograph. In the photo, the men are in a hotel room pretending to be doing their nails, pouring drinks, and pampering a large mustachioed man wearing a robe. Watson stands holding a pitcher, about to dump water on the large man's head—a devilish grin on his face and a cigar in his left hand. His jacket is off, exposing a white shirt and vest. Another photo shows two men, jackets off, wrestling for fun. Watson stands in a half-circle of cheering salesmen gathered around the wrestlers.

The salesmen performed for Watson. In 1911, NCR's sales of cash registers topped 100,000 for the year, more than double the sales of two years earlier.

Watson's success and popularity with the sales organization made him a star at NCR. Patterson embraced Watson, building a townhouse near his own, at 428 West First Street—Dayton's upscale neighborhood—and letting Watson live in the house rent-free. Patterson gave Watson a Pierce-Arrow car and introduced Watson to Dayton's elite, taking him to dinners and clubs. The two rode horses together, and at times seemed inseparable, often standing together at events, Watson towering over the compact Patterson.

Patterson, though, could change abruptly, and he never

tolerated challenges to his power. That became clear to Watson when he saw what happened to Chalmers, the man who plucked Watson from Rochester. Chalmers challenged Patterson's devotion to a health faddist who advised Patterson to impose rules about smoking, eating habits, exercise, and behavior. This was an age when businessmen usually filled meeting rooms with cigar smoke, downed cocktails at lunch, and enjoyed roast beef smothered in gravy. Chalmers, reading the dissatisfaction among employees, wanted it stopped. Patterson's reply was to fire Chalmers— along with six of his friends.

⪻

Growing up, Watson never dreamed he'd live a life of society dinners, expensive cars, and business success.

Born on February 17, 1874, to Thomas and Jane Fulton White Watson on the family farm in East Campbell, New York, Watson lived nowhere near anything that could be called a city. The nearest real town was Painted Post, a few miles west of Elmira and about 250 miles west of New York City. The farm, preserved as the Watson Homestead, was a flat piece of land settled in a dip between the region's rolling hills. The rocky ground made farming difficult. In back of the boxy, two-story house ran a stream, and nearby stood a barn that Watson's father built in 1825. (In the 1950s, an aged Watson built a replica of his childhood home on its original foundation. Between Watson's fading memory and inept contractors, the replica looked nothing like the real house of the 1870s.)

Watson's father never knew success. He combined farming and lumbering but fell victim to calamitous luck and his lack of business savvy. An early family home burned down. The depression of 1873 to 1879 kept the family struggling all through Watson's youth. The 1889 Johnstown flood killed a stand of trees the family owned for lumbering.

Thomas and Jane Watson had five children. The first four

were daughters: Jennie, Effie, Loua, and Emma. Tom—called Tommy—was the youngest and the only son. The family valued persistence and optimism. It couldn't have been lost on Watson that despite his father's many setbacks, the elder Watson never gave up hope that he could improve the family's life.

For his education, Tommy Watson only had to walk a few hundred yards to a one-room schoolhouse. Inside, six two-seater desks lined up on either side of a center aisle. A pot-bellied stove stood in the middle of the room, the only source of heat in the winter. As Watson entered his teen years, he moved on to The Addison Academy in Addison, New York, a tidy town a good half-day's walk from the Watson farm. Across from the school rose a tremendous Victorian-style house that belonged to a local banker. Watson boarded there and paid his way by caring for the family's horses, which were kept in a stable out back.[9]

The teenage Watson suffered from asthma and looked as skinny and bony as a goat's leg. His face had an angelic choirboy look, which made him seem younger than other boys his age. To friends, Watson was a playful prankster, but he also seemed overly responsible, always ready to take care of his sisters or his mother, whom he adored most of all.

Watson didn't seem to have any outstanding talents. He wasn't musical and wasn't at all athletic. He achieved good grades and could handle horses. He seemed to have his mother's warmth and a knack for being likable.

After Addison Academy, young Tom went to a training school called the Miller School of Commerce in Elmira. Finding little of value at the school, Watson returned to Painted Post in 1891 and took a job keeping the books at Clarence Risley's Market, a general store in the center of a one-block commercial part of town. One year later, Watson jumped over to Willard Bronson's hardware store, which looked out on the steel statue of a native American standing in the middle of the town square. Bronson loaded sewing machines and musical instruments onto a wagon, and sent Watson to call on potential customers—Watson's first salesman job.

The work frustrated him. Making little money, Watson quit and moved to Buffalo to try selling sewing machines for a manufacturer called Wheeler & Wilcox. Whether Watson could sell anything or not, he fit in with traveling salesmen of the day, wearing clashing, loud clothes; growing a mustache; and ending most days at a local saloon. One evening, according to Watson family lore, Watson stopped in a bar and stayed until closing. When he came out, his horse and wagon and the sewing machines on it had been stolen. Watson reported his loss to Wheeler & Wilcox and was promptly fired. Irrationally superstitious about personal disasters, Watson concluded that alcohol could never be mixed with business.

With his father's persistence, Watson tried selling shares in a building and loan company for a man named C. B. Barron, until Watson eventually figured out Barron was more of a huckster than a salesman. Next, Watson opened a butcher shop in Buffalo. The shop ran out of cash, and Watson had to sell it.

Hammered by failure, his confidence tattered, Watson trudged to the local NCR office to transfer the installment payments on his store's cash register to the butcher shop's buyer. Watson enjoyed talking to people in any situation, and at the NCR office he talked with salesman John Range. Watson asked Range for a job, and continued calling on Range until Range said yes. Watson began working for the company in November 1896 as a sales apprentice to Range, who pushed Watson hard and taught him salesmanship.

"He checked me every night and every noon," Watson said. "I was checked once or twice every day, and every man in his organization was checked to find out what we had been doing.

Watson said he told Range: "I didn't get any orders but I got some good business in sight."

"How far away is it?" Range barked. "Can you show it to me? Can I see it? Don't come and talk to me about business in sight. You bring in the orders so I can see the signature. That's what I want."[10]

Watson liked Range and soaked up everything Range could tell him about selling. Nine months after joining NCR, Watson moved up to full sales agent in Buffalo. Four years later, NCR assigned Watson to run its struggling Rochester, New York, office. Watson, only 27, turned the branch around and made it one of NCR's best, which caught the attention of the NCR brass. Watson had a chance to work with Chalmers, who 30 years later wrote Watson about their good times in Rochester, like "when we knocked out that Hallwood in Mr. Mutter's place." A Hallwood was a competing brand of cash register. In NCR lingo, *knocked out* meant that they got rid of the Hallwood and replaced it with an NCR model at that establishment, perhaps even by sabotaging the Hallwood—a not-uncommon NCR practice at the time. Those days made Chalmers think of Watson when NCR went looking for someone to run the secret operation.[11]

By 1912, Watson had traveled to Dayton, run the used–cash register business, and climbed to one of the most powerful positions at NCR. Watson became polished, finding a taste for impeccable clothes, fine horses, parties, and the luxuries that came with money. Always insecure about his roots, he was working his way into friendships at the top tiers of Dayton's establishment, searching for status by association—a trait that would follow him until he died. Watson became the treasurer of the Dayton horse show. He joined an exclusive group called the Club Men of Dayton. Its members included the top officers of NCR and many local company presidents, including Arthur Kittredge, who ran the Barney & Smith Manufacturing Company, maker of railway coaches. The club produced a book that is a collection of caricatures of its members. Watson is shown on a snorting horse. The caption says: "If there is any recreation Mr. Watson prefers to a spin in his automobile, it's a jaunt across the hills a-horse."[12]

Watson found a handful of lifelong friends inside NCR. Among them was Charles Kettering, who later moved to General Motors and became one of the greatest product developers in American history. Kettering's influence would later lead Watson to embrace research and development as a key driver of IBM's success. The two had an easy, fun, intellectual relationship all through Watson's time in Dayton. "Ket," as everyone called him, was two years younger than Watson. Tall, witty, and warm, Kettering had an engineering degree from Ohio State University. Watson's job as sales manager often put him in contact with engineers who were developing new features or products. Watson pushed for an electric cash register to sell. It would be modern and peppy, a machine of progress. Others had tried, but they couldn't come up with a motor that was small enough, or powerful enough, to slide out the cash register drawer at the push of a button. Electric motors of the day were designed to deliver a constant level of power over time, but this problem required a motor that would produce a strong burst of power. Kettering came up with a solution and took it to Watson for a demonstration. "Wonderful," Watson told Kettering, "but will the motor work when it's damp?" The machines would be used in fish markets and other places where it's damp all the time, Watson pointed out. Kettering, typically nonplussed, brought in a bucket of water, dropped his invention into it, and suggested they all go home and try the motor in the morning. Next morning, they pulled it out of the water, and it worked.

Kettering left NCR in 1909, but stayed in Dayton, starting an engineering company called Dayton Engineering Laboratories Company, or Delco. Henry Leland, president of the carmaker Cadillac, wanted a self-starter for Cadillac's 1912 models. Until then, cars had to be started by turning a crank sticking out of the front grill. The solution for a car self-starter was related to the solution for an electric cash register. It required a small motor that could deliver a powerful burst of energy, except that a car starter needed a much bigger burst than did a cash register drawer.

Under contract with Cadillac, Kettering worked on the invention in secret, unable to tell Watson until it was almost ready. He learned that Watson was due into Dayton on a 4 P.M. train. Kettering drove to the station in a Cadillac roadster, turned off the car, and waited. When Watson arrived, Kettering invited Watson to get in, and then slid into the driver's seat without turning the crank. "I started to laugh," Watson recalled. "I expected him to hand-crank the car. Instead, he pushed a button and it started, and I said, 'What the Sam Hill is going on?' " Watson was the first person outside Delco or Cadillac to see the starter in action.[13] Kettering sold his company to General Motors in 1916, then ran GM's research labs for 31 years.

Kettering proved to be an important bridge for Watson between engineering and sales by showing Watson how inventions could drive a business. Watson genuinely liked Kettering and found him fascinating. Their congenial relationship helped Watson, who was not naturally comfortable with science or mechanics, to learn how to work hand in hand with engineers and how to understand them.

Though Watson had numerous friends in Dayton, he didn't have a wife. Watson, according to family stories, broke off engagements twice. Watson insisted that he was choosy. He must have had plenty of opportunities with women. Watson's face had filled out and lost the look of a small-town innocent, making him more handsome than when he first arrived. He was well liked and well off. His most obvious quirk was his abstention from drinking, convinced that if he touched alcohol again, he'd be wrecked.

The Dayton social scene led Watson to one particular country club dinner party in the spring of 1912. A young woman he'd briefly met before, Jeannette Kittredge, meandered around the room, talking with guests. She was 29 years old, unmarried, and the daughter of Arthur Kittredge, one of the Club Men of Dayton and a person of stature. She had smiling eyes and cheekbones so high they formed a ridge on each side of her face. She dressed well but not stylishly. To Watson, Jeannette must have seemed quiet, proper, and shy. And aside from Watson, she was the only person at the party who didn't have a drink. As the party turned into dinner, Jeannette would always tell her children, she noticed that Watson never touched his wine glass. She decided she wanted to talk with him.

They began to see each other, and they fell in love. Jeannette turned out to be an excellent complement to Watson. She could modulate his ego, his energy, and his volatile temper. She was happy to remain in the background, but she could be, underneath her shyness, tough and protective—helpful to a man of power.

Later in 1912, Watson asked Jeannette to marry him, and she said yes. It was the best thing that happened to Watson at a time when the rest of his world came unglued.

⁓

On the morning of February 22, 1912, five inches of new, slushy snow covered Dayton, muffling its sounds and scrubbing the air. Charles Kettering, Arthur Kittredge, and the rest of the city's residents opened their newspapers to a sensation. The lead headline across the top of the *Dayton Daily News* read: "NCR Men Indicted by The Federal Grand Jury." Datelined in Cincinnati, the first paragraph bore the news: "Thirty officials and employees of the National Cash Register company of Dayton were indicted on charges of criminal violation of the Sherman anti-trust law by a special federal grand jury here." Two paragraphs down, the story listed those indicted. First on the list was John H. Patterson. A few names after: Thomas J. Watson.

Other NCR men charged included characters who were part of Watson's past or would be part of his future. They included John Range, who first hired Watson; Jonathan Hayward, one of Watson's best friends and a one-time roommate; Edward Deeds, a rival atop NCR; Joe Rogers, who had become another close friend; and Walter Cool, a mystical, elliptical NCR old-timer to whom Watson often turned for business advice.

The administration of President William Howard Taft was on an antitrust rampage. Working Americans felt uneasy about the growing power of business barons who were assembling giant corporations that could utterly control an industry. Taft's attorney general, George Wickersham, won antitrust suits against American Tobacco and Standard Oil and filed another against U.S. Steel. Wickersham sued two companies that allegedly sought to monopolize the butter industry, and he went after the manufacturers of sanitary enameled iron, dubbed by newspapers as the "bath tub trust."

NCR was not going to escape in that atmosphere. The company plainly dominated the cash register industry, controlling 90 percent of the business. Its rough tactics were widely known. Antitrust investigators had poked into NCR for years, but Patterson defiantly refused to worry about them. Now, though, Justice had a star witness: a bitter Hugh Chalmers, the executive whom Patterson had fired. Chalmers intimately knew about Watson's used–cash register operation.

The government filed three charges against each of the 30 defendants. The first count was built around restraint of trade, saying that NCR drove companies out of the cash register business by bribing employees of competitors and bribing transportation and telecommunication companies to

22

lose orders or damage equipment. The charge also said that NCR falsely damaged the credit of competitors and libeled competing machines. The second and third counts had to do with monopolizing the business using those tactics.

The government made the charges criminal. Almost all other antitrust cases had been civil—the companies could be fined or broken up, but the officers weren't threatened with fines or jail. However, for NCR, the government used a section of the Sherman Antitrust Act that allowed it to seek criminal indictments. Each of the three charges carried a maximum fine of $5,000 and a maximum prison sentence of one year. If guilty of all three charges, the NCR officials would each face a possible $15,000 fine and three years in jail.

Tom Watson could go to jail. He could go to jail for three years.

It's hard to imagine how horrific that must have been for Watson. He had risen from nowhere. He'd become a comet inside NCR. He had a house, a life, and a mother and sisters who often relied on him. After flying so high, Watson had to face the fact that he could wind up a criminal.

From February to November, the two sides prepared their cases. The trial, in U.S. district court in Cincinnati, began on November 19, 1912. It lasted three months—about 50 days actually in the courtroom. Patterson, Watson, and the others from NCR attended almost every trial day, at night staying at the Sinton Hotel in Cincinnati.

NCR got creamed in court. The government detailed practices that made NCR look like a gangster operation: NCR harassed competitors by using patent litigation, claiming rights to 14,000 patents when it owned just 140; NCR sold machines at a loss in certain regions to drive out rivals; NCR showed potential customers defective cash registers made by competitors and libeled those machines by saying they were all defective. Patterson's coarse language about

23

"knocking out" and "killing" competitors was quoted throughout the trial. Chalmers, safe from prosecution because of the statute of limitations on the law, took the stand and laid out the story of the used–cash register business and Watson's role in it.

The government did not show that Watson ordered or created the worst of the practices. Many of the practices had been part of NCR since the 1890s, the government said, ordered by Patterson. Still, Watson's organization carried out some of the tactics. If he didn't support the tactics, he also didn't stop them. When both sides rested their cases, the judge, Howard Hollister, made a point in his instructions to the jury: "These men are not on trial for what others may have done," Hollister said before sending the jury into deliberations. In other words, if Watson or any of the others were guilty, they'd have to be guilty because of what they did, not what their superiors or employees did. Watson believed unwaveringly in his innocence. Even later in life, he never acknowledged doing anything wrong.

On February 13, 1913, at about 10:30 P.M., word sifted through the Sinton that the jury had reached a verdict. Watson and the others gathered coats and hats and made their way into Judge Hollister's courtroom, which soon filled with spectators, reporters, curious Cincinnati lawyers, NCR supporters from Dayton, and family members of the defendants. Edward Morrow, foreman of the jury, would later tell reporters that every member of the all-male jury had made up his mind before deliberations began. On the first ballot, they unanimously voted for a verdict of guilty. All of the defendants except for one—Edgar Park—were found guilty on all three counts.[14]

The courtroom exploded with gasps and chatter. Patterson's daughter, Dorothy, and son, Frederick, walked to Patterson and cried on his shoulders. Nowhere is Watson's reaction recorded. However, the shock of the reality of a

jury proclaiming him guilty—of being labeled a criminal—
had a profound and lasting impact. If there was a single
moment when Tom Watson changed—when he decided
that a squeaky-clean image and reputation were paramount
in business and in life—this was that moment. "People
underestimate how badly that trial hurt him," said writer
Peter Drucker, who came to know Watson in the 1930s and
1940s. "He was portrayed as a villain. I don't think he ever
recovered from it."[15]

That Watson didn't recover was to his benefit. The trial
and verdict forced him to realize that there were bigger
things than his job and his advancement. It also gave him
something to prove—that he wasn't a self-centered crook. If
Watson had never been brought to trial, he wouldn't have
become the kind of leader who could build IBM.

NCR attorney John Miller immediately asked for a
motion for a new trial. The judge released the defendants on
$5,000 bail, pending sentencing. The next day, newspapers
across the nation blared the guilty verdict on their front
pages, spreading Watson's notoriety. In Dayton, the story
spilled all over every newspaper. The *Dayton Journal* treated
it as the ultimate defeat of Patterson. It's front page ran a
somber illustrated tribute to Patterson's family, titled "Patterson Made Ohio History."

At the sentencing, Hollister scolded the defendants.
"You have lost the opportunity given you by the methods
you pursued," he said. "In your desire for gain you forgot
everything else."[16] The NCR officials were, in the court's
view, guilty of behavior that has infected business through
the modern age. Hollister's disgust would've rung true 90
years later during scandals such as those at Enron and
WorldCom.

Hollister sentenced the defendants to one year in jail,
pending appeal.

The trial, the verdict, and the sentences were the biggest

news in Dayton so far that year. But those stories would pale compared with the gravity of the city's next event, which would take the lives of hundreds of Dayton residents, and perhaps save Watson's.

~

In the weeks after the verdict, life at NCR marginally returned to normal. Patterson continued running his company. The other 28 who were convicted, including Watson, went back to their jobs. All were convinced, or at least hoped, they'd win on appeal and that America's new president, Woodrow Wilson, might look more favorably on the company than did Taft.

On the morning of March 25, 1913, Watson awoke at the Waldorf-Astoria, a grand and elegant hotel on Park Avenue in New York. He was in the city on NCR business. Elsewhere in the hotel were Jeannette Kittredge, Watson's fiancée, and her mother, Mary Kittredge. Arthur Kittredge had been with them but had returned to Dayton. Jeannette and Mary planned to take a train to Dayton that day, but were halted by an urgent telegram from Arthur. Don't start for Dayton, the telegram informed them. Jeannette must have alerted Watson that something was wrong.[17]

In Dayton that morning, Patterson had been driving into NCR when he saw the local rivers swelling. Heavy spring rains were soaking Ohio. Patterson believed a disastrous flood was possible—he'd often told unresponsive city officials this would happen someday. He arrived at NCR and by 6:45 A.M. gathered a group of executives on the roof. The meeting lasted 15 minutes. Patterson ordered NCR into action. The company stood on high ground, a long gradual slope up from the main part of the city. If there was going to be a serious flood, NCR might be the only place of refuge. Patterson ordered the executives to collect food, medicine, drinking water, beds, and blankets. He ordered the woodworking department to drop everything and immediately start making flat-bottomed boats.[18] The executives thought Patterson was overreacting, but they wouldn't argue with him.

Patterson quickly set up a "Flood Relief Temporary Organization," with a pyramid of who would report to whom. Robert H. Grant, an up-and-comer at NCR, was made head of the Relief Supplies Committee. He worked directly at Patterson's side, in Watson's usual role. Watson, marooned in New York, was not listed on the pyramid.[19]

By 8 A.M., yellow running water coursed through the streets of Dayton. Residents ripped up rugs and hauled prize possessions and food to second floors. At 8:30 A.M., a crack startled the whole city as one of the levees broke. Waves of water raced through the town as giant whirlpools sucked in horses and wagons. The window of downtown's Harvard Clothing Store shattered and well-dressed mannequins floated out. Furniture, pianos, wooden shacks—all bobbed down Dayton's streets. The water kept rising—past first floors, to the tops of streetlamps.[20] It was the beginning of one of the worst floods in U.S. history.

By midmorning, train tracks in many parts of Ohio lay underwater. So many telegraph poles went down that few messages got out of Dayton. The city was all but isolated.

In New York, Watson hurried to NCR's offices at 1172 Broadway and found that the dedicated telegraph line linking NCR headquarters to the New York office still functioned. Watson started getting news of the flood from Patterson's office. As the *New York Times* reported, when Patterson couldn't get through to Watson's office, Patterson would wire the *Times*, which also had a link that was still working. Someone from the *Times* would then run the message over to Watson. By midmorning, Watson began hustling to secure a train and crew willing to attempt to carry relief supplies from New York to Dayton.

By the afternoon of March 25, water covered most of Dayton. "The principal corner, at Third and Main streets, is three feet underwater, and the classic old Greek courthouse is like an island in a sea of mud," wrote an eyewitness reporter from the *Cincinnati Times Star.* "The whole central portion of the city is flooded; the beautiful residence district lying east of the exclusive boulevard district is a Venice." The townhouses belonging to Watson, Patterson, and the Kittredges—all in that exclusive boulevard district—were flooded nearly to the second story.

NCR, on high ground, remained relatively dry. Residents rushed there by the hundreds. Handwritten signs pointed to a makeshift cafeteria, places to sleep, a barber shop, and a dental office. In one building, NCR created a morgue. As the woodworking shop finished flat-bottomed boats, men grabbed them and rowed out looking for others to rescue. At times, the scene was heartbreaking. "A big sturdy man is crying like a child here at the offices of the National Cash Register Co., where nearly 1,000 homeless flood victims are sheltered," reported the *Washington Times.* "He has been to the hospital, the schools, where refugees are housed, to the churches—at none of these is his family."

As the night passed, heavy, drenching rains layered on the misery. "Every time one of those big thick drops hit the water it made a bubble as big as an egg," a *McClure's* account said. The water continued to rise.

By the morning of March 26, Watson had a train ready. He'd roused officials of the food wholesaler Austin, Nichols & Company and had them stuff 39 truckloads of food into the railroad cars. Watson sent a Western Union telegram to Patterson: "Am arranging for relief train. Wire what you need most. Watson."[21]

That evening, a locomotive hauling four baggage cars and a sleeper pulled out of New York heading toward Toledo, Ohio. Watson had worked his contacts through the day, pulling in donations from businesses and wealthy individuals. On board were food, tents, overcoats, blankets, medical supplies, and one car full of bottled drinking water.

Two NCR employees traveled with the train: Lee Olwell and Watson's old friend Jonathan Hayward. Also on the train, according to the *Sun* in a next-day story, were a half-dozen newspaper reporters and a nurse who had a sister in Dayton.

Watson cabled Patterson: "Olwell left tonight New York Central via Toledo with special relief train, food, medicine, blankets, and water."

The train crawled as far as Liberty, Ohio, where a bridge was out. Someone—perhaps Watson or Patterson or citizens of Liberty—arranged to float the goods across on boats and load them on another train. The following morning, March 27, Watson cabled Patterson again: "NCR relief train passed Cleveland. Loading second relief train today. Our office here is headquarters. Send all information possible and instructions to me. Newspapers are looking to our New York office for information." From the wording, it sounds as if Watson, sensing his remoteness from the real action, wanted to make certain he was a prominent figure in the NCR relief drama.

By the time the second train was ready, sensational Dayton flood stories filled New York's newspapers, and many of them mentioned Watson's relief trains. New Yorkers started contacting Watson, ready to make donations. "New York City responding nobly to your appeals for aid," Watson cabled Patterson. At the same time, other cities—Detroit, Salt Lake City, Toledo—were sending Dayton their own relief trains.

By March 28, the floodwaters were receding and the publicity about NCR's efforts cascaded through the media. Patterson's actions during the flood were genuine. However, he also knew a great public relations opportunity when he saw one—particularly when he needed supporters so badly. Patterson brilliantly played to the press. He invited reporters to follow him around, sleep at NCR, eat there, use its typewriters, and send stories over its telegraph wires. When water covered the *Dayton Daily News* presses, Patterson let the

29

newspaper print on presses that NCR owned. Once again learning from Patterson, Watson from that moment understood the benefits of performing for the media.

Newspapers around the world portrayed Patterson as the "flood hero." His photograph appeared on the front pages of newspapers in Syracuse, New York; Cleveland, Ohio; and Salem, Massachusetts. The *Chicago Evening Post* wrote: "Patterson was revered by Dayton people before the catastrophe, but is now an idol for whom thousands would lay down their lives." The front-page story in the *Buffalo Evening News* was headlined, "Millionaire Who Aided in Relief." *Leslie's* magazine sent a writer, Edgar Allen Forbes, to do what amounted to a revisionist piece on Patterson. The central theme was that Forbes thought he'd encounter an abrasive, domineering bully, but instead found an unassuming, sociable man "without a trace of arrogance about him." Those who knew Patterson must have wondered if Forbes interviewed the wrong person.

The publicity was all Patterson's. Hardly anyone else from NCR was ever mentioned in the stories. Except for references to Watson's trains in New York newspapers, Watson wasn't mentioned, either. Later in life, when Watson recalled the Dayton flood, he was certain he played a crucial role. But at the time, he was not given much credit in the press.

Still, the wave of good feelings for Patterson aided Watson and the others convicted in the antitrust trial. The stories about NCR and the flood often contrasted the company's heroism with the fact that Patterson and his men might go to jail. By late March, pleas for a pardon showed up in major newspapers across the country. In Dayton, a petition circulated to send to President Wilson asking for a pardon. Patterson, still milking it for all it was worth, said he appreciated the gesture. However, he told any reporter in earshot, "I don't ask a pardon. All I want is a fair trial in a higher court. I am guilty of nothing. If I am guilty, I want to go to jail the same as any other man."[22]

Wilson asked his attorney general to look into the matter. By early April, the administration said it wouldn't pardon Patterson unless Patterson sought it himself and promised that he would accept it. Wilson didn't want to get set up by Patterson for a grandstanding refusal. Patterson wouldn't ask for a pardon, which would still leave him marked as a guilty man. Sensing that the swing in public opinion would greatly help his cause, Patterson insisted that his case continue on its way to the court of appeals. He seemed certain that he and the other NCR men would be cleared.

Jeannette Kittredge must have been pretty confident that Watson wouldn't land in prison. As soon as trains could again travel through Ohio, Jeannette and Mary Kittredge and Watson rode from New York back to Dayton. On April 17, 1913, Jeannette and Watson married in the newly scrubbed Kittredge townhouse, which had been under more than four feet of water during the flood. Only family and a few friends, including Patterson, attended. Hayward was Watson's best man. The couple then went on a honeymoon to the West Coast. Jeannette became pregnant almost immediately. When the couple returned to Dayton weeks later, Patterson surprised them by giving them a wedding present: a country house near Patterson's on what used to be the Patterson farm just outside of Dayton.

Compared with the dark days after the verdict, everything suddenly brightened for Watson. It didn't last long, though. Soon after showing Watson such generosity, Patterson decided he wanted Watson gone.

~≈~

Throughout his life, Watson would say that he chose to leave NCR. Some IBM documents dated after Watson's death say that he was fired, as do a number of Watson profiles in books and magazines. The only certainty is that Watson left the NCR buildings for the last time in late November 1913, and officially was no longer an employee as of December 1 of that year. Watson remained a director of NCR until February 10, 1914. After that, his association with the company terminated.[23]

What happened between April and November? How could the relationship between Patterson and his protégé go from sublime to sour in so short a time?

For one, the atmosphere at the top of NCR turned contentious. The officers had just gone through a few months that would have turned anyone inside out. Aside from Patterson, 28 of them sat through a difficult trial, and then found themselves guilty and sentenced to jail. Think of any workplace, and one can only imagine the tension between those 28 and other executives and managers who were not accused. Many in the latter group no doubt wanted to distance themselves from the supposed criminals. Amid all of that, the flood hit Dayton, further mixing up the dynamics atop NCR. Patterson emerged from the flood with a resurrected reputation and sense of power. New heroes and stars rose out of the crisis, among them R. H. Grant, who was not among those tried for antitrust. New patterns of bonding must have been formed among those in Dayton who gave their all in the relief effort. Watson, stuck in New York, played a heroic part, but he wasn't part of the Dayton experience.

A letter from Walter Cool to Watson hints at what must have been going on. Cool had been a regional sales manager under Watson, working out of Denver. He was older than Watson, and Watson admired Cool's Zen-like personality. In later years, Cool wrote to Watson describing a time around January 1914, after Watson had left NCR. Cool was still with the company. "Those were crucial and decisive days for me and I did not know it," Cool wrote. "You were gone from the NCR organization and insidious scheming and plotting was at work. I found out that nothing is fixed in this world."[24] Cool left NCR soon after.

Patterson turned on the executives who were his code-fendants in the antitrust case. Within a year after the flood, almost all of them would be gone. Perhaps Patterson decided to flush away any taint on NCR. Perhaps the changed dynamics from the trial and flood gave some executives an opening to scheme against rivals at the top of NCR.

Ed Deeds might have been just such a plotter. Both he and Watson would have been contenders to take charge of NCR once Patterson decided to leave, or died. Deeds could have whispered to Patterson that Watson was becoming too powerful. "The men love Watson," Deeds might have said. "They're more loyal to Watson than to you." If Patterson believed it, he would have rid NCR of Watson in a second.

Yet there are letters between Watson and Deeds, who eventually became president of NCR, that suggest other-wise. In September 1914, Watson wrote to Deeds asking for an advance payment on his contract, which Deeds granted.[25] If Deeds got Watson fired, and Watson knew, they probably wouldn't have dealt with each other. In a letter 20 years later, Deeds opened with the salutation "My dear Tom." Only friends addressed Watson by his first name. Deeds joked in the letter: "Maybe some time they will provide an institution for indigent business machine executives. If they do, I would like to pick out a bench that would hold a half dozen people. I would put you in the center, and I am sure the old veterans would have nothing on us." That doesn't reflect a rancorous relationship.[26]

Whatever schemes swirled around NCR, in the autumn of 1913 Patterson was making life uncomfortable for Wat-son. Patterson excluded Watson from decisions and meet-ings. At some point, according to one account, Watson arrived at work to find that his office had been given to someone else. The final blow came at a convention for NCR's Hundred Point Club. As sales manager, Watson was always at the center of such events. He loved rousing the sales force with grand dinners and go-get-'em speeches. At the 1913 convention, Grant spoke before Watson. Grant was the rising young executive who worked next to Patterson during the flood. Watson then took the podium.

Partway through his speech, Watson heard a trumpet-voiced shout from somewhere in the audience. Patterson stood, interrupted Watson, then turned to the assembled salesmen and effusively praised Grant. Patterson ranted for some time, humiliating Watson. Watson got the message. He'd just been publicly stripped of power. He had no choice but to leave.

Did he quit or was he fired? Like many instances when a top executive suddenly leaves a company, it was a little of both. Patterson made sure Watson left but Watson apparently "voluntarily" resigned. The parting wasn't so bitter that Watson would hold Patterson in contempt. In following years, he'd often talk about Patterson in meetings and speeches, always in a generous way. Yet, even though Watson couldn't hate Patterson, he would be driven to beat his one-time mentor.

Toward the end of November 1913, Dayton enjoyed unusually mild weather. Temperatures hovered in the sixties for more than a week. Occasional showers kept the air damp. On one of those days, Watson, impeccably dressed in a suit, stiff white collar, and richly textured tie, walked out of NCR's main entrance, past the white pillars that had so impressively welcomed him on that first secret trip to Dayton, and stood on the sidewalk outside. With him were Joe Rogers and Robert Houston, two sharp men closely associated with Watson at NCR. Back when Patterson fired Hugh Chalmers, he also fired six of Chalmers's friends. It was Patterson's way of purging. Similarly, Rogers and Houston were kicked out right along with Watson. Before leaving the NCR property for the last time, the three of them commiserated. Watson, according to stories passed down through IBM, turned and looked over NCR's buildings, then told Rogers and Houston that he was going to go out and build an even bigger business. There's no way to know if those words were spoken, but the sentiment foretold what was to come.

First, however, Watson had to face his grim situation. He had been at NCR for 17 years. They were mostly wonderful years, sweeping Watson from nothingness to a position at the top of society and business. NCR was where he found many of his closest friends and where he found his business father in Patterson. Now he had to leave behind the company he loved.

He had to leave Dayton, too. The place was too small. Watson would always carry the stigma there of Patterson's deposed executive, and Dayton wouldn't likely have a range of new opportunities from which to choose.

At the age of 40, Watson lost his job and felt the need to leave the city he'd adopted as home, while his wife was about two months shy of delivering their first child.

Worse, he still had a jail term hanging over his head. What company was going to hire a top executive who might soon go to prison?

At least his situation wasn't desperate. Patterson had given Watson a generous $50,000 in severance, and he let Watson keep the Pierce-Arrow car.

Watson left Jeannette at the townhouse and started making trips to New York to see what he could find.

"WHY THEY CALL US IBM"
(To the tune of "A Little Bit of Heaven")

Have you ever heard the story—how the IBM was named?
I'll tell you so you'll understand from whence this Big Three
    came.
No wonder we are proud of this successful company.
For here's the way Old Father Time revealed the tale to me.
Samuel Hastings came from Dayton with Computing Scale one
    day.
Met George Fairchild and financiers of old Wall Street and
    Broadway.
They owned Hollerith Tabulating Systems—wondrous line.
And International modern methods of recording time.
Sure, immediately they recognized that Moneyweight meant
    "dough."
With Hollerith and Bundy—this triumvirate would go.
Then they found a genius, Watson, greatest leader of all men.
Now this great and prosperous company is known as IBM.

—Songs of the IBM

2

LIT BY FLINT

HE INTERSECTION OF BROAD AND WALL STREETS IN New York pinpointed the center of the American financial universe in 1914. The corner carved a piece of real estate that J. P. Morgan had bought a year earlier so he could build his financial headquarters. Morgan paid more per square foot than anyone had ever previously paid for land. The four-story building going up looked like a white fortress constructed to protect the money inside, and it looked directly across at the New York Stock Exchange, the centerpiece of the stock market. It was adorned on the outside with grand pillars, gleaming marble, and bas-relief figures of naked men carved along the top ridge.

Approximately 100 yards from J. P. Morgan's corner, at 25 Broad Street, stood a building nowhere near as imposing as the stock exchange or Morgan's half-finished hunk of stone, but it had its own elegance. It rose 20 stories. Two white pillars out front framed a double-door entrance. Beyond the doors, the building's long front hallway sparkled with grandeur: a white marble floor; a ceiling of intricately decorated plaster set off by gold leaf. On a winter day in early 1914, Watson stepped through the doors and out of the cold. His shoes clicked on the marble floor as he walked straight ahead about 40 steps to an oddly shaped, dark oak reception desk, which looked a bit like a large, polished lifeboat. A receptionist pointed Watson to the elevators behind the boat. Up those elevators were the offices of Flint & Co., where Watson had an appointment with Charles Ranlett Flint, who would change Watson's life with a job offer.

Flint stood about five feet, six inches tall and looked more like a man of the nineteenth century than the twentieth. He wore a mustache and bushy muttonchop-style whiskers, which helped hide scars on each cheek—the scar on the right from falling through a window as a child, and the one on the left from a blood poisoning incident as an adult. His wavy, gray hair defied combing, and his eyes burned with a sense of impatience. Sixty-four years old when he met Watson, Flint had already packed his life with more adventures than a roomful of ordinary men.

Born into a family of shipbuilders and captains based around Thomaston, Maine, Flint started his first dockside business at 18, then won a job with trader William R. Grace by approaching him on a ferry and saying he'd initially work for him for free. In 1872, Grace organized W. R. Grace & Co. as a shipping and trading firm, and asked Flint to join as a partner. Eight years later, Grace would be elected mayor of New York, becoming another Flint friend in high places. W. R. Grace & Co. is still in business after 130 years. In the interim, W. R. Grace established the Marine Midland Bank, sent the first commercial ship through the Panama Canal, introduced shrink-wrap packaging to the food industry, and grew into today's chemical and construction materials conglomerate.

At Grace, Flint got involved in South American shipping and politics. An opportunistic arms trader, Flint retrofitted commercial ships with dynamite guns and sold them as battle ships to warring South American nations and smuggled Pratt & Whitney torpedoes across Colombia to his military customers in Peru. "I had sat up many nights trying to find some general article of commerce that would hold a dirigible torpedo, and I had discovered that oilcloth folded in the ordinary way weighed just about the same as a layer or two of oilcloth with a torpedo inside," Flint wrote.[1]

When the Spanish-American War loomed, Theodore Roosevelt, then Secretary of the Navy, asked Flint to use his skills to help the United States obtain warships. Flint and Roosevelt became pals. By the time the calendar rolled over to the 1900s, Flint had been a friend of Presidents Roosevelt, Harrison, and McKinley; an acquaintance of dictators and royalty around the world; and a sportsman who hunted and fished with steel magnates Andrew Carnegie and Charles Schwab. Flint liked to tell funny stories, usually about somebody like Carnegie or Roosevelt. He especially liked to tell funny self-deprecating stories about himself. Jovial and supremely self-confident, he rarely failed to deliver on promises, no matter how outrageous. Yet, in contrast to his risk-taking reputation, Flint didn't indulge in vices. He believed smoking was "injurious to health" and rarely drank alcohol or coffee.

He loved inventions and gadgets. He latched onto automobiles soon after they were first sold to the public and funded a race car in the late 1890s. He had one of the first incandescent lights installed in a New York City residence. He put it behind an aquarium, illuminating the tank so he could show off both his light and his fish. He saw the potential of airplanes and got involved with the Wright brothers, cutting a deal to sell their airplane overseas. Orville Wright became another of Flint's famous friends. Flint would get invited to Dayton as Orville's guest.[2]

Flint's international trading led him in 1872 to start pulling together rubber exporters until he eventually created a monopoly trust called U.S. Rubber. He delved into forming other trusts—a trust was a combination of companies in the same industry, intent on gaining monopoly power so it could control the industry—and became one of the best-known advocates of trusts. Over the following 30 years, Flint put together 24 trusts, including National Starch, American Caramel Company, and United States Bobbin and Shuttle, which dominated the business of making certain sewing machine parts. Trusts were tolerated and seen by many at the time as beneficial. Years later, attitudes toward trusts would take a dramatically darker turn.

Among his trusts, Flint had hits and misses. One of his last was one of his worst, and it would be the unlikely and inglorious beginning of IBM.

Starting in 1900, Flint attempted to create two trusts. One was built around recording time clocks. At a factory, when an employee arrived or left, he could punch in using a recording time clock, which would stamp the time on a piece of paper. The device helped employers keep track of hourly wages. After a series of buyouts of every recording clock entity he could find, Flint formed International Time Recording Company (ITR), based in Endicott, New York.

Around the same time, Flint bought Dayton Scale Company, Detroit Scale Company, Moneyweight Scale Company, and other firms that made computing scales, which weighed items sold by the pound and added up the total cost of whatever was placed on the scale. Flint pulled all those companies together into the Computing Scale Company of America, based in Dayton, Ohio.

Over the next few years, ITR grew modestly. In 1908, the company employed a few hundred people in a white, two-story factory in a cornfield outside Endicott. Computing Scale, awkwardly assembled by Flint and poorly managed in Dayton, listed like a sinking ship.

So Flint therefore decided to try something new. He could define a market not as time clocks or scales, but as information recording machines for business. He could merge Computing Scale and ITR, creating a bigger entity that might salvage his two beleaguered trusts. Flint had been looking at a third company, which he thought might fit into his new information recording trust. That company was Herman Hollerith's Washington, D.C.–based Tabulating Machine Company (TM), which added up and sorted information recorded as punched holes on rectangular cards. Hollerith machines were the first commercial computers—forefathers of mainframe computers of the 1960s and 1970s and the computer servers of the 1990s and early 2000s.

In 1911, Flint bought out Hollerith, and merged Computing Scale, TM, and ITR into one company based in Endicott and New York City. Flint unimaginatively called the merged company Computing-Tabulating-Recording Company (C-T-R).

It didn't work. C-T-R started life bloated with debt and spread among Endicott, Dayton, Washington, Detroit, and New York. It achieved no economies of scale and no market advantages of a trust, and the leaders of the three companies either ignored or antagonized one another. By 1914, Flint desperately needed someone to come in and save his experiment. That's when Watson walked through Flint's door.

Watson and Flint first talked in Flint's office, where photographs of Flint's famous friends looked down from the walls. The two men talked while dining at some of New York's finest restaurants. Flint learned about Watson's NCR past, and was probably particularly interested in Watson's situation and frame of mind since leaving NCR. Something of a scoundrel himself, Flint gave Watson the benefit of the doubt.

A mutual Rochester friend, George W. Todd, had suggested to Flint that Watson might be right for the C-T-R position. Todd knew Watson from Rochester, where Todd ran a business. In 1916, once Watson had run C-T-R for a couple of years, Flint would tell Todd: "Watson is living up to your predictions. If in your travels you run across another Watson, I hope you'll remember me again."[3] Watson had good reason to check out the C-T-R opportunity. His pending jail sentence no doubt scared away many potential employers. Watson got offers to be a manager at Remington Arms and submarine maker Electric Boat, which thrived thanks to the war in Europe.[4] But Watson wanted to run a company, and he was primarily a sales expert. Sales didn't play an important role in the submarine business.

He considered starting a business, but didn't have enough capital. The antitrust verdict guaranteed that Watson would find it hard to borrow money or lure investors. So Watson hoped to land a position running a company that was still small but already funded, greatly narrowing the possibilities.

While Jeannette seemed to support Watson's quest for the right position, Watson must have felt pressure to quickly settle on a job. He had become a father in January 1914, a few months after he left NCR. While still living in the Dayton townhouse, Jeannette had given birth to Thomas J. Watson Jr. Weeks after the birth, Watson and Jeannette put most of their belongings in storage in Dayton and took the train to New York with the baby. First they stayed in the Vanderbilt Hotel in Manhattan. Soon after, they found a roomier and less costly place, the Edgewood Inn in Greenwich, Connecticut. It wasn't much of a home for a young family.

What did Flint discover while interviewing Watson? He found a charged-up package of energy and charisma, and a man who shared similar ideas about the desirability of monopolies. They knew some of the same people in Dayton, where Flint operated Computing Scale and visited the Wrights. They both knew Western New York State, where Watson grew up and Flint operated ITR. Both men loved cars, and at their first dinner together, they no doubt discovered their common views about abstaining from alcohol and smoking—although Watson was fond of an occasional good cigar.

As they talked, Flint must have liked the freshness of Watson's try-anything attitude, shared by much of the wartime generation. As World War I consumed Europe, the U.S. economy went into a dive. Young men and women talked about the old order getting demolished. Suffragettes pushed for women's right to vote, and dancer Isadora Duncan broke through the manners and prudishness of the Victorian era. Music invented by African Americans— ragtime—grabbed hold of a new generation with its swirling syncopation. Model T cars made the middle class mobile, and Henry Ford started paying his workers the unheard-of salary of $5 a day. Webs of electric wires were being strung atop poles over the streets of cities and towns, supplying the energy to light up increasing numbers of businesses and homes, and making possible inventions such as the refrigerator and washing machine. Anything, it seemed, could happen, and Watson's mind continuously calculated what *he* could make happen. In that way, Watson seemed a lot like Flint in his younger days.

Flint discovered Watson's entrepreneurial zest. Examples of that are captured in letters between Watson and his chief business conspirator at the time: his father-in-law, Arthur Kittredge. Kittredge by then ran his own business in Dayton, The Kay & Ess Company, which made paint and varnish. In their letters, the two men exchanged ideas about the economy and the war in Europe. ("It is hard to realize that such a thing could happen right in the center of civilization," Watson wrote.[5]) Often, they bounced business ideas off one another. At one point, they looked at a new kind of paper packaging that Kittredge thought would be ideal for shipping fruit. They discussed a cash register, invented by a couple of young men they knew, that tracked customers' credit. They looked at a new kind of carseat patented by a man named A. G. Cordley.

One exchange was about a product called Petrolief, made by Kay & Ess in limited quantity and apparently given only to friends and family, who considered it something of a miracle concoction. On a drive from Albany to Rochester, New York, Watson and two colleagues stopped their car by the roadside to talk with two women who paused while motoring to New York. "One of the ladies was very badly sunburned—in fact, the skin was peeling off her nose, and she was complaining bitterly about her appearance," Watson wrote to Kittredge. So Watson went to his car, grabbed a jar of Petrolief, and gave it to her. "I instructed her to use it not only for sunburn, but for anything that might happen to her in the future."[6]

Not long after, Watson received a letter from the woman, Miss M. E. Barbeau of Toledo, Ohio. She wanted more jars. "It is a wonderful composition and should be on the market for the public to have the advantage of," she wrote. That prodded Watson to write Kittredge: "It seems strange that we cannot figure out some way to 'cash in' on this remedy." Kittredge said that he was open to suggestions. Eventually, they dropped the idea, having decided it wouldn't be worthwhile.[7] They also never invested in the packaging, cash register, or carseat, finding those options lacking. Still, Watson's business mind constantly raked through ideas and inventions.

While Flint probed Watson, Watson learned all he could about Flint and the situation at C-T-R. Watson must have quickly recognized that Flint needed someone willing to take a big risk. C-T-R was in precarious shape. It had 1,200 employees spread over far-flung locations, a total market capitalization of $3 million, and a burden of $6.5 million in debt—more than double the value of the company. The fractured leadership and internal battles stalled progress.[8] Eugene A. Ford, chief engineer at the Tabulating Machine Company, remembered: "We who knew the inside figures of the corporation never could figure how the new company could be a success. Two very high-grade businessmen had tried their hands at managing the new concern and it was still headed for the rocks."[9]

The more Watson learned, the more he was convinced that struggling little C-T-R had a chance. He could understand its products. Like cash registers, they automated a business process and recorded data. Coming from the NCR culture, he also knew the value of patents for warding off competitors, and Watson found that C-T-R locked up patents covering time recorders and tabulating machines.

To find a new leader for C-T-R, Flint had created a search committee, headed by one of the company's largest shareholders, A. Ward Ford.[10] (A. Ward Ford was not related to Eugene Ford.) Ford met and interviewed Watson and other candidates.

The more Flint and Ford learned, the more they liked Watson. Both decided to risk hiring Watson, despite the antitrust conviction. Other C-T-R board members weren't so sure. One director allegedly barked at Flint: "Who's going to run the business while he serves time in jail?"

In April, Flint and Watson cut a deal. Watson would get a salary of $25,000 a year—not a lot for a top position at the time—and 1,200 shares of stock worth about $36,000. Watson would also get 5 percent of C-T-R's profits after paying taxes and dividends. It gave Watson great financial upside, especially because of the cut of profits. However, Watson would own less than 1 percent of the 104,572 C-T-R shares outstanding. Flint protected himself by making Watson general manager, not president, even though Watson would act as the top operating officer from day one. After the jail sentence was overturned, according to the deal, Watson would be named president.

On Monday, May 4, 1914, Watson rode the train from Greenwich into Manhattan, made his way to the island's southern tip, and approached C-T-R's headquarters at 50 Broad Street—across the street and 48 paces from Flint's offices at 25 Broad. C-T-R occupied the top floor of the 20-story sandstone building bedecked with 10 carved-stone cherubs over the front entrance. Watson found his office—a small and plain room, with white walls, worn Venetian blinds, a polished oak desk, and a candlestick-style telephone. There, he began his first day as the head of C-T-R.

The experience was almost immediately miserable.

The company treasurer told Watson he would deduct one day's pay from Watson's salary because Watson started work on Monday, May 4, instead of Friday, May 1. So much for welcoming the new leader.

Over the following few weeks, Watson got to know two men who, from Watson's point of view, were the business equivalent of a couple of impacted molars. Herman Hollerith and George Fairchild would obstruct Watson's plans and shackle his ambition for nearly a decade, and there was no way to get rid of either of them.

Of the two, Hollerith was the more consistently difficult. A brilliant, glowering German with a thick mustache, Hollerith invented the tabulating machine. At the age of 15, Hollerith entered college; at 19, he got a graduate degree in engineering from Columbia University. He went to work for the U.S. Census Bureau as a statistician, helping count the 1880 census—a laborious task done by hand. While there, a manager suggested that there ought to be a machine that could count the population more quickly. Hollerith agreed and thought he could build one.

Hollerith took a position teaching mechanical engineering at the Massachusetts Institute of Technology, and kept working on his machine. In 1884, Hollerith applied for a patent on tabulating machine and punch card technology. He took his invention back to the government and won a contract to build 50 of them for the 1890 U.S. census, which turned into his breakthrough. The Census Bureau expected that it would take two years to hand-count and analyze the 1890 population of 62,622,250. Hollerith's machines did it in three months, saving $5 million.

Hollerith formed the Tabulating Machine Company in Washington, D.C., and won census contracts in Canada, Norway, and Australia. For the 1900 U.S. census, Hollerith presented a steep bill to the Census bureau, which then decided Hollerith was too pricey. It assigned one of its own engineers, James Powers, to create an alternative tabulating machine. Powers turned into Hollerith's chief competitor, in 1911 launching the Powers Accounting Machine Company—a seed of a company that in various forms would challenge Watson's IBM for more than 40 years.

In the spring of 1911, Flint approached Hollerith with a purchase offer. Hollerith resisted, but knew his company was falling apart. Hollerith treated customers contemptuously, believing that customers should be honored to pay to use his machines. His raging temper alienated his best employees. Hollerith's health kept him from focusing on the company. Fond of rich food and cigars, Hollerith kept gaining weight and suffering from headaches. He visited a heart specialist in Washington, D.C. All the while, Powers began winning customers from TM.[11]

On July 6, 1911, Hollerith agreed to sell to Flint, who paid $2,312,100 for the 5,138 shares outstanding. Hollerith received $1,210,500 for his 2,690 shares, keeping most of the cash and subscribing to just $100,000 worth of stock in the new combination, C-T-R.

Hollerith, though, would not walk away. He asked for and got a contract that hired him as a consulting engineer for 10 years at $20,000 a year. He also demanded two contractual clauses that would haunt Watson. One said that all design changes to tabulating machines must be submitted to Hollerith for approval. The other said that Hollerith "shall not be subject to the orders of any officer or other person connected with the company."[12] Watson couldn't make Hollerith do anything, yet Hollerith could paralyze product development, which Hollerith chose to do from time to time.

Hollerith would not go to New York to meet with Watson. When asked by Watson, Hollerith refused to help engineer new machines to compete against Powers. Hollerith acidly told acquaintances he was deeply wounded when a protégé, Otto Braitmayer—who had come to work for Hollerith at age 15 as an office boy—left him to become a loyal Watson lieutenant. Years later, Braitmayer wrote: "Dr. Hollerith referred rather disparagingly of me and of others connected with the Company." He added: "I have never myself understood what it was I did that gave him offense."[13]

Yet Watson needed Hollerith on board. The Hollerith name was synonymous with tabulating machines, much like Ford and automobiles. Customers called his products "Hollerith machines." He was a brand name. Watson stifled his annoyance and massaged Hollerith's ego. When Hollerith threw a fit and threatened to resign from TM's board, Watson coaxed him back. Watson wrote to ask if Hollerith liked his office space in Washington. "If there is any change that you would like to have made, let me know and we will endeavor to meet your requirements, not only in regard to the offices, but in regard to everything else pertaining to your connection with the business."[14] Managing Hollerith remained a difficult part of Watson's job for years.

Then there was George Fairchild, who wasn't so much difficult; he was simply always in Watson's way.

Fairchild, who was 20 years Watson's senior, wore a bushy mustache, and a forlorn, serious look on his face. He tended to be intellectual and reflective, which friends said often made him seem indifferent or distracted. When Watson joined C-T-R, Fairchild was the chairman and the largest stockholder, while at the same time serving as a member of the U.S. House of Representatives—a conflict of interest tolerated in the early 1900s. In fact, the presence at C-T-R of respectable Congressman Fairchild helped make investors less worried about Watson's criminal conviction.

Fairchild came to C-T-R by way of International Time Recording. ITR began in the Auburn, New York, workshop of Willard Bundy. In 1889, Willard and Harlow Bundy set up a business in Binghamton to make and market Willard's time clocks. The brothers needed investors. A. Ward Ford, an in-law of Harlow Bundy, put up some capital. Bundy also worked business connections in nearby Oneonta, New York. Fairchild, who owned the *Oneonta Herald* newspaper, agreed to become another investor. The new company was launched as Bundy Manufacturing Company, which eventually got vacuumed into Flint's whirl of time clock mergers. When the financial dust settled, Fairchild held the most shares in C-T-R, and Flint asked him to be chairman.

Fairchild didn't want to actually make decisions or issue orders, but he did want Watson to keep him informed about every single move he wanted to make, often in excruciating detail. Worse for Watson, Fairchild was often inaccessible. He constantly suffered health problems. He complained of a mysterious swelling "from imperfect circulation." Another time, he was ill "with an obstruction of the bowels" on a train from Chicago to El Paso, Texas. Fairchild wrote to Watson one New Year's Day: "First, Happy New Year to you and your family. Secondly, I have been ill in bed with an apparent nervous breakdown for several days." It's not hard to picture Watson rolling his eyes with a sigh.[15]

Watson pinched off his ego and tried to handle Fairchild with tact. "I want you to feel that I will do everything in my power to act in accordance with your ideas, as they were expressed to me the last time we had a talk," Watson wrote to Fairchild.[16] It was typical of Watson's deference, even if he was not sincere. Watson, it seems, rarely followed through on Fairchild's ideas.

Watson hoped that he'd have better luck with the rest of the executives and employees of C-T-R—and, in fact, some of them became his best hope.

﹏

At least Flint liked Watson. Support from Flint helped when Watson started making moves to organize and stabilize C-T-R.

Flint at first kept his offices at 25 Broad Street, sending messengers to run the short distance to 50 Broad Street to give Watson punchy, telegraphic notes, usually scrawled in red ink on torn-off pieces of paper. Flint addressed the notes to TJ, TJW, or TW.

"TJ: After your talk re J, I was 'calm, cool, & collected,' " Flint wrote on one ripped corner of stationary. No telling who J was or what the note meant. Another note read: "TJW—I have to go to Washington tonight but want to see you re . . ."—and he drew an arrow pointing to a note about needing factories in Europe after World War I.

Flint, who during his career had dealt with a series of egotistical characters, seemed to brush off the protests of Hollerith and the whining of Fairchild. He consistently threw his support behind Watson. When in 1914 Watson wanted to postpone dividends so the cash could be put back into the business, Flint backed Watson while Fairchild howled.

In Watson's first year, C-T-R fell deeper into trouble. The company ran out of cash and paid bills six months late. The war in Europe hurt overseas sales. Watson received a memo from Tabulating Machine officers, saying that because TM didn't have a machine that printed results on paper, and Powers and another firm did, TM was in danger of losing high-paying customers in the insurance industry. "We cannot very well afford to lose this business," the memo said.[17]

As Watson dug into C-T-R's organization, he found that Flint's many mergers had created a chaotic structure. Some subsidiaries were empty shells and some so-called manufacturing assets turned out to be toolsheds. Watson tried to streamline the company, ease the financial strain, and hire engineers for an Experimental Department, which was to design a printing tabulator in a hurry.

But Watson chose *not* to take radical action, such as immediately selling a division to raise cash. He didn't wipe out old management and bring in his own team. The only people he brought with him were Robert Houston and, eventually, Joe Rogers, his NCR friends. Watson didn't storm in with a vision. He certainly did not proclaim that he saw tabulating machines as C-T-R's path to greatness. The only vision Watson communicated to C-T-R in those first months was that the company was going to become a glorious institution. Considering C-T-R's condition, that pronouncement was enough to convince a lot of C-T-R employees that the new boss was a nut. Like inventor E. A. Ford, many who had been with C-T-R saw a company in decline, not one of greatness.

The restraint showed Watson at his best—a charismatic, forceful leader who because of circumstance chose to apply patience and savvy. Watson's force of personality, though, would not stay in reserve for long.

⤛⤜

On Monday, December 7, 1914, 30 salesmen from the Tabulating Machine Company sat in stiff wooden chairs set up in rows in a conference room at a New York hotel. Most of the men looked to be in their 30s and 40s. Scattered among the men were C-T-R executives who would become important players in Watson's career, including Otto Braitmayer, Walter Titus, Walter Spahr, and Sam Hastings. Two of those executives would in later years become problems for Watson. Everyone in the room wore the formal business style of the day: a dark, vested wool suit; a high, white detachable collar; and a dark tie. The men waited for Watson, anxious to get a sense of the new general manager.[18]

Gershom Smith, general manager of TM, stood and introduced Watson, calling him "a man of national reputation as a sales booster."

Watson walked to the podium and promptly announced that he didn't know anything about tabulating machines, or how to sell them. One can imagine the soft titters.

Then, instead of telling the men what they were going to do, Watson turned it around. He asked them what *he* should do. It was unheard of at the turn of the century. Executives never admitted ignorance. Bosses were bosses and they issued

53

orders to their underlings, who were expected to obey. Bosses didn't listen to those below them—especially those far below them. In case the men didn't get what he meant, Watson spelled it out: "Every supervisor must look upon himself as an assistant to the men below him, instead of looking at himself as the boss," Watson said. He described the flat business organization 75 years before authors and consultants made it popular.

Watson's attitude sent a charge through the room. The men opened up and shared ideas. Two men excitedly discussed why the company was missing a chance to convince department stores to use tabulating machines for accounting and inventory tracking. In another conversation, the men talked about customers' complaints that putting information on punch cards is too cumbersome. Watson turned to Spahr and asked, "Is there any way that you could get that information on those cards in a little shorter form?" Spahr said yes. Watson urged him to get the engineers to work on it.

Watson, though, did not only listen. He loved to talk— actually, he loved to preach. At a number of junctures during the conference, Watson slid into lengthy homilies, delivered in his deep, rumbling voice. He didn't scold or demand. He talked, for instance, of personal success, trotting out a theory about enthusiasm. He told the men that they have to be enthusiastic to be successful, and the path to enthusiasm is intimate knowledge of a subject. As an example, Watson talked about the relationship between himself and golf. "Why do some men do it for 36 holes, chasing a little white ball? I have done it myself. Now, why am I not enthusiastic about golf? Never played the game, don't know anything about golf, and I am not an enthusiast." But, he said, if he did know a lot about golf, he'd be enthused. The men swallowed their first dose of Watson's theology.

Watson preached company-wide success, telling the men to push their products as hard as they could, "always having in mind that this business has a great future, and that everybody has a bearing on the future of this business."

Watson delivered a message of unity. C-T-R would never get anywhere as a loose collection of three companies that often seemed at war, he told his audience. He introduced the men to Hastings from the scale division, and brought in other executives from other parts of C-T-R. No one, apparently, had ever done that before. Each executive gave a brief talk. The TM men asked questions. They got to know one another.

"We want all of our subsidiary companies to feel that they are all one thing, one big family," Watson said to the men in the room. "We want you all to get together and everybody have their shoulder to the same wheel and everybody push in the same direction."

Some doubters among the TM men probably dismissed Watson's message, perhaps whispering to one another that he'd be in jail this time next year, or that Watson wouldn't fare any better than others who'd tried to run C-T-R.

A month later—January 25, 1915—Watson took the same message to ITR, giving a lecture at the division's Endicott, New York, factory. He trotted out the same golf analogy. Over and over, he hammered at his desire for the company's pieces to align. "There is one thing that is just a little more important than anything else, and that is cooperation, team play," he told the ITR group. "We must all pull together in this business just the same as horses attached to a whiffletree. It is necessary with a three-horse team to have them all pull together or results will not be satisfactory. So it is in this business."[19]

During that talk to ITR, Watson laid out what he called "The Man Proposition." On a large paper tablet, he wrote job titles one under the other, vertically:

The Manufacturer
General Manager

Sales Manager
Sales Man
Service Man
Factory Manager
Factory Man
Office Manager
Office Man

Then Watson crossed out all of the letters of the job titles except for the word *man*. Using the gimmick, Watson said that everyone in the company was important and every man was equal. "We are just men," Watson continued. "Men standing together, shoulder to shoulder, all working for one common good."

Like a pop music star never tiring of playing an early hit, Watson spoke of The Man Proposition in IBM meetings and speeches for the next 42 years. Yes, it was simplistic and forced and in later years seemed impossibly old-fashioned. But so important was this sentiment to Watson, he would leave a version of The Man Proposition as his last message to employees, in the last year of his life.

In the autumn of 1914, lawyers for NCR filed an appeal of the antitrust verdict in the United States district court of appeals in Cincinnati. Newspapers ran headlines expressing awe at the sheer volume of the appeal: 2,000 pages long, alleging that the presiding judge in the original trial had committed 393 errors. The appeals court took four months to work through the case.

At 12:10 P.M. on Saturday, March 13, 1915, Arthur Kittredge sent Watson a telegram: "District court verdict set aside. New trial granted. Congratulations." It was the first Watson knew of the decision. He quickly wired back: "Thanks for your telegram. Celebrating tonight. Love to you all."[20]

The Wilson administration could have decided to try the case again, but instead offered the defendants a deal. It drew up a consent decree that was little more than a wrist slap for the NCR executives, yet would allow Wilson to say he wasn't a pushover for big business. If Patterson and the rest of the defendants signed, the government would not pursue another trial. All the defendants signed except Watson. He said that signing it would be an admission of guilt and that he was not guilty of any crime. It was a calculated risk, driven by his stubborn refusal to believe he'd done anything questionable. The government probably wouldn't go to the expense and trouble to try only Watson, and, in fact, it never did.

On Monday, March 15, the C-T-R board met and named Watson president.

On March 23, Watson got a letter from Deeds, by then general manager of NCR. "In this morning's paper I saw a notice of your election to the presidency of your concern," Deeds wrote. "This gives us all pleasure here and I want to extend my congratulations and good wishes."

There was no such letter from Patterson.

Watson finally broke free of the worst episode of his life. But the desire to bury his past now consumed him. He had to prove Patterson made a mistake, and he had to prove to the world that he was a moral and straight-shooting businessman. To do that, Watson needed to build C-T-R into a great and admired company, instilled with the high moral values of an orthodox religion.

In 1915, anyone who knew C-T-R would have thought that goal no more plausible than if the governor of Jamestown in 1608 pronounced that the settlement was the beginning of a great nation. C-T-R was a wheezing, minor company. Watson was either a prophet or a fool.

⟨⟩

The Maverick and His Machine

(To the tune of "Pack Up Your Troubles")

Pack up your troubles—Mr. Watson's here!
And smile, smile, smile.
He is the genius in our IBM.
He's the man worth while.
He's inspiring all the time
On Wall Street—he's sublime! Fine.
He is our own, our matchless President!
His smile's worth while.

—*Songs of the IBM*

3

A MESS
SPELLED
C-T-R

RED NICHOL, JUST 23 YEARS OLD AND A WIRY PACKET of energy, marched across the hall from Watson's office at C-T-R headquarters and into the office of Robert Houston, the former NCR colleague whom Watson brought to C-T-R. "As you know, he didn't like your attitude in the meeting yesterday," Nichol immediately said, referring to Watson's take.

"I don't want to talk about it or discuss it in any way," Houston snarled. "Unless he instructed you to say certain things to me, I don't want to talk about it."

The early days of C-T-R ground Watson and those around him to their raw nerves. Watson worked with intensity, determined to turn C-T-R around and drive the company toward growth. He pushed hard on his executives. Those who believed in Watson put up with his demands and temper flare-ups. Those who didn't fled.

Houston had had enough of Watson. At a tense meeting the day before, Watson had become frustrated at a lack of intelligent input from the executives gathered in the room. As too often happened, no one challenged or disagreed with Watson. A year into his tenure, many of the men were afraid of the boss or were holding back while trying to figure him out. Watson hoped that Houston would feel free to speak up, but Houston hadn't, and Watson blew. Watson bullied Houston in front of the other men.

Nichol, Watson's dutiful secretary, hoped to ease the tension between Houston and Watson. "He didn't instruct me to come in and talk to you," Nichol said. "But after the meeting and at the meeting yesterday, he was angry, and he said some things to me, and said I could tell you if I wanted to. I think it's a friendly act on my part. I'm doing what I think I should."

"Well, you can tell him that if he wants to talk to me today, he can get me at my house," Houston said. He told Nichol that he was going home in the middle of the workday. "My nerves are in no condition to talk today. It's my physical condition. I haven't slept for a week." Houston added: "I am and have been just as dissatisfied as he is. I've felt the strain for the last six weeks."

Nichol repeated that he was only trying to help, which again set off Houston. I work harder than anybody, Houston fumed, and if I don't talk in a meeting, it's for a good reason. "I have the greatest respect for Mr. Watson's ability," Houston said, "but no man, no matter how big he is, can upbraid and humiliate me as he has."

"The main thing yesterday was that you didn't talk at the meeting," said Nichol.

"I know it! And I didn't talk because I didn't have anything to say!" Houston yelled. "There's been too much of that talk with nothing to stand on around here."

"You'd better go home and calm down. Your nerves are all wrought up, and you're in no condition to talk today," Nichol conceded.

"That's exactly what I'm going to do."[1]

Houston put on his hat and stomped out, though not for good. He liked Watson too much to leave him.

❧

In the decades to come, Watson would run his company like a tyrant. However, in 1914, he pulled together an exceptional, loyal team that would help to build C-T-R into a lasting entity.

Watson took charge of C-T-R during one of the most difficult periods to run an American company. As Germany and the Central Powers dug in against the Allies in 1914 and 1915, trade with Europe dropped off a steep cliff. In early 1917, the United States entered World War I, pulling resources and young men (including Nichol, much to Watson's dismay) out of businesses. In 1918, the so-called Spanish flu killed 21 million people worldwide and 675,000 in the United States—10 times more than the number of Americans killed in World War I. The sheer misery of death sometimes overwhelmed the conduct of business. A postwar economic surge gave companies a pop, until a dreadful crash in 1921 took almost all of it away.

Keeping C-T-R steady through the tumult was challenge enough. During this stretch of time, Watson also spent a great deal of time and energy looking for the right people to add to his team. He didn't launch any programs to find the right executive talent. When it came to people, Watson ran on seat-of-the-pants instinct. He reached into every corner of C-T-R to find talented executives. He did not look outside of the company.

"When I joined the company," Watson said in a speech years later, "our three divisions were not disorganized— they were unorganized. There were plenty of ideas lying around, but many of them seemed too big for the organization to handle. The directors told me, 'You'll have to go out and hire outside brains before you can build up this company.' I told them, 'That's not my policy. I like to develop men from the ranks and promote them.' "[2] Watson believed that lifelong employees were more likely to live and breathe the company, and remain dedicated to giving their all.

Among the first to join his team was Otto Braitmayer, a round-shaped, kind, and lovable man who had been practically glued to Herman Hollerith. When he was just 15 years old, Braitmayer went to work for Hollerith in the Tabulating Machine business. At first he was Hollerith's secretary, often seen hustling alongside the inventor, feverishly writing down orders as Hollerith snapped them out.[3] Hollerith treated Braitmayer like a son and protégé—at times, Braitmayer even lived in Hollerith's home. Over time, Braitmayer learned nearly everything about the Tabulating Machine company and could run the business when Hollerith was away or ill.

But the two men were very different. Hollerith came off as gruff, harsh, and humorless. Braitmayer was the opposite. With his big jagged smile and a head lacking much hair, Braitmayer was buoyant, funny, and thoughtful. People liked him and felt they could talk to him. As Hollerith grew more temperamental and unpredictable, Braitmayer stabilized the business with his dependability. So Watson courted Braitmayer, offering him the chance to jump into C-T-R's inner circle.

Braitmayer felt more comfortable than most with Watson. Perhaps after working for a buzz saw like Hollerith, Watson's edges seemed soft by comparison. Braitmayer could tease and joke with Watson, but he did it breezily. Braitmayer once sent Watson a memo with a page from a seed catalog advertising what the catalog called a Watson watermelon. "Of course, while I appreciated that while one so talented as you might perhaps have a cigar named for him," Braitmayer ruefully wrote in the accompanying note, "I confess to some surprise on finding the enclosed, showing how your qualities had been translated even into watermelon terms."[4]

Watson entrusted Braitmayer with some of the company's most urgent assignments. Braitmayer helped create and manage C-T-R's engineering labs. Years later, when Braitmayer's wife died, Watson handed to Braitmayer the task of expanding internationally, sending him around the world to open markets and, along the way, escape his grief. Braitmayer's personality comes out in letters sent back from overseas. In one letter to his brother, Joe, Braitmayer told of rickshas pulled by "old men that you would expect to see drop of heart disease any minute." With characteristic humanity, he added: "I simply could not bring myself to ride in them on account of having to look at the poor devil running along in front of me."[5]

Seventeen years after joining with Watson, Braitmayer was elected to the board of directors. He cabled Watson from Germany to say the appointment was "fulfilling a secret ambition of years."

Watson kept looking for talent. He found Samuel Hastings in the Computing Scale division. Older than most of the men atop C-T-R, Hastings brought competence and wisdom to Watson's team. From the Time Recording camp, Watson latched onto A. Ward Ford, who had led Flint's search committee. Ford owned a large block of C-T-R shares and sat on the board, but he was not involved in management. He became one of Watson's most trusted advisors, and a friend. "I have found him a businessman of the first rank," Watson said of Ford. "He is a real, big, honest businessman."[6] When Watson needed to get away and relax, he would sometimes do so with Ford at places such as the Pinehurst resort in North Carolina. Ford lived and worked in Binghamton, New York, near the growing Endicott factory, so Ford could be Watson's representative in the region.

Although Watson rarely recruited from beyond C-T-R, his single most significant hire came from outside. That was Fred Nichol.

Nichol was 17 when he met Watson. The teenager already had a career. At 14 he landed his first job, as a clerk for the New York & Ottawa Railway Company. He took successive jobs as a stenographer and clerk at other railroad companies before being introduced to Watson in New York when Watson was NCR's general sales manager. Watson hired Nichol to be his assistant secretary. In the antitrust aftermath of 1913, the two went separate ways but kept in touch. When Watson joined C-T-R, Watson lured Nichol back to be his secretary. "I have been in his vest pocket ever since," Nichol said years later.[7] Houston would tease Nichol by saying, "You were born under T.J.'s desk."[8]

Nichol became as indispensable to Watson as oxygen. Short, slight, and as energetic as a two-year old full of sugar, Nichol was reliable and organized. Watson would fling out orders and ideas, spontaneously change his schedule, and let papers pile up on his desk. Nichol took care of it. He was like caulking, filling in the cracks in Watson's style to keep things from falling apart. Nichol was the kind of person who would never forget who was doing what, who needed to be contacted, and who had a birthday coming up. Watson craved lavish praise, and Nichol dispensed it like a drug dealer. Watson trusted Nichol completely, to such a degree that Watson began sending Nichol to conventions and trade shows to speak on his behalf.

Nichol was not only loyal to Watson, he revered the man. Nichol wrote to Watson: "No other man has ever received more blessings from another than I have from you . . . and no other man could possibly be as grateful, and as devoted to you and yours, as I am."[9] In turn, Watson protected and guided Nichol. In answer to one typewritten letter from Nichol, Watson wrote: "Pardon me for mentioning the pen and ink corrections made in your letter to me. I note there are eight corrections. This gives your letter a very bad appearance. I thought I would mention this to you, as I know you are always anxious to receive suggestions."[10]

As their years together passed, Watson promoted Nichol to ever higher positions but always kept him no more than a few steps away. When Nichol died in 1955 at age 63, Nichol's wife Adair told Watson: "He was constantly speaking of you in a most affectionate manner. He used to say you were like a father to him."[11]

Not everyone worked out so well.

G. Walter Spahr looked like he had all the right tools for success in the Watson regime. A handsome man—interestingly, many of the men atop C-T-R were not—with bold features and penetrating eyes, Spahr had worked in a number of top sales positions at the Tabulating Machine Company before leaving in 1919 to become general sales manager at another company. Less than a year later, when Watson and Hastings needed someone to run the day-to-day operations of the scales division in Dayton, they rehired Spahr as general manager of Computing Scale.

Spahr came in determined to become a star. The scale division had a good year in 1920. Spahr quickly delivered to Watson a broad plan to shake up the division, consolidate manufacturing and offices, and raise the company's visibility. Spahr promised $15 million in sales in 1921. On their end, Hastings and Watson apparently told Spahr the division was expected to generate $1 million in profits, and Spahr's salary and bonus would be tied to profits. However, in 1921, sales dove to $3.5 million, and profits vanished. Spahr had already been complaining about his compensation—for 1920, the good year.[12] He got paid even less for 1921, and continually needled Watson for more money.

Spahr came across as selfish and coarse. When Spahr wanted lower electricity prices from Dayton Power & Light Company, he engaged an attorney to demand action from the Public Service Commission of Ohio. Watson was appalled, and he told Spahr to take up the matter personally with the power company. "My main point is that we would not care to have one of our customers make a demand for decreased prices in such a manner as this," Watson scolded Spahr in a memo. "We do not want to take any action that we would not want taken against us."[13]

In December 1923, an unhappy Spahr left C-T-R to join

Dayton Rubber Company. Spahr was out of step with Watson and the culture at the top of C-T-R, and the culture ejected him.

James Ogsbury steered himself from a golden future with Watson to the bottom of an abyss. When Watson first walked in the door at C-T-R, Ogsbury was the conglomerate's general auditor. Watson instantly found him to be highly capable, a hard worker, a financial wizard, and a clever manager. Ogsbury looked tough and athletic, with a prominent forehead, deep-set eyes, a strong jawline, and broad shoulders. Watson's early inclination was that Ogsbury could be his right-hand man. Watson even picked Ogsbury over all of the others to be the first man from Watson's team to join the board of directors.

But soon, Ogsbury crossed Watson in two ways that permanently damaged Watson's faith in Ogsbury. In the first instance, Ogsbury, Fairchild, and another man allegedly tried to manipulate C-T-R's stock price to make a quick profit. The men apparently bought and sold shares among themselves to create the illusion of increased demand for C-T-R shares, which in turn would raise the stock price. When the price got high enough, the men planned to sell their shares, taking a profit. As soon as their fake trading activity stopped, the stock price would have plummeted, perhaps hurting C-T-R investors. By the standards of the time, their plan wasn't outrageous. Financial markets were barely regulated in the early 1900s, and as a criminal act, stock schemes ranked about even with a barroom fistfight.[14]

Watson, however, still felt shadowed by the antitrust verdict. A mere whiff of scandal could ruin his reputation for good. When he learned what Ogsbury and Fairchild were doing, he angrily confronted the men and convinced them to end the scheme.[15] Apparently, Watson didn't consider it a firing offense, or perhaps didn't feel he yet had the political capital to fire a longtime, well-liked C-T-R man. Ogsbury stayed on Watson's team, but Watson never forgave him.

Decades later, Ogsbury—who denied his role in the stock scheme—wrote to Watson about the grudge that Watson carried: "Apparently you cannot forget and you cannot forgive something that happened more than thirty years ago, and I feel that you have always held that against me."[16]

Around the same time, Ogsbury quit as a director. He told Watson he didn't want the responsibilities. To Watson, it was an act of disloyalty—a terrible sin in Watson's eyes. Ogsbury wasn't just any appointment to the board—he was Watson's *first* appointment to the board. Ogsbury's resignation embarrassed Watson. The board must have thought, Is this what we can expect of Watson's judgment?

Ogsbury was finished in Watson's eyes. "Of all the men who started with me when I came with this company, you were the closest, and my right-hand man and confidential man," Watson later told Ogsbury. "And if you had had the confidence in me that I had in you, and had been as loyal to me as I was to you, you would today be my right-hand man in addition to having a substantial fortune. You had a greater opportunity than any other man in this business."[17]

Watson moved Ogsbury out of headquarters, assigning him to run C-T-R's operations in Canada. Ogsbury was made president of the scales division in Dayton in the late 1920s, after the division was in hopeless decline. Ogsbury was miserable, complaining that he was second-guessed in business and that his family was unhappy in Dayton. "There is very little hope of any bonus being earned from the scale business," Ogsbury wrote to Watson. "I am also sure that the executives at 50 Broad Street do not realize conditions in the counter scale business."[18] Watson sold Computing Scale to Hobart Manufacturing in 1933. Ogsbury stayed with Hobart for two years, leaving to become president of an aerial photography company run by George Fairchild's son, Sherman. Ogsbury always thought Watson would hire him back, but Watson never did. Ogsbury, by his own admission, suffered nervous breakdowns in the 1930s. He died in

February 1950, having not heard from Watson in more than a decade. Watson sent his family flowers and a telegram of condolences.

⮾

Watson could be a very hard man to work for.

On a Monday morning in December 1916, at the 50 Broad Street headquarters in New York, eight C-T-R executives, including Houston, Ogsbury, and Tabulating Machine executive Gershom Smith, sat around a conference table in Smith's office discussing an upcoming sales convention. A few minutes into the conversation, a glowering Watson burst in, followed by the ever-present Nichol.

"I am ashamed of every member of the tabulating organization that attends this meeting," Watson began, an iciness to his tone. "To think that you men hold a Monday morning meeting here, and you haven't got this in front of you," Watson said, tapping a sheaf of papers that showed the previous week's sales activities.

Watson had noticed that a large number of tabulating machine installations had been discontinued just months after being put in. C-T-R leased tabulating machines, sorters, and card punches. C-T-R would install and maintain them and, in return, get a monthly fee. If a user didn't want the machines anymore, C-T-R would be called to come take them out. Putting them in and taking them out cost C-T-R in labor and time, so frequent turnover added costs and cut down on profits. C-T-R made better margins on long-term installations.

No one had reported any increase in turnover to Watson, so he assumed his executives didn't know about it. "I have preached and preached and preached to you men here to study the business, study the business—but it seems impossible to get you to study the most important part of this business," Watson told them.

Watson read down the sales report. Feil Manufacturing

ended an installation in a few months, saying it didn't have enough tabulating work to justify the rent. Ohio Varnish ended an installation after three months. Griffin Wheel Company dropped its machines in less than two months because the setup was "too expensive and volume of business too small."

"Now just think, gentlemen, of men going out and taking an order where the volume of business is too small to justify the use of our equipment," Watson said. "This sale is credited to . . . two men that we are paying salaries to, and a district manager to supervise them and all that, and they go out and put a machine in—a tabulator and sorter—and in less than three months they're discontinued and they personally give us the reason that it was too expensive and the volume of business too small. Now is it possible for a man, if he has got his eyes open, to put a machine in where the volume of business is too small? Can't he find that out?"

The eight executives mostly sat in silence. A couple of them tried to defend themselves.

"I want you people to think a little and quit arguing," Watson said sharply. He lectured them about the importance of reading and discussing the sales reports every Monday. It was good management to know what was going on.

That same Monday afternoon, Watson instructed Nichol to round up the same group of executives. They gathered in Watson's corner office, where the windows looked out on downtown New York and boats chugging around the harbor.

Watson had read the report wrong. Dates on the report were written as "5-15" or "9-14." Watson thought that meant May 15 or September 14 of that same year, 1916. However, the numbers stood for the month and year, so 5-15 was May 1915 and 9-14 was September 1914. Installations that Watson thought had been discontinued in a few months really had been in place for a year or more.

Watson admitted that he was wrong, but now Watson got *madder* than in the morning. He was upset because the executives didn't know enough about the report to *correct* Watson, or if they knew they didn't speak up.

"Don't accept what I say as being law because you know I'm not infallible," Watson told them. "Let's know what we are talking about. Then, if I'm talking about something and I'm in error, why, you men want to have enough knowledge of it to correct me. Don't let me get away with a talk like I did this morning without any foundation."

Gershom Smith spoke: "There is enough foundation in what you said, Mr. Watson."

Watson was incensed by Smith's fawning. "There was no foundation for the big points I was making!" he roared. "You know you're not always wrong. You could get up there and fight your battle with me."

Suddenly, Watson seemed to catch himself. "The fact that I criticize some one or two or three little things doesn't mean that you men haven't been working and haven't been trying. It doesn't mean that I am dissatisfied with all of you, either, but, in a business, especially in a business like ours where there are so many things to take into consideration, it behooves every man to analyze every report that comes out."

The meeting lasted another 20 minutes as they calmly talked about the value of analyzing sales reports. Then Watson dismissed the men.[19]

C-T-R had no discernable culture when Watson arrived. The various divisions each had their own way of doing things. No cultural adhesive held the units together.

So the strong-willed refugee from NCR imposed on C-T-R the culture of Watson, idiosyncrasies and all. That culture would later become Watson's most important contribution to the evolution of business in America.

It started on the surface, with appearances.

Watson liked fine clothes. He developed a taste for expensive suits as his income increased at NCR. The clothes covered his poor rural roots and lack of formal education. He could put on a tailored dark wool suit and vest, a detachable high white collar, and a heavy silk tie, and look as respectable and prosperous as any bank president.

Watson never issued an order for all employees to dress like him. In fact, he expressed concern that lower-paid employees would feel pressured into buying clothes they couldn't afford. However, Watson spread his philosophy and made it clear what he desired: If you're going to call on important people, you've got to dress like them. It was part of the sale—part of winning people over. Watson didn't like people who overdressed or wore flashy vests or jewelry. Again, it was part of the sale: You want the customer to focus on your sales talk, Watson would say, not on your fancy watch fob. As it became apparent to employees that Watson was at C-T-R to stay, and that advancement within the company probably depended upon his approval, Watson dress-alikes spread through the company. Before long, conservative business suits became part of life at C-T-R.

Watson also renovated C-T-R's physical appearance. Early on in his tenure, Watson visited a sales office on the 11th floor of the 50 Broad Street headquarters. He found, as he described it, a room with an old, scarred oak table and three or four chairs of different styles. Watson shot off a memo to his staff. "I feel very badly to find that we were conducting any department of any branch of our business in such a manner," Watson wrote. "There were none of our products to be seen, and while I was there a man came in who was formerly sales manager for the H.O. Company. He looked around, asked one or two questions and got out as quickly as possible." Watson was not going to stand for such sloppiness inside his company.[20]

Because of the theft of his rig outside the saloon years earlier, Watson didn't drink. Yet in the 1910s, businessmen generally thought nothing of drinking at lunch, or sharing a drink in their offices. C-T-R was no different in its pre-Watson days. Coming in the door, Watson could not possibly have banned drinking at the company. He would have become instantly unpopular with employees. The first two conventions held by C-T-R served wine at meals. Though every fiber of Watson believed the wine was a mistake, he kept quiet and allowed it for political reasons.

About two years into his tenure, Watson began to push his point of view—though he didn't then issue an edict on drinking. At one 1916 meeting in his office, Watson, Houston, Ogsbury, Nichol, and three other executives were planning an upcoming convention. Watson brought up the topic of serving wine.

"I am not a temperance lecturer," he began. Yet, he said, if he were employing a young salesman, he'd tell the man he must not drink during business hours. Therefore, Watson said, it makes no sense if C-T-R tells new employees that drinking isn't good, and then serves wine at the convention. The new employee would think, in Watson's words: " 'Why, these people are not sincere in what they say. The man who hired me gave me a long talk about not drinking too much. Now they want me to drink everything in sight because they keep putting it before me all the time.' It isn't fair."[21] Watson pointed out the need for a consistent message.

As happened with the dress code, employees took note of Watson's personal habits and beliefs and began to follow. From there, the drinking policy took on a life of its own. A manager would never want to shoulder blame for a subordinate's drinking, so he'd enforce a no-drinking rule, and that would get replicated all up and down the chain of command. Whether Watson ever set down a rule about alcohol—and there's no evidence that he did—it became a de facto part of the culture. No one at C-T-R was to ever drink on the job, or ever be in front of a customer after drinking, and it was risky even to drink off the job, in private.

Well beyond drinking and dress, Watson pushed his

personal values onto the company. At a TM sales convention in January 1917, Watson took the stage to address the employees. He preached about health—a topic far afield from a typical business presentation. He told the audience: Get enough exercise and fresh air, eat the "proper quality of food at the proper time," and get enough sleep.[22]

A whole package of Watson-like traits began to percolate through C-T-R. In reaction to his close encounter with prison time, Watson evangelized integrity. He demanded employees always act with honor and decency, especially when dealing with competitors. Formality and politeness were required, whether it meant using good manners at a dinner or addressing each other using Mr., Mrs., or Miss. Watson, however, didn't always practice what he preached. When he lost his temper, politeness escaped him.

Watson carried the culture of his old company, NCR, inside of himself. He transplanted aspects of it into C-T-R. Watson lifted the idea of Patterson's Hundred Point Club and at C-T-R created the Hundred Percent Club. In both companies, salesmen who met or beat their quotas became club members for that year, attending a week-long annual convention. Eventually, Watson would reconstitute other NCR cultural artifacts, such as the employee country club, a schoolhouse for training, and a company-wide newspaper that served as a propaganda organ.

Watson pushed to infuse optimism into the culture of C-T-R. He wanted everyone to share his faith in the company's future. Most of the people inside of C-T-R never had a reason to think grandly about the company. C-T-R had been falling apart. But Watson wanted employees to see what he saw. "The C-T-R has a vision of something way beyond our present conception of what it will mean to be a member of the Computing-Tabulating-Recording Company," he said at a meeting of Computing Scale executives in Dayton. "I think I know what is in the minds of the management of this company—some of the things they have in view for the future. All those things mean unlimited opportunities for every one of us who started in the business."[23]

Slowly, Watson won converts to his religion.

⁓

Contrary to his popular image, Watson had a sense of humor. Sometimes.

A half-dozen C-T-R and Tabulating Machine officers joined Watson in his 50 Broad Street office for a meeting. As they settled in and chatted, a man named Olsen ducked in carrying a portfolio of papers.

"Is that your speech, Mr. Olsen?" Watson teased, looking at the thick bundle in the man's hands.

"No, I'm sorry, I haven't prepared any," Olsen said, taking Watson literally.

Two others entered the room. Both were assistants to J. L. Hyde, an executive involved in customer service.

"Here comes the real working crowd," Watson said. "They're always late, because they have so much work to do."

"I'm sorry we kept you waiting," one of Hyde's assistants said.

"We know it's because you're busy," Watson said. "The rest of the people here don't have so much to do, so they can always get around on time." Watson turned to William "Mac" MacLardy, a Tabulating Machine executive at the meeting. "I think now would be a pretty good time to take up a collection for your potato farm."

The room bubbled in laughter. No one mentions why this is funny.

"I told you the other day, Mr. Watson, that it was a sore spot on my heart," MacLardy said melodramatically, tickling another round of laughter out of the group.

"Is everybody here?" Watson said.

Houston shot out a wisecrack: "Yes, there are sixty-five, a pretty good crowd." Ten people were in the room.

Finally, Hyde arrived. "Now we can start," Watson said. "There is a chair we've been saving for you, Mr. Hyde, right there."

"The witness chair," Houston said.

"Take the witness chair!" Watson said with a flourish.[24]

The meeting started. The group discussed ways to encourage employees to buy War Savings Stamps and to get involved in other company efforts to help in World War I.

⁓

As Watson remade C-T-R, he remade his personal life—and began to blur the lines between the two.

A bachelor at the end of 1912, by 1919 Watson was the father of four: Tom Jr., Jane, Helen, and Arthur (nicknamed Dick).

Just before Helen was born, the Watsons moved into a castle-like Tudor home on five acres at the top of a rise in Short Hills, New Jersey, about 20 miles from Manhattan. They bought the place for $19,500, and then turned it over to contractors for three months for major renovations that altered the living room, added stonework to the outside, replaced the plumbing and fixtures in all but one of the bathrooms, and added a stairway.[25]

At the Short Hills home, Watson could be surprisingly playful. Family stories tell of Watson play-acting in costumes, and sometimes Jeannette's clothes. He'd come down the stairs in a dress, hat, and heels, talk in a high-pitched voice, and make the children squeal and giggle.[26] In films taken on retreats to a cottage in Langhorne, Pennsylvania, Watson looks like an ordinary vacationing parent, except he never gets out of his business suit. He bounces Dick on his knee on a porch swing, then arranges Dick and Helen on the swing for the camera. Watson grins and cuddles with the children. In another film, he piles a group of kids into a pony cart and leads the pony around. They stop, and one by one the children hold Watson's two hands so he can flip them over, landing back on their feet.[27]

"When I was little, I thought he was the liveliest father imaginable," Tom Jr. wrote in his autobiography.[28]

Watson, though, was highly attuned to image. He manipulated what was caught on camera, family members attest, to make sure that he'd be seen as a happy family man.

Watson demanded nearly as much of his children as he did of C-T-R executives. They were to display manners, behave, and do well in school. When the children misbehaved, Watson flew into rages that would send the children scampering to Jeannette for protection.

In Short Hills, Watson led the life of a proper, well-heeled executive. He joined the Short Hills Episcopal Church, though he was reared as a Methodist. He joined the tennis club, despite having little aptitude for tennis. He indulged in automobiles. In 1917, he bought a Packard Twin Six and owned a Ford Model T wagon, adding a Packard limousine a couple of years later. He squabbled with Packard over repair bills, once getting into a standoff over a $12 charge for a repair that Watson says the mechanic never did. "I'll gladly pay you when I get value for the money," he wrote to the Packard company.

He maintained his lifelong interest in horses and rode whenever he could. He bought and bred dogs. He clipped an ad from *Country Life* magazine about Newfoundland puppies, and ordered one for $80. A month later, he ordered a second.[29]

While living in Short Hills, Watson endured two personal tragedies that affected the time and strength he put into work.

The first was the death of his mother, Jane Watson. Watson felt especially close to her. He looked a lot like her—the same thin lips, jutting chin, and high cheekbones. She always treated him, her youngest, as a favorite. After Watson's father died, Watson moved his mother to Rochester, New York. He paid her rent, sent her money, sent money to the church she attended, and visited once a month. He took her to business dinners and once bought her an electric car.[30] Watson also bought one for Jeannette. Electric cars were popular among wealthy women in the 1910s, when gasoline-powered cars still had to be started by hand crank. Turning the crank required more strength than many women could muster. Coincidentally, Kettering's electric starter for gasoline cars directly led to the demise of the electric car market. Watson's mother had contracted pneumonia just after the New Year in 1917, and Watson rushed to Rochester. He was with her during her last days, and she died on January 11, 1917. When Watson's old friend and mentor, John Range, heard of Jane Watson's death, he wrote Watson a letter of deep sympathy. "It's hard to bear up, but I am glad you were with her at the last, as you always were everything in the world to her," Range wrote. "And your treatment of her made us all think more of you."

Watson's grief must have carried over into work, distracting him and making the load seem heavier. Watson at this stage worked long hours, and he extended those hours by scheduling a constant whirl of business dinners, events, and travel—perhaps staying so busy in part to ward off the pain. About a year later, some of the C-T-R executives became extraordinarily concerned about Watson. After Watson had been out sick for a week, Harrison Chamberlain, general manager of the Time Recording division, spoke for them. "I have been afraid and am afraid that you will have a breakdown unless you get more positive rest and absolute change from business," he wrote to Watson. "You are an absolute essential to this company now, and they should realize it is for their interest for you to take intermittent rests so that you will not be forced by illness to take a long rest."[31]

Two years after Watson's mother died, fire destroyed the family's home in Short Hills.

On February 20, 1919, Watson and his family settled in at the house for the night. Tom Jr. was five; Jane was three; Helen, one-and-a-half. Jeannette was seven months pregnant with Arthur. On that winter night, Watson asked a new houseman named Carlo to stack logs in the fireplace and light them. Watson watched and decided that Carlo didn't know how to correctly build a fire. Watson nudged Carlo aside, built a tremendous log structure in the fireplace, and lit it.

Tom Jr., in bed in an upstairs room, started crying. Watson volunteered to go up and settle down his son. When Watson came up the stairs, Tom Jr. yelled that he saw a funny light outside his window.[32] The fire had burned through the chimney and set fire to the roof.[33] Watson and Jeannette got all of the children out and safely to a neighbor's house. Watson and probably Carlo went back into the house and started hauling out everything they could—furniture, paintings, rugs, lamps. In letters to friends, Watson would claim they saved nearly everything on the ground floor. By the time the Union Hose Company trucks, 15 firemen, and two chiefs[34] arrived, they could do little but let the fire burn itself out.

The family lost much of what it owned. In Watson's closet had been 12 suits, two pairs of flannel trousers, 10 suits of underwear, 12 white nightshirts, six colored nightshirts, four silk shirts, two Panama hats, nine Yeager woolen undershirts, one Knox outing hat, one suit of silk pajamas, one silk dressing robe, one "couch robe," and two bathrobes. Total value: $1,717. In Jeannette Watson's closet were two evening gowns, six dresses, two suits, three skirts, two smocks, two sweaters, two furs, six French nightgowns, six Italian undervests, three union suits, 12 pairs of silk stockings, five hats, three ostrich feathers, and a handful of other items. Jeannette also lost her white-satin-and-lace wedding gown. Total value: $1,585.

The family lost thousands of dollars' worth of other belongings, ranging from a mission-style oak table to a cherry four-poster bed, a Singer sewing machine, a Navajo rug, two cribs, a camera, and $100 worth of business books.[35]

For four days after the fire, the Watsons stayed at a neighbor's home. Watson by then found a furnished house in Short Hills that they could rent. As all of this was happening, Tom Jr., Jane, and the pregnant Jeannette caught severe colds and were confined to bed. The illnesses hung on through mid-March. At that point, Watson wrote to Fairchild: "I have not been feeling first-class myself for the past few days and yesterday I stayed at home in bed all day. I feel better today. One of my assistants from the office comes to my house every day to take up with me whatever matters need my attention."[36]

Imagine the strain on Watson as he dealt with the house, illnesses, and a baby due to be born. Watson had to deal with insurance companies and lawyers. Architects descended on him asking if they could build his new home. Real estate agents sent him piles of notices about luxury homes for sale.

Watson decided to rebuild on the same property, and acted as his own prime contractor. He engaged a specialized service to load stone from Netcong, New Jersey, onto a train to be delivered to Short Hills. He researched and decided to put in a central vacuum cleaning system. (The vacuum pump sat in the basement and hoses ran to round outlets in every room.) He made decisions on everything from shrubbery to roof tiles, and he often went to the site to check on the work. More than a year went by before the Watsons moved back in, but that wasn't the end of the ordeal. Watson fought with builders over the type of nails used in the roof, a fireplace that smoked into the room, and the kinds of screens on the windows. From the tenor of conversations in business meetings, it seems that the stress at home made Watson even more volatile and impatient at the office.

～

"We are going to have different cooperation in this business," Watson snarled. He had corralled 13 of his executives in Tabulating Machine President Gershom Smith's office. Minutes after starting the meeting, Watson went off on a tear. "There is going to be no more of this old-woman's gossip, no more knocking, no more round-the-corner whisperings, no more back-biting. Everybody has got to put their cards on the table face up who stays in this organization from now on, gentlemen."

Of all the things Watson tried to do to point C-T-R in the right direction, none proved more stubbornly difficult than getting executives from the different divisions to work in harmony. But Watson believed they had to become a cohesive team to succeed.

"I have just worn myself out trying to help you people, trying to make this a real organization, a big organization, and still I find that going around on the quiet there is this undercurrent of knocking and criticizing and fault-finding. Gentlemen, it has got to stop, and I want to say right now that I am prepared to accept resignations of any men who can't make up their minds today to cooperate with everybody else in this business."

He hammered on the point. "You are pulling and hauling sort of like pulling a cat by the tail. You know, all trying to pull in different ways. Get in the same boat and get in stroke and pull in the same direction. Then you begin to get pleasure out of your organization."

No one offered to resign. Watson left the meeting, then Houston instructed the executives to put their work aside and go home or to their offices and "have a little talk with yourselves."[37]

Though Watson felt frustrated at times, C-T-R was growing. From 1914, when Watson took over, to 1917, annual revenue doubled from $4.2 million to $8.3 million. Revenue climbed to $9 million in 1918, then $11 million the next year, and $14 million in 1920. Most of those years, the U.S. economy grew briskly, helping to pull C-T-R along. The number of employees held steady at around 3,000 from 1917 to 1920.[38] Still, the company walked a financial tightrope, borrowing heavily to build factories in Endicott, open branch offices, and develop new products.

As Watson looked for ways to grow C-T-R, he saw both opportunity and trouble in the Tabulating Machine Company. Chicago retailer Marshall Field adopted tabulating machines to keep track of inventory, and much of the retailing industry was beginning to follow. Journals of the accounting profession published studies on the use of the machines, spreading the word to every company with a large payroll. During World War I, the U.S. government created the War Industries Board, which soaked up a large chunk of C-T-R's tabulating machine production to help the board manage wartime production.[39] Railroads, banks, and insurance companies began to rely on tabulating machines.

The trouble was that C-T-R offered tired technology, and most of its patents were about to expire.

At the time Watson joined C-T-R, the company had only two senior technical people: Herman Hollerith and Eugene Ford. Hollerith, living and working in Washington, D.C., increasingly refused to develop new machines. Ford worked in Uxbridge, Massachusetts. If Ford invented or improved a feature, far-away Hollerith had to approve it, and often he would not.

As Hollerith dithered, Powers Accounting Machine Company rushed into the void. James Powers had taken over the development of tabulating machines for the U.S. Census after Hollerith lost the contract. Like Hollerith before him, Powers used that knowledge to start a tabulating machine business. By the late 1910s, Powers offered products that were more innovative than C-T-R's.

A typical tabulating machine installation consisted of three essential pieces: (1) The tabulating machine read the cards and added the figures. (2) Equally important were mechanical sorters, which dropped cards into different hoppers by category. For instance, the Army used sorters to run through cards of all its servicemen looking for 600 chauffeurs who spoke French.[40] (3) The keypunch punched holes in the appropriate places in the cards.

Powers's machines were easier to use than C-T-R's. For instance, Powers's keypunch worked much like the familiar typewriter; C-T-R's keypunches worked in a unique way and required special training. Also, Powers's machines sensed the holes in the cards by a mechanical method, versus C-T-R's electrical method. In the 1910s, Powers's method ran faster.

C-T-R dominated the tabulating machine market, but Powers was gaining share. Better technology translated into sales. Thinking of the lessons from his friend Charles Kettering, Watson decided to fund a laboratory full of engineers like Kettering.

Watson convinced Hollerith's engineer, Eugene Ford, to move from Massachusetts to New York. Watson rented laboratory space in a New York loft and assigned Ford to start recruiting the best engineers he could find.

Ford hired Clair Lake, who was designing automobiles for Locomobile in Bridgeport, Connecticut. Lake built the company's first printing attachment for tabulators—a device that helped C-T-R catch up to and surpass Powers in making user-friendly machines. Lake also standardized tabulating machines so they could be made more efficiently. In 1922, Otto Braitmayer figured that Lake's design saved the company $100 on the manufacture of each tabulator. Lake would play a role in product design into the computer age.

A year after Lake joined C-T-R, Fred Carroll, who designed cash registers at NCR, wrote to Watson asking to work at Watson's new company. Watson jumped at the chance to get him. Carroll worked on tabulating machine designs, but ultimately made his biggest contribution by building the Carroll Press. It was an automated system for printing, cutting, and trimming the punched cards that C-T-R would sell to users of its tabulating machines. Like razor blades in a razor, the cards accounted for between 5 and 10 percent of C-T-R's revenue and, in some years, up to one-third of the profits. A single Carroll Press could churn out 1,000 cards per minute, allowing C-T-R to mass-produce the cards inexpensively and make wide profit margins selling them.

In 1917, Watson recruited James Bryce, who would come to rival Kettering as one of the most important product developers of the century. Brilliant and moody, with a dry sense of humor, Bryce started out as chief engineer for the International Time Recording division in Endicott, and later was named C-T-R's chief engineer. He worked on or directed nearly every new tabulating product over the next two decades. He ended up with more than 400 patents to his name, and in 1936 he was honored by the U.S. Patent Office as one of the 10 greatest living inventors.

Together, they led a remarkable team that became the engine of C-T-R. Powers couldn't match C-T-R's laboratory personnel or its spending on product development. C-T-R's technology breezed past Powers's, helping C-T-R lock up a near monopoly in tabulating machines and punched cards.[41]

Watson didn't just hire this group and leave them alone. He assembled them in a laboratory, then created rivalries by simultaneously giving two or three groups the same assignment, sometimes without even letting each group know that others were competing. At the conclusion of an assignment, Watson, Bryce, and perhaps other executives would choose a winner. When C-T-R needed a printing tabulator, for instance, Watson assigned development to both Lake and Carroll. (Lake's design won.) When the company needed to develop cards that could hold more information by using more holes, he handed the job to Lake and J. Royden Peirce, another top engineer brought into the lab. (Lake won again.) The groups competed ferociously, creating a sense of urgency even when the company controlled the market and had virtually no outside competitors.

On the downside, engineers felt frustrated and burned out when their designs didn't get chosen. Watson, though, wasn't about to let them quit out of dissatisfaction. He assigned good guy Braitmayer to oversee the labs and baby the engineers. Braitmayer would send a man on an exotic vacation paid for by the company, or hand out $5,000 bonuses at a time when the engineers' annual salaries were between $10,000 and $20,000. At one point, Carroll wrote to Braitmayer saying he'd had to sell some of his stock in the company to pay off a loan. Braitmayer wrote a note to Watson suggesting that they give Carroll 100 shares for all he'd done. The note came back to Braitmayer with Watson's scribble at the bottom: "Suggest 200 shares stock."

The engineers appreciated the gestures. After getting a bonus, Ford wrote to Watson: "At times I have felt discouraged when my recommendations have been turned down and opinions overruled, but now that I know you have not looked upon my defects as evidence of incompetence, I shall strive harder to justify your good opinion."[42]

Many of Watson's early management tactics paid off. As Watson put it years later, he simply experimented. "I found when I tried the first experiment years ago that the organization responded to such an extent that I was justified in trying another," Watson said at a dinner for IBM employees in 1940. "I had the same results on the second experiment, so I have kept on."[43] He was beginning to find a formula that would guide his company to greater heights.

⟨≈⟩

In 1920, C-T-R was a small company: $14 million in revenue, $2 million in earnings, 2,731 employees. However, it was growing more than 20 percent per year. In twenty-first-century lingo, C-T-R was a hot growth stock.

So in 1920, Watson called in his management team and told them to double the size of the business in 1921. No debates. Double it. "Think in big figures," he told executives attending a training program that September. "A few years ago we were thinking in six million dollar figures. Now we're thinking in terms of twenty millions." He added, "I shall thank you in advance for what I know you are going to do in carrying out your part of the program for the coming months and next year."[44]

It was a bad call at the wrong time. The company started boosting production, building up inventories, and adding employees in preparation for its all-out assault—just in time for a sharp recession that slammed the U.S. economy from late 1920 through 1921, continuing to hurt business into 1922. C-T-R's revenue dropped 30 percent in 1921. The biggest calamity was the scale division. Led by Spahr, who was gunning for $15 million in revenue for 1921, business dove to about $3 million, leaving the division with too much inventory and too many employees.

Watson resorted to layoffs and salary reductions to try to get by. This was not the Watson remembered by later generations for never laying off workers.[45] In one meeting, Sam Hastings told Watson how hard it was to deliver the news of 10 percent salary cuts to workers already short of cash. He talked of one young woman making $16 per week and paying $10 per week to live at a YWCA. For her, a cut of $1.60 per week "presented a real problem, and the handling of such a situation as this was not a very pleasant task."[46]

Watson began thinking about getting rid of the scales business. Time and again, he expressed his disappointment in the business and its prospects. At one tense meeting with scales executives in Dayton, Watson ran through the figures for the division, then told those assembled: "You men in eight months have dissipated a lot of money. It certainly does not look like sound business."[47]

Contrary to the Watson legend, he did not immediately see that tabulating machines were his company's future. He did not start out with a vision of a company focused on information processing. He arrived at that point by making sensible business decisions, one at a time. Computing Scale was rapidly becoming a business that was not worth owning, so Watson wanted to sell it.

In those grim months of 1921 and 1922, Watson maintained his unwavering faith in a good outcome. In November 1922, as C-T-R closed out the second of two rotten years, Watson lingered in his office with only his friend, Joe Rogers, and with Harry Evans, a spunky, fast-rising executive. Watson grumbled that every American company was sending out signals that "business is bad." Executives, bankers, newspaper reporters—they were messengers of gloom, and that wasn't helping the economy, he said. "What we want to do as a company and as individuals in this company is to get back of this better business and advertise it," Watson told his colleagues.[48] He followed through, proclaiming in ads, speeches, and interviews that "business is better." In his 1922 Christmas message to employees, Watson concluded: "We are entering a new period of prosperity—not the boom of the war period, but a time of substantial progress toward better business."

He was right. Business boomed for the rest of the 1920s. Being right about that made Watson more confident than ever.

≈

The company name—Computing-Tabulating-Recording Company—ate at Watson. For one, the name reflected the names of the three divisions. If Watson rid himself of what had been the Computing Scale Company, that would leave an awkward naming problem. Should he keep the whole C-T-R name, because the company was becoming fairly well known? Or drop the first word so it would be the Tabulating-Recording Company? What then if he sold off International Time Recording? Would the word Recording have to be ditched, too?

Second, Computing-Tabulating-Recording Company didn't have the heft that Watson wanted. He dreamed of building a giant—an institution. Such companies had names like General Motors, American Telephone & Telegraph, and United States Steel. They were names that invoked limitless expansion and power.

In 1917, as Watson tried to reorganize and streamline C-T-R, he consolidated three Canadian subsidiaries into a single subsidiary. Instead of calling it C-T-R Canada, he gave it a new name: International Business Machines. It was to be an umbrella for operations abroad. In 1923, Watson applied the name to C-T-R's Latin American subsidiary.

Watson liked the name. It didn't box him in. It had the ring of an institution. On February 5, 1924, he submitted an application to list International Business Machines (IBM) on the New York Stock Exchange, and C-T-R disappeared.

Not everyone was pleased. A number of shareholders wrote to protest. Many of their letters read like this one from F. P. Furlong, a vice president at The Hartford Aetna National Bank: "The name Computing-Tabulating-Recording Company is to the writer much more euphonious, and would impress me as being a more impressive and substantial name than the one you have changed to, to wit: International Business Machines Company."[49]

Watson had a standard reply: "We have found it a very euphonious and suitable name, regarded as indicating that our machines are aids to business big and little, ranging from the accounting departments of railroads to the ordinary transactions of retail stores . . . and they go practically over the civilized world." Euphoniousness was important to people in those days.

International Business Machines was still an upstart little company. In 1924, revenue climbed to $11 million—not quite back to 1920 levels. (An $11 million company in 1924 was equivalent to a company in 2001 with revenue of $113 million, which would not be even half the size of Internet media company Real Networks in 2001.)

Inside IBM, 1924 handed Watson one more significant event. George Fairchild still held the title of chairman of the board, but he had become increasingly detached as his health slipped from him. On December 31, 1924, the last man Watson would have to treat as a boss died.

IBM became Watson's—and in a short time, Watson would become IBM.

(To the tune of "Columbia, the Gem of the Ocean")

T. J. Watson, we all honor you,
You're so big and so square and so true.
We will follow and serve with you forever.
All the world shall know what IBM can do.

—*Songs of the IBM*

4

BRINGING UP BABY IBM

T HE *NATIONAL CYCLOPEDIA OF AMERICAN BIOGRA-phy* planned to include an entry on Watson in its forthcoming edition, so it sent Watson a questionnaire. His answers showed that he was in the early stages of a couple of tendencies that would worsen as he grew older: self-absorption and overconfidence.

One section asked for physical and mental characteristics. Watson answered (in the third person): "A tall erect figure and dark direct eyes that appear to see through people and situations at first glance, and with complete understanding, are probably the two physical characteristics that dominate one's initial impression of Mr. Watson. His manner of speaking is to the point. Eyes and speech tell of a keen mentality that is always alert and searching."

Another heading was "Special gifts and avocations." Watson answered: "Mr. Watson has a pronounced gift for public speaking and . . . he is continually being called upon to exercise it. His avocation is that of gentleman farmer and dairyman. He owns a model farm and dairy in Lebanon, N.J., on which he raises thoroughbred horses and cattle."

Under "Dominating personal characteristics," he answered: "Tremendous vision; indomitable will; unswerving determination."[1]

On October 30, 1925, Watson planned to hold a board of directors meeting in Endicott, New York, which was becoming IBM's manufacturing center. This board, finally, would be *his* board.

After George Fairchild's death at the end of 1924, Watson awarded that seat to Fairchild's son, Sherman. A restless, clever inventor, Sherman Fairchild adored aviation and devoted almost all of his time and talents to it. He made the first successful aerial camera, taking photographs that resulted in tremendous leaps in mapmaking. His Fairchild Aviation built airplanes, and Sherman would later have a hand in the founding of Juan Trippe's Pan American Airways and American Airlines. Although Sherman was very good at aviation, he was very bad at—or perhaps just uninterested in—business. His companies often struggled in disarray. He was not likely to think up ideas for IBM. Sherman posed no challenge to Watson on anything.

The board now was stuffed with Watson appointees and fans. It included Watson's lifelong friend, Christopher "Kip" Smithers of Delray Beach, Florida; and a newer friend, New York lawyer George Post. Old-timers Flint, Sam Hastings, and A. Ward Ford stood squarely with Watson. The others would generally go along with whatever Watson wanted.

As the date of the Endicott meeting approached, Watson's office received notes about members' plans. Post, who lived in Somerville, New Jersey, intended to drive the nearly 200 miles to Endicott and offered to take another member with him. Charles Smith, president of Citizens National Bank of Oneonta, New York, decided to drive from Oneonta and stop by the Arlington Hotel in Binghamton, so he could give board members who would be staying there a ride to Endicott, about five miles away. Most of the other directors boarded a special railcar from New York that Watson reserved.

Charles Flint, the financier who hired Watson, stayed home. As could only happen to Flint, a few months earlier he thought he had appendicitis and hurried to the hospital. Doctors cut him open and found that while he didn't have appendicitis, he had fluid collecting in that region, suggesting an infection that might have killed him. By October, he felt much better and wanted to attend the board meeting in Endicott. "But Mrs. Flint feels that I would run the risk of taking a cold," Flint wrote to Watson's secretary, George Phillips. "As she so recently saw me through one siege, I am complying with her request and am giving myself up entirely to business in New York and to home consumption."[2]

Around the same time, IBM lost the two men who knew Watson best: his former NCR colleagues Joe Rogers and Robert Houston. Rogers quit to run a small business machine company called Addressograph. Houston had already left IBM for another company. Rogers had been the only person left in IBM's top ranks who could face Watson as a friend and equal. The other executives bowed to Watson every time. Nobody was left who could argue with him.

⸻

Watson in the 1920s faced a world that he never could have imagined when he took charge of C-T-R a decade earlier. In a flash, two-thirds of homes had electricity, half had telephones, and one-third owned radios. Consumers bought refrigerators for their kitchens, and at train stations ate sandwiches they pulled out of the first coin-operated vending machines. Charles Lindbergh flew across the Atlantic and made everyone think the world was shrinking. At dinner parties, educated men and women talked seriously about rays—X-rays, death rays, health rays, and ray guns. A new generation threw its arms around science, gadgets, automation, and invention.

Society took a U-turn from the ways Watson had known. Young people wanted to be sassy and outrageous. Women raised hemlines, bared shoulders, and jiggled their bodies doing the Charleston. Men packed into speakeasies, kissed women in public, listened to raucous Louis Armstrong music, and used Sigmund Freud as an excuse to talk about sex in mixed company. Cars, highways, national magazines, and advertising campaigns knitted the nation together.

The economy soared, growing 6 percent one year, 13 percent the next, and showing no signs of slowing. President Calvin Coolidge bestowed his blessing on companies by pronouncing that the business of America was business. Industrial stocks, widely distrusted by the general public just a few years earlier, turned into everybody's fantasy. Get in and get a rocket ride to riches, they thought. Children came to know what a stock ticker looked like. A hero could get no higher an honor than a ticker tape parade, rolling through the clefts between New York's skyscrapers while the by-products of wealth floated down on him. Businessmen felt they were gods. Many of them believed they were revolutionaries ushering in a new age.

As Watson saw it, scales weren't going to usher in a new age. Time clocks weren't going to make him a god. Those products would not excite Jazz Age socialites, daredevil investors, or national magazine writers.

Tabulating machines would.

They were clunky, ugly, noisy, and erratic. They were increasingly becoming known as "punch card machines," because they recorded information using holes punched through rectangular cards—a peculiar language that no one but a specialist could read. The machines, performing functions like figuring insurance actuarial tables, which bored most people silly, were stuck in back rooms visited mainly by corporate accountants. Yet tabulating machines had a quality that caught people's imagination. Other machines automated physical work, making hands more productive; tabulating machines automated mental work, making brains more productive. There had never been anything quite like them.

"They are machines which seem actually to think," Flint told people as a way to explain his company's product.

Because there had been nothing quite like these tabulating machines, and because they were only beginning to be adopted by industry, the field in the 1920s lay wide open to new ideas. For this reason, Watson increasingly turned his attention toward data processing, as he called it well before most anyone else. Watson, then in his 50s, loved coming up with data processing ideas, which he then dropped like hand grenades onto his beloved engineering teams.

Watson pressed his engineers to develop a railroad ticket printing system. He shot them a memo describing his idea. It would be a complete system for printing and tracking tickets and passengers. A ticket seller would push some buttons to punch information on the ticket about the destination, train number, mileage, amount paid, and taxes. Conductors would have other devices to punch other information about the passengers and fees charged on board. The cards could later be counted and sorted by railroad headquarters to figure everything from commissions for the ticket sellers to whether a particular rail line needed more or fewer passenger cars.[3]

Sometimes IBM's engineers couldn't carry out Watson's ideas. Five years after Watson's train ticket memo, the engineers still hadn't built what he'd described, and he was still carping about it.

Watson wanted to get tabulating machines into bank branches. Tellers did most of their business on handwritten pieces of paper, which accountants in back rooms had to read and record. Why not push automation right to the point of contact with customers? Watson proposed a machine to install at each teller window, so the tellers could record transactions on punched cards. In the back, a tabulating machine system could do the accounting, and sorters could help a bank to identify delinquent loans or figure out which branch offices were underperforming. In this idea, too, Watson got ahead of both the market and engineering. One bank president told Watson that each transaction would take a teller too long to complete. IBM's engineers weren't certain that they could build a bank system at reasonable cost. Watson pressed on. "I still think I am right, although nobody agrees with me," he said in a meeting with Braitmayer and engineers Lake, Bryce, Peirce, Carroll, and Ford. "We can hop right into this bank business, and I think it is something we have got to go into."[4] Almost 10 more years would pass before IBM would offer a bank system.

Watson didn't dream up only big concepts for punch card machines; he paid attention to surprisingly minute aspects. From the reports of servicemen in the field, Watson noticed that punch card machines tended to break down more in damp weather. He encouraged the engineers to come up with a heating lamp that could be fitted inside a machine, so the lamp could keep parts dry. Whether the engineers thought this was the best solution, they carried it out.

Punch card machines—how to improve them, how to apply them, and how to sell more of them—ate up an increasing share of Watson's time. What occupied Watson would occupy the rest of the company. He appropriated more executive time, more engineering manpower, and more money to punch card machines. In 1924, Bryce sent Watson a two-page engineering report. The first page-and-a-half detailed new punch card machine products and improvements. By contrast, about one-third of a page was devoted to Time Recording developments. The scale division got two sentences.[5] A laboratory report a few years later showed IBM spending, in six months, $83,411 on developing tabulating machine products, $13,393 on scales, and $9,850 on time clocks.[6]

On Monday, October 17, 1927, Watson called a meeting in the IBM boardroom. Braitmayer, Bryce, and Nichol took seats, as did 12 other executives from the top levels of the company. Watson, looking older, his hair nearly white, the skin on his high cheekbones beginning to sag, began the session by stating: "The object of this meeting is to talk about the future."

He made his leanings clear. The scale division got nothing but his disgust. "There is absolutely no common sense in this scale business going along and making no money."

The Time Recording division was well managed and making a profit, but the potential for growth seemed limited. IBM's marketers couldn't find many new ways to apply time clocks, and engineers could improve the products only incrementally. Time Recording's managers ran a steady, decent business, but it was not explosive. "The time clock business is a little harder problem than anything else," Watson told the men, sounding apologetic about the static nature of what was once the centerpiece of C-T-R. "There isn't very much there we can give the men in the way of anything new."

Watson then pointed to where he wanted IBM to go. "There isn't any limit for the tabulating business for many years to come," he said. "We have just scratched the surface in this division. I expect the bulk of [increased business] to come from the tabulating end, because the potentialities are greater, and we have done so little in the way of developing our machines in this field."

Underneath that statement lay a number of reasons—other than the thrill of new technology—why Watson zeroed in on the punch card business. When seen together, the reasons clicked like a formula for total domination. IBM would never be able to make sure it was the world leader in scales or time clocks, but it could make certain that it was the absolute lord of data processing.

The formula began with patents. Watson had learned the value of patents while at NCR and from Kettering. Inventions would drive sales, and patents could keep competitors at bay by preventing them from introducing similar inventions. It's a formula in full boil in the technology industry of the 2000s. From the beginning at C-T-R, Watson was aware of the value of the patents that Hollerith held. Bryce later pushed Watson to become aggressive about patents. Bryce's lab generated many of IBM's patents; Watson acquired more by buying upstart competitors. For instance, IBM bought J. Royden Peirce's fledgling punch card machine company to get Peirce's patents—and to get Pierce, who would go on to win more patents as an IBM engineer. Controlling the key patents on tabulating systems helped make life difficult for the competition because competitors would have to invent entirely new technology or license IBM's patents, which IBM could refuse to do.

Another ingredient in the formula was the punch card. The rectangular pieces of thin cardboard, seven and three-eighths inches by three and one-quarter inches, were the data storage devices for tabulating machines—the equivalent of a hard drive on a twenty-first-century computer. By the late 1920s, IBM had embraced Clair Lake's new and pantentable card design. Lake's cards lined up spaces for punched holes in 80 columns of 12 spaces under each column. A hole in a specific position represented a bit of information—possibly a letter in a name or a dollar figure in a paycheck. To fit all 960 spaces on a card, Lake made the holes narrow and rectangular, instead of round, as they were previously.

Lake's new IBM cards only worked on IBM machines. IBM offered a reproducing device that transferred information on old punched cards to the new versions. Once an IBM customer put all of its old information on IBM's proprietary cards, and stored more and more of its new information on those cards, the customer became locked in. Switching to a competing data processing company would require transferring the information on millions of cards to that company's cards. Some insurance companies, for instance, literally had entire floors devoted to the storage of punched cards. The cost of transferring all those cards would have been prohibitive; so the cards coerced IBM customers to remain IBM customers.

The card lock-in would prove to be powerful. Competitor Remington Rand would later introduce a 90-column card, which could hold more information than IBM's 80-column card for the same price. But IBM's customers would choose not to switch, and Remington Rand wouldn't dent IBM's dominating position.

IBM also manufactured the cards. It had to, IBM insisted. The company needed to ensure that the cards would work with its machines. It didn't want a customer to buy cheap cards from someone else, and have the cards tear or jam inside a machine. IBM forced customers to buy cards from IBM, a situation that allowed IBM to inflate prices and make chunky profits on punch cards.

Data processing was a young technology, Watson realized. Clever engineers would be able to improve punch card machines; clever salesmen would find new applications and new customers. The company that could fund the best research and development *and* the best marketing could outdistance any competitor. IBM was the one company that could afford both.

Watson had no epiphanies. No voice spoke to him about the future of data processing. He didn't have a grand vision for turning IBM into a punch card company. He got there little by little, one observation after another, over a period of 10 to 12 years. If Watson did indeed possess tremendous vision, an indomitable will, and unswerving determination, the traits served him by helping him toil through more than a decade of figuring out what his company would be.

One kink wrinkled Watson's plan: reliability. Punch card machines, which were becoming critical to the operation of businesses, broke down far too often. Springs snapped, typing elements stuck, and magnets misaligned. Printers at one point randomly printed 9s throughout documents. A customer in Paris balked at paying a full month's rent for its machines, telling IBM: "(The machines) often during a good part of the month cannot be used."[7] Braitmayer wrote a letter to Lake about repairs, saying: "I dislike exceedingly to be passing on to you so many complaints, but I certainly got an ear full this past week from the field force."[8]

Improving reliability meant improving the design of the machines, but it also meant improving the factories and the people who worked in them. That turned Watson's attention to Endicott, where in the process of strengthening his business, he met a man who taught him about love.

⟨⟩

On the south side of the railroad tracks that ran through Endicott, New York, lived the English-speaking natives—the families that were there before the place turned into a boomtown. In 1910, Endicott's population was 9,486. By the early 1920s, that number had tripled. Most of the new residents lived on the north side, and most of them didn't grow up speaking English. They had trekked from Greece, Poland, Italy, Russia, and the Slovak regions, sifted through Ellis Island, boarded trains, and disembarked in this town bordered on one side by the Susquehanna River, enclosed on the other sides by forested hills and topped by a sky that almost always filled with gray clouds. The ethnic groups tended to cluster in their own neighborhoods, but they blended together on Washington Street, which was lined with scores of specialty grocery stores, plus two bakeries, four barber shops, three drugstores, eight clothing stores, one florist, three hardware stores, two hotels, three banks, and an undertaker. A trolley clacked down the middle, a lively farmers market opened every morning at 10:00, and the police chief kept watch by riding up and down the street in a motorcycle sidecar.

Just beyond one end of Washington Street hummed the Endicott-Johnson (E-J) shoe factory complex, churning out nearly 175,000 pairs of shoes per day, making it one of the world's biggest and most successful shoe producers. It made women's fashion shoes, men's dress shoes, farmer's work-boots, and shoes for children. The company's imposing red-brick structures and towering smokestacks stretched out over 10 acres. Other E-J buildings peppered the region. The company operated tanneries, rubber factories for athletic shoesoles, and a factory that made ice skating boots and baseball shoes. It owned and operated two hospitals, two firehouses, a public library, and, for a while, a minor-league baseball team. Endicott-Johnson was the region's economic force. The town of Endicott took its name from the plant, not vice versa. A bordering village, once called Lestershire, was renamed Johnson City.[9]

The shoe company and Endicott owed their success to one of the most progressive chief executives in business history, George F. Johnson. Watson first met Johnson in 1914, soon after Watson was named to run C-T-R. Watson had traveled to Binghamton to visit the International Time Recording factory. Binghamton was the larger, older city; Endicott, the blossoming town. They stood a few miles apart and shared the same labor market and the same dreary weather. Johnson was already the industrial king of the region. Watson was a recently fired NCR executive facing a jail term and running a company that, as Johnson's son would later say, "had to all intents and purposes collapsed."[10] Despite the gap between them, Johnson met with Watson and offered Watson encouragement and assistance. "We talked together for over an hour," Watson recalled. "I found he was deeply interested in our little business, which was very small at the time."[11] Watson would always say how much he appreciated it, but at the time he developed only a cordial, business-like relationship with Johnson.

Like Watson, George Francis Johnson knew what it was like to be poor. He was born October 14, 1857, in Milford, Massachusetts, the son of Francis A. Johnson, a captain in the Civil War and a career-long boot tree-er—a job that entailed stretching freshly manufactured boots on wooden boot trees and rubbing the leather with a dressing to give it a finished look. To find work, the elder Johnson moved from factory to factory, town to town, dragging the family with him, barely making enough to subsist. George Johnson went to work at 13 as an apprentice at Seaver Bros. Bootmakers in Ashland, Massachusetts, and followed his father into treeing. In 1881, George landed a job as a treeing foreman at the Lester Bros. shoe factory in Binghamton. Seen as an effective boss, George Johnson gained increasing responsibility.

Henry B. Endicott, a stiff, no-nonsense investor who knew nothing about running a shoe business, bought out Lester Bros. in 1890 and gave Johnson a shot at running the factory. In two years, production soared from 1,000 pairs of shoes per day to 18,000. In 1899, Endicott sold Johnson half the business and gave him free reign to run it.

Johnson proved to be a manager like no other of the era. In an age of carpetbaggers and all-powerful business barons, Johnson felt a company should be a community of equals, all working toward the same goals and all sharing in the wealth created. "I don't believe that a man can own a business," Johnson told a biographer. "It belongs to the customers, to the workers, to the community, to the public." One of his oft-repeated slogans was, "I'm out to make all I can OF this concern, not try to take all I can OUT of it."[12]

He put everyone on a first-name basis—a stark contrast to the era's accepted business formality. Every worker and manager called Johnson by the name George F. He built homes and sold them to employees at cost. He offered free meals in a company restaurant, free legal aid, and medical care. He built glorious, extravagant parks and left them open to the public. He eliminated hourly salaries in favor of piecework, believing piecework empowered employees by letting them decide how hard to work and how much money they'd make. In 1919, Johnson instituted a plan that he dubbed "profit sharing," modestly commenting that it was "a comparatively new idea in industry"—an idea that is common today. He decreased the workday from nine and one-half hours to eight, prompting 12,000 employees to spontaneously rally around his colonial-style home to thank him.

While unions gathered momentum in many industries, they couldn't get a toehold at Endicott-Johnson. By all accounts, Johnson created a happy, productive, loyal workforce, and he became famous for it. In a lengthy feature story in 1917, the *New York Herald* said that Johnson governed "the nearest possible approach to a Utopia."[13] President Woodrow Wilson passed through Binghamton, stopping to tell a crowd of Endicott-Johnson workers: "If the same spirit which exists between you and [management] existed everywhere, there would be no question, no trouble, no difficulty as between the employer and the employee."[14] Johnson never stopped winning the reverence of his workers and the communities in which they lived. As time went on, he used money from E-J and his personal fortune to build one of the world's largest public swimming pools, a pavilion that attracted top acts such as Benny Goodman, and a series of carousels that he donated on the condition that they forever be free for anyone who wants to ride them. A few of them remained operating and free to the public into the twenty-first century.

Watson's management approach in the 1910s came nowhere near Johnson's. IBM ran its factories for efficiency. Although IBM didn't treat manufacturing employees any worse than most companies of the day, it didn't treat them particularly well, either. When IBM was still C-T-R, Rogers approached Johnson to ask if Endicott-Johnson would take over the Time Recording factories in the area because C-T-R couldn't compete with E-J in the labor market. As Johnson later recalled, Rogers wanted to move C-T-R production to Patterson, New Jersey, "where they could hire and fire." Johnson said that he advised Rogers to keep C-T-R in town, "and pointed out that I believed in the long run our (E-J's) policy was correct, and he would be benefited,

as we expected to be benefited, by a liberal, fair consideration of the partner Labor."[15] Between the lines, Johnson was
saying that C-T-R fell short in the "liberal" and "fair"
departments.

Although the C-T-R factories stayed in Binghamton and
Endicott, for some years Watson didn't buy into Johnson's
way. Their relationship remained stiff, with letters beginning "Dear Sir" and exchanges stuck in business-like patter.
As late as 1923, Watson still considered selling the factories
to E-J. An independent report prepared for Watson starkly
told him that C-T-R created its own manufacturing difficulties in the Endicott area—particularly the factory's inability
to keep good workers. "The condition of the plant, due to
the local management, has been responsible for the attitude
of the people toward the company, and hence their lack of
desire to be employed there," the report said.[16]

Still, Watson and Johnson continued to get to know one
another. Of the two, Johnson clearly had built up greater
wealth—his fortune was estimated at as much as $50 mil-
lion. Johnson ran the bigger company and wielded more
power. Photographers often caught them together in Endicott, capturing their physical differences. Watson, as usual,
looked thin, angular, and stiff. Johnson, a star baseball
pitcher in his youth, looked like a round, owlish favorite
schoolteacher. Standing just under six feet tall, Johnson had
broad shoulders, a portly midsection, and thick, muscular
hands. His moonlike face crinkled at the corners of his gray-
ish blue eyes. Random streaks of red tinted his otherwise
gray hair.

When Watson in the late 1920s focused on punch card
machines, he realized that to win in that business, he needed
loyal, happy employees who could put out high-quality
machines. To get there, something would have to change.
His factories sat in a labor market where most people—particularly the best workers—wanted to work for Endicott-

Johnson. The residents weren't so sure about IBM. The smart thing for Watson to do in Endicott would be to follow Johnson's lead.

One other issue helped convince Watson to borrow from Johnson: Endicott-Johnson had kept unions out by keeping employees happy. Johnson continually bested whatever unions demanded of employers. Watson wanted to keep unions from organizing inside IBM, and Johnson provided a template.

IBM began to pay more, offer benefits competitive with E-J's, and add a greater sense of respect to factory jobs. Watson traveled to Endicott more frequently and enjoyed roaming the grounds and visiting the factory floor, where he'd stop and ask a worker to explain his job and ask if he had suggestions for making production better or more efficient. Workers got the message that Watson considered them to be important. In the mid-1930s, as IBM's growth took off, Watson matched Johnson by building a golf course for employees. In a reflection of their personalities, Watson's course was challenging and made players walk up an incline, dubbed Cardiac Hill, steep enough to give someone a heart attack. Johnson's golf course was purposely flat and easy, so that dog-tired factory workers of any golfing ability could enjoy a round.

Eventually, Watson even trumped Johnson, constructing an industrial schoolhouse for ongoing training, and offering hourly factory workers two weeks' paid vacation. Upon hearing of the vacation benefit, Johnson wrote to Watson to express his admiration and his sadness that E-J was not in a position to offer the same. Endicott-Johnson, Johnson explained, had too big a backlog of orders and couldn't spare workers for that long.[17]

The men disagreed on some points. Watson felt that piecework—pay based on how many items the worker finishes—demeaned workers and hurt quality, because workers would try to finish items quickly, rather than expertly. Johnson believed a factory couldn't be run from afar, while Watson kept his base in New York.

Still, Johnson saw Watson as a convert—a disciple who could spread Johnson's ideas across the Endicott and Binghamton region and beyond. For years, Johnson kept up gentle but none too subtle pressure on Watson. He made sure that Watson felt their two companies were linked in a cause. Johnson pointed out that E-J and IBM were "disposed to be fair and liberal as possible—disposed to encourage neighborly kindness and human friendship."[18] He played on Watson's desire to wash away his earlier antitrust taint. "I am firmly convinced, Tom, that the only happiness we are going to get out of our life's work is the happiness of doing kindly, considerate things for those less fortunate in this world's goods."

Johnson really got to Watson, and not only in business and management. Johnson's warmth melted into Watson on a personal level. The two men began writing and speaking to each other frequently, effusively complimenting one another in speeches and during interviews with newspaper reporters. Their correspondence transformed over the years from business stiltedness to friendliness, their greetings becoming "My dear George F" and "Dear Tom." Watson told Johnson he was "one of the greatest sources of inspiration one could have."[19] Johnson told Watson, "I admire you greatly, and love you more."[20]

When Johnson came down with pneumonia, Watson sent flowers, demanded regular updates on Johnson's health, and expressed relief when Johnson recovered. The two men exchanged Christmas presents—Johnson sending Watson shoes; Watson giving Johnson a smoking jacket.

Their relationship was among the most touching of Watson's business life. The emotions crystallized in a moment on April 25, 1938. Watson had been visiting Endicott but already left town. Not knowing that, Johnson's son, George W. Johnson (yes, known as "George W"), telephoned the manager of IBM's Endicott factories and said his father wanted to see Watson.

The manager said that Watson had gone. A disappointed George F then picked up the phone to say how much he regretted missing Watson on this trip.

"Why?" the manager asked Johnson.

George F. Johnson said into the telephone, "One of the things I want to tell Mr. Watson is that I love him."

The manager typed up a note saying exactly that and sent it to Watson in New York.

⟵⟶

Eleven IBM executives took seats in Watson's office on an autumn day in 1928. As the meeting got underway, they might have experienced any number of emotions for their chief executive, but probably none of them at that moment were love.

"I have definitely concluded that you gentlemen do not realize even in a small way what the future is going to demand of you in connection with sales of your products," said a furious Watson. "And incidentally, I might add that I am going to demand more of you, because I've got to."

In 1927, the company made a $4 million profit on $14 million in sales. In the fall of 1928, IBM was on its way to making $5 million profit on $15 million in sales for the year. Almost any businessperson would be impressed by a 25 percent increase in profits in a year. But Watson had ordered his executives to grow the company to at least $20 million in 1928, and then he wanted sales to rise to $28 million in 1929. He fumed at his executives because they were off the pace he'd set.

In that state, anything could have set him off. The spark on this day was his executives' failure to answer a call to dedicate a company-wide sales push during the last four months of 1928 as a tribute to Otto Braitmayer, who was celebrating 40 years with the company.

They'd all received telegrams from Watson about it. In 1928, if you wanted to communicate with another person immediately and convey a sense of urgency or importance, you sent a telegram. When that piece of paper labeled "Western Union" landed on a desk, its message printed in block letters minus punctuation could not be ignored. No one could ever use the excuse, "I didn't see your telegram."

Yet none of IBM's executives responded to Watson's Braitmayer telegram. More than likely, they didn't think that there was any need to respond—Watson didn't ask for their input, and the dedication seemed only symbolic. Yet Watson lit into those present, letting the hyperbole fly.

"I never in all my experience in business worried as I have since last Tuesday morning because I did not hear from you men. Not one of you even mentioned it to me," Watson said. "You men don't know what you are trying to do. Why is the tabulating division in such an awful condition?" The executives must have been thinking: It's not in awful condition! Though they wouldn't dare show it in their faces, much less speak it aloud. "Because you fellows don't know what you want to do. Last month was the biggest month we had, over a half-million dollars net for August. That ought to have been a million dollars. And you should have gone after it. It's right out there waiting for you."[21]

In that mood, if they'd netted $5 million, Watson would have been mad that it wasn't $6 million. He always pushed himself to chase near-impossible goals, and he had little patience for anyone who didn't do the same. This stance was reflected in two of his many business aphorisms, which were often posted in IBM offices and factories: "They can who know they can," and, "Never feel satisfied."

Watson felt he could unleash tirades at his managers

with impunity, and for the most part he could. No one dared question or cross him. Executives rationalized his behavior by telling each other, "If you weren't worth putting together, he didn't bother to tear you apart."[22] They were willing to take it because they wanted to be part of IBM. They were building machines that had never before existed. They worked with brilliant engineers and sharp managers who blended together to form this odd but magnetic cult of sober people who made the company their life and ambition. Few other American companies offered the promise and excitement of IBM—or such an opportunity to get rich. In 1928, Watson received a letter on IBM stationery saying that the undersigned were impressed with the "rapidity" of IBM's stock increase during the year. "We feel it is only proper to tell you at this time just how deeply grateful we are to you . . . for making it possible for us to become stockholders and prosper with the business." It was signed by 20 midlevel IBM executives.

Many felt blessed to be able to follow Watson. He was such a strong personality, so sure of his leadership and so driven. People hitched themselves to him like railcars to a locomotive. Once they did—and once they proved their loyalty—Watson gave back, whether it was with bonuses, quick promotions, paid vacations, or compassion during an illness or family crisis.

The fear of getting cut off from all of that shot ice through executives' arteries. Harry Evans, the peppy young executive, knew exactly how that felt. He believed he was wronged when IBM chose not to give him a bonus for landing a major deal with the U.S. Census. Evans aired his complaint to Watson, who sent back a scathing reply. "I feel very sorry to learn that after your long term of service you seem to be so unhappy regarding your connection with the company," Watson wrote.

That was all Evans needed to hear. Petrified of Watson's disapproval, he wrote back immediately. "I have always been and am now very happy in my work for and with every division of our company and all our executives and representatives," Evans wrote. "No one could be happier in serving with you and for you than I am. I believe I have enthusiastically proved on all occasions my whole-hearted loyalty and joy in cooperating with your good self . . . to the best of my ability." Whatever Watson decided about the bonus, Evans promised he would "cheerfully abide" by it.

Watson's dictatorial tendencies were served by his inability to create an effective management structure suitable for a large company. When C-T-R was small and spunky, decisions funneled through Watson—big ones about new products or factories and little ones about the wording of an advertisement or the seating at a convention. He would listen to members of his team and rely on their input, but he wanted the final say. As the company grew, decisions continued to go through Watson. To be sure, IBM managers had plenty of responsibility; however, the company revolved around its president, who at any time might undo a decision or promotion made by an executive.

An organizational chart from the period looked like bird tracks in the snow, jammed full of lines, tiny squares, and initials. With subsidiaries, legal entities, and international entities, IBM consisted of 13 different companies, including the umbrella IBM Corporation. A matrix of the top executives involved in running IBM listed the 13 entities across the top and 14 executive titles down the left-hand column. The boxes formed by the intersection of a company and a title (Tabulating Machine Company and treasurer; Dayton Moneyweight Scale Company and secretary) were filled in with the initials of the person who had the job. Eighteen different individuals held 182 jobs among them. A matrix of IBM directors was even more difficult to follow. There was no chain of command at IBM, but something more like a web, with Watson as the spider.

Watson continually pledged—usually to Nichol—to simplify the structure and push more duties off his desk and onto others, but he found it difficult to do either. Watson was not a systematic man, nor was he one who easily gave up control. However, he easily gave up credit. In speeches and interviews, he would never fail to put the spotlight on others, whether honoring Braitmayer for 40 years of service, naming every IBM inventor in a business club speech, or publicly thanking the Endicott factory workers. To Watson, though, credit was one thing; control was something else entirely.

As the checks on Watson disappeared, he had fewer ways to find out when he was deluding himself. He believed he was a powerful speaker who could rouse a sales force or draw tears from a dinner crowd. For the audience, however, many of his speeches were dull and long. He often spoke in a flat voice and had a habit of loudly clearing his throat every few minutes. He sometimes read from prepared texts; other times he referred to brief notes typed vertically on the backs of unpunched punch cards. At times he spoke extemporaneously. However he prepared, he never hesitated to vary from whatever he'd planned to say. Generally, he spoke about broad concepts and generalities, rarely using anecdotes. The result was that many of his speeches meandered aimlessly and went on far too long for the audience.

Though Watson had a sense of humor, his speeches were humorless. He sometimes opened with one of a few tired jokes. He'd stride to the podium after Nichol or someone else gave him a flowery introduction, and say the introduction reminded him of a funeral he went to. The minister went on and on about the good qualities of the deceased, Watson would explain. Finally, a man tiptoed up and peered into the casket. "I asked him why he did that," Watson would say, closing in on the punch line. "He said, 'I thought I was at the wrong funeral.'"

Another opening joke: "Why is a public speaker like the

wheel of an automobile? The more he spoke, the bigger the tire." Then, with no sense of irony, Watson would speak too long.

Watson also started to believe he was as important outside of IBM as he was inside the company. More than once, he sent a conductor to order the engineer to stop a train so he and his party could view the scenery. On one trip from New York to San Francisco, the engineer cranked up the train's speed to make up for falling behind schedule. Watson, who had booked the entire train for a party of IBMers, overheard one passenger say, "Mercy, we're just whizzing along, aren't we?" Watson suddenly feared a wreck, and yelled for a conductor—who tried to explain that the train was traveling at a safe speed.

"Don't talk to me!" Watson said. "If you don't slow up this train, I'll pull it down myself." He reached for the cord that would trigger the emergency brake.

"If you touch that cord you're likely to hurt somebody," the conductor said.

"Listen, who's boss of this train?" Watson bellowed.

"I am," said the unimpressed conductor.

"Well, I'm paying for it. I'll have you fired!"

"Maybe you will," said the conductor, "but you won't touch that cord."[23]

That time, Watson lost the argument. But clearly he felt that in any situation, he should be able to do as he wished.

❧

Watson bought a farm in rural Lebanon, New Jersey—a little less than 200 acres previously known as the Amos Crater Farm. He had only owned the place about a month when he and his family went out there for a spring respite. Watson kept dogs on the farm, and they had wandered off across the fields onto a nearby farm owned by a Mr. Smith. Concerned that the dogs might cause damage or disturb his animals, Smith fired at them with a shotgun, meaning only to scare them off. Though Smith didn't realize it, he wounded a female dog.

Another man who lived in the area, Winfred Green, heard the shot and saw Watson's dogs running. Green called on Watson and told him what happened. Watson checked and found that one of his dogs was missing, so he and two of the children went to Smith and asked to search his fields. There, near a stump pile, they found the dog, alive but severely wounded.

Watson lifted the dog and carried it to his car. He called a veterinarian, who came by the house and suggested he take her to a hospital in Summit, New Jersey. X rays showed she had 37 shots in her hind quarter, but none of the shots hit the intestines or stomach. Watson and the family nursed her back to health.

Watson could have been furious. Instead, he went back to Smith and told him that if the dogs came around again, Watson would pay him for any damage they might do. He asked Smith not to shoot at them. Smith agreed. In a letter to Green, Watson called it "a very satisfactory talk."

In appreciation for notifying him, Watson sent Green a check for $25.[24]

The farm continued to be a source of odd distractions. One winter day, a letter arrived at Watson's IBM office from a real estate agent named Wilmer N. Tuttle. "We have had a Mr. Lear out here looking for property who represents a nudist society who are seeking a [30- to 40-acre] summer place," the letter began. "He seems to be interested in the 40-acre Farley place which adjoins your property."[25]

Noting that Watson might object to a nudist colony in his backyard—not exactly a great leap of judgment—Tuttle thought he'd give Watson "the opportunity to acquire the property yourself if you care to."

Watson didn't buy the property; nor did any naked rompers take over the Farley place. The farm next door remained a farm.

Watson's wealth had ratcheted up over the previous decade. He was a millionaire, able to afford the big Short Hills house, the New Jersey farm, a chauffer, a caretaker, a cook, and a few horses and ponies. The once-poor farmboy enjoyed the things money could buy. Jeannette, who'd grown up with money, seemed more conservative about the family finances.

In 1927, Watson revised his will, sorting out his priorities at the time. The will stated that when Watson died, $50,000 should go to each of his four children. Watson's three sisters would each receive $25,000, and $10,000 was to go to Asbury Methodist Episcopal Church in Rochester, New York, which his mother attended in the last years before she died. Two nieces and a nephew would receive $5,000 each. George Phillips would receive $5,000, but only if Jeannette did not survive Watson, because then Phillips would have become guardian of Watson's property and of Watson's minor children—an enormous and unusual show of trust by a boss in his personal secretary. Each of three domestic employees would receive $1,000. The rest would go to Jeannette.[26]

The family had money to spare. As the nation exulted in Lindbergh's flight, cheered Babe Ruth's drive to 60 home runs, and puzzled over Calvin Coolidge's decision not to run for reelection, the Watson's vacationed at the Montana Ranch Club in Cameron, Wyoming. For entertainment at home over a weekend, the family rented films. One weekend they rented *The Olympic Games,* a comedy featuring Spanky, Alfalfa, and the rest of the Our Gang characters; another film called *Will Rogers in Dublin;* and a short documentary about a small-town Wild West sheriff. Total cost for the film rentals came to $20.[27]

Watson bought a seven-year-old black gelding, 14 hands, for $500. He also bought a 1928 Stutz Seven-Passenger

Speedster, model BB, including wire wheels, tonneau windshield, and slip covers. The car cost $4,300.[28]

He started thinking about owning a yacht.

～

Thomas J. Watson Sr., the serious man in serious clothes, loved to sing and dance.

A film, shot at Watson's house on a brilliant summer day, opens by showing the Watson children playing on some rocks. The camera pans to Watson, who is dressed in a light suit and wearing a brimmed strawhat. Other men in suits and women in dresses mill about, invited there for a picnic. The children ride bicycles and hop through three-legged races, then gather on the porch and attempt to do the Charleston, their limbs flailing as they giggle. In a moment, the children clear the porch and Watson stands there, lips silently moving as he talks to the deaf camera, Jeannette positioned next to him, wearing a white dress and looking bashful and uncomfortable. Music must be playing off to the side. In a sudden, spontaneous move, Watson turns to Jeannette, grabs her, pulls her toward him, and begins dancing to a quick beat. Jeannette, laughing and embarrassed, needs a few seconds to get in sync, then begins moving her feet with him. He leads her back and forth across the porch.

At another time—a Thanksgiving—again a number of formally dressed men and women walk around Watson's property. They stiffly try to figure out what to do for the movie camera. Watson enters the frame, chatting and smiling. Abruptly, he seizes a woman and begins dancing. She seems delighted. They dance for a couple of minutes, then he partners with another woman, this time doing a sublimely silly dance.

In those moments, vanished is the Watson who appears so somber at the podium, or who shreds his managers in a meeting room.

He delighted in singing as Jeannette played the piano. People more commonly sang in the early part of the century. The first radio broadcast skipped through the air in 1920, and until then music didn't arrive from the outside—it had to be generated inside. People sang in their homes, they sang in their cars, they sang in small groups, and they sang in large gatherings. Watson enthusiastically participated.

If Watson sang, IBM would sing. As with the dress code, Watson didn't order IBM to sing. That bit of corporate culture started with Harry Evans. Outgoing, attention-seeking, good-natured, wired with energy, and shorter than every other man in the room, Evans was always the guy with the joke, or the guy willing to laugh at a joke. Watson liked him and promoted him.

Evans loved to sing, and he enjoyed setting his own lyrics to popular tunes. He'd try to make the words funny or about someone familiar. Sometimes he'd make the lyrics up on the spot; other times he'd first write them down. He'd sing his songs solo to entertain his colleagues or friends; other times, he'd teach his lyrics to a group and get everyone to join in.

As the years went on, Evans informally assembled quite a few songs about IBM or people at the top of IBM. In 1925, he went to Watson and proposed printing a booklet of his IBM songs so that any of the employees could sing them at gatherings. It might be fun, Evans said. Watson liked the idea. At company sales conventions and other gatherings, employees already sang patriotic numbers and songs of good fellowship. Why wouldn't they want to sing about IBM?

Evans went to work. One number was sung to the tune of the World War I fight song, "Over There."[29]

IBM/ Sing again
Give a cheer/ for our great/ IBM
We make time recorders/ and tabulators
And Dayton scales for business men

118

Evans—along with Nichol, who contributed a few lyrics of his own—wrote lyrics about nearly every top manager in the company: Braitmayer, Sam Hastings, Ogsbury, Bryce, and many far lesser executives. Some of the songs must have made their subjects wince, like the one for inventor J. Royden Peirce, sung to the tune of "My Bonnie Lies over the Ocean."

> His mind is a fine laboratory
> Our problems he solves with great ease
> Unmatched his creative ability
> All IBM patrons to please
> (chorus)
> Patents! Patents! J. Royden Peirce has them by the score
> Inventions! Inventions! Each day he creates more and more

When the booklet was printed, two songs were about Watson. A few years later, Evans wrote a third, to the tune of "Auld Lang Syne."

> T. J. Watson/ you're our leader fine/ the greatest in the land
> We sing your praises from our hearts/ we're here to shake
>   your hand
> You're IBM's bright guiding star/ you're big and square and
>   true
> No matter what the future brings/ we all will follow you

To Watson's ears, the songs were inspirational. They cemented a sense of togetherness and loyalty to IBM. Singing became one of those odd cultural fragments that made the company so different and noteworthy.

Evans remained dedicated to IBM's singing tradition until his last breath. Fifteen years after creating his songbook, Evans led the salesmen at a 1941 convention in several songs. After the session, Evans retired to his hotel room, collapsed from a heart attack, and died.

The tradition survived for another 20 years. The generation of employees who listened to Elvis Presley on the radio had little interest in publicly singing outmoded tunes about their company. Nobody thought to write IBM lyrics set to the tune of "Heartbreak Hotel." The songs faded out.

~

On October 17, 1929, crusty old Flint—still around and still an IBM director—received a letter from Watson regarding the next regular board meeting, scheduled for 3 P.M. on October 29. It would be held at the Endicott factory, followed by a lavish dinner to celebrate A. Ward Ford's 40th anniversary with the company. An IBM-chartered train was to leave from Jersey City, New Jersey, at 10 A.M. on October 29, and Flint, his wife, and the many other invitees traveling to Endicott from New York or New Jersey were welcome to ride.

Although the upcoming event was intended to honor Ford, Watson just as much wanted to celebrate IBM. In the rocketing stock market of the late 1920s, IBM emerged as a star. Its stock performance couldn't match Radio Corporation of America (RCA), which zoomed from $85 a share in 1927 to $573.75 in 1929, but IBM made a lot of investors happy and wealthy. Its stock began 1927 at $54 a share. At its peak in 1929, it was more than four times that. The company hummed with growth. The first nine months of 1929, profits were up 29 percent over the first nine months of 1928. IBM operated factories in Endicott and Dayton, with manufacturing outposts in Toronto, Canada; Sindelfingen, Germany; Paris, France; and London, England. The company sold scales, meat grinders, clocks, employee time recorders, coupon printing devices, tabulating machines, sorters, punches, and punch cards. IBM still wasn't an outsized presence in American industry, but it sizzled with an energy and vitality that few companies could match.

Seven days after Flint got his letter, the stock market's

crash began. On Black Thursday, October 24, 1929, hysterical investors and speculators decided the market was overvalued. The New York Stock Exchange opened at 9 A.M., as always. By 11 A.M., stocks had lost $9 billion in value. (About $95 billion in value in 2002 dollars.) New Yorkers crowded onto Wall Street. The grand old banker, J. P. Morgan, emerged from his building and announced that he and other bankers would help stabilize the market, and all would be fine. The market rallied and cut the day's losses to $3 billion.

The market remained stable on Friday and Saturday. Monday, it headed back down. A. Ward Ford's party was scheduled for the next day.

Tuesday morning, October 29, 1929, Nichol, Bryce, Hastings, Evans, Phillips, and dozens more men and women drifted into the Jersey City Terminal for the trip to Endicott. The train would stop in Paterson, New Jersey, to pick up Watson. The men wore suits, topcoats, and fedoras. The women wore droopy dresses hemmed about midcalf, and flapper-style hats. Some wrapped themselves in fur. Many of the men and women puffed cigarettes. Each traveler brought with him a folded, pocket-size white card, which outlined the trip on the IBM Special: "Seating of guests on train, according to own preference. Facilities for playing Bridge will be provided." It told them that lunch would be served and their baggage checked and delivered to their hotel rooms. At the Arlington Hotel in Binghamton, "a page will conduct you to your room. It is not necessary to register. You will find your key in your door, and your baggage in your room." The celebratory dinner, the card informed them, would be at 7 P.M., announced by trumpet call.

In the hour spent on the platform and boarding the train, from 9 A.M. until 10 A.M., panic was gripping Wall Street. Sell orders instantly overwhelmed traders. Nearly 650,000 shares of U.S. Steel were sold in the first three minutes after the market opened. Stocks plunged at an unprecedented rate, quickly wiping out the market's gains for the entire previous year.

At midday, as the train clacked through Upstate New York's forested countryside, all those on board gathered in the dining car. They started lunch with vegetable soup and salted almonds. The main course was a choice of filet of sole with tartar sauce, or lamb chops with a rasher of bacon. After the white-jacketed waiters cleared the meal away, they set down a dessert of mince pie with cheese.

As the travelers ate, the market rallied in New York. Investors expected Morgan and his bankers to again jump in to prevent a meltdown. They didn't, and the market went into free fall.

On a railcar moving through scenic hills in 1929, there was no way to get news. The travelers were clueless about the crash for the duration of the five-hour ride.

In the early afternoon, the IBM Special stopped near the freight entrance to the factory in Endicott. There was no train station or platform, just bare dirt and gravel. The men and women streamed out of the cars under a cloudy sky. The IBM Band lined up nearby and struck up a welcome march. The band—trumpets, trombones, French horns, clarinets, and drums, all played by men wearing band uniforms and hats—escorted the arriving group on the walk to the factory, blaring the whole way. Watson, age 55, bounded out to the front of the crowd, leading them onward like a military general overrunning captured territory. When they arrived at the IBM plant, the two-story main entrance was draped in red, white, and blue bunting. A large sign said "Welcome." The entire group—executives, wives, friends, the band, with Watson and Ford front and center—lined up for a panoramic portrait. Afterward, some of the executives and wives took a tour of the factory. Watson and the other directors pealed off to conduct their board meeting. In the meeting, nearing 4 P.M., they must have learned the full measure of what was happening on Wall Street.

By the close of trading, 16,410,030 shares had traded hands, a record that would stand until 1968. Perhaps $15 billion, maybe more than $30 billion, in market value had been lost—no one could tell because the volume of trades was so great that stock tickers could not keep up. Frantic traders on the exchange floor tried to liquidate their holdings before the closing bell rang, creating a sound that one observer described as a constant, ear-ringing roar. The damage flashed out across the nation on telegraph wires, and investors watched their net worth spill away. One man died of a heart attack while reading the ticker in a brokerage office. John Schwitzgebel of Kansas City, Missouri, shot himself twice in the chest, saying, "Tell the boys I can't pay them what I owe them."[30]

In Endicott, the only certainty among Watson and his directors was that the carnage had been great. Most of them probably first thought of their personal concerns—they all held considerable amounts of IBM stock, which had taken a beating like all other stocks. What the crash meant for IBM as a company they could not fathom.

But while much of the business world worried and tended to its wounds, Watson put on a tuxedo and went to a banquet. At the Arlington Hotel, the trumpets blew. The doors to the Spanish Ballroom opened as the IBM band played a rousing march. The 600 guests found their places among long rows of white tables. An attendee described the scene: "Jeweled pendants hanging from the chandeliers flashed the rich colors of rubies, emeralds, and sapphires. Candle flames gleamed among the warm tones of autumn flowers."[31] The band gave way to the IBM Factory Orchestra, which played Broadway tunes. As guests picked up the menu, many of them chuckled. The names of the items were given a twist using IBM jargon. First came a Labor-Saving Consommé. It was followed by a choice of Dayton Scaled Fish with Electrically Controlled Potatoes, or Key-Wound Breast of Chicken Eugene with Mechanically Perfect Potatoes and Brussels

Sprouts with Counting Attachment. Dessert would be Lacquer-Finished Ice Cream and Key-Verified Cake. Dayton Ground Coffee would finish the meal.

Before dessert, Harry Evans took the stage and led the hall in IBM songs. A group of executives put on a skit poking gentle fun at Ford, parodying him and a golf foursome as they arrived at a country club. Moments later, four waiters appeared bearing a giant cake topped by 40 candles, followed by 40 waiters each carrying a normal-size cake topped by a single candle.

Watson played toastmaster. He made brief remarks, then began introducing the speakers who would pay tribute to Ford. Watson invited 16 men to speak, from Braitmayer to the mayor of Endicott. Each told stories about Ford and detailed his accomplishments. For the audience, it must have seemed interminable. When the 16 speakers finished, Watson took his turn.

As he wound toward a conclusion, Watson engaged in the kind of kitschy pomp he was coming to adore. Two silk curtains hung behind the head table. Watson paused dramatically, stepped to the side and pulled a cord. The curtains parted to reveal a trio of outsized photographs of Ford and his family. The crowd applauded enthusiastically. For his grand finale, Watson named Ford's son a vice president of the Time Recording division. E. E. "Tink" Ford had been the division's sales manager.

At no point in the evening did a single speaker mention one word about the stock market crash. Not a hint.

The next morning, October 30, America woke up to the dull pain of a new economic reality. The *New York Times* headlines screamed the news: Under banner headlines, the first paragraph called the day "the most disastrous trading day in the stock market's history."[32] However, in Binghamton and Endicott, Watson delivered alternative medicine. The banner headline at the top of the *Binghamton Press* read, "American Business Sound, Notwithstanding Stock

Crash, IBM Head Says Here." Watson spoke to reporters about the crash. "This flurry, which has brought large paper or actual losses to many persons, has seemingly left a large portion of the public in a more or less befuddled state of mind, and perhaps in some instances has resulted in a loss of confidence in the stability of American business," Watson pontificated. "I see absolutely no reason why the public should feel alarmed over the situation—nor get the idea that a money or business panic might be impending."[33]

Watson was wrong. The stability of American business was in question, and so was IBM's future.

⤐

(To the tune of "Round Her Neck She Wears a Yellow Ribbon")

We're proud to be all IBM star salesmen.
The records prove conclusively—our quotas we have made.
We all enjoy that grand and glorious feeling
Expressed in Mr. Watson's smile. Oh, boys! It's truly great!

—*Songs of the IBM*

5

DARING
AND LUCK

ONDAY, NOVEMBER 18, 1929, WATSON CALLED HIS top executives into the boardroom at headquarters. They came gladly, anxious to hear anything from Watson. He had disappeared after the stock market crash 20 days earlier.

"Gentlemen, I thought we would get together this morning, as there have been a great many things happen in the last few weeks," Watson began. "Some of our people have had to give a lot of thought to their finances, which has distracted their attention from the main issue. That main issue, of course, you all know with us, is building the IBM and making it a bigger and better business."

The crash rattled the nation and left businessmen with a hollow ache in their guts. Stocks kept falling. Companies quickly cut workforces. Financial institutions struggled to stay afloat. The economy seemed instantly, shockingly crippled. For those 20 days, when this group of men needed Watson to stand tall and assure them, he disappeared. Had he given up? Was IBM sunk? Was he busy planning a way out of the mess?

"I have been thinking this over very carefully over the weekend, and that is why I have called you all together this morning, so we can get to thinking along sane and sound lines," Watson told them. "I have not done anything in the interests of this business for the last three weeks."

The executives must have gasped. That didn't sound like good news.

"You know I have not talked with any of you about sales, money collections, et cetera," he continued. "I have run a stock broker's office for three weeks."

It dawned on them: Probably every one of those men individually had gone to see Watson since the crash. They had built their lives and finances on IBM stock, which so far had almost exclusively gone up. As it hit new highs in the summer of 1929, some executives used their holdings as collateral for margin loans to buy other stocks. But now the value of their IBM holdings had been cut in half, and the share price kept falling. Margin calls might have wiped out some of the men, leaving them in need of loans or salary advances. Other executives might have only wanted to hear that the company was sound and the stock would recover. They paraded into Watson's office seeking help or comfort or both. He took the time to give it to them, in a gesture that said that his men *were* the business. He had to steady his executives before he could steady his company.

He'd had enough of that, though. The Watson stock brokerage office was closed, he told the group. "I have now opened up on the IBM company with a vengeance, and I want all of you to get your heads up and tails over the dashboard," he said. "We have a big job to do, a hard job to do, and the only way is thinking and working constructively, and we must start it immediately."

He put the situation on the table. IBM's business was going to dip, Watson admitted. Every U.S. business was about to experience, as he put it, "a temporary slowing up." But IBM would not sit still and await its fate. It would find ways to keep the business growing. IBM had to open new markets for its machines, selling to businesses and entities that might never have thought they needed data processing.

The company had to push harder in foreign countries. "We are not going to wait for something to happen—we are going to make something happen," Watson said.

He went around the room, handing out assignments. Drawing on his belief that engineering could drive sales, Watson ordered the research department to come up with marketable inventions. It was a remarkably different reaction than that of CEOs, throughout history, who often slash research and development budgets to try to save money during down times. Watson then told the manufacturing executives to tighten costs and boost productivity. The finance group had to beef up its ability to collect on bills because the economy was going to leave a lot of companies in arrears. Purchasing, sales, service—boom, boom, boom—he hit every department. It was time to get serious, and they were going to have to do it together.

"I hope that every man in this room feels that he can start doing a bigger job than he has done before," he said as he was winding down. "And if there is any man in this meeting who doesn't feel that way and will come to me alone, I will be glad to talk with him and help him, because now is the time to make the most of everything."

It wasn't a threat. It was a call to rely on each other, not tear the organization apart.[1]

⊸⧉⊶

One evening in Endicott, Watson took the stage to speak to hundreds of assembled employees and guests. He stood behind the lectern, began his talk, then plowed on incessantly. In the front row sat his wife, Jeannette Watson, wearing, as she often did, a simple boxy dress, a hat, and a choker of a double strand of pearls. Seated next to her were two men of no great stature: Russ Ingraham, an employee in the Endicott factory, and Bob Novak, who ran the IBM Club, an employee recreation and athletics organization in Endicott.

On stage, Watson would not stop speaking. He rambled on.

Jeannette took out a piece of paper, wrote on it, folded it, and handed it to Ingraham. She told him to put it on the lectern.

Ingraham opened the note. Jeannette had written, "Shut up!"

Ingraham turned to Novak and showed him the note. Ingraham didn't know what to do. He was, as Novak would recall, looking extremely uncomfortable. Ingraham turned back to Jeannette and told her, as respectfully as possible, that he couldn't give the note to Watson. Jeannette looked at Ingraham with bullets in her eyes. "Put it up there," she said.

Ingraham slithered onto the stage and placed the note in front of Watson, who never broke his stream of words as he picked up the paper and read it. Showing no sign of surprise or indignation, Watson didn't even finish his sentence. He simply said, "Good night," and left the stage.[2]

Jeannette Watson often seemed an enigma—a kindly, sweet, silent-shadow figure who accompanied Watson like a dedicated golf caddy. To Watson, though, she was an anchor to reality. Without her, Watson's worst tendencies would have gone completely unbridled. At times, he could only see his effect on people through her eyes. She protected him. Watson could show an inability to understand the petty politics and sensitivities of mere mortals. She made sure that he didn't trip over them.

Even inside the marriage, the relationship could seem baffling. Although Jeannette at times could stop Watson with a word or hard look, she was also afraid of him. Olive Watson, who married Tom Watson Jr. in 1941, remembers Jeannette always seeming nervous around the senior Watson, afraid to say something that might put a match to his temper. Yet Olive Watson also remembers that Jeannette adored her husband. Eleanor Irvine, who as a young woman knew the Watsons well, never understood the relationship between the two of them. While they would appear together on many occasions, "they would be there, but as individuals," Irvine said.

Jeannette Watson was not particularly pretty. As she aged, her face became increasingly plain. Her cheekbones rode high up under her warm eyes. Nearly a foot shorter than Watson, her body retained its petite, fit shape throughout her life. She had little sense of style, preferring muted or plainly patterned dresses with a modest V neckline and a length cut to midcalf. Rarely did she appear without a hat. She wore little makeup and often wore white gloves.

In public, she almost never said a word. When she felt overly stressed, she would disappear into a women's restroom and lie flat on the floor.[3] She was practical. Early in their marriage, when Watson admitted that he didn't know how to check a furnace or do anything handy around the house, Jeannette learned how to do it herself. She could get flustered by Watson's spontaneity. The two of them once hopped in their car and drove to Hyde Park to visit Eleanor Roosevelt. When they arrived, Mrs. Roosevelt wasn't home.

"Tom, did you tell her you were coming?" Jeannette said to her husband.

"No, I thought we'd just drop in," he answered. Jeannette grew furious.[4]

In 1939, Jeannette visited Alice Denton Jennings, who billed herself as a character analysis expert, and had Jennings analyze her hand. Jeannette Watson saved the written analysis, probably because it was fairly accurate. The analysis said that Jeannette Watson had "a talent for appreciation," which doesn't sound like much of a talent. The term might have been a nice way to say Jeannette was very good at admiring Watson. She had "a horror of discord and dissension" and often found herself in the role of mediator, which fits with her role inside the family. The report continued: "You are not especially demonstrative, but sincere and true and will make great sacrifices for loved ones." She had "exceptionally good judgment, a well-balanced brain, judicious and practical reasoning powers, as well as a strong will."

Jeannette protected Watson even in small ways. Eleanor Irvine saw that firsthand. Irvine graduated from Cornell University and began working at IBM in 1937. As a young single woman, Irvine lived in a small cottage in Upstate New York. Following a company picnic, Watson and Jeannette visited Irvine there. Watson noticed an unusual corner cabinet in the kitchen. "He thought it was so interesting," Irvine said. "Well, it was full of liquor. I thought, my gosh, I hope he doesn't open it, because he'd do that kind of thing, just because he was interested." If Watson had discovered the liquor, he would have at least been disappointed with Irvine, and he might have held it against her when considering her career at IBM.

Watson moved toward the cabinet, his hand poised by the handle.

"Tom, don't you do that!" Jeannette said sharply. "This is a young lady's home."

Embarrassed, Watson turned away and left the cabinet alone.

Jeannette Watson could be a behind-the-scenes operator. Twice a year, the Endicott factory held a massive employee banquet to give awards for company sporting events. The Watsons attended every one, and Watson would hand out 300 trophies over the course of an evening. Jeannette wanted to be able to monitor the people around him, so she stationed a man in the projection booth high up in the cavernous banquet room. The man had a telephone and a seating chart. By her place at the head table, Jeannette also had a telephone. If she wanted to know who someone was, or what a certain person was doing, she called the projection booth to get the information.

"She was a very brilliant lady," said Bob Novak, who sometimes manned the projection booth for Jeannette. "She could detect everything."

Outside of IBM, Jeannette held Watson's home life together. She ran the household and did the majority of the day-to-day parenting. As Tom Watson Jr. recalls, until he went to boarding school at age 15, she was the main presence in his life. "She was much more accessible than Father, and always made us feel protected and loved," he recalled.[5] The four children grew close to her in ways they could never approach with Watson. Some of Jane Watson's letters to her mother over the years show the depth of her affection. "You do so much for us that I feel overwhelmed," she wrote as an adult. "I could never imagine a more perfect mother." In another letter, she wrote: "I get quite weepy as I write you. You mean so terribly much to me, and I think you are SO wonderful."

As a child, Tom Jr. began to get upset witnessing the way his father could treat Jeannette at home. As Watson began to feel more powerful at work, he would come home and order Jeannette around, as if she were a secretary or middle manager. She would push back. From behind the couple's closed bedroom door, the children would hear angry voices arguing.

Watson's treatment of the boys, Tom and Dick, could sometimes horrify Jeannette. She could only stand by, feeling helpless, when his temper blew. Ben Wood, a close family friend, said he'd heard Watson "scold his boys in ways that made me weep. When he got mad, his reason and everything else vanished."[6]

Fifteen years into their marriage, Jeannette told Watson that she wanted a divorce. The arguments, the absences, the unpredictable temper—Watson's behavior had worn down Jeannette. Her dedication to the marriage, though, finally cracked because of Watson's thoughtlessness. He would, for instance, arrive home unannounced with four or five guests—usually customers or business associates—and expect Jeannette to entertain. She would scramble and do her best, but would resent the clear signal that Watson considered IBM before he considered her. She'd had enough, and told Watson so. Watson reacted with horror and devastation, as Tom Jr. and other family members recalled. He was so upset, Jeannette dropped the subject and never again brought it up. Jeannette thereafter survived in the marriage by doing less of Watson's bidding. She would, for example, tell unexpected guests that they could make themselves sandwiches.[7]

Watson would have been lost without Jeannette. She was his sixth sense, and she was the fiber that connected him to his children.

Late in life, Watson carried a black-leather, single-fold wallet, trimmed at the corners in gold and engraved with his name in gold letters. Inside the wallet, along with money and a driver's license, he kept two pieces of paper. On one, his 11-year-old grandson, Tom Watson Buckner, had written out the Boy Scout oath. Watson's messy, urgent handwriting covered the other slip of paper. He had written:

Dearest Jeannette:

Always know I have always loved and adored you, as the best wife, mother, friend, and humanitarian, and possessing qualities not found in any other woman of the world.[8]

He signed it: Tom.

Peter Drucker first met Watson in the early 1930s in Europe. Watson was to give a speech, and the young Drucker, then a reporter for a German newspaper, had come to report on Watson's comments.

After the speech, Drucker said, "I interviewed him and he was exceedingly nice to young people. Gracious and nice. He began talking about something called data processing, and it made absolutely no sense to me. No one knew what data processing was. I took it back and told my editor, and he said Watson was a nut, and threw the interview away."

Drucker continued: "He was fantastically good at establishing direct contact. It's hard to describe the warmth of the man. He could turn it on. It was an art. But if there had been a *Harvard Business Review* (during the 1930s), it would have run stories about him, and he would've been considered a nut or a crank."[9]

⌒

Watson bet the company in the early 1930s. He bet it on his unwavering optimism. He bet big, too—either IBM would grow and prosper, or it would disintegrate.

Melancholy had seized most of the business world. The U.S. economy contracted by 8 percent in 1930 and by another 7 percent in 1931, and it showed no signs of getting better. More than 3,000 banks failed. Unemployment rose by hundreds of thousands of people each month, on its way to 12 million unemployed, or more than 20 percent of the population. Soup lines stretched around blocks. Companies closed factories and cut production, each act sending another shock wave through the system, causing suppliers—and suppliers of suppliers—to cut back and lay off workers. President Herbert Hoover couldn't stop the decline. The most successful people seemed to be the gangsters who ran a booming illegal liquor industry in the age of prohibition.

Companies were in no position to install new tabulating machines, time clocks, or scales. Wage levels dove, so hiring an ocean of clerks to handle information was no more expensive than getting a single machine to do it. The market for office equipment plunged 50 percent in 1930 and kept sinking.

Watson knew the facts about the broken economy. But the situation didn't fit his plan, so he decided to bulldoze through the facts. His words always reflected optimism—in public, in executive meetings, and to IBM's employees. Endicott-Johnson was one of the few companies still going strong in the early 1930s, and Watson would go to Endicott, stand side-by-side with George F. Johnson, and show that there was no reason to give into the darkness of the Depression. Watson welcomed invitations to speak at almost any event, just so he'd have a platform for spreading his viewpoint.

"When is industrial progress going to start again?" he said in a typical speech, this time before the Rochester Chamber of Commerce. "I say it never stopped. Some people may not believe that, but it is a fact. You are going to find as we get further out of the Depression—and we are on our way out—that inventive genius, progressive ideas, progressive people, have been more active than ever. Industrial progress has never stopped."

An April 1, 1930, issue of *Forbes* magazine details Watson's view that businesses had become too efficient and well run to drift into a deep depression. "I see no signs of a severe recession," he told the interviewer. "As a matter of fact, I think 1930 will end up as a very good year."

Watson's actions backed up his words. He made two dangerous decisions: (1) He would keep the factories running and lay off no one, and (2) he would increase spending on research and development (R&D), even as companies around the world slashed their R&D budgets. The decisions came within a sliver of ruining the company.

First, the factories.

In the *Magazine of Wall Street*, John C. Cresswill wrote a column about an interview with Watson. "Mr. Watson has the idea that the troubles of the times are not so much due to overproduction as to underproduction," he wrote. Businesses didn't need to cut back because they were making more goods than it was possible to sell. Quite the contrary, businesses needed to work harder to make more goods and sell more goods, which would in turn restart the economy and move things in the right direction. "Selling more machines would attack the problem on one front, and keeping up wages as far as possible would attack it on another," Cresswill wrote, reflecting Watson's comments.[10]

IBM could beat the Depression, Watson believed. He reasoned that only 5 percent of business accounting functions were mechanized, leaving a huge market untapped. Surely there was room to keep selling machines, even in difficult times. Watson also reasoned that the need for IBM machines was so great, if businesses put off buying them now, certainly they'd buy them later, when the economy picked up. His logic told him that the pent-up demand would explode when companies decided to buy again. He wanted IBM to be ready to take advantage of that demand.

He'd keep the factories building machines and parts, stockpiling the products in warehouses. In fact, between 1929 and 1932, he *increased* IBM's production capacity by one-third.

Watson's greatest risk was running out of time. If IBM's revenue dropped off or flattened because of the Depression, the company would still have enough money to keep operating for two years, maybe three. If IBM's revenue continued to falter past 1933, the burden of running the factories and inventory would threaten IBM's financial stability. Watson later recalled what he said to his executives about continuing to make machine parts: "I said, 'No, conditions in this country are going to be better, our sales force is going to get stronger, and later on we are going to be able to do more business . . . I will take my chances on selling enough machines later to absorb those parts.' "[11]

Watson's logic led him to make what looked to outsiders like another insane wager. On January 12, 1932, Watson announced that IBM would spend $1 million—

nearly 6 percent of its total annual revenue—to build one of the first corporate research labs. The colonial-style brick structure in Endicott would house all of IBM's inventors and engineers. Watson played up the symbolism for all it was worth. He would create instead of destroy, despite the economic plague. At the groundbreaking in July 1932, he dramatically posed for news photographers with IBM officers. Watson, wearing a double-breasted suit, picked up a shovel on the empty hard-dirt site and scooped up a mound of earth. Next to him, A. Ward Ford, in a light-colored suit and with a cigar clamped between his teeth, drove a pick into the ground. Behind them stood Braitmayer, Nichol, and six other IBM officers. All froze as the cameras snapped.

The lab, completed in 1933, was a scientific haven, and it became a model for the great corporate research labs of later ages, including Xerox's Palo Alto Research Center and Microsoft Research. In the front foyer, rich wood paneling covered the walls, contrasting with an elegant black-and-white tiled floor. Marble stairs rose up to the left, leading to the Gold Room—a beautiful art-deco conference room adorned with delicate sconces and intricate woodwork. On the top floor perched a scientific library with a vaulted, wood-beamed ceiling; a stone fireplace; and a view of Endicott's rolling hills. Watson stocked the engineers' offices with any piece of scientific equipment they felt they needed. The basement contained a weather room that could reproduce the temperature and humidity of every region where IBM sold machines. Tunnels ran from the basement under North Street and into the IBM factory on the other side of the road, so the engineers wouldn't have to get cold in Endicott's harsh winter when they wanted to try something out on the factory floor. For the humid summers, the entire building had a feature still rare at the time: air conditioning.[12]

How could Watson justify this? He spent $1 million for

something as amorphous as research and development when businesses were falling apart and nearly one-quarter of Americans barely had enough to subsist. But building the lab had a logic to it. Somehow, Watson had to stimulate demand. He had to come up with products that companies couldn't resist, whatever the economic conditions. Again, thanks to Charles Kettering's influence, Watson believed that R&D would drive sales. So Watson decided to build a lab, pull engineers together, and get them charged up to push the technology forward.

Throughout the 1930s, IBM cranked out new products and innovations, finally getting its technology well ahead of Remington Rand or any other potential competitors. In the early 1930s, IBM introduced, for instance, the Type 405 Alphabetic Accounting Machine, a breakthrough that allowed IBM systems to process 150 cards per minute and print out tabulated information in words, not just numbers. The company introduced the 600 series of punch card machines, which for the first time handled multiplication and division. In 1934, IBM unveiled a system of machines aimed at banks—a version of the system Watson described in the 1920s. It was big, expensive, and powerful. If the machine spread throughout the banking industry, every check would be an IBM punch card—and sales of such cards would become a massive profit center. As it turned out, major banks slowly adopted it and smaller banks never did. Checks remained on paper, not IBM cards.

Within a few years, Watson's gamble on manufacturing and research looked disastrous. As IBM pumped increasing amounts of money into operations and growth, revenue from 1929 to 1934 stalled, wavering between $17 million and $19 million a year. IBM edged toward insolvency. In 1932, IBM's stock price fell to 1921 levels and stayed there—11 years of gains wiped out. The board of directors discussed ousting Watson, but put it off.[13]

As Drucker observed about Watson: "He didn't know how close he'd come to collapse."

≈

Amid critical decisions and tense meetings, odds and ends of executive life floated past Watson. A letter from John Herbert, a New York attorney, landed on Watson's desk on October 17, 1932.

"I have been invited . . . to see a demonstration of 'television' on next Thursday evening . . . when we can see both the Columbia Broadcasting and Photo Lyte Sound demonstrations of 'television,' " wrote Herbert. "I am told that both of these are worth the effort of accepting the invitation."

Watson turned down his first chance to see television, replying: "I am in receipt of your letter inviting me to see a demonstration of a 'television' machine. But I have already accepted an invitation for that evening that I do not feel that I can break."

On another occasion, executive Red LaMotte sent Watson a novelty: One of his speeches recorded on a Speak-O-Phone, which etched sounds on a brittle disk. LaMotte only sent the disks. "No doubt you can rent the machines from a radio store out there, and the best kind to use is the combination radio-victrola, because they have the voice amplifier attachment," LaMotte wrote.[14]

As Watson vacationed in Camden, Maine, in the summer, his secretary, Phillips, sent Watson a note about a number of little things going on in New York. A board member was sailing for Europe, and Phillips sent him a gift basket as a bon voyage. Phillips had sent Watson a suit and cigars, as requested. Also, Phillips enclosed an invitation for Watson to join the Committee for the Consideration of Inter-Governmental Debts. Phillips added: "Judging from the names of those already on the committee, I believe you will be willing to accept."[15]

Jim Birkenstock was one of two recent graduates from the University of Iowa hired by IBM in 1935. To begin his career, he joined 66 other new hires in the square, brick IBM schoolhouse built next to the new engineering lab in Endicott. IBM almost exclusively hired fresh young people, and indoctrinated them into the IBM culture through classes in Endicott. That way, the recruits would grow up pure IBM, untainted by the ways of some other corporation. Birkenstock, in Endicott for six weeks of instruction, was in class number 125.

Only a couple of days into Birkenstock's stay in Endicott, Watson appeared for class 125. Watson showed up at least once for every new class attending the schoolhouse. He'd come in, stand behind the lectern, tell the men old stories about IBM, and talk about how he cherished IBM's values. Watson thoroughly enjoyed those sessions.

About two weeks into class 125, its 67 young men buzzed with excitement when they saw 25 young women—"girls," as everyone called them at the time—gathering at the schoolhouse. Previous classes at the IBM school had been all male. But a young college student, Anne van Vechten, had asked Watson to explain why there were hardly any career paths for women in American companies. Watson immediately decided that there was no good reason, and ordered the school to start training women—though women would still only be trained for certain positions, such as helping customers to learn to use their machines and human resource management.

"Watson was like a kid—I shouldn't use that word—OK, he was enthralled he'd brought these women in," Birkenstock recalled. "He started appearing weekly."[16]

Birkenstock continued: "He was so taken with the women. Every weekend we had a party, some co-sponsored by us and Watson, and sometimes the girls put on the party. Watson would always show up. One of the last parties the girls threw, the setting was a slumber party, and they wore those (long flannel) Dr. Denton's pajamas. A lot of the men chuckled a lot. Watson got a big kick out of it."

The men's and women's classes graduated at the same time. Watson spoke at the graduation and publicly bet the head of the school—the bet was a hat—that a marriage would result from this first coed school session. "There was more than one," Birkenstock said.

Both the men and women graduates scattered to IBM field offices across the country. As the next few months went by, IBM's field managers balked at accepting the women. Watson became furious. In an angry fit, he ordered the firing of all 67 men in Birkenstock's class. They hadn't done anything wrong, but if those men were unavailable, the managers would have to accept the women graduates, or they wouldn't get anybody. Watson would force his point.

Watson called two executives into his office and told them to carry out that order. One of them excused himself to go to the men's room to throw up.[17]

A few of the male class members, including Birkenstock, were protected by wily upper-level managers, but the rest lost their jobs. They were cut loose and left in the void of the Great Depression. Birkenstock went on to work for IBM for 38 years, most of that time at the top levels, side-by-side first with Watson and later with Tom Watson Jr. Yet in conversation decades later, it was clear Birkenstock never forgave Watson for this act of management brutality.

"Watson did a terrible thing," Birkenstock said. "He got away with it because there weren't any officers at IBM in those days who stood up and would say, 'Mr. Watson, you're wrong.' Good people were let go for no cause at all— leading guys from Harvard or Yale suddenly had no job."

He paused for a second, seeming to focus on friends

made long ago in a bright classroom in a little town that most of the students' families couldn't have found on a map. "I was pure lucky," Birkenstock said.

⤳

Before Watson, hardly anyone paid attention to corporate culture—traditions and values that make an organization unique. NCR's Dayton campus had a unique set of quirks and values that added up to a culture, but it was barely acknowledged as such by NCR management. A few other companies represented pockets of corporate culture. Still, businessmen didn't consider a culture to be important or strategic. It was just there, a by-product—like manure on a farm.

IBM's culture was a whole new species—a great evolutionary leap from what had come before. In its own way, the culture of IBM became the key to the company's success. IBM was not the best in the world at any particular part of its business. It was not the best at technology innovation. As with Remington Rand's 90-column card versus IBM's 80-column card, IBM could take a product that wasn't quite as good and still crush the more inventive competition. IBM was good at manufacturing, but Ford Motor was better. Even IBM's vaunted sales organization didn't have any noncultural advantage, such as smarter salesmen or some special technology, over other companies' sales divisions. What Watson's IBM did better than any company in the world was to create and manage a strong, cohesive— and *successful*—corporate culture. In turn, that culture wove together the pieces of the business and drove employees forward in ways that competitors couldn't beat.

Watson never sat down and said, "Hey, let's create a culture," and dictated that it will have this feature and that feature. In the cultural void of the old C-T-R, Watson began to impose his idiosyncratic personality on the company. The combination of his style and values simply worked and drew to him others who either shared his style and values or bought into them. As that cultural core permeated the whole company, Watson grasped the importance of the culture, supported it, and stoked it to ever-greater levels. By the 1930s, it was often said that Watson and IBM were inseparable and indistinguishable from one another.

International Business Machines became famous as a company where men wore stiff white shirts under impeccable suits, vowed to avoid alcohol, and sang Harry Evans's songs at meetings. Such elements helped to identify the company to outsiders, taking on the role of artifacts such as kilts in Scotland or Kabuki theater in Japan.

Watson created institutions. He wanted the Hundred Percent Club to be the pinnacle of achievement at IBM. A salesman had to meet 100 percent of his quota to get in for that year. Getting in meant promotions, public adulation, and a trip to Endicott for the annual Hundred Percent Club rally, billed inside IBM as the most important event of the year. The Hundred Percent Club drove IBM's sales culture the way the World Series drives millions of baseball players to learn the game and try to be the best.

To spread the culture, massage it, and renew it, Watson built up an internal media and propaganda machine. His main mouthpiece was *Business Machines,* a weekly broadsheet newspaper that borrowed its look from the *New York Times*. It ran news about Hundred Percent Club conventions, major promotions, and Watson proclamations and speeches. Editorials hammered home messages about meeting quotas, staying loyal to IBM, and working with enthusiasm. Rarely in *Business Machines* was there any bad news. In 1935, Watson took his publishing tendencies a step further, creating a monthly magazine called *Think*. It featured essays by well-known writers and businessmen, innocuous stories with headlines such as "Air—What Is It?", photographs of art exhibits, and sermons from Watson about IBM and its values. Not only did *Think* circulate inside IBM, but about 60,000 copies were sent to customers, politicians, and anyone else Watson deemed important.

IBM had a symbol—a symbol important to the culture in the way that the Eiffel Tower is important to France or the kangaroo to Australia. That symbol was the word THINK.

Around IBM, a rectangular sign simply saying, in all capital letters, THINK, could be found absolutely anywhere. It was in every executive's office, in meeting rooms, on factory floors, on building entranceways, in cafeterias, and on company documents and stationery. It was such a strange thing—this constant admonition to think—that writers and cartoonists started telling the public about it and poking fun at it. One famous cartoon shows a middling worker at his desk, which is adorned by a THINK sign. Behind him is his more successful boss, whose sign says SCHEME. By the mid-1930s, the THINK signs were well known to Americans, and immediately identifiable with IBM and Watson. Moreover, THINK was probably more renowned than the company. An ordinary man on the street could probably have told you that THINK was on those signs at IBM, but wouldn't have been able to describe IBM or its products.

THINK originated at NCR—a fact lost to almost everyone inside and outside IBM. According to Lee Olwell, Watson's longtime friend who worked with him at NCR, it began in an NCR meeting room on a cold, damp, foggy day in December 1911. Watson ran a meeting of the sales and advertising departments, and none of the participants volunteered ideas. Olwell, who was there, saw Watson spring from his chair and bound to the front of the room. "The trouble with every one of us is that we don't think enough!" Watson hollered angrily. "We don't get paid for working with our feet—we get paid for working with our heads." He lashed out at the group for about 10 minutes. As he finished, he turned to a large pad of paper on the easel next to him. "The trouble with us, the trouble with the agents, the trouble with everybody, is that we don't—." He wrote in blue crayon on the pad: THINK. After the meeting, Watson told Olwell to make a placard with the word THINK in bold letters, and post it the next morning on the sales department's wall. Watson, always fond of making the complex seem simple, loved how a whole basket of behaviors were loaded into that one five-letter word. He sold NCR President Patterson on the signs, and pushed them throughout the company. When Watson joined C-T-R in 1914, he brought THINK along with him.[18]

As THINK grew into a symbol of IBM, Watson became the company's George Washington. He stood for something identifiable, and everyone at IBM could point to him and say: That's what we're about. Straight-arrow. Competitive. Driven. Creative. Spirited. Dedicated above all to the company. The lines blurred between the real Tom Watson and the Watson who was a symbol of IBM. As each year passed, the latter grew stronger at the expense of the former.

Because he was a symbol—and because he was the human face of a quirky, unusual company that made machines that seemed to think, as Flint called them—Watson started to become famous. He encouraged it. He talked to journalists whenever he could. He'd call Drucker out of the blue when Drucker was an editor at *Fortune* magazine. He got close to Henry Luce, founder of *Time* magazine, and never hesitated to call or write him about stories or issues of the day. He made friends with Frank Gannett, owner of a chain of newspapers in New York State. In 1932, Watson was quoted or written about 15 times in the *New York Times;* 26 times in 1937. IBM didn't have money to pump out a lot of advertising, so Watson became the advertising.

When, in 1933, fourteen-year-old Seymour Harris of Cedarhurst, New York, asked Watson for his autograph, Watson obliged.[19] He liked that he was famous enough to be treated like a baseball star.

To further raise his profile, Watson mixed with the right people. Gannett was certainly one of them. He held black-tie parties at his house in Rochester, New York, or his Miami Beach winter home and invited top industrialists from around the country to eat dinner and discuss the Depression, or Prohibition, or the Republican Party platform. Watson was always invited.

A political chameleon who later turned solidly Democratic, Watson made friends with Herbert Hoover and Franklin D. Roosevelt. He came to know Hoover, a Republican, in the mid-1920s when Hoover was Secretary of Commerce, and was invited by Hoover to his 1929 inauguration as president. More than a decade later, Hoover asked Watson to review a manuscript for a book he was writing, entitled *The Problems of Lasting Peace,* and invited Watson to a World Series baseball game. Watson didn't go, citing a sinus problem.

Watson acquainted himself with Roosevelt, a Democrat, when Roosevelt was governor of New York in 1931 and 1932. Watson was Roosevelt's guest at the 1933 inauguration. He wrote the new president long letters about the national debt, capital gains taxes, and other topics; got invited to White House dinners; and by the late 1930s maintained a regular flow of correspondence with Roosevelt.

IBM's size and importance did not preordain that Watson should get audiences with U.S. presidents. By force of personality, Watson made that happen, and he leveraged it for greater fame and more high-level contacts. It all helped him bear the standard of the IBM culture—*his* culture.

IBM's culture created a club that only the best people with the right values could join. That created cohesiveness. If you got in and stayed in, other IBMers knew you were special. You were one of them. "We do a great many things in our business that strike outsiders as being unusual," Watson said. "Sometimes, young men disagree with our ideas or our policies because they believe they know better ways. Such young men never make a success with us."[20]

The culture built a discipline inside the company. Instead of having to be told what to do, most employees *felt* it, the way most Americans know to be tolerant of religions or know that pancakes are appropriate to serve at breakfast in a U.S. home while smoked fish is not. The discipline of IBM's culture allowed Watson to get away with governing his company with his haphazard, dysfunctional spider-and-web management structure. His secret was this unseen force that permeated the entire company and got people to do his bidding without his constant attention.

The culture was Watson's brilliance. It saved him from his inadequacies.

Then, too, Watson was saved by extraordinary good fortune.

In 1934, Watson's favorite hunting dog was named Lucky. Good old Lucky, standing by Watson's side, tail wagging, ready to help. A movie scriptwriter couldn't have dreamt up a better metaphor.

≈

In the worst economy in American history, Watson got rich. In order to be an upstanding member of the wealthy executive class, he decided to get into yachting. In June 1931, Watson bought a 17-foot Dark Harbor class knockabout for $750 so Tom Jr. could learn to sail. The following month, Watson chartered a 42-foot yacht called *Caribou*, moored in Salem, Massachusetts, from July 14 to September 14.

In 1932, he bought the 64.5-foot *Poseidon* and hired a captain to sail her. The *Poseidon* was still far from *really* being big time. J. P. Morgan had a 343.5-foot yacht named *Corsair*; film and aircraft magnate Howard Hughes had the 320.5-foot *Southern Cross;* and General Motors President Alfred Sloan owned the *Rene*, at 234 feet 10 inches.

Also in 1932, Watson sent a proxy, A. L. Anderson, to Helsingfors, Finland, to check out the sleek, fast, 9.6-meter Finnish First Class Shark Boats built there. Through Anderson, Watson decided to buy 13 Shark Boats for $700 to $875 each, and bring them to the Camden Yacht Club in Camden, Maine, where Watson sometimes sailed. Watson sold 11 of them, keeping 2 for himself.

In 1935, Watson bought *Fontinalis II* for $20,000, paid in cash. The 94-foot yacht had two mainsails, two main staysails, two fore staysails, and two jibs. He renamed the boat *Aeolus* [pronounced EE-ol-us, after the Greek god of the winds]. Watson hired a captain for *Aeolus,* paying him $100 a month, and put the *Poseidon* on the market for $15,000.

Watson spent little time on any of the boats.

In mid-June 1935, Tom Jr., then 21, set off in *Poseidon* on a lengthy cruise with the captain, Sigurd Hansen, at the helm. Watson sent a letter to Hansen ahead of Tom. "There is an absolute rule that no guests or members of the crew shall ever be permitted to have any kind of beer or liquor on board the boat," Watson wrote. "I have no objection to what any guests do while on shore, or what any members of the crew do within reason while on shore. If at any time you have occasion to use this letter you may do so."[21]

In 1942, during the war, Watson loaned *Aeolus* to the Coast Guard because, as Watson said when turning her over, he wasn't going to use her anyway "in these conditions." Once Watson got *Aeolus* back in 1943, he put it on the market and wound down his yachting career.[22]

⇌

Watson's continued success—IBM's success—depended on opening new markets for its wonder machines. For nearly two decades, Watson thought of IBM's tabulating machines as devices that could handle tangible quantities—money, inventory, army troops, and so on. Never did he consider that numbers could be used to represent and simulate *absolutely anything,* whether the movement of the stars, music, chemical reactions, or the growth pattern of a human embryo. In the later decades of the twentieth century, most people took for granted that computers, the electronic descendants of tabulating machines, could be tools for science and art as well as for business and accounting. In IBM's early years, though, that wasn't obvious—not to Watson, and not even to his crack engineering team.

Watson learned it from a shy, awkward, poorly dressed Columbia University professor in a meeting that altered the course of IBM. Watson scheduled the meeting in the Century Club, a stuffy businessmen's establishment in New York, and reserved a private dining room for one hour. He'd responded to a letter from Columbia's Ben Wood about the possibility of using tabulating machines to score the kinds of standardized tests that might be given to thousands or millions of students. However, Watson didn't expect much. Wood wasn't a college president, armed with a check to buy machines. He was some unknown professor with an idea. Watson would give him one hour.

After joining Columbia, Wood had pioneered standardized testing. He did it first as an academic exercise, a way to compare and study the educations offered in different places. The findings led educators in New York and Pennsylvania to use Wood's tests to try to create minimum levels of learning across their states. That led to the problem of scoring tens of thousands of tests at once. Wood took to hiring hundreds of young women and packing them in Columbia's Hamilton Hall, where they'd mark the tests by hand at a cost of about $5 per test. Clearly, Wood thought, there had to be a better way. He sent letters to the presidents of 10 corporations that made business machines. Nine failed to reply. Wood recalled the curt phone call from the tenth, Watson:

"I'm Thomas Watson. I'm very busy and can spare only

an hour. Be at the Century Club promptly at twelve. I have an engagement at one." And that was it.[23]

Arriving at the club for the meeting, Watson, who put so much stock in appearance and personal presentation, must have taken one look at Wood and decided this was going to be a lost hour. Woefully timid, Wood was visibly trembling. Watson had brought along a young male secretary, whom he left outside the dining room door with instructions to interrupt at 1 P.M.

Wood began talking about test scoring, but seeing Watson's scornful face decided to broaden his approach. He began explaining how IBM machines could be used to measure intellect and psychology. It's all quantifiable, Wood told him. Anything could be represented by mathematics—numbers and formulas. Biology, astronomy, physics, or any other science could be aided by IBM machines. "There is no aspect of life to which these IBM machines cannot make a basic and absolutely essential contribution," Wood said to Watson.[24]

That was sweetness to Watson's ears. All along he had measured IBM's potential market by its share of the accounting and record-keeping functions of business and government. This nervous professor was telling Watson that IBM's potential market was almost limitless. The secretary stuck his head in at 1 P.M.; Watson shooed him away. Watson grilled Wood until 5:30 P.M.

Two days later, three trucks pulled up at Columbia University to deliver all the tabulators, sorters, and punches Wood might need.

Watson embraced Wood and his work at Columbia, and would drop by, unannounced, to see what Wood had accomplished and how he'd used IBM's machines. Watson invited Wood to IBM to talk to engineers and sales managers about the potential role of IBM in science, and Watson put Wood on the payroll as a consultant. IBM started working with Columbia's astronomy department, which eventually led to the establishment of the Watson Astronomical Computing Laboratory at the university. The company quickly grasped its new opportunities and began selling machines to every kind of scientific lab.

Wood and Watson were always an odd pair: the ultimate academic and the ultimate businessman. But they liked each other. Watson asked Wood to give tests to evaluate the Watson children, and Wood tried to help Tom Jr. find ways to master academics. Tom was smart, but unconventionally so. He often had difficulty with traditional ways of learning.

Watson paid for Wood and his wife to vacation in Maine, he gave the Woods gifts of jewelry and furniture, and Watson and Wood stayed friends through the rest of Watson's life.

$\approx$

By 1934, Watson needed a miracle. He had been counting on a prompt end to the Depression—an end that was nowhere in sight. The New Deal had created some big new accounting problems for the government, so it needed more IBM machines. That helped business a bit. But since 1930, IBM had continued to extend itself while its business stayed flat. It expanded factory capacity, built the engineering lab and schoolhouse in Endicott, and increased the number of employees from 6,346 in 1930 to 7,613 in 1934. Products and parts were piling up in warehouses, costing IBM a fortune. In 1933, IBM bought the Electromatic Typewriter Company in Rochester, New York—IBM's entry into the typewriter business.

In about the only move to lighten IBM's load, Watson finally sold the struggling scales division, unloading it on Hobart Manufacturing.

On February 13, 1935, Charles Flint died. In the background, events made the world bleaker still. Hitler was militarizing Germany, and Japan had become an aggressor in Asia, slowing or cutting off trade around the globe. Dust storms roiled over the Midwest, wrecking crops and farms. Any chance of pulling out of the Depression was being flushed away by soldiers and nature.

His back against the wall, Watson's greatest stroke of luck dropped in to save IBM.

Franklin Roosevelt's New Deal had been taking shape over the previous year. Watson, continuing his relationship with FDR, had been able to watch the President's program unfold up close. In fact, Watson was one of the few businessmen who supported Roosevelt. Most despised the president, believing he was socialist and antibusiness.

On August 14, 1935, Roosevelt signed the Social Security Act. No single flourish of a pen had ever created such a gigantic information processing problem.

The act established Social Security in America—a national insurance system that required workers to pay into a fund while employed so they could draw payments out of it once they retired, or if a wage-earning spouse died. To make the system work, every business had to track every employee's hours, wages, and the amount that must be paid to Social Security. The business then had to put those figures in a form that could be reported to the federal government. Then the government had to process all those millions of reports, track the money, and send checks to those who should get them.

Overnight, demand for accounting machines soared. Every business that had them needed more. An officer of the store chain Woolworth told IBM that keeping records for Social Security was going to cost the company $250,000 a year.[25] Businesses that didn't have machines wanted them. The government needed them by the boatload.

Only one company could meet the demand: IBM. It had warehouses full of machines and parts and accessories, and it could immediately make more because its factories were running, fine tuned, and fully staffed. Moreover, IBM had been funding research and introducing new products, so it had better, faster, more reliable machines than Remington Rand or any other company. IBM won the contract to do all of the New Deal's accounting—the biggest project to date to automate the government. Maybe Watson's relationship with FDR helped, but to what other company could the government have turned? IBM was the only real choice.

This period of time became IBM's slingshot. Revenue jumped from $19 million in 1934 to $21 million in 1935. From there it kept going up: $25 million in 1936, $31 million in 1937. It would climb unabated for the next 45 years. From that moment until the 1980s, IBM would utterly dominate the data processing industry—a record of leadership that was unmatched by any industrial company in history.

Peter Drucker asked Watson years later if he had anticipated the Social Security Act. Watson said he hadn't. Of course, the act was debated and written about well before it was passed. But Watson said that he had no idea it would impose such a record-keeping burden on business and the government. No one did—otherwise, Congress might never have passed the act. Watson did not foresee that the act, combined with IBM's readiness, would not only save IBM, but propel it toward tremendous growth.

Watson borrowed a common recipe for stunning success: one part madness, one part luck, and one part hard work to be ready when luck kicked in.

～～

IBM made a high-living handful out of Aunt Fan.

Fannie Hale was Jeannette Watson's aunt. Not long after Watson joined C-T-R, she apparently started buying sizable amounts of the company's stock. By 1927, the stock made her rich. She turned into a shrewd stock trader. She held onto her IBM shares and raked in thousands of dollars in dividends paid to IBM stockholders, then used that money to buy other companies' stocks, such as American Steel Foundries, Pennsylvania Railroad, and Vick Chemical, maker of Vicks VapoRub. She adroitly rode the market up in the 1920s.

However, Aunt Fan didn't want to be bothered handling all that money and all those transactions. In 1927, she gave power of attorney to Watson and essentially put her money in his care. In turn, Watson assigned Aunt Fan and all of her demands to secretary George Phillips. It must have been one of Phillips's least favorite jobs.

"My dear Mr. Phillips," Aunt Fan wrote on one occasion, "I do know that you have worked awfully hard to do something for me. Mr. Watson said you had given more attention to my money than your own."[26]

"My dear Mr. Phillips," she wrote from a posh San Francisco hotel called The Clift, "You will have to send us another statement of what we are worth, for if tonight's paper is correct about IBM, our fortune has increased considerably."[27]

In 1929, she ran into trouble with the Internal Revenue Service and wound up owing nearly $2,000 in back taxes and fines. Phillips had to sort out all of that.

She had bought and sold and saved enough to never lose a step, despite the Depression. More important, she had enough IBM stock to keep a river of dividends flowing into her account. Wall Street's crash crushed IBM's stock price, but IBM's steadiness in the early 1930s and its growth in the second half of the decade allowed IBM to keep paying hefty dividends. Aunt Fan sailed through the thirties, traveling between California and Florida, buying houses and furniture, living well all the time, and constantly sending requests to Phillips in her neat script written on clean white note paper. Aunt Fan could afford to sound chipper. "Thank you so much for the telegram about Mr. Watson speaking on the radio," she wrote Phillips in 1938. "I am telephoning some of my friends, and we will have a real party listening to him. Isn't he wonderful?"[28]

Aunt Fannie Hale lived the miracle of IBM's 1930s performance. Almost everyone associated with IBM benefited from the company's growth. Hundreds of stockholders, many in pockets around Endicott and Dayton, accumulated considerable wealth. For A. Ward Ford, the annual dividends alone on his stock were $88,903.50, equal to more than $1.1 million in 2002.

Inside IBM, for Christmas in 1935, Watson gave all factory workers who'd been with the company at least one year a bonus equal to one week's pay. Appreciation poured into Watson's office. An entire department signed their names to a letter thanking Watson. He received telegrams such as this one: "Gratitude hearty greetings to you— employees Gear Cutting Dept. #4."[29] In 1937, IBM factory workers got a raise of 5 cents per hour.

A solid IBM salesman who made the Hundred Percent Club a few years running could make $25,000 annually, the equivalent of $315,000 in 2002. In those dire times, when most businesses could only dream of awarding bonuses, Nichol got a bonus of $20,000 (equal to $251,000 in 2002); Braitmayer, $10,000; and Phillips, $2,500.

Watson's pay, though, took on a meaning all its own. He never owned much of IBM—his shares of stock never came to more than about 3 percent of the company. But when he was hired in 1914, he cut that deal that gave him a percentage of the profits. In the 1910s, that didn't amount to much. By the 1930s, though, IBM's profits were enough to give Watson an enormous paycheck. Riding the New Deal fervor for monitoring and distributing wealth, the newly formed Securities and Exchange Commission (SEC) began tracking the incomes of corporate executives making more than $15,000 a year, and listing the highest paid in order. The SEC released the first of the reports in 1935. Newspapers everywhere ran the news on the front page: At number one on the list stood Watson.

Anyone who hadn't been familiar with Watson by that

point now knew who he was. Watson's pay was $365,358. Americans were shocked. Instantly, wags slapped Watson with the label of the Thousand-Dollar-A-Day Man. The nickname was both worshipful and derogatory. The nation's citizens, worn down by the Depression, could fantasize about making $1,000 every day. But the news stirred up popular criticism: People muttered that one man should never be paid so much money. The issue concerned stockholders, who wondered if Watson's salary hurt the company. It was the kind of debate familiar to business watchers in the early 2000s, when the public buzzed about outsized executive compensation during a time of layoffs and plummeting stock prices.

As the news of Watson's salary spread, Tom Jr., then in his 20s, found that suddenly women found him much more attractive.[30] Watson's friends got in touch, sometimes to rib him. Harvey "Bill" Harrison, an old friend from Buffalo, New York, sent Watson a clip from the Buffalo newspaper. The headline said, "$1000-a-day-man." Under it was a photo of Watson. "You are getting a little older, but I want to say you still have that distinguished look of 25 years ago," Harrison wrote. "At the price they mention in the paper, I suppose I ought to send you a check for going over these brief lines."

The following year, the House Ways and Means Committee expanded the salary list to include all Americans, not just corporate officers. Some famous names popped up on the list, including movie magnate Samuel Goldwyn and the enormously popular cowboy humorist Will Rogers. Watson was still number one, making $364,432. Rogers made $324,414. In other words, the head of a midsized company beat out Will Rogers—now, that was news. Better-known businessmen running bigger companies made a good deal less than Watson. Sloan of GM made $201,693. Walter Chrysler, founder of the Chrysler car company, made $197,568.

Watson felt embarrassed. He did not want to be known for his wealth. He wanted to be known for his company. Two weeks later, at IBM's annual shareholder's meeting, Watson devoted an entire speech to justifying his pay. He ran through the company's history since he'd joined in 1914, detailing IBM's growth under his leadership. "When I took charge of this company 22 years ago, it was agreed that if I could develop some new things I would receive a percentage of the money made," he told the audience. "This agreement has been renewed several times, and today I draw a salary of one hundred thousand dollars and get five percent of the net profits after dividends of six dollars a share." Watson's pay structure, still based on the deal that had been cut long ago when the possibility of good-sized profits seemed like a joke, resulted in a mountainous paycheck when the company prospered.

The day after the annual meeting, Phillips wrote to IBM director Smithers, who'd been absent, to report on the proceedings. He mentioned Watson's "dignified talk" about his compensation. Phillips noted: "It seemed a good thing to do in view of the reviving publicity as to the high point in his income, which apparently they keep on publishing."

To promote IBM, Watson wanted to become famous. Suddenly, he shot past his contemporaries to become the most famous businessman in America.

❧

"TO OUR IBM GIRLS"
(To the tune of "They're Style All the While")

They've made our IBM complete and worthwhile.
They work and they smile—so sweetly they smile.
Tall, short, thin, and stout girls—they win by a mile
With heavenly styles all the while.

—Songs of the IBM

6

FRIENDS, HEROES, SYCOPHANTS

"ERE I AM WRITING YOU THIS LETTER AT THIS HOUR of the morning because I can't sleep," Anne van Vechten wrote to her parents. "Yesterday was the most exciting day I have ever had in my life." Her excitement entirely centered on Watson.

She was 21, effervescent, ambitious, and fearless. She had attended Bryn Mawr College—she didn't graduate because of poor grades—where she made friends with Watson's daughter, Jane. In 1935, while at the college, she typed a note to Watson, mentioning her acquaintance with Jane. "I am taking the liberty to ask if you would be willing to give me some advice concerning my future opportunity in business," she wrote. "If you would be willing to grant me an appointment, I should appreciate your kindness."[1]

She received a note from Watson secretary Byne Waters, setting an appointment for an upcoming Friday at 3 P.M.[2]

During the conversation in his office, van Vechten asked why big companies didn't offer women professional career paths. At the end of the interview, Watson told her that she was right—IBM should hire women and train them for more prestigious jobs, and van Vechten was to help him. She was hired. This sparkling young woman got caught in Watson's whirlwind and landed in Endicott as part of the first class of women at the IBM school.[3]

163

At 3:30 A.M. on August 6, 1935—during the night after her first full day at the school—van Vechten gave up on sleep, got out pen and paper, and began describing for her parents all that had happened to her.

She'd started the previous day at 7 A.M. with a golf lesson at the IBM Country Club. Afterward, the 25 women classmates went over to the IBM school and joined the 67 men in Jim Birkenstock's class, plus another 90 male students on other tracks, in one large classroom. Watson appeared and walked to the lectern, waving at van Vechten as he strode across the room. "That was my first thrill of the day," van Vechten wrote. "Then in front of 180 students he made a speech in which he paid great tribute to me, thanking me for giving him the idea, and he told all the girls that I was responsible for their being there. I got redder and redder." In his speech, Watson called her his "great pioneer woman." Van Vechten wrote: "I really felt like kneeling down and praying or weeping!"

At lunch, Watson sat and talked with van Vechten for 30 minutes. When afternoon classes ended, a lot of the men vied to play golf with her. She seemed very aware of why she'd become so popular at school.

Evening rolled around, and Watson threw an outdoor dinner party for the students and a number of IBM executives. Elegant tables glistened with silver and crystal under a canvas awning on the IBM grounds near the school. Before the dinner, Watson had sent each woman in the class a corsage, which they all wore—as if they had a choice. When Watson arrived, he looked for van Vechten, and asked to see her inside the building. She had no idea what he was up to, or if she'd done something to displease him.

"I was scared skinny," she wrote. "He took me in, and there he had 25 Whitman's Samplers [boxes of chocolates] and 25 cartons of cigarettes for the girls. How a man with such big thoughts can think of all the niceties in life, I don't understand."

At dinner, Watson asked her to sit with him at the head table, and throughout the meal he rambled through his collection of stories about IBM and his early days as a salesman. She was completely charmed.

After dinner, the IBM Band played. "Mr. Watson danced with me first," van Vechten wrote. "He is a wonderful dancer, too! I don't know whether it was the politics or not, but I got the most wonderful rush." By that, she meant that after her dance with the boss, a rush of one man after another kept her dancing all night.[4]

By that point, Watson had won her devotion and swept her off her feet.

Watson loved women and women loved him. That was not a tawdry equation. No one has ever suggested that Watson had sexual encounters with women other than his wife, Jeannette, or even wound up in a compromising situation. That has not surfaced in any letter, interview, article, or book. But Watson thoroughly enjoyed women—especially attractive young IBM women and, in a niche category by itself, opera singers. He liked having such women around and liked to impress them. He often made sure that a young woman employee or two accompanied him to a business lunch meeting, on a long car ride, to the theater, or sometimes on a lengthy business trip. He always had a reason: He wanted the woman to write a report on the trip, wanted to show other male CEOs that IBM was training women to be managers, or he simply had an extra theater ticket that ought not go to waste. But Watson apparently never behaved in a way that suggested the woman was an object of his desire.

Instead, Watson had a feminine side. He enjoyed beauty and fashion, fine clothes, shoes, and dancing. He loved to shop. He loved to be close to people and touch them and get inside their heads. For the most part, he couldn't indulge that side of himself with Jeannette. She cared little for beauty, clothes, shopping, or dancing, and she was not the stereotypical chatty, touchy, gossipy female. If that's what Watson wanted, he had to find it elsewhere—in a safe way that would never risk his all-important image as IBM's upstanding, moralistic leader.[5]

Watson, who was 61 when van Vechten arrived at IBM in 1935, paid van Vechten considerable attention from the start. Later in 1935, he assigned her to the department that ran IBM's schools and education. In 1941, when van Vechten was 27, he named her manager of the personnel department. She often joined him at company events and on trips. She attended many of the top-level executive meetings at headquarters, to the delight of some of the 50- and 60-year-old long-time IBM officers and the annoyance of others. She left the company in 1942 to get married. From the 1920s to the early 1940s, IBM's policy for women managers dictated that they resign when they married.

(The policy is somewhat explained in a 1934 letter from Phillips to Braitmayer. Phillips, ever the stickler, sorted through punch cards representing each employee's benefits. He noticed one woman who had been recently married. "Unless there are extenuating circumstances to warrant the retention of female employees after they have married," Phillips wrote, "we feel that their husbands should assume the responsibility of their support and thus cause a vacancy for some deserving person who is sorely in need of employment." Phillips added that the rule especially applied "at this time when so many families have no income at all."[6])

Eleanor Irvine was another young woman who got special attention from Watson. After graduating from Cornell University, about a 45-minute drive from Endicott, she entered the IBM school in 1937 with 23 other women. Among the men at the school that year was Tom Watson Jr., then 23 years old and just out of Brown University. Like van Vechten before her, Irvine wound up on the staff of the education department in Endicott. While working at the school, Irvine lived at the Homestead, the rambling country house in the hills above Endicott. IBM had purchased it and turned it into a combination of lodge, minihotel for visitors to IBM, and second home for Watson.

One evening, as Irvine walked outside the Homestead, she noticed a car coming toward her, motoring up the long, winding driveway. The car pulled up to the building's entrance; Watson popped out and, before going inside, noticed her. Later, on a stairwell in the building, Watson introduced himself to Irvine and mentioned that he'd seen her outside. "I sensed he immediately liked me," Irvine said. Later, someone told Irvine that Watson said she had "an ethereal quality."

Irvine was a slight and beautiful young woman, with small, refined facial features, bright eyes with a hint of devilishness, and a way of moving that suggested graceful strength, like a ballerina. Watson pulled her into his orbit. He let her continue to live at the Homestead for free. When he'd arrive there, he'd have one of his secretaries find Irvine.

"I'd drop everything," she said. "It would not be for anything important. He just wanted to chat and talk."

If customers were around, Watson would ask her to join the group in the living room. Sometimes he'd go from Endicott to New York by car, and take Irvine along for the ride. Watson took Irvine to Kansas City, along with a few other IBM women. "He had some kind of meeting there," she recalled. "All the top businessmen of Kansas City were there. He just wanted us to be at his table. We were in our twenties. I think he was showing them they should have women in business."

On a miserable, rainy day in New York, Watson whisked Irvine and three other IBM women all around the city for appointments and other stops. By the time the group arrived back in front of IBM's headquarters, the weather had soaked the women's shoes. With the enthusiasm of a boy about to pull a prank, he steered the group away from IBM's front doors and over to a shoe store next to the building. Watson told the salesman: "These gals have been out in the rain this morning and have ruined their shoes. They each need a new pair." Watson stayed and enjoyed himself. "He was having an awfully good time buying three women shoes," Irvine said. Watson even approved when Irvine picked out the flashiest shoes in the store.[7]

A few years after meeting Irvine, Watson encountered Ruth Leach. She was born in Oakland, reared in the San Francisco Bay Area, and in 1937 graduated from the University of California at Berkeley. In February 1939, she began a temporary job demonstrating IBM machines in a pavilion at the San Francisco Golden Gate International Exposition, a 400-acre West Coast version of the World's Fair.

That October, Watson visited the exposition, hauling along behind him Tom Jr., daughters Jane and Helen, Fred Nichol, and a handful of other executives. All that week, the Watson entourage and the demonstrators and salesmen at the IBM pavilion came together for lunch. After one lunch, Watson approached Leach and asked her to show Tom Jr. around. She and Tom Jr. hit it off and spent a couple of evenings dancing at San Francisco nightspots. At the end of the week, Watson told Leach and the seven other women demonstrators they were hired on a permanent basis.[8]

The following year, Leach and her colleagues traveled across the country to Endicott just as the weather in Upstate New York turned cold and damp. As Christmas of 1940 approached, Leach and four of the women who had family in California realized they wouldn't get home for the holiday. They decided to travel to New York City, cram into a single room at the New Weston Hotel, and see all of the tourist spots. Early on the morning before Christmas—way too early for five revelers who'd been getting to know New York's night life—the telephone in the room rang. One of the women shook off sleep, picked up the phone, and heard a voice say, "Good morning, girls, this is Mr. Watson speaking."

The woman started giving the caller a hard time, thinking

it was a friend playing a prank. Her tone changed as she realized the caller really was Watson. Leach claimed she never knew how Watson found out they were in that hotel in New York. Watson invited the women to his home in New York for Christmas Eve dinner. They accepted politely. It's not hard to imagine the women hanging up the phone, and then all five of them shrieking in delight.[9]

Once Leach completed the IBM school, IBM assigned her to the company's office in Atlanta, Georgia. On a visit to Atlanta in the spring of 1941, Watson grilled Leach about her job. Not knowing any better, Leach challenged some of his ideas about how to teach customers to use IBM machines. As Leach's boss squirmed in his seat, a testy Watson lectured Leach about the proper way to teach customers.

Impressed by her pepper, Watson called Leach a few days later, and asked her to come teach at the Endicott school.

Years later, Leach was named by Watson to be an assistant vice president at IBM. In December 1943, Leach would become the first woman vice president at IBM, and one of the first women at that executive level in any major industrial company.

Aggressively hiring and promoting women exposed one Watson weakness. Although women managers were not immune to Watson's temper or his demanding style, if he started berating a woman manager, and she cried, Watson would soften, and sometimes back out of whatever he'd just ordered the woman to do. Watson could not deal with tears.

In one area of his life, though, Watson could be immune to emotional appeals. For his political beliefs, he was willing to endure the scorn of his peers.

⌒

President Franklin Delano Roosevelt was despised by nearly every businessman and person of wealth. If they didn't despise him the moment he was elected in 1932, they definitely did after his first 100 days, when the Roosevelt administration pushed through more than a dozen laws that inserted the government deep into the economy and launched the New Deal. J. P. Morgan would not allow Roosevelt's name to be mentioned in his house. Students at Harvard—Roosevelt's alma mater—jeered him as a turncoat to the upper class.[10] During the Roosevelt administration, income taxes on the richest Americans shot up from under 10 percent to as high as 60 percent, and corporations complained that new taxes on business were onerous. The business community believed that Social Security's safety net for the aged and unemployed would destroy the work ethic because people wouldn't feel they must work to survive. Politically active industrialists, such as newspaper baron Frank Gannett, plotted incessantly to rid the country of Roosevelt in the next election. Any businessman who even voted for Roosevelt risked the wrath of his peers. Watson not only supported Roosevelt, but became a friend and mouthpiece.

Watson and Roosevelt met while Roosevelt was governor of New York. IBM's headquarters was in New York City, and much of its manufacturing was in Endicott, adding up to more than 4,000 IBM employees in Roosevelt's state by 1932. As Roosevelt revved up his first presidential campaign, Watson prudently contributed money. In the summer of 1932, Roosevelt met with Watson a number of times, apparently to talk about campaign issues and how they would affect business.[11] Watson's invitation to attend Roosevelt's inauguration as president of the United States came from Roosevelt personally.

Year by year, the relationship wrapped tighter, though how close they got is hard to know. IBM documents and Watson's authorized biographers say the relationship was important to Roosevelt. Yet major biographies of Roosevelt fail to even mention Watson.[12] In 1937, when Franklin

Delano Roosevelt, Jr., married chemical heiress Ethel DuPont in the most lavish social event of the year, Watson was not on the guest list.[13] More than likely, the relationship meant more to Watson than it meant to Roosevelt.

Still, the relationship existed. During 1933, Watson wrote Roosevelt long, ponderous, business-like letters about the national debt, capital gains taxes, waste in government relief programs, and other issues. On February 12, 1934, Watson and Jeannette dined at the White House for a formal event. By 1936, warm telegrams and notes reflected a relationship that had turned friendly.

"I am sending you a memorandum of a few of my thoughts before sailing on the *Europa* tomorrow," Watson wrote to Roosevelt in a cover letter for a package of memos on the upcoming reelection campaign. "I recommend these thoughts as being important enough for you to read personally." Watson included himself on Roosevelt's campaign team, making liberal use of the pronoun *we*. "We must all keep in mind that we are running a different type of campaign from the other side," Watson wrote.[14]

Roosevelt wired a telegram back to Watson: "Thanks for your letter and suggestions. Have a fine trip. I want to see you when you get back. Franklin D. Roosevelt."[15]

During Roosevelt's second term, Watson's secretary kept the secretary to the president, Marvin McIntyre, abreast of Watson's travels and schedule. Roosevelt would at times ask Watson to entertain a foreign dignitary visiting New York. Watson's notes and suggestions were at times given personal attention by Roosevelt. "That is a good idea of yours about having certain people come to the United States during the World's Fair," Roosevelt wrote to Watson. "I am following it up."[16]

Roosevelt benefited from the relationship. Like an emissary to a hostile land, Watson acted as a bridge to the business community. Watson could inform Roosevelt about attitudes in business. When Watson delivered speeches, he often talked about Roosevelt's New Deal and why he supported it. "There is no question in my mind but that the New Deal will mean certain restrictions in regard to some methods that have been employed by certain people and corporations whereby they, perhaps, will not be able to profit as much for the benefit of the few," Watson said in a 1933 talk to all the employees at IBM headquarters. "In our own business, I am looking forward to an era, under the New Deal, in which we shall be able to pay everybody more money—and I am looking for that in every industry. I believe it is coming."[17] Talk like that amounted to heresy among corporate chief executives.

What did Watson get out of it? The New Deal created Social Security and other massive programs that generated demand for IBM machines. The government became a large and growing customer. One might think that Watson, who had supported Hoover while the Republican was president, was an opportunist, jumping to the Democrats to seek favor when selling to the Roosevelt administration. However, on the chessboard of business, Watson thought ahead more moves than that.

For one, currying favor with Roosevelt might have helped IBM win government contracts, but by entwining himself with Roosevelt, Watson stood to lose more than gain. When selling to the government, it's better to be apolitical. Administrations change, and if a different party wins the next time, an executive or company wouldn't want to be punished for supporting the previous administration. Watson understood that. He stood by Republican Hoover, supported Democrat Roosevelt, and later befriended Dwight Eisenhower, who became a Republican president.

Anyway, IBM didn't have to lobby for sales. During the Roosevelt administration, even if the government wanted to buy from another company, it couldn't. IBM was the only company capable of supplying the New Deal with all of the tabulating machinery it needed.

Watson was attached to Roosevelt for reasons deeper than machine sales. In the early 1930s, Watson was just achieving the kind of success for which he'd been driving ever since getting ousted from NCR by his mentor, John Patterson. Patterson had been Watson's North Star. He built NCR by buying a tiny company and making it into a large, successful corporation. Patterson did it by creating a near-monopoly for NCR, emphasizing engineering, and running rah-rah sales conventions. Patterson became wealthy, and he wielded considerable power in Ohio.

If Watson had a Patterson checklist, somewhere between 1930 and 1935 it was done. Turn a tiny company into a big company—check. Build a near-monopoly; base it on good engineering; build a culture—check, check, check. Acquire wealth and regional power—check.

Watson wanted to overtake Patterson on Patterson's playing field, playing by Patterson's rules, and he did it. For more than 15 years, Watson focused entirely on building IBM until he beat the ghost of his mentor. Having won, business was no longer challenge enough. He'd caught up to his North Star and passed it. He'd done what he was compelled to do. He was faced with a big Now what?

The answer: Watson wanted a place in history, and he wanted a role on the world stage.

Roosevelt knew how to command both, and do so with a decisive, magnetic, action-oriented style that appealed to Watson. In the mid-1930s, when Watson needed a new North Star, he set his compass to Roosevelt.

Watson found a lot to like in Roosevelt, and often talked about how Roosevelt turned him into a supporter and admirer during their first meeting after Roosevelt took office. "People realized they were listening to a man who had a new idea," Watson said, describing what he admired about Roosevelt. "And a man who was not afraid to stand before them and say, 'This is the truth as I see it,' regardless of precedent—because precedent had proved itself to be wrong."[18] That image of a lonely, fearless pioneer always appealed to Watson.

Watson chose to see aspects of himself in Roosevelt. At IBM, Watson practiced paternalism and preached that managers, salesmen, and factory workers were equals. He provided insurance and benefits that went far beyond the norm. To a degree, IBM was an industrial New Deal. Watson believed that he was a dynamic speaker, a no-nonsense leader, and a man given to acting first and worrying about it later—traits often ascribed to Roosevelt. All of that helped Watson believe that Roosevelt's success could be his. If Roosevelt could take hold of the world, so could he.

Watson changed after becoming involved with Roosevelt. He previously avoided controversy, but after coming to know Roosevelt, he did not flinch from it. He had avoided politics, but now became deeply embroiled in them. He began to think of IBM as more than a company. It could be, he decided with a sense of grandeur, an institution that would improve the world and promote peace, capitalism, and democracy. He increasingly acted and thought of himself as a great historical figure on the level of presidents, kings, and popes.

Watson caught up to one hero. He was certain he could catch up to another. This time, however, he was wrong. He wasn't in Roosevelt's league. He overestimated himself. That's always dangerous, and in Watson's case, it led to trouble.

⁂

The world knew that Watson was wealthy. Year after year, his salary kept him among the top 10 earners in the nation. He was not, in fact, one of the nation's richest men. Unlike barons such as John D. Rockefeller of Standard Oil or Andrew Carnegie of U.S. Steel, Watson didn't start his company or ever own much of it. In the 1930s, he owned 7,500 of 855,400 shares outstanding, or less than 1 percent of the company. That didn't matter to the public, though. The stories of his salary were convincing enough. Newspaper photographers often caught him looking splendid in a tuxedo and mixing with famous industrialists, leading politicians, and leading ladies of the theater and opera. The pictures added to his image as an upper-crust gentleman. One newspaper columnist wrote about how he wanted to ask Watson for $10,000, conjecturing that Watson would hardly miss even that much money.

As Watson got richer, the Depression brutalized millions. Among those hurt were dozens—perhaps hundreds—of people who'd known Watson as a child in Painted Post, New York, or who were part of his extended family growing up. Others had crossed paths with Watson when he prowled Upstate New York as a salesman, or worked for him as he shot toward the top of NCR. During the Depression, many of those people lost their jobs, lost their savings, and lost their pride. In their desperation, they wrote to Watson asking for a job or money. At one point, Watson received a request for a job from an unemployed Hugh Chalmers, who was Patterson's second in command at NCR before Watson vaulted into that role. Walter Cool, the enigmatic veteran NCR salesman who advised Watson from the sidelines in the early days of C-T-R, asked Watson to help with money. Others who wrote included many who had only a tangential relationship with Watson.

Hundreds of letters crossed Watson's secretaries' desks. Watson was a busy man. He could have rationalized turning away from those who sought his aid. Yet in an extraordinary number of instances, he tried to help, usually sending $25 or $50 checks. Even though he had a staff that could take care of the letters for him, Watson paid personal attention to at least some of the requests.

He offered nothing to Chalmers, who Watson detested for testifying against NCR in the 1913 antitrust trial. But Watson was generous to Cool. In the late 1930s, Cool neared 90 years of age and had no money. Watson told him: "I never want you to be in need of anything that will add to your comfort and happiness." He sent cool $330 a month to cover expenses.[19]

Watson got a letter in 1934 from a Pittsburgh man named F. E. Lippincott, who worked for Watson in NCR's second-hand cash register business from 1906 to 1908. Lippincott described his hopeless state and asked Watson for $50, the equivalent in 2002 of nearly $650. Watson sent it, and over the years sent more when Lippincott continued to write, begging for cash. Watson barely knew the man.[20]

Watson sent money to more people than he could count. At one point, he wrote in a letter, "The Depression has brought so many of my relatives and friends to a point where they have to depend on me to a large degree."[21]

Such was the case with a childhood pal named Erford Gorton. The public, feasting on stories of Watson's riches, never got to see the side Gorton brought out. Watson and Gorton found each other as teenagers. Both attended the school in Addison, near Painted Post and the Miller School of Commerce. Gorton kept a photograph from when they were 15 or 16 years old, showing eight boys and a teacher posing in their best suits. When Gorton sent Watson the photo 50 years later, Gorton wrote that he remembered an incident when Watson gave Gorton one of his cuff links. Gorton recalled that he and Watson had the highest marks in the school. A glance at the photo would suggest reversed future roles for Gorton and Watson. Gorton stands at one end, leaning in, looking dashing and sure of himself, like the boy who owned the class. Watson stands in the center, tall and gangly. He looks immature compared with the other boys—the brainy, quirky kid who would get teased by the others.

Gorton stayed in Upstate New York, and he and his wife, Nora, opened a small general store in Hornell. When the Depression rolled in, the town's two banks failed, leaving the Gortons with no savings and no credit for buying goods to stock their shelves. They had to close the store. Nora separated from Gorton, which Gorton never told Watson, and later Gorton was injured in an automobile accident. By 1934, Gorton was left without a wife, a job, good health, or a car. In his despair, he wrote a humble and apologetic letter to Watson.

"Everything I've tried, for the past two years, turned out no good," Gorton wrote, explaining all that had happened. "I hate to bother you, if it is a bother, but I'm surely, desperately in need of a living." He didn't ask for money, or even imply that he wanted a donation or loan. He asked for a job. "I'd do almost anything," he wrote, signing the letter, "Your old friend, Erf."[22]

Watson had been traveling and didn't see the letter right away. When he replied, it was four weeks later. He expressed sympathy, but told his old friend: "I have canvassed our situation and there is nothing we could offer you that would be of interest." IBM rarely hired older people, though Watson didn't say as much to Gorton. Along with the reply, Watson sent Gorton a check for $100.[23]

Over the next few years, Gorton worked little, except for a couple of short-lived, abysmal sales jobs. He continued writing Watson to say he was "in the same old boat." Watson continued to send checks, usually for $25, never calling the money a loan and never belittling or chastising Gorton for his poverty. In January 1939, Watson sent another $100 check. Six months later, Gorton wrote asking for $100. With Watson traveling, Watson's secretary, Phillips, decided on his own to respond by sending Gorton a check for $50 out of Watson's account. That time, Gorton had the nerve to write back thanking Phillips, but complaining it was half of what he requested. Watson later sent the other $50.

A year later, Watson paid for Gorton and six other childhood friends to visit New York. Watson put them up at the first-class Waldorf-Astoria, ate with them in IBM's elegant executive dining room, and took them to the New York World's Fair as his guests. In a photograph of the seven men in Watson's office, the guests look uncomfortable and bashful in their suits and ties amid the corporation's dark paneling and rich furnishings, the way first-grade schoolchildren might look if plunked down amid a sixth-grade class.

Gorton continued to cling to Watson. At one point, a collections agent visited Gorton demanding $187.51. Watson paid the bill for Gorton. Watson sent a note to Phillips saying that after that incident, he "then would be through with any further donations" to Gorton.[24] Still, Watson sent other checks when Gorton would write complaining of destitution.

Gorton died on March 4, 1945. Afterward, Watson received letters from two of Gorton's four adult children, further explaining Gorton's sad life.

"We have none of us been very considerate children," Marjorie Gorton Hyatt, of Penn Yan, New York, told Watson. "Dad was very lonely but I don't think any of us realized how lonely. I can't tell you of the conditions he lived under but they were pretty bad."

The daughter ended her letter this way: "What I have been trying to say is that we greatly appreciate all the kindness that you gave him. We all feel that he imposed upon you and I'm afraid he did, but nevertheless I am very grateful that he had a friend like you that was so kind and generous with him. He used to say that no brother could have been better to him than you were."[25]

❧

Watson lived each day as if he controlled time the way a great painter controls color. He challenged its rules, stretched it to its limits, and used it as it suited him. As he felt increasingly invincible, Watson felt he could bend the forces around him to his will.

His mastery of a given day began a little after dawn in his bedroom at 4 East 75th Street, on New York's Upper East Side, less than a block from Central Park. The Watsons bought that townhouse in 1933, and by the late 1930s lived there most of the time. Surrounded by more quaint and relaxed-looking Manhattan brownstones, the Watson residence stood the width of two typical townhouses and faced the street with a white stone front that was as plain and stark as a sheet of ice.

Upstairs, in the bedroom, an awakening Watson would go to his dresser to get out his clothes, pulling open little drawers, each one neatly holding a different item—socks, underwear, a stack of white handkerchiefs perfectly folded. A top drawer hid his stash of gum, LifeSavers, and sometimes chocolates, all among his favorite treats.

Once Watson slipped off his pajamas, he put on long underwear, whether it was winter, summer, or any time of year. He always claimed to be cold otherwise. Over at his closet, he surveyed his beautifully tailored suits, most of them dark and stoic but lined inside with boldly patterned silk. "Funny dresser," recalled his granddaughter Lucinda Watson. "Very conservative yet very wild under it all." He dressed completely, including vest, jacket, tie, shoes, and pocket watch, before setting foot outside the bedroom. Hardly anyone ever saw Watson descend the stairs wearing a bathrobe.[26]

The domestic staff readied Watson's breakfast, often oatmeal. Jeannette would sometimes join him at the table, if she hadn't already left the house. All around Watson was a house that was serious and formal—and extremely white. In the entranceway of the first floor, bright white marble walls surrounded a black-and-white marble-tiled floor. A grand staircase of white marble edged by elaborate black iron railings rose to the second and third floors. A great room opened up on brilliant marble that encased floor-to-ceiling windows. The room was precisely furnished with couches, French-style chairs, and a baby grand piano. In the dining room loomed a massive portrait of Watson, and near it hung smaller but still sizable portraits of Jeannette and of Tom Jr., by this time a tall and imposing young man. In the home's library, shelves along one wall held books stacked so neatly, they looked as if they were not supposed to be touched. In later years, Olive Watson, Tom Jr.'s wife, would declare that there wasn't a single cozy room in the house.

When Watson finished eating, he would walk out the front door, where a chauffeur waited with a car—unless he needed to think through an idea. He wouldn't go into the office unless he had thought through four or five items he wanted to get done. If it meant sitting with a cup of coffee for an hour or two, that's what he'd do. Then Watson would head out to the car.

In 15 minutes, depending on traffic, the car would arrive at IBM's world headquarters at 590 Madison Avenue. Earlier in the 1930s, IBM had burst out of its original building at 50 Broad Street. In 1933, Watson moved the company to three leased floors in a newly constructed building at 270 Broadway, but looked for a more permanent, stand-alone presence in New York. Watson negotiated the purchase of a rundown, unremarkable corner building at 590 Madison Avenue, in the busiest part of Manhattan. IBM renovated the building into the kind of showy headquarters befitting Watson's style. As the car carrying Watson pulled to the curb, Watson could see INTERNATIONAL BUSINESS MACHINES—in all capital letters—spread across the front of the building.

Once inside, Watson would pass through an ample first-floor showroom—open to the public and displaying IBM's products. On his way to the elevators, he'd hear "Good morning, Mr. Watson," from any IBM employees present. Watson would step on the elevator and take it to the 17th floor, stepping off into an elegant central hallway, paneled in oak and with black-and-white marble floors. As Watson walked to his office door, five male secretaries greeted him. Most of Watson's contemporaries in other companies employed women as secretaries. Watson believed that was a mistake. Pretty young woman secretaries were distracting. They could lead to improprieties or, at least, the question of improprieties. In addition, they weren't serious enough. If you wanted to be successful, Watson told his executives, you must have male secretaries. He could be superstitious about sticking with what worked, and because Watson had been successful and always had male secretaries, in his mind there must have been a link.

From the door of his office, Watson had to cross 30 feet of deep-pile blue carpet to get to his desk. The corner windows offered a view of the East River and the Queensboro Bridge, except Watson almost always kept the red velvet drapes nearly closed. Every morning, every day, his beautiful mahogany desk suffered the indignity of heaping piles of papers, books, binders, and magazines—so many stacks so thick, he could not possibly have known what was in them. He often would not read his mail for days. Watson had no interest in keeping his papers orderly. It was not the way he thought or organized himself.

Aside from the papers, on his desk were photographs of his family and a chrome paperweight that said, "REFLEX-IONE." Above him, against the mahogany paneling, hung a THINK plaque and a number of signed photographs of famous people, including politicians, entertainers, and businessmen. The photos helped confer status on Watson from their places on the wall.

He sat down and attacked his list of things to do—the list he thought up before riding to the office. Watson would choose an item from his list, and then pick an executive. Sometimes it was the obvious choice, sometimes not. He'd rely on instinct to choose the man to buzz in.[27]

As the day unfolded, Watson talked with three men more than any others. All had been with him for decades.

One, of course, was Nichol. Another was Phillips, who had become far more than a secretary. He was an aide-de-camp, a caretaker, a butler, and, because of his gatekeeper role with Watson, a man of considerable power inside IBM. The third key man was Charles Ogsbury, a jovial, outgoing, highly dependable workhorse of a manager who started with C-T-R in 1914 as a mechanical serviceman. (His brother was James Ogsbury, the executive who had a falling out with Watson in the 1920s.) All three of them did Watson's bidding uncritically, although Ogsbury was slightly less concerned with pleasing Watson than the other two. Whether by chance or design, all three stood at least six inches shorter than Watson.

Over the course of a morning, Watson could usually clear his to-do list. He'd then breeze out to a lunch at one of the businessmen's clubs, or to a gathering where he was to speak. He came back, many days, two hours later.

Upon returning to his office, Watson might close the door behind him, stretch his long frame out on a leather couch, and nap. If he couldn't lie down, perhaps because he had to get to an appointment on Wall Street, he'd put his head back during the car ride downtown and instantly fall asleep. Arriving in the financial district 20 minutes later, Watson would awaken and jump to life like a toy that just got new batteries. CEOs of later eras generally considered daytime sleep to be a sign of weakness or laziness. Watson treated naps as time management. He slept when it was most convenient.

On the ride back to headquarters, Watson might constantly bark directions to the driver about where to turn or which lane to get into. The driver probably liked it better when Watson wasn't conscious.

Midafternoon, Watson's energy ran at full power. Though he was in his mid-60s, Watson at full power awed many of his contemporaries. "I have often wondered if others knew what an incredibly driven man Mr. Watson was," wrote Ruth Leach, who had to try to match his stride for a couple of decades. "So inquisitive, and with such boundless energy. Sometimes I found it exhausting just working for him, always having to run just to keep up."[28]

He liked to be moving. He could stay in his office for a while, pushing buttons behind his desk to summon secretaries and executives, whose offices were rigged with buzzers linked to Watson's buttons. But every other week, if not more often, he felt the need to get out of there. Once or twice a month, he'd board the train for Endicott, stay a day or two, then return. When he didn't go to Endicott, he'd travel farther afield, off on a tear through IBM sales offices in the Midwest, the South, or the West Coast. He'd cause local managers to sweat; on a whim, he'd promote talented but obscure salesmen; and he'd criticize the way IBM's machines were displayed in the windows. Then Watson would gather all of the managers and salesman in that office and host a dinner—he called them "family dinners"—at the nicest restaurant in town. Throughout the meal, he'd tell the guests all about his philosophy of business and life. Once or twice a year, Watson would mount a mission to Europe, blowing through major cities at the rate of one every day or two, giving the European branch offices the same treatment he meted out to the domestic branches. Everywhere he went, Watson engaged customers and dined with dignitaries. On a few occasions, Watson took his whole family—Jeannette and the four children—with him on a European trip, sailing off for a couple of months, driving his staff crazy with the logistics of such an entourage.

Watson refused to fly. He dismissed this new way to save time even while pushing to do more in less time. In the second half of the 1930s, executives increasingly boarded airplanes to get from city to city. Douglas Aircraft's 21-seat DC-3 revolutionized the air travel industry when it was introduced in December 1935. Compared with anything that had come before, the DC-3 was safe, comfortable, and speedy, cruising at 160 miles per hour. Flying, however, scared Watson. It wouldn't be accurate to say he was afraid of flying, because he never flew. He often told the story of taking his family to a country fair in the 1920s, when airplanes were new, exciting, and dangerous. An enterprising pilot sold rides for $5. Watson had never been up in a plane and decided to try it. He waited in line, and was the next to go when his children asked him to get them ice cream. Watson relinquished his place in line to go to the ice cream stand. Before Watson could return, the plane crashed, killing three people. That kind of event fed his superstitions and absolutisms. It was similar to when he had his rig and goods stolen because he drank in a bar, afterward deciding never again to touch liquor. When Watson nearly lost his life because of an airplane ride, he decided never to fly. Time be damned—he would go by rail or sea, however long it took, and no one could change his mind.

Wherever Watson went, once he arrived he still moved constantly.

"We spent a typically strenuous week in Endicott," Leach reported. "Mr. Watson, a human dynamo, went on and on through the day and night, talking all the time, on less sleep than anyone I ever knew. He made an average of two speeches a day, spent hours in the factory, gave a luncheon each day, ate with the girls in the class and talked to them each night at the Homestead into the wee hours. Then, after that, he wanted to report to me about his impressions of the class."[29]

Watson used coffee like rocket fuel. He downed it in quantity. Occasionally, he skipped a cup of coffee and instead swigged a bottle of Yoo-Hoo chocolate drink.[30] He was a junk food addict. He couldn't resist peanuts, milkshakes, hot dogs, almost anything chocolate, and a long list of other sweets and fatty foods. He never had to worry about getting fat. He burned calories the way a speeding locomotive burned coal.

Whether in New York or on the road, Watson's business day ended at 6 or 7 P.M., though that was not the end of anything for Watson. Nearly every evening, he attended or hosted a dinner, joined business guests at the theater or opera, or spoke at an event inside or outside IBM. If he didn't do any of those things, he brought business guests to the Watson home for dinner. In any location, unfortunate souls who ended up with Watson at the end of the evening had no choice but to listen to him for another hour or two. He would talk, and the listeners dared not escape. Eleanor Irvine witnessed that when Watson stayed at the Homestead in Endicott. "He'd hang out with [guests] in the living room, sometimes until 2 A.M.," she said. "And he did all the talking. They'd all be yawning."

Eventually, far past the hour of exhaustion for most humans, Watson said goodnight, loosened his tie for the first time since that morning, changed into his pajamas, and caught just enough sleep to rejuvenate for the next day.

As with any job, Watson had work that he tackled day in and day out. That included decisions, budgets, meetings, and memos. Some of the trivialities were the stuff of office life. Phillips was unhappy that a group of executives always met for breakfast at a nearby restaurant and failed to show up for work until 9:30. Office hours, Phillips griped, began at 9:00. The company hired a cook for the executive dining room, which launched a discussion of whether the executives who ate there should pay $10 per month toward the cook's salary. Another time, Phillips sent around a memo: "It seems to me we have an enormous increase in the amount of telephones serving the departments," he wrote. "Our telephone switchboard is extremely busy and where it is possible to cut down the number of extensions in a department without affecting the efficiency of that group, we must do it immediately."[31]

One other daily task soaked up a large portion of Watson's schedule: ruthlessly manipulating his executives.

Watson did so with skill and precision. Often, he applied extremes of kindness and cruelty. The touching kindnesses made executives love him; the cruelty inspired fear of crossing him. IBM's success, the monetary rewards, and Watson's charisma stoked their desire to stay in Watson's circle. Together, the dynamics created a faithful staff of people desperate for Watson's approval.

Watson enchanted an executive named Walter Titus. On January 2, 1939, Titus wrote a letter to Watson that perfectly reflected the conflicting, off-balance feelings Watson inspired.

"It seems to me that years ago I used to be 'scared to death' of you and that even now I view approaching contacts with apprehension," Titus wrote. "But the more I think about why I should assume such an attitude, the more I pin the blame on myself. It really never was you that I had to fear. Certainly my treatment at your hands has been kindly and considerate in extreme, and you are, in truth, the best friend I have. No, the trouble with me has been my own deficiencies and the fear that they would be found out."[32]

His best friend? At the time, Watson was trying to lose him.

Energetic, smart, and witty, Titus had started with C-T-R around 1909 and over the next two decades became a star in sales. In the early 1930s, he was pulled into Watson's circle as an executive assistant. Watson dished out rewards to Titus. In 1933, he sent Titus on a scouting trip to Europe to analyze IBM's prospects in that part of the world. From February to July, Titus went to Madrid, Naples, Berlin, Oslo, London, Warsaw, Prague, Paris, and Dublin.[33]

On at least one occasion, Titus got invited out to Watson's New Jersey farm. He was given a $1,000 bonus in 1934. In 1935 he made $18,000; the next year he made $25,000 plus a $2,000 bonus. By that point, Titus was a faithful Watson soldier. So Watson promoted him to vice president, sending him to Endicott to supervise all operations there.[34]

Titus's skills in sales and at headquarters didn't transfer to managing a manufacturing plant. Watson got mad when Titus didn't pay the factory workers more than union scale. Watson, who wanted to keep unions out of IBM, forced Titus to raise pay levels. Titus gave public speeches without clearing it with headquarters, angering Watson, who said Titus sometimes talked about "subjects that I feel are dangerous to the interests of the company." Watson became outraged about a report that Titus was indifferent to the fact that Endicott managers and executives were supposedly behaving badly by drinking and having "immoral relations with IBM girls."

In each case, Watson ripped Titus. As a frustrated Watson wrote in a letter to Nichol, "I regret to say that he (Titus) has not given me his cooperation in the way that a man must do in that position."[35]

In January 1939, at the time when Titus called Watson his best friend, Nichol and Ogsbury—under Watson's orders—were completing an investigation of Titus, detailing all of his many alleged wrongs. The wrongs were all disagreements with Watson, not necessarily bad decisions or morally questionable acts. At the conclusion of the investigation, Nichol and Ogsbury demoted Titus and sent him to California to run the Pacific division, which was primarily a sales organization. Only then was the spell of Watson broken for Titus. That left him dispirited, as if a part of his soul for so many years had been carved out of him. After a miserable two years on the West Coast, Titus resigned, and joined Sperry Gyroscope, where he eventually became a vice president.

Watson's manipulations took different forms for different reasons. Jim Birkenstock experienced some of Watson's methods firsthand. In 1939, Birkenstock was probably unknown to Watson. Birkenstock worked at the time as an

IBM salesman in St. Louis, Missouri—hardly a position that would get the attention of headquarters. Driving with his young family near Peoria, Illinois, Birkenstock suffered a car accident. He broke his sternum and jaw. His wife sustained a concussion. Their one-year-old son was killed. While recovering in the hospital, a despairing Birkenstock was visited by IBM's Peoria branch manager, who handed Birkenstock a telegram from Watson. In an era before comprehensive health insurance, Watson had authorized a $5,000 account to pay for the Birkenstocks' hospital bills. "This was my first introduction to Watson Sr.'s compassion toward his employees," Birkenstock said, and it won Birkenstock's lasting affection for Watson.

But years later came a far different experience. In an executive meeting in Watson's office, Watson asked Birkenstock, by then an executive in headquarters, to tackle a major project with an impossible deadline. In that public setting, Birkenstock refused, saying it couldn't be done. Watson turned to Birkenstock's assistant, gave that man the assignment, and told the assistant that he would personally help work on it. The meeting broke up, and Birkenstock went to his office. Soon after, one of Watson's secretaries came by to tell Birkenstock that Watson felt Birkenstock needed a vacation. It was all set up and all expenses paid. Birkenstock and his family would go to a resort in the Pocono Mountains in Pennsylvania. This was in May—a damp, chilly, muddy season in the Poconos. The secretary had already called Birkenstock's wife and told her to pack. A car would pick them up at 3 P.M. and drive them to the resort, where they would stay for a week. Birkenstock had no choice but to go, disrupting his family's life. He was sent away for what amounted to a house arrest. The resort was empty. The weather turned worse. Birkenstock got the message: He was not indispensable.[36]

No one escaped Watson's games, not even those closest to him. After Tom Jr. joined the company, father and son would have casual conversations at home, and Watson would spring a trap. "He'd say, 'What do you think of the new sales plan?' or 'What do you think of Mr. Jones?' " Tom Watson Jr. recalled. "No matter how I responded, he'd listen for a minute and then come back with something terribly cutting like: 'You know, you are really not experienced enough to have an opinion on Mr. Jones.' I think Father must have enjoyed these petty emotional exercises. Maybe he was trying to test me, but it was a test no one could pass."[37]

Watson's psychological ruthlessness was his way of getting things done. It helped him push people to their limits. It was his way of testing his son. His employees were, in a sense, willing accomplices—they could see what Watson was doing, and they continued to play Watson's game.

Ruth Leach recalled how she was indoctrinated into the Watson way in the fall of 1944. World War II had turned for the Allies. Watson wanted to jar his staff, which had been completely focused on war-related business, to think about IBM after the war.

Leach ran IBM's Systems Service group, the women's management track begun in the 1930s. Watson called her to his office and asked questions about how many women might leave IBM after the war, and how many women might continue in sales. Leach hadn't thought about it. Watson generously suggested she do an analysis and write it up. After she finished the report, Watson called a high-level meeting. He held it in his home because he'd been suffering from a cold. Watson contacted Leach beforehand and told her to bring her report. Upon arrival, she noticed that no one else had a report—her first clue that Watson was up to something.

Watson launched a discussion of postwar planning. "[Watson] asked, 'Have any of you gentlemen thought about if the war ended tomorrow, how that would affect your department?' " Leach recalled.

189

No one said a word.

Watson said: "I just cannot understand why no one here this morning has even thought about the future of this business when the war ends." He went into a rage. As his voice rose to a crescendo, Watson turned to Leach and said, "Miss Leach, what do you have in your lap?"

She whispered, "An analysis of the Systems Service personnel, sir."

"Well, will you please read it aloud?"

She had been set up. She recalled being so upset she could barely read the report. She worried that the other executives—all men and all senior to her—would think she knew about the setup and willingly went along.

When she finished, Watson said, "Miss Leach has put all of you to shame!" He continued to rant at the men.[38]

Leach felt horrible. After the meeting, she began apologizing to her colleagues. Not surprisingly, they knew exactly what had happened and weren't angry at her. They'd seen Watson's tactics before, and knew they'd see them again.

⁓

In the early days of C-T-R, Watson listened to the executives around him. He had to. He didn't know the business, and he didn't have control. As time went on, he imparted his philosophies and barked commands, but he also continued to ask questions, especially when sitting around the table with engineers. He soaked up information from any resource available to him.

In the 1930s, Watson still sought information. He made a habit of ordering reports on any question that popped to mind, and when he traveled to IBM outposts, he'd converse one-on-one with a salesman or factory worker, politely asking the nervous employee ever more detailed questions about his job.

But management meetings took on an entirely different tone. If a meeting lasted 60 minutes, Watson might lecture for 50, leaving the other 10 minutes for Nichol or another servile executive to praise Watson's comments. As one Watson contemporary put it, IBM managers didn't attend meetings with Watson; they submitted to them.

Such was the case on a Monday morning when sales, manufacturing, and customer service executives gathered in a conference room at 590 Madison.[39] This is what it was like to submit to a meeting with Watson.

Watson settled into his seat and launched his first missile.

"I had a very interesting meeting with an outside man this morning," he said. "The young man telephoned me and said he would like to come up and talk with me because he had been doing a lot of work improving the efficiency and appearance of various (IBM) machines."

If an unknown outsider wrote or called, and the person struck Watson as interesting, Watson would ignore his calendar and take the meeting, throwing a dozen executives' schedules into disarray. Inevitably, Watson would glean some little nugget from the meeting that he'd bring up with his executives later.

In this case, the visitor showed Watson photos of a desk he was selling for use with IBM's tabulating machines. It had slots and other features that helped a user organize the heaps of punched cards.

"Do we use them here in our building?" Watson asked everyone sitting around the table in the meeting.

"No, I don't think so," said one of the managers.

"Nobody is doing any thinking about it. You just want the old-fashioned desk and keep the cards in the backyard, I suppose, or some other place," Watson said cuttingly. He couldn't believe that not only was IBM failing to use this man's desks internally, but that some other company—not IBM—was making money selling an IBM-related product. That relatively small transgression lit Watson's gunpowder. "I don't care what you think about if you will only think

191

that we are asleep on a lot of things. Think about that,"
Watson said. "I think that it is a disgrace. I think it is a
reflection on every man connected with the sales end of our
business. I am going to give that man (the desk maker) a
present. I don't even know his name. What is his name,
Waters?"

Byne Waters, Watson's secretary, said simply: "Strum."

"That is what is wrong with everything. Let's see if we
can't be different. We have been different in the IBM in a lot
of things. This THINK sign—where is it?" Watson looked
around the conference room. There was no THINK sign.
The executives in the room probably braced for Watson to
react with the ferocity of a mama grizzly bear that had lost
her cubs. This time, Watson's reaction was mild. "I guess
somebody took it down. What do you know about that?
Find out, Mr. Waters, when that was taken out of this room
and have four put in."

Waters wrote that down.

"Now, this THINK sign, gentlemen, means a lot to me,"
Watson said. "I am going to talk about myself for a minute.
I am going to tell you that that THINK sign is responsible
for what little success I have made in this world. That is
why I keep it around, hoping to help other people."

Watson then abruptly switched direction, without telling
the men much about the THINK signs.

Watson had heard about violations in the reporting and
use of overtime as dictated by the Wage and Hour Law. On
a two-hour car ride with Nichol, he decided that any manager who violated the law, or allowed someone working for
him to violate the law, would immediately be fired. IBM
would not—ever!—be caught breaking the law. For Watson, this was an absolute, forged during his NCR antitrust
trevails. Beyond that, Watson, who risked ostracism by supporting Roosevelt, could never let his company defy the
New Deal.

"If you think that is arbitrary or unfair, tell me so,"

Watson said to the others. "It is going to stand unless you men can tell us this morning that it isn't fair to you or the business."

The executives didn't comment—not then or anytime during the meeting. Watson said, "Now we will drop that."

Without a pause, he continued: "I wonder if anybody has ever talked to you gentlemen about getting your duties right down to a simple formula so you all know what you do. Did anybody ever tell you right out just what your duties as executives are? Well, I will tell you."

At that signal, the executives might as well have ordered popcorn and slipped off their shoes. They would've known that it was going to be a long one.

"Your duty, first, is to employ men," Watson said. He dove into an anecdote about meeting an IBM employee working in a factory in San Antonio, Texas. The worker was from Owego, New York. Why wasn't this man working in Endicott, near his family? Watson wanted to know. After telling a long story, Watson made the point that managers have to be smarter about who they put where.

He continued on about employment, telling his executives to look for character, which was more important than a first-class education. Watson said that he knew an engineer 30 years ago who was one of the best engineers in Dayton, and that man had quit school when he was 13. Then Watson told another long story, this time about Lawrence O'Brien, who was last in every class at the IBM school, but had great character.

"Now where is he?" Watson asked. "He is one of our outstanding young men, a hundred percent dependable. He does a good job, takes good care of his customers."

Oh, Watson said, and another thing about employing people: "Make sure that he is really crazy about this business. Because if he doesn't love what he's doing, he'll do a bad job, and that will make you—the managers—less successful."

He had talked about employment for more than 10 minutes. But that was only the first point.

"Now, supervising comes next—supervision—and I could talk to you all day on supervision."

Oh no!

"But I am not going to. But I am going to tell you one thing. The best way to supervise your men is from their reports that they make out." Study their numbers and base your decisions on their results, he said, somewhat contradicting his pronouncement that character is more important than sheer performance. Don't give automatic raises based on tenure, Watson instructed the men in the meeting. "Treat each case as an individual case, and give every man an opportunity to earn just as much money as he is capable of earning." Anyone in the meeting who knew Watson's background—his lack of formal education, his failings until NCR's John Range gave him a chance—would have understood how much of Watson's management philosophy grew out of his early experiences.

Watson moved on to the next point: promotion. He told a story about an IBM man whose aunt he'd met in Berlin. The aunt told Watson that the nephew invented a button machine. When Watson returned to New York, he inquired about this man and met him. The man had been working in an IBM service department helping customers use their IBM machines productively. Watson plucked the man—whom he never named—from service and put him in engineering, where he became a fantastic success. "I got him just by accident," Watson said in the meeting. "I never would have thought to ask him or any other young man that I meet about whether he ever thought about inventing anything." So, find out what your workers are best at doing. Perhaps Watson was thinking of his career boost when Patterson gave him the chance to run the used–cash register operation.

Watson made one last point about the executives' jobs: "Discharging," Watson said. "That is a disagreeable one, but unfortunately it has to be considered."

Watson humbly told the group that he hates firing people. "I have never done a good job at that." Any attendee still awake might have slyly thought: How could he be bad at it after so much practice?

Watson continued, saying that when you fire someone, tell that person exactly why and "give him a little piece of advice so that he can try to do better in the next place."

By that point, the meeting had gone on for about 45 minutes. The only real accomplishment had been to tell the managers about the policy concerning the Wage and Hour Law. The number of words spoken so far by someone other than Watson was 24.

"So there is the simple formula," Watson finally said, winding up his management lesson. "If you take one of those away, you are whipped."

Was he done?

No.

"The reason I feel so good and want to talk so much today is that I have just been out in the field a couple of weeks calling on offices and learning something about this business."

Imagine the stifled groans, though no one in the room would dare show the slightest sign of boredom.

Watson talked about the value of getting out and seeing the business. "How many offices did you visit last year, Army?" This was directed at the head of education for IBM, George Armstrong.

"I have been in quite a few," Armstrong said. "I'm just trying to think of them. Detroit, Chicago, Toledo, Cleveland, Philadelphia, New York."

"My point is, Army, go to more this year," Watson said. "Go to twice as many this year as you went to last year."

Watson looked down at some notes he'd brought with him, and remembered another point he wanted to make. In more rural territories, where one salesman might cover hundreds of miles, it would make sense to train one person to handle both sales and service. "Take up in Vermont; take Bangor, Maine. There are a lot of fine jobs for good first-class customer servicemen who show a little sales ability." He hammered on the point for a number of minutes.

Watson again looked at his notes. "Wage and Hour, I have talked about that. Research, ideas for inventions. I don't know that I have anything else. Would any of you men like to ask me some questions?"

They probably wanted to get the hell out of there. No one asked a question.

"I would like to thank you, Mr. Watson, for that fine talk," said an executive named J. L. Turney. "I know we all got a great deal out of that, and it will be a great thing for the customer service organization."

Watson reiterated his decision about compliance with the Wage and Hour Law. He turned to Fred Nichol. "Mr. Nichol, have you anything to say?"

Ever the sycophant, Nichol restated some of Watson's points, then said: "I say that Mr. Watson has covered this so thoroughly, he has given you not only a program for this meeting, but he has given you sailing orders for the rest of your job." He mentioned that a stenographer was recording the meeting and the notes would be available. "I would carry this talk with me, if I were in this position, as my bible. I would keep looking at it. He has laid out your jobs thoroughly."

Watson broke back in to talk about the importance of good customer servicemen, then suddenly veered into a question about someone in one of the factories deciding to cut punch cards "a little bit short so they would expand to the right length." In hot and humid climates, the stored cards would expand a bit; however, in cooler climates, they didn't. A customer whose cards were too short complained. Watson wanted to know who made such a stupid decision. "Find out who it was, who didn't think, and then give him a job that doesn't require thinking," Watson said.

The meeting came to an abrupt end with Nichol saying, "We'll get down to work now."

The meeting lasted at least 90 minutes. Watson talked for almost all of it. He reinforced a number of facets of his management philosophy: Give people a chance to do their best; be open to innovation and ideas; fire people when you have to; get out in the field as much as possible; and above all, be upstanding citizens. Through the entire meeting, none of the executives even slightly challenged him, or asked a question, or offered a suggestion. They might have been thankful that this was one of the more pleasant meetings. At least Watson wasn't angry. He didn't embarrass anybody. The men in the meeting sat mute, some of them, perhaps, soaking up Watson's words of wisdom, while others daydreamed or doodled. Either way, it was an act of submitting to a man who increasingly expected nothing less.

<hr />

(To the tune of "Glory Glory Hallelujah!")

Overseas we also make our marvelous machines.
Round the globe in every land, our service is supreme.
IBM's fine products are the joy of kings and queens.
We serve humanity.

—*Songs of the IBM*

7

ENEMIES
AND
DELUSIONS

UTSIDE THE BORDERS OF WATSON'S GROWING empire, events of the grandest magnitude shoved the world closer to a cliff. Europe was coming unglued. Adolf Hitler consolidated power in Germany in 1934, started openly repressing Jews in 1935, formed the Axis with Japan and Italy in 1936, annexed Austria in 1938, and conquered Czechoslovakia and Poland in 1939, teeing up a world war. Benito Mussolini, stridently anticommunist and laughably pompous, became the fascist leader of Italy, then invaded and took over Ethiopia. General Francisco Franco led Spain's army in rebellion against its government, fought a brutal civil war with the help of Italy and Germany, and by 1939 won the war and a seat at the table of tyrants. In the Soviet Union, Joseph Stalin terrorized or murdered anyone who might challenge his power, pinning the communist nation under his thumb.

Similar forces wrenched Asia. Japan, increasingly run by aggressive military generals, expanded its empire piece by piece, and invaded northern China in a horrible storm of destruction, mass murder, and rape.

In the United States, the misery of the Depression continued and dust storms tore up the Midwest. Sit-downs, walkouts, and violent strikes at General Motors, Ford, steel

201

plants, and even Broadway theaters created a chasm between labor and management.

At the same time, inventions and engineering feats promised a spectacular future. Air travel sprouted and began making distant places seem far less distant. The first television sets arrived on the market, as did Technicolor movies and the first animated feature, Walt Disney's miraculous *Snow White*. An explosion of skyscrapers, bridges, and dams—and the emergence of Louis Carrier's air-conditioning machines—altered where and when people worked, lived, and played.

While events loomed large, Franklin Roosevelt always seemed larger. He won in a landslide reelection in 1936. He could stand with England's Winston Churchill and against Hitler and Mussolini, and still battle the economic rot at home. He could and would shape a new world. He made things happen that affected millions of lives. Though he enraged his enemies, to most Americans he remained respected, admired, and, to a great extent, loved.

Watson believed he could become a businessman's version of everything that Roosevelt was, and his rising stature gave him a chance to prove it. He ran a company that was increasingly recognized and important. IBM made "thinking machines" that fascinated the public and revolutionized the way business and government did accounting and record keeping. In the headwind of the Depression, IBM grew stronger. Revenue increased 81 percent from 1935 to 1939, billowing from $21 million to $38 million. Profits climbed 29 percent—from $7 million in 1935 to $9 million in 1939. IBM spread around the globe. It operated factories in Sindelfingen, Germany (opened in 1924); Vincennes, France (1925); Berlin, Germany (1933); and Milan, Italy (1935)—which left IBM straddling all sides as fascists rose to power. The company also operated foreign subsidiaries— mostly sales and service organizations run by natives—in every major country in Europe, most of the countries of

South America and North America, and Japan. Though IBM in the 1930s still did not rank among the biggest American companies, its impact was felt widely.

Watson achieved celebrity status. He'd become famous because of his salary and his peculiar culture. He spoke in front of hundreds and sometimes thousands of people. He climbed into the nation's business elite and New York's social elite. He communicated regularly with the U.S. president.

Now Watson wanted to ascend to a higher level. Businessmen had rarely been successful in American politics. Business and politics seemed to be two separate forces that needed but often repelled each other. Yet Watson wanted to match Roosevelt as a statesman, effect historic change, move world events, and be welcomed by heads of state. He chose to do so while running his beloved IBM, using it as his lever. It was the only way that made sense to him.

Watson had already reached toward history. He helped finance Admiral Richard Byrd's expedition to the South Pole, making important contributions to Byrd's success. When Byrd flew over the South Pole and back in November 1929, a three-deck headline stretched across the entire top of the *New York Times*'s front page. In 1935, Watson held a luncheon in Byrd's honor. When Byrd spoke, he told the audience that Watson was the first man who realized what the expedition was trying to do for science.

After such extra-IBM successes, Watson stepped fully onto the global stage by taking on the presidency of an organization called the International Chamber of Commerce (ICC). Watson intended to use the position to influence world affairs, and that's where his ambition backfired.

The ICC had cachet in the 1920s and into the 1930s—a time when international organizations attempted to end war. After World War I, U.S. President Woodrow Wilson conceived of and set up the League of Nations, which was to act as a political forum for international disputes and the creation of international laws and principles. Some saw the ICC as a business equivalent, focusing on trade, tariffs, patent disputes, and other commercial issues. Most developed nations recognized the body. Still, the ICC was essentially powerless; before Watson, it hadn't been used as a pulpit from which to evangelize the value of global business.

Watson got involved with the ICC in the 1920s, after an IBM board member, Willis Booth, became ICC president.[1] In 1937, the ICC needed a new president, and no one much wanted the job. The heat and turmoil of the times made it too perilous.

The 1936 Olympics in Berlin had fed worldwide audiences an unsettling dose of Germany's militarism and belief in a superior race. The American public, wanting no part of another war, stood firmly behind isolationism. Yet American companies over the previous 15 years had become increasingly global and increasingly reliant on profits from afar. Most major U.S. companies sold to Nazi Germany, and many ran factories inside the country. Those companies included Standard Oil, Colgate Palmolive, Quaker Oats, International Harvester, and the three big automobile manufacturers: Ford, General Motors, and Chrysler. General Electric maintained some of the deepest ties, forming a partnership with the German company Krupp. Companies tried to keep operations going and held onto stakes in subsidiaries even after Germany began blocking Reichsmark profits from leaving the country. Part of the thinking at the time was that Germany might eventually overrun much of Europe, and if a company pulled out of Germany now, it might end up walled off from Europe later.[2]

IBM owned 90 percent of its German subsidiary, called Deutsche Hollerith Machinen Gesellschaft, better known as Dehomag. The unit had been started in 1910 by Willy Heidinger, an enterprising German who licensed the right to sell Hollerith's machines. Heidinger agreed to pay Hollerith's company 10 percent over the cost of the machines that Dehomag imported, plus a 25 percent royalty on its revenue from rentals. In the 1920s, Germany's economy collapsed. Runaway inflation left Heidinger deeply indebted to what was then C-T-R, and unable to meet payments. Watson, certainly taking advantage of the situation, offered to keep Heidinger in business if he ceded a controlling interest in Dehomag to C-T-R. Eventually, that interest ratcheted up to 90 percent. Heidinger controlled the other 10 percent and ran the company as a quasi-independent subsidiary.[3] In the mid-1930s, IBM counted the resurgent Germany as its second-biggest market after the United States.

The sum of Watson's risks in taking the ICC presidency was enormous. Amid all the no-win conflicts cascading down on the organization, the ICC's 1937 congress was to take place in Berlin. There, the new president would be installed in a ceremony watched by the world and manipulated by the brilliant Nazi propagandists.

Watson, though, held firmly to his optimism. It had guided him through C-T-R's early struggles, and it allowed him to beat the Depression. He believed that he could use the ICC and IBM to avert a world war. He stepped up and took the job. If somebody had to sell peace to Hitler, Watson figured he was more qualified than anyone.

⌘

On June 24, 1937, Watson and his wife, Jeannette, stepped off the train in Berlin. They arrived from London, where Watson had been a guest of George VI, crowned as king of England only one month earlier. A few days after the Watsons disembarked in Berlin, Tom Jr., 23 years old, joined them there.

Upon arriving, Tom Watson Jr. immediately sensed that "the atmosphere in Berlin was highly charged."[4] Jeannette pulled Tom Jr. aside to tell him that their friends, the Wertheims, were about to sell their department store for almost nothing and flee the country. This was no minor bit of news. Wertheim's, the name of the store in the center of

Berlin, was celebrated around the world. Built in 1896, it dazzled visitors with a glass-roofed atrium, chandeliers of crystal and Bohemian glass, 83 elevators, window displays glowing under thousands of lights, and luxurious goods from every corner of the globe. The Wertheims were one of the city's wealthiest families, and they were Jewish. In 1935, Nazi youth gangs ran through Berlin smashing windows of Jewish businesses, including Wertheim's. Ever-escalating persecution convinced the family to leave for Sweden, the family told Jeannette Watson. Their personal possessions filled six railroad cars. The Wertheims made the Watsons tangibly aware of the Nazi treatment of Jews.[5]

Watson pressed on with his purpose. The ICC congress officially anointed him president of the organization in a ceremony attended by 95 executives of U.S. companies and 1,515 delegates from 43 other nations. Then began several days of meetings, politicking, and partying.

Watson's moment of intersecting with world history came three days into the ICC congress. On June 28, Nazi officials escorted Watson into an elegant room in the Reich Chancellery. At a low pedestal table set with elegant teacups sat Hitler. Watson and Hitler were joined by four others: F. H. Fentener van Vlissingen of the Netherlands, who was the outgoing ICC president; Abraham Frowein, the round, goateed president of the German sector of the ICC; Lord Riverdale, an honorary president of the ICC; and Hitler's interpreter. The men settled into the stuffed floral chairs and took tea with the Führer. What was said during the meeting was not recorded. When Watson emerged afterward, he stood in front of anxious reporters from all over the world and told them that Hitler had given him his "personal promise" that "there will be no war. No country wants war, no country can afford it. Certainly, that is true of Germany."[6] That was exactly the message Watson wanted Hitler to buy into. Watson felt triumphant.

That night, as guest of honor at the German Opera

House, Watson listened as an orchestra played Beethoven. Nazi banners and flags hung overhead. When Hitler walked into the vast chamber, the Germans stood and bellowed out the *Sieg! Heil!* salute, arms pumping skyward. In the excitement, most of the delegates from Europe and North America joined in. Watson, according to one report, almost joined the salute before realizing what he was doing and pulling back.

Over the next couple of days, Watson listened to Nazi speeches and attended elegant parties in the homes of Hjalmar Schacht, minister of the national economy, and Hermann Goering, Hitler's air force commander. Watson's visit culminated in an opulent party thrown by propaganda minister Josef Goebbels in what had been Friedrich Wilhelm III's eighteenth-century castle, a short drive outside of Berlin. A reported 3,000 guests ate, drank, and sang German folk songs, until Goebbels and Schacht quieted the crowd and summoned Watson before them.

It's not hard to imagine Watson swept up in the moment. He had strived for this. He was being treated as a world leader in one of the great capital cities. Beyond his wildest dreams, he'd convinced Hitler, he believed, that business was better than war. Watson thought he might have just nudged history off a course of destruction and toward one of commerce and prosperity. As a father, he probably thought of his two sons, Tom Jr. and Dick, both of military recruitment age. If war came, one or both could see action.

So did Watson feel guilty being hailed by Nazis as he walked to the front of that room? Did he think for a second that he shouldn't be there? Probably not. His optimism and his sense of accomplishment blinded him to any downside. He didn't see the Nazis for what they were. He saw them for what he wanted them to be. He had looked through the same faulty prism to see Patterson, and later would do the same when regarding his young son, Tom Jr.

In the sudden silence of that ballroom, the guests could hear the whir of film churning inside newsreel cameras. Outgoing ICC president van Vlissingen—a slim, plain man with a crooked nose and thinning hair—was called up front along with Watson. Schacht unfurled a red, black, and white ribbon attached to the Cross of Merit of the Decoration of the German Eagle with the Star, a medal that represented Germany's second-highest honor for foreigners. The gold and white enamel cross was adorned in each corner by a German Eagle resting on a swastika. With the cross came a separate six-pointed star to be worn pinned on the left breast. Schacht began his speech, addressing the outgoing and incoming ICC presidents.

"In your work for the International Chamber of Commerce, you have also worked for Germany," Schacht said. He went on to thank the honorees and the ICC for trying to repair global trade, and he thanked them for bringing the ICC congress to Berlin. Shacht made it abundantly clear that Germany was awarding the medals to Watson and van Vlissingen for their work with the ICC—and, really, for simply being there, which by itself helped buff the darkened German image. Schacht didn't mention IBM, Dehomag, or punch card machines. Whether the German Reich appreciated IBM's products, it didn't give Watson a medal for making them.[7]

Schacht slipped the ribbon over Watson's head and left arm, draping it from his right shoulder across his chest to his left hip. The medal on the ribbon settled on Watson's chest. Schacht decorated van Vlissingen with the same medal in the same way.

"Please accept this presentation as a pledge [by] Germany of our sincere desire to cooperate with all our means in the reconstruction of world trade in the interest of the economic and cultural welfare of all nations," Schacht said.

The onlookers applauded. Watson beamed. He remained blissfully unaware of his atrocious political blunder.

After leaving Berlin, Watson continued through Europe, visiting another 11 countries, pitching his slogan "World peace through world trade," and believing he could make commerce trump war.[8] Watson stopped in Florence, Italy, where he added to his political mistakes. Addressing an IBM sales convention there, he gave his blessing to the Italian dictator.

"I want to pay tribute this morning to your great leader, Benito Mussolini," Watson told the group, most of them Italians. "The thought came into my mind that your Mussolini is a pioneer. Under his leadership, Italy, one of the oldest of all countries, is showing signs of becoming a very new country. I feel that the present generation in Italy is going to benefit greatly as a result of the pioneering work of your leader, Mussolini."

Yet Watson was not naïve. He was never naïve about much of anything. Watson spent more than a month traveling in Europe and meeting kings and prime ministers, and in the prickly atmosphere of 1937, every conversation must have turned to Germany and its mistreatment of not only Jews, but of Catholics and anyone not considered a member of Hitler's master race. Watson regularly read newspapers and magazines, which reported the Nazi atrocities. He received information from IBM's European offices. He knew about the Wertheims. He knew more than most Americans about the events in Germany.

Still, Watson, like many Americans in 1937, felt ambivalent about the Nazis. The worst of Hitler's program had not yet begun. The United States would not declare war on Germany for almost five years, and U.S. business leaders still saw Germany as a vital market. Just prior to the Berlin ICC event, a roomful of top U.S. executives welcomed the new German ambassador to the United States at a luncheon at the Ritz-Carlton in New York. As the elite group dined, American and Nazi flags flew side-by-side over the tables. In July 1938, four months after Germany annexed Austria,

Henry Ford arrived in Berlin to receive the Grand Cross of the German Eagle, the Nazis' highest honor for foreigners—a step above the medal Watson received one year earlier. Ford, in fact, was a known anti-Semite whom Hitler admired. One month after Ford received his medal, the Nazis gave the same one—a Grand Cross—to James Mooney, a senior executive at General Motors. The Nazis appreciated GM and its German subsidiary, Opel, which manufactured trucks and aircraft for Hitler's military.[9] Watson's friend, GM Chairman Alfred Sloan, defended GM's continued operations in Germany as sound business management. An even more prominent American received a Nazi medal around this same time. Charles Lindbergh, the American flight pioneer, visited Germany in 1936 and 1938, praising Hitler for rebuilding the nation and creating the impressive Luftwaffe, the German air force. Lindbergh accepted a medal of a lower level than Watson's.

Watson was still traveling through Europe on August 18, 1937—a month and a half after his Berlin medal ceremony—when he stopped in Geneva, Switzerland. From there, he wrote a letter to Schacht. Watson attempted to tiptoe across the slimmest of lines between criticism and helpfulness. "As a friend, I would not be fair to you or your country if I did not try to convey to you some idea of the situation as I see it," Watson wrote, "and bring to your attention the fact that in the United States, the racial question and the conflict with the churches in your country have alienated many friends of Germany." In careful words, Watson told Schacht that Nazi persecution of Jews and Catholics would hurt trade and political relations with the United States. Watson wrote objectively, telling Shacht of anti-Nazi sentiment in America, but purposefully avoiding writing that he, personally, opposed the Nazi policies. He tried his best to avoid angering Shacht. "I am prompted by the sincere desire to be constructive and helpful," Watson wrote.[10]

Watson's moral compass, so true in business, spun uncertainly when used in politics and world affairs.

~

A question has hovered over Watson's legacy: Aside from the ICC and the medal, what was his and IBM's relationship with Nazi Germany in the late-1930s?

More than 60 years later, a book by Edwin Black charged that Watson and IBM collaborated with the Nazis, actively and knowingly helping the Hitler regime devise punch card machines that could track Jews for elimination and make the German army more efficient. Those inclined to see Watson as a collaborator believe Watson received his Nazi medal for far more than his ICC role. At the other extreme, Tom Watson Jr. and others have portrayed Watson as a right-minded man duped by Hitler into thinking Germany would not start a war or inflict genocide with the help of IBM machines. Other theories bounce around in the middle, some making Watson into an amoral capitalist who didn't purposely help the Nazis, but who was more than willing to take the regime's money and ignore the probable uses of IBM's products.

The truth is more complicated than any one of those labels. Certainly neither Watson nor IBM actively collaborated with the Nazis. As a person, Watson's powerful morality would never have allowed him to knowingly help anyone kill or destroy others. Even if the subjectivity of judging someone's character is removed, there's no reason to believe Watson formed an alliance with Germany. No documents prove such a link. On a pragmatic level, cold business calculations would have prevented Watson from colluding with Nazis. The company had more to lose than to gain from such a relationship. IBM's culture was its most important asset—a culture that was built on American churchgoing values of decency, respect for individuals, egalitarianism, and patriotism. Collaborating with the Nazis for financial gain would have cut directly counter to those values, ruining IBM's culture like toxic chemicals dumped into a clear stream. Such a blow to the culture would have imperiled IBM's standing among customers, hurt its relationship with the communities surrounding its factories, and disillusioned its employees. Considering that Watson created the IBM culture and embodied it, taking any action that might jeopardize that culture would have been the equivalent of slashing his own wrists.

At the time, the company's revenue and earnings were soaring anyway. Though Germany ranked as IBM's second-largest market, the absence of income from Germany would not have substantially slowed IBM's growth. The company didn't need to bust its moral conscripts to aid Nazi atrocities for the sake of money.

And yet, IBM in New York continued to do business with Germany and retain its majority ownership of Dehomag until 1940. Why?

One slice of the answer lies in the context of the times. Looking back from the twenty-first century, Hitler was a blatant villain, and American companies should have immediately broken ties with Nazi Germany. But amid the uncertainty of late-1930s geopolitics, American companies kept their German businesses alive and protected their stranded assets through backdoor deals, Swiss bank accounts, clever barter trade, and a lot of secrecy. IBM was a member of that club. For example, when currency could no longer be exchanged between the United States and Nazi Germany, IBM's German subsidiary would ship machines to European markets, and get paid for the machines in credit against its debt owed to IBM in New York. No money would exchange hands, but business would continue. That went on until 1938, when the Nazis stopped it, wanting to prevent valuable goods from leaving the country for payment of, essentially, nothing.[11]

IBM's relationship with Dehomag, its German sub-sidiary, became strained and complex through this time period. IBM completely owned and controlled its opera-tions in other parts of the world, but Willy Heidinger's 10 percent stake in Dehomag gave him the clout to operate the German subsidiary with some autonomy. Heidinger hated Watson, forever believing that Watson stole Dehomag when it was helpless in the 1920s. As a consequence, Heidinger wanted his company back, and latched onto any way to wrest more control from IBM headquarters.

Heidinger wrote a series of letters to Watson saying that Dehomag would be better off as an independent German company.[12] He engaged in almost childish acts of rebellion. IBM officials in New York complained that Dehomag refused to send copies of the minutes of management meet-ings, even when requested.[13] Over the next few years, the relationship between Dehomag and IBM disintegrated, as did the relationship between Heidinger and Watson. The Nazi government threatened that if IBM New York wouldn't give up its stake in Dehomag, the Nazis would create and fund a competing data processing company in Germany. The Nazis could then direct the German military and businesses to buy only from the German-owned com-pany, with the intention of choking off IBM's subsidiary.[14] Phillips wrote to U.S. Secretary of State Cordell Hull, com-plaining about Dehomag: "As a matter of fact, so far as controlling the operations of the company, we have practi-cally no control under present conditions."[15]

By the late 1930s Dehomag had become a self-contained business. It operated factories, designed its own products, licensed patents from IBM New York to build other prod-ucts, and ran its own sales organization. Dehomag special-ized in one product that is chilling in retrospect: It made the world's best punch card machines for taking a census. Dehomag's census machines were so good, IBM in the

213

United States stopped making census machines, preferring to import Dehomag's. In 1938, when trade with Dehomag was cut off, IBM executives in New York and Europe panicked. "Since Endicott has discontinued making the Printing Counting Sorter, we do not seem to have any machine particularly adapted to census work," wrote IBM Geneva manager J. C. Milner in August, 1938. "We have always figured on being able to get machines from [Germany] for forthcoming census work. During 1940, the census will be taken in several countries, and we expect a number of orders." J. T. Wilson, manager of IBM's foreign division in New York, added that if IBM in Endicott couldn't quickly develop and build a census machine, possibly the IBM factory in France could "economically construct a machine equivalent to the German Census Tabulator."[16]

Inside Germany, the Nazis treasured Dehomag's Census Tabulator. In 1933, shortly after Hitler came to power, the Nazi government began a census that, in part, tracked race and religion. Clerks tabulated, sorted, and collated the census information using Dehomag's machines. The efficiency of the machines made it easier for the Nazis to sort their census to find Jews, and in the following years the government applied that capability in Poland, the Netherlands, and other countries that Germany conquered. As the Nazis established concentration camps, they further perfected the use of Dehomag and IBM machines to track and sort prisoners.

More than likely, Watson didn't know in 1937 how the Nazis were using Dehomag or IBM machines. Though the Nazis had oppressed Jews and other non-Germans, few outside of Germany knew about Nazi plans for genocide, and even fewer knew about the inner workings put in place to carry out those plans. German intentions became clear to Americans in November 1938, when the rage of *Kristallnacht* swept across Germany. Nazi gangs, directed by Hitler, shattered the glass of every building owned by a Jew, set fires and looted Jewish homes and businesses, and beat

Jews in the street. American newspapers rang out with banner headlines, and American public sentiment turned sharply against Hitler.

At that point, Watson's stance showed him to be a Nazi appeaser. He again wrote carefully worded, spineless letters to the German leadership. The letters made note of public opinion in the United States following *Kristallnacht* and said that Germany would cripple trade between the two countries unless, as he euphemistically stated, "the Jewish situation today is not improved." Watson wanted the Germans to come to their senses, and he clung to the possibility that they would. His excessive optimism betrayed him.

As a businessman in this situation, Watson was a pragmatist. He tried to protect IBM's assets in Germany, and thus protect IBM's long-term viability in that country. IBM's late-1930s letters and memos concerning Dehomag are almost all about holding onto IBM's stake in Dehomag and preventing the Nazis from setting up a competitor. Those actions, as Watson saw it, were his duty to shareholders. The president of IBM treated the Nazis in 1937 and 1938 as a business problem.

All in all, Watson failed to do the *right* thing. Watson was a rare American who had an audience at the top levels of the Nazi party. His words of condemnation would have been heard in Berlin, and the world's media would have repeated them. He could have made a powerful statement—and perhaps a difference in history's outcome—by pulling IBM out of Germany and speaking out against Nazi oppression. Prewar corporate America would have said that Watson was taking a huge, shocking risk—but that's what heroes do.

Watson wasn't evil, and he wasn't a fool. He didn't work with the Nazis, but he failed to work against them. As he tried to rise to the stature of Roosevelt on the global stage, Watson abandoned one of the traits he admired in the President: courage.

In private, Watson treated the Nazi situation differently than in public.

In the spring of 1938—months before *Kristallnacht*—Watson received a letter from Armand May, an acquaintance who was chairman of the American Lecithin Corporation in Atlanta, Georgia. (Lecithin was an emulsifier used to thicken food and cosmetics.) May asked why Watson accepted the Nazi medal and what his feelings were about the Nazi persecution of the Jews. Reading their exchange is like listening to Watson defend his actions, and it reveals the little-known fact that Watson helped a number of Jews escape from Europe.

Watson responded first by saying the medal recognized his ICC role. "Every decoration which I have received has been given me in recognition of my efforts toward developing world peace through world trade," Watson wrote. "I might add that on my trip last year, in addition to Germany, I was decorated by Sweden, Yugoslavia, Belgium, and France." Watson added: "I am an internationalist. I cooperate with all forms of government, regardless of whether I can subscribe to all of their principles or not."

Watson went on: "As to my feeling in regard to the Jewish race, it is well known throughout the world that I have always put forth my best efforts to assist them in every way." He mentions "two young men I brought out of Germany," and who now work for IBM. He pointed out that the managers of IBM in Hungary, Czechoslovakia, Holland, Yugoslavia, and Romania were Jewish. "Two weeks ago, we got three Jews out of Austria, and by cable a day or two ago, I started a movement to get four others out, who are very badly in need of help." Watson asked May to aid him. Watson would pay to get one family of four out of Europe and to Atlanta, if May would employ the 50-year-old father.

Watson concluded his self-defense: "I do not feel that it is necessary for me to answer any question as to whether I am in sympathy with the movement against the Jews, because what I have been doing for the Jews is so well known, and, furthermore, no real American could subscribe to any principles of government that discriminate against race or religion."[17]

To an extent, Watson deluded himself. It's hard to call his aid to Jews "well known" when not a single article in any major publication mentioned it. Watson's antidiscrimination stridency didn't match his public stance at the time. It's commendable that Watson showed his values in small but meaningful actions. Still, Watson's true feelings make his guarded appeals to the Nazis seem more disappointing.

May did not respond to Watson and did not offer to help take care of the Jewish refugees. In November, after *Kristallnacht,* May wrote again to Watson, questioning the Nazi medal. "It seems to me, irrespective of dollars and cents, since I know you are not in sympathy with the persecution that is going on, that as an individual if you would return this decoration it could not help but be of great benefit to humanity at large," May wrote.

May concluded by saying he understood the reasoning, which Watson put forth in the April letter, for accepting the medal. "But I don't believe the International Chamber of Commerce can close its eyes to this terrible scourge . . . and nothing finer in your whole career could be done than to return this decoration. You would have the satisfaction of knowing that you did something for humanity."[18]

May had pushed Watson's most sensitive button. Watson shot back: "I cannot understand on what grounds you feel that you have a right to take the position of telling me what to do."

Watson parried May by castigating him for failing to help care for the Jewish refugees. Watson mentioned five Austrian Jews whom he had helped travel to Turkey and who were awaiting a chance to get to the United States. "There is also a long list of others that I have personally promised to take care of as soon as possible," Watson wrote.

"This Jewish refugee problem is more serious, I believe, than most people realize," Watson added. "I feel that it is the responsibility of all of us to try to do something to help the situation."[19]

It was like a man possessing a steam shovel choosing to move earth using tweezers. Armand May was right: Watson was in a position to do something for humanity. Instead, Watson eased his conscience by doing something for a few humans.

However, as the world learned more about Hitler's barbarism, Watson began to refill his drained bottle of courage. His previous appeals to the Nazis had been sent to Schacht, the economics minister. In early 1939, Watson addressed a letter directly to Hitler, noting "a loss of good will to your country," which was sure to damage trade between the nations. "I respectfully appeal to you to give consideration to applying the Golden Rule in dealing with these minorities."[20]

Though the language was meek, it was an important step: This man who had received high honors from the Nazis dared criticize the leader.

The letter never reached Hitler, and was returned to IBM unopened. Those who wish to see Watson as a Nazi collaborator point to the returned letter, and say that Watson purposely misaddressed it so he could claim he rebuked Hitler, yet avoid the consequences of actually doing so. But first of all, how could Watson or anyone misaddress a letter to Hitler? If an envelope only said, "Adolf Hitler, Germany," it's a good bet that any postmaster would know where to send it. So it's hard to know why the letter was returned. Even so, the Watson/Nazi conspiracy theorists must have missed a brief follow-up letter dated March 7, 1939, and signed by Watson's secretary, Byne Waters.

"Prior to leaving for a trip to South America, Mr. Watson forwarded you the enclosed letter which has been returned undelivered," the secretary wrote. "It is being enclosed with this letter, which explains why it has not reached you sooner." It was correctly addressed to Hitler and marked "Personal." It apparently arrived at its destination.

⁓

In the spring of 1940, Germany had taken Poland and the Netherlands and was marching on France. The Nazis herded Jews into ghettos and camps as Hitler talked of his Final Solution.

Dehomag seemed lost to IBM, and discussions at 590 Madison centered on whether to give up its majority interest to the Germans in order to preserve a healthy German entity, which IBM might reclaim when the Nazis were driven from power.[21] The Nazi medal started to look more like an anchor around Watson's neck. It would come up in conversation when Watson attended business functions. A crisis public relations firm wrote Watson to offer its services: "With the intensification of hostilities in Europe, the public reaction to your retention of that medal has grown," wrote M. E. Zerwick of Planned Publicity Service. "There is the possibility that it will affect the good will of the International Business Machines Corporation."[22] As Watson prepared for an IBM event at the World's Fair in New York, Jewish leaders cancelled plans to take part. J. X. Cohen, of the New York Board of Jewish Ministers, returned his invitation to Watson, saying he was "shocked and wounded" that Watson accepted a decoration from Hitler.[23]

In late May of 1940, Tom Watson Jr. enlisted in the Army National Guard. The fact that his son intended to fight against Hitler pushed Watson to act.

On June 6, 1940, Watson packaged up the medal and sent it back to Hitler. In the enclosed letter, Watson pointed out that Hitler lied to him about avoiding war and about developing trade with other nations. The five-sentence letter ended: "In view of the present policies of your Government, which are contrary to the causes for which I have been working and for which I received the decoration, I am returning it."

Watson released the letter to the press, and his words appeared in newspapers worldwide. Congratulations swamped Watson's office, coming in on business stationery, handwritten letters, postcards, and telegrams. Cohen, who had turned down the IBM Day invitation, sent a telegram: "Deep satisfaction in the action which you have seen fit to take." A telegram from a woman named Gertrude Powell read: "Marvelous heartiest congratulations returning trophy." Erwin Burris, manager of Grand Central Art Galleries in New York, sent a letter: "You seem always to be able to do the right thing at the right time. The men who were with me on the train this morning shared my admiration for your action."

Watson learned how much the act helped him regain faith inside IBM. Sam Hastings, who had been in Watson's executive suite since 1914, sounded relieved when he wrote: "I was thrilled and delighted to read in the *Chicago American* that a certain U.S. citizen had returned a Hitler peace medal. You do the right thing always at the right time, and your fellow citizens throughout this great country will applaud your action."[24]

The broad impact of Watson's entire Nazi adventure was brought into perfect focus by Ruth Chudnow, who had no connection to Watson other than operating an IBM machine in her workplace at a company in Milwaukee, Wisconsin. She wrote:

Dear Mr. Watson:
Ever since I first began to operate the various machines of the International Business Machines Corporation at my

place of employment, I've been wondering who was at the head of such a mighty organization.

Soon I learned that Mr. Thomas J. Watson was the president and he had all my respect and sincere appreciation and awe for having the superhuman courage, foresight, energy, and ambition to head a concern of such importance and worldwide scope. I know it just didn't happen by accident overnight. Mr. Watson, you must have worked harder than all those countless other millions who aren't in your place.

Then, Mr. Watson, you received a severe setback. I read that a certain Rabbi had refused your invitation to participate in a peace conference because you had accepted an award from the world's greatest menace to civilization, and in such acceptance you left one no alternative but to believe that you were in complete accordance with the principles and aims of Europe's Madman.

Mr. Watson, I don't think I ever was so shocked in all my life. I could hardly believe it. Everyday, at work, I was reminded of the fact by my close contact with your machines. To me, you were the spirit of America, one of the greatest workers, and stood for all that America stands for—freedom and peace and life and liberty. How could such an important and distinguished and prominent American as you ally yourself with the enemies of such doctrines and so openly?

I felt you mocked all Americans until, Mr. Watson, a few days ago, I read the startling and very welcome news, "Watson returns Nazi decoration to Hitler," and the reasons you returned it. I'm so happy and although I don't know you, Mr. Watson, you have restored my faith and once again reign as the Symbol of Greatness and Honor in our country."[25]

Watson kept the letter.

Germany heaped spite on Watson. Furious, Hitler declared that Watson would never again set foot on German-controlled soil. The Nazi leadership renounced IBM, and Dehomag officials exploded in anger at Watson. IBM Geneva sent reports back to New York headquarters about reaction to Watson's act. "All German officials are aware of the matter and associate it with our company in various countries," said one memo. Another said Dehomag "can be considered a company working within Germany which is hostile from the head."

Dehomag feared for its existence. "This stupid step of Mr. Watson's opens up a number of possibilities," said an internal Dehomag memo. "It is not improbable that such a step may harm the company and all of us very seriously sooner or later since it must be considered as an insult to the Fuhrer and thereby of the German people."

In that memo, Dehomag proffered theories about Watson's act. "It appears Mr. Watson is surrounding himself with a group of Jews who fled Europe," the memo said, adding that the Jews are "beginning to affect his mind and to impede his judgment." The memo added a note of concern: "This step is indicative of great excitement in America, and thereby the danger that America may enter the war is somewhat closer." In that case, Dehomag would welcome a separation from IBM New York. "I have the feeling that Mr. Watson is sawing the branch on which he and his IBM are sitting," the note concludes.

Debate and bitter arguments ricocheted between Dehomag in Berlin, IBM's Geneva office (which continued to monitor Dehomag), and IBM headquarters in New York. This continued through 1940, growing increasingly vicious through 1941. The debate ended on December 7, 1941, when the Japanese bombed Pearl Harbor, Germany declared war on the United States, and the United States declared war on Japan and Germany. In his own way, for his own reasons, Watson declared war on Hitler.

As a statesman, Watson had failed. His "World peace through world trade" campaign had all the impact of a fistful of beans hurled against a barn door. He had misjudged the power of commerce, misread the Nazis, and missed an opportunity to make a difference. They were the biggest mistakes of his life.

It's important to note that the impact wasn't obvious at the time. From the distance of history, Watson's entanglement with Nazi Germany seems like it must have been a defining, all-consuming event in his life. Yet standing in Watson's place and time, the Nazi medal, Dehomag, and the ICC look like a subplotline in a textured play. In the United States in the late 1930s and the beginning of the 1940s, while events concerning the Nazis unfolded, Watson otherwise stayed very busy trying to become the king of capitalism.

❧

(To the tune of "Yankee Doodle")

T-H-I-N-K spells THINK—
Our President Watson's motto.
It saves mistakes, lost time, and ink.
You'll then do what you ought to.

—*Songs of the IBM*

8

KING AND CASTLE

A N IMPRESSIVE LINE-UP OF 13 IBM EXECUTIVES ASSEM-
bled around a conference table in the boardroom at headquarters. Tom Watson Jr. sat
smooth-faced and young in one chair, there
because his father wanted him to get exposure to the company's inner workings. Others present included Charley
Kirk, Jim Birkenstock, and Al Williams—all men who
would become IBM's next generation of leadership, eventually taking over from Ogsbury, Nichol, Phillips, and the
others rooted in the C-T-R era. A light chatter perked
around the room as the executives exchanged greetings and
necessary office tidbits, the way people do before a meeting
begins. The affable Kirk probably made a wisecrack or two.

In whooshed Watson. The men started to get up from
their chairs.

"Don't bother to stand up," Watson said, apparently in
an impatient mood. "It takes up too much time and it
breaks your trend of thought. I don't like it."

Slam! In three sentences, Watson pinned those 13 executives and established total control over the room.

"Now, what's the news?" Watson said, briskly opening
this high-level meeting.

"We're aiming to win that speed contest," said one of
the men.

They were there to discuss, of all things, a typing competition. Didn't these guys know a world war was brewing?

"Aiming to? We're going to win it. When is it?" Watson said.

"The nineteenth—two weeks from now," came the reply. "We're planning to have a full force out there ahead of time to handle the publicity, both we and the home office here. Now, we've worked up some newspaper advertisements to follow it. We have two or three alternatives— Miss Hamma may win and set a new record. Miss Pajunas may win and set a new record. One may win and not set a new record—so we have to be quite varied here with the planning."

"If everything should go wrong—," Watson said. "If someone outside should win—?"

"Then we won't come back! We'll just keep traveling!" one executive said.

Everybody laughed.

The competition was the annual International Commercial Schools Typing Contest, an obscure event that IBM was about to overrun and inflate in a move as ill-proportioned as the New York Yankees showing up to compete in a Little League baseball game. IBM made typewriters—among the first electric typewriters—and Watson wanted to be able to advertise that his company's typewriters worked the fastest. To prove it, IBM needed to find a legitimate, third-party typing contest, dramatically play up the event in national ads, and make sure the winner typed on IBM typewriters.

IBM found the fastest typists in the world and hired them—just to competitively type. The company's hopes rested with Margaret Hamma and Stella Pajunas. It also hired a 1909 world-champion typist (a male) to coach Hamma and Pajunas. The coach drilled the women all day, every day, honing their skills so it would not be possible for them to lose.

"Have you talked to Miss Hamma?" Watson asked the group.

"She feels that she's all tuned up. Miss Hamma believes she is going to win. We're not so sure. We have another contestant (Pajunas) who's also good."

"Has she ever sat in a speed contest with Miss Hamma?" Watson said.

"Yes, they're training together."

They were training in a building on Fifth Avenue, blocks from IBM.

"Have they trained in front of a group?"

"No, it's been secret and all alone, so far, with the instructor."

Competitiveness sizzled through Watson, and it could excite every molecule in his body until he almost vibrated from it. The typing contest would give IBM an advertising edge—a legitimate reason to say it had the fastest typewriters. Beyond that, though, Watson wanted to *win*.

There was Watson—the famous businessman, the friend of presidents, the international lobbyist for peace through commerce—devoting a large chunk of his time, and the time of 13 well-paid and busy subordinates, to ensuring victory in the International Commercial Schools Typing Contest.

"Would it be much trouble to go down there?" Watson said excitedly. He wanted to rip up his schedule for the day so he could get closer to the action. "Let's go down."

"Do you think there will be a new record?" an executive said. "That's the ideal thing—if there can be a new record."

"We don't need to think," Watson said. "We can find out. These girls can write so many words per minute. I would like to go down and sit there while they do."[1]

In the end, Watson got his victory. Hamma won, banging out 149 words per minute. It was, indeed, a world record.

Five years later, Pajunas, typing for IBM, beat Hamma's

record, hitting 216 words per minute. As of this writing, Pajunas's record stands unbroken.

∽

Watson wasn't just the best business story at the end of the 1930s; he had become a great American success story that captured the popular imagination. He ran a company that beat the Depression, and the company was unlike any other, from its culture to its products to its grandiose image of itself.

"Probably no businessman in the country gets his name and picture in the newspapers more often than he does," wrote journalist Gerald Breckenridge in the *Saturday Evening Post*. "Watson makes hundreds of public appearances every year at banquets, university commencements, the opening of art exhibits, and similar occasions. He makes good copy, not alone with his cultural projects; with simple statements on matters of public interest, he carries ever onward the twin banners of peace and prosperity. And he makes all of his extracurricular interests profitable to his stockholders.

"Within his organization, his executives say that President Watson *is* the International Business Machines Corporation."[2]

Everything clicked. Watson felt like a king.

And what better place to celebrate the king of the world than a World's Fair? One just happened to be available.

At 3:12 P.M. on April 30, 1939, President Roosevelt balanced himself on handles hidden behind a podium on an outdoor stage in Flushing, New York, and officially dedicated the New York World's Fair with a speech about the value of peace and the promise of tomorrow's technology. Behind Roosevelt stood Boy Scouts in uniform and dignitaries in top hats. In front of him, an RCA television camera picked up Roosevelt's image and beamed it out as the nation's first commercial TV broadcast. When Roosevelt looked beyond the camera, he could see the fair's central

Watson *(standing, center)* at the Miller School of Commerce, near Watson's birthplace of East Campbell, New York. His classmates included Erf Gorton (top left), who Watson later helped support during the Depression. Watson never got a formal college education. *(IBM Archives.)*

Watson at age 21, and a few years later, in his early days as a National Cash Register employee. He was a disaster in his early business ventures, but The Cash, as the company was known, molded Watson into a successful salesman. *(IBM Archives.)*

Watson felt deeply attached to his mother, and cared for her long after his father died. Watson was the youngest of five children, and the only boy. This undated photograph is probably from around 1910. *(IBM Archives.)*

At NCR, Watson moved up to the top ranks by becoming a favorite of President John Patterson *(center, with moustache)*. Watson, a sales manager, sits to Patterson's right. Edward Deeds, Watson's chief rival, is on Patterson's left. *(IBM Archives.)*

Months before Patterson fired him, Watson helps run a session under a tent at NCR. Patterson *(standing)* tore pages off the easel, dropping them at Watson's feet. *(IBM Archives.)*

Rascally financier Charles Flint *(left)* created C-T-R in 1911, then hired Watson in 1914 to save it. Herman Hollerith *(right)* built the first tabulating machine. He sold his company to Flint but retained control over tabulating machine development. *(IBM Archives.)*

By 1919, Watson found a core of executives to help him run the Computer-Tabulating-Recording Company. *Left to right:* James Ogsbury, Joe Rogers, C-T-R Chairman George Fairchild, Watson, Sam Hastings. After Fairchild died, Watson became more of an autocrat. *(IBM Archives.)*

At the time Watson took over C-T-R, the company was a minor presence in the Endicott and Binghamton area. Shoe manufacturer Endicott-Johnson reigned as the region's business power, as depicted in a postcard circa 1910. *(Courtesy Beth and Eric Sullivan.)*

C-T-R's presence in Endicott consisted of a couple of low-slung buildings in an open field, shown in a 1912 postcard. *(Courtesy Beth and Eric Sullivan.)*

C-T-R's headquarters at 50 Broad Street, New York, lacked the refinement that Watson later demanded. Here he dictates to his secretary, Fred Nichol, circa 1916. Watson promoted Nichol to the top levels of IBM in later decades. *(IBM Archives.)*

Anne van Vechten prodded Watson to create a management path for women. *(IBM Archives.)*

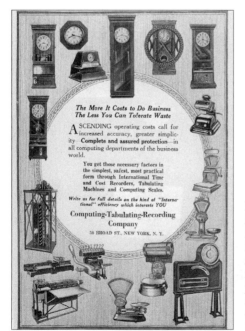

In 1920, C-T-R created this ad for its product line of computing machines, which included factory punch clocks at the top, meat scales, and tabulating machines. Eventually, Watson jettisoned the scales and time recording businesses to focus on tabulating machines. *(IBM Archives.)*

The Watson home in Short Hills, New Jersey, before it burned down in 1919. The reconstruction of the house distracted Watson for the next year. *(IBM Archives.)*

Watson traveled often to the heart of IBM: its manufacturing center in Endicott, New York. In the late 1920s, a crowd of IBM employees gathers outside the factories along North Street. Watson stands and speaks to the crowd on the far left, facing the sousaphone of the IBM Band. *(IBM Archives.)*

Watson opened a new IBM headquarters building in January 1938. The ornate offices at 590 Madison Avenue, New York, greeted visitors with Watson's hopeful prewar slogan: "World peace through world trade." *(IBM Archives.)*

By the 1930s, Watson was holding Hundred Percent Club conventions in tent cities erected on IBM property outside Endicott. While other companies suffered during the Depression, IBM kept growing—thanks in part to the information needs of President Roosevelt's New Deal. *(IBM Archives.)*

By the 1940s, tent city had grown to fantastic proportions. The tents are upper left. In the foreground are the Homestead and a big-top tent for speeches and entertainment, erected on the Homestead's parking lot. *(IBM Archives.)*

Among business structures, the Homestead in Endicott was unique—a combination lodge, retreat, gathering place, and satellite headquarters. Watson loved to settle into the living room of the old mansion and hold court with customers and employees until 2 A.M. *(IBM Archives.)*

IBM employees could belong to the Country Club for $1 per year, which gave them access to golf, swimming, tennis, and social events. *(IBM Archives.)*

When in Endicott, Watson enjoyed lecturing classrooms full of new employees, who went through intensive training in the ways of IBM. He stands at the podium in the IBM school, speaking to a noticeably all-female class. *(IBM Archives.)*

Watson's house on East 75th Street in New York, a few steps from Central Park. It was the most plain-faced house on the block. Watson's daughter-in-law, Olive, said the house had no warmth. After Watson died, his wife, Jeannette, quickly sold the house, saying she never liked it. *(IBM Archives.)*

Ben Wood showed Watson that computing machines could be used for far more than accounting. Here Wood works with his test scoring machines at Columbia University. *(IBM Archives.)*

Watson married Jeannette Kittredge in 1913 in Dayton, Ohio. This photo is from their honeymoon. Jeannette agreed to the marriage even though Watson still faced possible jail time for the antitrust conviction. About six months after the wedding, Patterson drove Watson out of NCR. *(IBM Archives.)*

Jeannette was a fixture at IBM throughout Watson's tenure, often traveling with him and appearing by his side at company functions. In 1950, Watson and Jeannette arrived by ship in New York after a trip through Europe. *(IBM Archives.)*

In the 1920s, Watson and Jeannette oversaw a growing young family. *Sitting, left to right:* Jane, Jeannette, Helen, and Dick. *Standing:* Watson *(left)* and Tom Watson Jr. *(IBM Archives.)*

The postwar Watson family. *Standing, left to right:* Nancy and Dick Watson, Olive and Tom Watson Jr., Helen Watson Buckner, and Walker Gentry Buckner. *Sitting:* Jeannette, Watson, and Jane, who would marry John Irwin in 1949. *(IBM Archives.)*

George F. Johnson, president of shoe company Endicott-Johnson, influenced Watson's management style and became a close friend. Johnson showed Watson that generosity and fairness to employees paid off. The lessons influenced Watson to build IBM's Country Club and to institute liberal policies, such as two-week paid vacations in an age when such benefits were rare. *(IBM Archives.)*

At NCR in the early 1900s, Charles Kettering taught Watson that invention and engineering could drive sales, leading to Watson's lavish spending on research and development. Kettering went on to lead R&D at General Motors. The two remained lifelong friends. *(IBM Archives.)*

Watson's early-1930s management team helped him continue to grow IBM during the Depression, and then launch the company into hypergrowth during World War II. In 1933, they posed for the groundbreaking for the engineering lab—a monument to defying the Depression. Some key members, *left to right:* Fred Nichol, holding both hands and his hat in front of him; inventor Clair Lake; Watson; executive Otto Braitmayer; sales executive Red LaMotte; director A. Ward Ford, with the pick. *(Courtesy Robert Schumann.)*

Watson looks to be making a sly remark to New York Metropolitan Opera diva Lily Pons while posing for this shot. Watson was particularly fond of Pons and hired her to sing at numerous IBM events. Charley Kirk *(far left)*, true to form, seems to join in on the joke. Next to Kirk is Fred Nichol. James Melton *(center)*, was another Metropolitan Opera star. *(IBM Archives.)*

Watson rarely took time for recreation and never mastered golf, but he insisted on hitting the first ball every spring at the IBM Country Club. Here he shows his terrible form in 1944. *(IBM Archives.)*

Few photos remain of Watson's fateful 1937 visit to Berlin for the International Chamber of Commerce congress. In this one, he stands on the upper platform, just below the ICC banner, as he presides over the final session of the congress. *(IBM Archives.)*

During the Nazi years, Watson and Willy Heidinger, the head of IBM's German subsidiary, Dehomag, became bitter adversaries. Heidinger always believed Watson stole Dehomag from him in the 1920s. The German tried to regain control as trade between the United States and Germany grew more difficult. Here Watson walks with Heidinger in Atlantic City, New Jersey, circa 1924. *(IBM Archives.)*

The Watson family sings at their home on East 75th Street in New York. By no means was such harmony a typical scene around the house. Watson was rarely home, but if he and Tom Watson Jr. were in the same room, they usually ignited each other's combustible tempers. *(IBM Archives.)*

Watson loved big events, and he put on one of his most lavish as the stock market crashed in 1929. This dinner honored A. Ward Ford at the Arlington Hotel in Binghamton. The tone of the event was an unintended precursor to a decade of IBM defying the Depression. *(IBM Archives.)*

In his quest for social status, Watson had a weakness for medals, no matter how obscure, from organizations and nations. Here he looks pleased to get the Haitian Order of Honor and Merit in the Rank of Grand Officer from the Haitian ambassador in New York. *(IBM Archives.)*

For the landmark 1939 World's Fair in New York, Watson spent extravagantly on an exhibit that he hoped would make IBM seem like a big, important company. IBM, though, still ranked as a pipsqueak compared with exhibitors such as General Motors and General Electric. *(IBM Archives.)*

Watson was determined to leave IBM to his two sons, Tom Watson Jr. *(left)* and Dick Watson. This photo was taken two months before Watson died. *(IBM Archives.)*

Grandchildren became one of Watson's greatest joys outside of IBM. Months before his death, he is surrounded by all 15 grandchildren, his wife, and his four children and their spouses. *(IBM Archives.)*

Watson dictates to a secretary in his office at 509 Madison Avenue at the height of his power. Unlike many chief executives, Watson never kept a clear or neat desk, instead piling up papers, magazines, binders, and mail. *(IBM Archives.)*

After the war, Watson pulled General Eisenhower into his orbit, and convinced Eisenhower to be president of Columbia University, where Watson served as a trustee. The two remained friends and mutual admirers, even after Eisenhower won the U.S. presidency. *(IBM Archives.)*

As he aged, Watson spent increasing time at the sprawling house in New Canaan, Connecticut. *(IBM Archives.)*

IBM's 701 was the first factory-built computer. At the dedication, Watson pushed some buttons for the cameras, though he had little knowledge of how to operate a computer. *(IBM Archives.)*

To show off IBM's push into electronics, Watson ordered the monstrous SSEC erected in the IBM headquarters lobby, which was open to the public and could be seen through large sidewalk-level windows. The three walls and three consoles make up one SSEC computer. *(IBM Archives.)*

By the mid-1950s, Tom Watson Jr. ran IBM with his hand-picked team, which included Al Williams *(left)* and Red LaMotte, flanking Watson Sr. *(IBM Archives.)*

When the 702 computer replaced the 701 in IBM's lobby, Tom Watson Jr.'s assumption of leadership took on a visible manifestation. Tom Jr. ushered in the bold colors and minimalism of modern design. *(IBM Archives.)*

Watson in full regalia. Late in life, he at times seemed a parody of himself, clinging to baubles, ceremonies, and praise that reminded him of the power and success he'd achieved. *(IBM Archives.)*

At an IBM event honoring Watson, Nichol, at the podium, rolls out a larger-than-life reproduction of the scribbles Watson made when first delivering what Watson called The Man Proposition. Watson was an autocrat, but he preached egalitarianism until the end. *(IBM Archives.)*

Most of the burdens of IBM lifted, Watson manages a warm smile and a soft look, with Jeannette at his side. *(IBM Archives.)*

mall, leading to a statue of George Washington and, just past it, the magnificent centerpiece of the fair: the Trylon and Perisphere. The soaring Trylon, a three-sided white obelisk, poked its nose toward the clouds. Huddled beneath it was the mammoth white Perisphere globe. The world's longest escalator carried mortals inside the structures.

No one ever saw anything like this fair. Corporate pavilions the size of city blocks, all designed in the art-deco modernist style, displayed eye-opening technological wonders—some real, some imagined. General Motors built an exhibit called "Futurama." Thousands of people constantly jammed the winding walkways in front of the GM building. Once inside, they rode an elevated conveyor, moving them over a simulated future landscape of superhighways and bucolic suburbs, making the riders feel as if they were flying across time. At the RCA pavilion, television cameras outside sent electronic pictures to closed-circuit TV screens inside, and visitors went home bearing cards that said, "I was televised." The "Electric Utilities" exhibit teased housewives by showing a dream kitchen of electric dishwashing machines, robotic food slicers, and mood lighting. Nothing escaped the future. In the Borden Company Building, visitors learned about the "Dairy World of Tomorrow." In every corner of the fair, visitors were bombarded by the message that the future was going to be a wonderful place.[3]

While technology inspired the public's dreams, a yearning for peace stirred its soul. Visitors to the World's Fair were invited to see peace among nations all around them. Gleaming pavilions from various countries stood side by side, all coalescing in harmony around the vast Lagoon of Nations. They worked as one, yet proudly displayed their cultural differences. As a stark reminder of the cost of war, the Czechoslovakian pavilion stood closed and shuttered. Unopened packing cases were piled inside. Hitler had overrun the country before it could set up for the fair.

A walk along the lagoon, ending in the main plaza, left fairgoers thinking and hoping that maybe the world could hold together long enough for the future to have a chance.

Expectations for the fair had run high. The project was a product of Fiorello LaGuardia's New York. The city's mayor and his driven Parks Commissioner Robert Moses seemed to be able to do anything. They had turned New York into the best, cleanest, most vibrant city in America. They'd built highways, parks, and the Triborough and Bronx-Whitestone bridges. Anyone who lived in or visited New York had faith that LaGuardia and his citizens could turn a smelly garbage dump in Queens into a living masterpiece.

Watson certainly believed. He signed up for the fair early. He offered his help. IBM donated money. Though a fraction of the size of GM or Ford, IBM planned to build an exhibit alongside those of the automakers. In return for his support, Watson got to hijack the World's Fair for a day, two years in a row.

He'd host a King Watson the First coronation in 1939, inviting what was essentially his court of executives. A year later, he'd do it bigger, for all his IBM subjects. At this point, he had yet to give back the Nazi medal and he still believed "World peace through world trade" might prevail. But those issues could be set aside for a while. Watson loved pomp and grand events. He had put on fabulous, extravagant banquets for A. Ward Ford, Otto Braitmayer, and others vital to IBM's early success. Now it was his turn, and this was going to be colossal.

⁓

May 4, 1939—four days after the World's Fair opened—happened to align with the 25th anniversary of Watson's first day at C-T-R. Watson coaxed the fair's governing body into anointing May 4 "IBM Day." The company ran a full-page advertisement in the *New York Times*: "Whereas the International Business Machines Corp. typifies in its worldwide organization the spirit of intellectual understanding," the ad began. After tossing in a few more haughty clauses, the ad proclaimed IBM Day.

IBM didn't build a pavilion of its own. A stand-alone structure would have cost millions of dollars, and IBM's total revenue the year before the fair was $34 million, with profits of $9 million. The company was hardly producing enough cash to afford something like "Futurama." So IBM bought space inside the Business Systems and Insurance building, a stark edifice dominated by a half-circle of massive square pillars. A little before 9 A.M., some of Watson's 4,000 invited guests gathered under a cement awning, just outside the building's main doors. The guests included IBM officers and major stockholders, presidents of some of IBM's biggest corporate customers, and officials of New York City and of the World's Fair.

The guests heard the clop of horses hooves on asphalt, low and in the distance. The multipart rhythm meant it was not one or two horses, but a number of them moving on the empty road approaching the building. As the sound grew louder, a small cavalry appeared. Seventeen horses bore 17 men dressed in glowing white outfits with dark jackets. White cowboy hats, white gloves, and white pennant flags flapping over the riders' heads created a spectacle. The last of the horses rounded the bend, immediately followed by a bulbous black automobile. The horses lined up to the side, as if in a military review, while the car pulled around in front of the crowd in the entranceway. The riders saluted as the car disgorged Watson, who looked nonchalant, as if he always arrived with such a flourish. The men in suits reached out to shake Watson's hand and utter a few words of praise for IBM Day, or for the bleached palace guards Watson had brought along.

The crowd moved inside to the IBM exhibit hall. In the center of a large open area, a glass bubble enshrined a tabulating machine. Around the floor stood accounting machines, sorters, card punchers, and other IBM products. On the walls hung paintings by artists from each of the 79 countries in which IBM did business. The art was a gimmick ordered up by Watson, who fancied himself a patron of artists and an educated art buyer. Critics said the most remarkable thing about the collection was its consistent inoffensiveness. Chairs had been set up in rows in the room, and the guests found seats. Watson and World's Fair President Grover Whalen sat in chairs on a small, low-rise stage. As the audience quieted, Whalen stood and spoke as he unrolled a proclamation. Amid flowery praise for Watson, Whalen dubbed this day IBM Day. Watson got to his feet, accepted the proclamation, rolled the document back up, and began speaking extemporaneously.

In a conversational cadence and tone, he talked about the idea of the fair—to share the best of each country. "What are you going to get out of it?" he said to the IBMers in the audience. "Educational value better than anything I ever came in contact with." He shook his fists and made his voice more blustery. "Tell your friends and family to come" he said. "Why do I emphasize this? Because my heart is so full of this world peace subject which is so important to all of us." He ran through a few platitudes about world peace, concluded his comments, then sat down to applause.

To the surprise of everyone, Watson stood back up.

He'd overlooked something, he said. "When I get off on world peace, I forget about everything else." He thanked all those who helped him over 25 years at IBM. But, he said, IBM's past accomplishments are not as important as what IBM will do over the next 25 to 75 years. "We do not consider the IBM as a business or a corporation, but as a great world institution."

Satisfied with that statement, he sat down and stayed sitting down.[4]

As the day went on, the guests were treated to intellectual lectures, special tours of some of the pavilions, and a concert by the Philadelphia Orchestra, led by well-known composer Eugene Ormandy. The orchestra played Bach's Prelude and Fugue in D-minor, followed by a piece by Sibelius—one of the few Finnish composers—and concluding with a piece Watson commissioned composer Vittorio Giannini to write: *The IBM Symphony.* It had three movements, and the third blended national anthems of various countries with IBM's most revered company song, "Ever Onward."

For Watson, who could tear up with sentiment about his company, the day was an emotional experience. That night would be even more so.

The 4,000 guests gathered for a banquet in the grand ballroom of New York's Waldorf-Astoria. Men in black tie and women in shimmering evening dresses crowded into rows and rows of tables, each table nearly buried under flowers, leaving barely enough room for plates and silverware. Banners draped from the balconies of the immense hall reminded everyone of Watson's favorite word: *Think!* All around hung flags of the nations where IBM did business. The IBM Glee Club sang IBM songs from the perch of one of the balconies. Fred Nichol acted as master of ceremonies, pouring out an endless stream of compliments to Watson in his clipped, nasally voice, and introducing a wearying number of speakers. After about two hours of tributes, the waiters rolled in a cake nearly the size of an automobile. In a grand finale, Nichol pulled a cord, a drapery on the wall fell away, and the crowd gazed at a commanding oil portrait of Watson—his 25th-anniversary gift from IBM. The guests rose to their feet in a sustained ovation.

Before beginning his speech of thanks, Watson had to visibly compose himself.[5]

⁓

The next IBM Day got messy. Watson had far more ambitious plans for the second IBM Day, on May 13, 1940. He

235

invited all of IBM's midlevel managers, salesmen, and factory workers, and their spouses, to the fair. Ten thousand decided to attend. IBM would pay for everything. It would bring them to New York on 12 chartered trains, put them up in Midtown hotels for three nights, buy all their meals, pay for their tickets to the fair, and stage all kinds of events for them. Watson took out full-page ads in New York newspapers to try to build IBM Day into a media event. The ads showed hurtling locomotives and blared: "They are all coming on 12 special trains!"

IBM Day cost $1 million dollars, more than 10 percent of the company's profits for the year. Watson wanted IBM to make an impact on the fair and everyone who attended. He felt IBM Day would help the company stand among the corporate giants.[6]

Anyway, that was the plan.

On Friday, May 12, IBM factories and offices everywhere in the United States fell silent, their doors closed. Employees, dragging suitcases and dressed in their best clothes, crowded into train depots in Endicott and Rochester, New York, and Washington, D.C. (The pockets of employees in field offices around the country took regular seats on scheduled trains.) It was a joyous party. Many of the employees had never been to New York. Friends boarded together, laughing and talking about what they were going to do in the city.

Everything was perfect until the trains reached Port Jervis, New York, a small community on the Delaware River. Two of the trains had passed through the town. The third stopped there. The fourth, going too fast, rounded a bend that had an obstructed view of the stopped train. The engineer pulled the brakes, but not in time. At 8:44 A.M., the train slammed into the rear of the stopped train, the engine partly mounting the last coach.

The impact sent shock waves through the cars of both trains, throwing passengers from their seats and knocking down anyone standing. Suitcases, purses, books, newspapers, food, and drinks flew through the air, hitting people and walls. Windows and overhead lights shattered, raining glass on everyone. "It was so sudden, I couldn't tell you anything about it," William Tilton, age 31, told a reporter.[7]

After screams and a few moments of disorientation, the passengers got their bearings and looked around. Most everyone was okay. They climbed out of the trains and sat on the tracks, waiting for help. About 400 suffered cuts and bruises. No one was killed, but 35 of the passengers were badly hurt.

Not long after the crash, the telephone rang in Watson's house at Four East 75th Street. He learned the basics of what happened, and that some employees were injured. IBM Day was supposed to start the next morning. Watson had to be a gracious host and deliver speeches. Yet, apparently, Watson didn't hesitate: He called his driver and ordered his car to pick him up right away. He called Nichol and told him to be ready to be picked up. He asked his youngest daughter, Jane, to come along, to have another Watson to comfort the hurt employees. Watson made one more call—to IBM's public relations people. He ordered them to keep the incident out of the newspapers, though that would prove to be impossible. Within 30 minutes, the car was speeding out of Manhattan carrying Watson, Jane, and Nichol.[8]

As cruel as Watson could be to his executives, he truly did think of IBM employees as his family. Just as he expected unerring loyalty and extraordinary deeds, he reciprocated, giving IBM his complete loyalty and nearly all of his energy. He learned from George F. Johnson that love and business could profitably go hand in hand, and Watson practiced it as much as any prominent businessman at the time.

The Port Jervis accident happened long before business schools developed theories of crisis management. No one taught CEOs to jump in immediately, take control, and appear to be doing the right thing no matter the difficulty or cost. It was also an era before widespread liability lawsuits. At the dawn of the twenty-first century, a CEO who put employees on a company-paid train for a company event would expect a blizzard of lawsuits after a crash like that. In 1940, it was unlikely that even one of IBM's injured employees considered such an action. Watson's reaction to the accident wasn't calculated or learned. Watson worked on gut instinct, and his gut told him that his family needed him, and he had to be there.

By the time Watson's car arrived in Port Jervis—the drive took at least two hours—the injured had been moved to two small Port Jervis hospitals. Watson and Jane made the rounds, talking to all of the IBM employees who were there. Watson and Nichol made furious phone calls back to New York, telling their staffs to get in touch with doctors and put them on trains to Port Jervis to help the overwhelmed town hospital. IBM arranged trains to get the employees stuck in Port Jervis to New York, and to have medical care ready at the New York hotels where the employees would stay. Watson ordered flowers delivered to every injured person.

Watson didn't get back home until late into the night before IBM Day. The next morning, tired and angry, he was a terror, ripping into IBM managers right and left. Apparently, his reserves of employee love had been temporarily emptied in Port Jervis.

The rest of IBM Day went much better. Employees saw the World's Fair and visited the IBM exhibit. As many as 30,000 people packed into a courtyard on the fair grounds to see an IBM-sponsored show featuring opera stars and, once again, The IBM Symphony. Watson spoke at 2:30 P.M.

The only other hitch came during a speech by Mayor LaGuardia. He talked of the miracle of IBM's machines, and the popular mayor added: "Mr. Watson's machines will do everything but kiss your wife for you, and, for all I know, they may even do that." To Watson, the remark was inappropriate, and he steamed about it all day.

In the world outside the fair, war news dominated. British Prime Minister Chamberlain resigned, and Winston Churchill took over. The Nazis moved on Belgium and Holland. The Allies bombed Germany's Krupp Works factories and industries in the Rhineland region. Real war had begun.

The New York World's Fair closed in September 1940. It had become a worldwide phenomenon—a much-needed celebration at the tail end of a painful economic depression and the start of war. For almost anyone who attended, the fair was a marker in their lives.

A young reporter from Europe was among those who never forgot the fair. Peter Drucker, who would become the twentieth century's foremost writer on management, had been assigned to write about IBM's exhibit and activities at the fair. When interviewing Watson, Drucker noted that other companies exhibiting at the fair dwarfed IBM in size. How could Watson justify IBM spending so much money to be there?

"He named a figure of how much it cost," Drucker said. "He said, 'If I spent that on newspaper and radio advertising, I might reach 1,000 people. Do you know how many people saw our pavilion? Two-and-a-half million!' "[9] Long before companies would regularly put their names on golf tournaments and cultural events, Watson had figured out the calculus of corporate sponsorship.

⤙⤚

Thomas Watson was volatile and self-aggrandizing. He could be domineering, unbending, demanding, and a maddening micromanager.

His company, however, projected an aura of classiness, excitement, and strength. IBM was a darling of American business. It had marshaled monopoly control over tabulating machines and automated accounting systems, which had become critical to the operation of companies in every major industry. The company's traits and successes attracted the most talented people coming out of universities. Those elite men and women in turn built better products, came up with better ideas, and managed their departments more effectively, making the company yet more successful, which attracted more talented recruits—over and over in a virtuous cycle. IBM was gaining the momentum of a great company.

How could a man burdened with so many glaring faults build a great company? How could he be a great *man*—or if not great, at least a man who legions of people inside and outside of IBM revered and loved?

Many of the reasons are packaged in the World's Fair episodes.

Watson inspired loyalty. He came through for people when they needed him, and did more than they expected. He took extraordinary action during the Dayton flood, and similarly acted when Birkenstock's son was killed, when Erf Gorton lost everything, and when the trains crashed in Port Jervis. He did smaller versions of such deeds often. The beneficiaries never forgot, and the effect of those acts rippled out. The stories got around. People understood that Watson was that kind of man.

As much as he promoted himself and thought the world revolved around him, Watson also generously gave credit to others. He would publicly name those who came up with a great idea. He lauded his engineers whenever possible in speeches to audiences outside IBM. He rarely failed to thank and praise the thousands of employees in "the IBM family." To honor those who meant the most to him, Watson would insist on banquets and splashy write-ups in IBM's internal newspaper, *Business Machines*.

Watson was blessed with charisma. On an intimate level, he drew people in with an intangible magnetism. People who met him often ended up telling him secrets as if he

240

was a best friend, or accepting his advice as if he was a father. On a public level, he could walk into a room and immediately become the center of attention, before uttering a word. Maybe it was his height, or his bearing, or his eyes. Different people were drawn to him for different reasons, but *something* made everyone want to look at him—and many to follow him. Watson always appeared to be commanding and important.

Except for factory workers, IBM almost exclusively hired young college graduates. The company paid them well, treated them well, and gave them big opportunities at a young age. Birkenstock, Ruth Leach, Charley Kirk, and many others landed in high-level positions when they were in their twenties or thirties. When a fresh graduate was hired, he or she was first sent to the IBM school in Endicott for as long as 12 weeks. They learned about products, sales techniques, and management methods. While the students were there, the school—and the Endicott complex all around it—sautéed the students in the cult of Watson. Lecturers taught IBM's history and Watson's management philosophy. Watson's simple sayings—"Self-supervision is the best supervision"—were posted around the classroom. His photograph hung in every IBM office. The students saw Watson speak at big events. At some point, Watson appeared in the classroom—the legend up close. The cult was so fervent, students either bought into it, or eventually resigned. Once the nonbelievers were sifted out, the company was left with an army instinctively devoted to Watson and IBM.

That common devotion and passion inside IBM, combined with the values and institutions, such as the Hundred Percent Club, which Watson set up early in the C-T-R years, bred IBM's potent culture. The culture machine drove IBM. It was powerful enough to smooth over the worst or most excessive Watson acts, which actually gave Watson the freedom to behave badly. He could promote an underqualified field manager to a headquarters position because he liked something the man said, or berate a talented executive for missing an obscure detail. Once the culture became strong enough, not even Watson could dent it.

Success didn't come from the culture alone, however. It needed a magic ingredient that would light up the culture and turn IBM into a business rocket—a pinch of something that would make all the difference in the world. That ingredient was Watson's daring. He made big decisions and took big risks, and then he stuck by them. In C-T-R's early days, those decisions included focusing on tabulating machines instead of time clocks or scales, and pouring relatively great amounts of capital into engineering. Watson gambled with the Depression and won. He spent a dangerous amount of money on the World's Fair, and made it pay off in publicity, high morale, and goodwill. Some of Watson's small decisions and actions were horrendously bad. But the big ones, he got right.

In 1940, Watson turned 66. Crinkles extended from the outer edges of his eyes. A canal-like furrow had formed above the bridge of his nose. His hair had thinned to wisps and turned nearly white. His hands, with their close-cropped, meticulously clean nails, were acquiring the visible veins and uneven coloring of an older person. Watson had slipped past the age when many people stop working. Yet still he had almost two decades left at IBM. Over those coming years, IBM's culture would have a number of chances to save itself from its creator. Watson would make countless more small and bad decisions—and, much later, one damaging decision. He also had two more big and right decisions to come.

᷒

Every king needs his Camelot. Watson had Endicott. At the start of the 1940s, the U.S. economy chugged to life, fueled by demand at home and orders from the Allies for war equipment and supplies. The Nazis stormed Paris and bombed London. The Japanese attacked Pearl Harbor and conquered the Philippines. Men went to war and women took traditional male jobs in factories. Ernest Hemingway wrote *For Whom the Bell Tolls,* Frank Sinatra launched his career by joining the Tommy Dorsey Band, and Orson Welles made *Citizen Kane.* The nation delighted in the feel of renewed energy.

IBM felt the surge, too. Business turned upward for manufacturers of war products, and that in turn gave a boost to companies that supplied raw materials and services. As one big company after another shook off the Depression, many ordered more punch card machines, or got their first ones. In the hard times, some had put off investing in IBM systems, and the upturn released pent-up demand. The U.S. military swelled, and it discovered the benefits of using IBM machines to help manage men and material. Demand began to outrun supply, until government orders mandated that all new or refurbished IBM machines must go to the military or to companies connected to the war effort.[10]

At the time, Watson's seat of power resided in New York at 590 Madison Avenue, a building IBM managers started calling "galactic headquarters" as an inside joke playing off Watson's ambitions. The spiritual, cultural, and manufacturing center of the company remained in Endicott. For that reason, Watson always loved going there. It was his respite and his second home. More than anything, it was where he could ride down the street and bathe in the success of his kingdom.

Endicott never qualified as a picturesque tourist stop. It lived and breathed manufacturing, dominated by the mighty old giant, Endicott-Johnson, and the rising star, IBM. Endicott-Johnson was still by far the bigger of the two companies. It finished and shipped thousands of shoes a day and, in the 1940s, won orders for hundreds of thousands of military boots. Its smokestacks, on a day when the wind blew just right, gave Endicott its acidic, leathery perfume. The company built most of the town's parks and many of its houses, which were sold to E-J factory workers at cost. The town center hadn't sprouted around a pretty, old village green or square—it sidled up to the E-J site, where the stores, restaurants, and bank branches could serve the streams of workers pouring out of the buildings at the end of each day.

When IBM started building factories in Endicott, it put them in a logical place: on a tract of land next to E-J. Nearby were the services of downtown and, on the back side of the property, the railroad yards. Tracks laid to serve E-J could also serve IBM. A main road—North Street—ran past the front of both companies.

As IBM grew, a constellation of shiny, clean IBM factories lined up on one side of North Street, one after another. On the other side of North Street stood the IBM schoolhouse and the engineering lab, both quaint little buildings that didn't much look like they belonged with the factories. The company attached loudspeakers to buildings and telephone poles so it could fill the sidewalks with music during lunch breaks. All of IBM's Endicott-based manufacturing and business functions clustered on that one property.

A different side of IBM could be found just outside of Endicott. IBM spread out on 870 acres of a wooded hillside that rose from the Susquehanna River and commanded a view looking south, over the region's rolling, wooded hills. IBM owned two main buildings on the property, the IBM Country Club and the Homestead. Watson considered the whole complex his little slice of heaven.

The IBM Country Club stood at the bottom of the hillside, next to the road that ran from Endicott to Johnson City. From some angles, the building looked like an old, white, wooden hotel. From other angles, it resembled a barn at a state fairground. Across from the building stretched a wide green field, where bands marched, batters hit baseballs, and kids ran and squealed. To one side of the Country Club, families splashed in the swimming pool. In the early 1930s, soon after the club opened, an employee complained that the pool was too small. Watson ordered it doubled in size. Around back of the club building, an 18-hole golf course crawled up the hill. Every spring, Watson insisted on hitting the course's first ball of the season. Amid a crowd of golfers ready to play, Watson would stroll up to the first tee wearing his suit and street shoes. Every year, he'd set up the ball, get in his stance, swing, and watch the ball dribble out about 50 yards. The golfers would try not to giggle. Watson would grin, incapable of being embarrassed, then make his way back inside.[11]

Watson visited often—usually at least twice a month. As Watson walked through the Country Club, he'd nod to the groups rolling balls down the eight bowling alleys, say hello to the children eating hot dogs in the restaurant, and check out a cavernous room that could be turned into a gymnasium, a banquet room, or a theater for a performance. Sometimes the entertainment was first class, such as National Basketball Association games and some of the most popular big bands. In that big room, Watson hosted the annual Watson Trophy Dinners. All year long, IBM employees would compete in organized sports ranging from baseball to shooting. Those who won were invited to the dinner. Watson each time personally handed out 300 to 400 trophies.

The Country Club became the employees' social hub. The IBMers could belong for $1 per year. Watson once estimated that it cost the company $100,000 per year to subsidize the club—money Watson considered well spent. The Country Club, Watson told employees, "is not something I have given you. It is something you have earned by being loyal and doing a fair day's work for a fair day's pay."[12] The club always hummed with activity. To Watson's pride, it was for its time an amazingly egalitarian place. As unions and management fought bitter battles at big companies, Watson kept IBM union-free by offering pay and benefits far better than the unions would demand. At the Country Club, managers didn't get preferred tee times over factory floor workers. The whole range of employees swam in the same pool and ate the same food. Rank, for the most part, melted away in the kind of workplace social structure Watson always imagined and sought to create.

Watson adored the Country Club—but not nearly as much as he loved the Homestead. The Homestead didn't look like anything that could be associated with corporate America, which is one reason it was so effective. It looked like a very large old country lodge, plopped in a clearing cut into a stand of soaring pine trees. Watson bought the building and its 430 acres in 1935, after he'd opened the Country Club below. He then added a wing that was divided into 40 narrow sleeping rooms, each fitted with cots and a bathroom shared with the room next door. The wing had the feel of a military bunkhouse, yet IBM managers and customers slept there without, apparently, too many complaints.

If a guest arrived at the Homestead on a typical weekday evening, he'd find the place alive and busy. As the guest walked in the Homestead's doors and to the left, he'd find an expansive and tasteful living room. It had a tile fireplace at one end, Persian carpets on the floor, bookshelves packed with books for guests to read, and a picture window that looked out over the valley. A cluster of IBM customers might be found talking around the fire. IBM invited customers to attend classes at the IBM school on the operation of IBM accounting systems, and while in town they stayed at the Homestead. Everyone staying there had to wear name badges, which quickly identified the customers.

Just off the living room, in an octagonal drawing room, Charley Kirk, who at this point ran IBM-Endicott, often played the baby grand piano, leading a group of visitors in popular songs, the sounds reverberating throughout the building. In a little alcove to the right of that room, a customer and an IBM salesman would wordlessly stare at a tabletop chess board, plotting their moves. At the other end of the floor, a visitor would come across a long, communal dining room, where yet more people gathered.

From the middle of the main floor rose a grand stairway that stopped at a landing and then split, curling back until it set the visitor on the second floor. Over the years, IBM installed a number of foreign government leaders, U.S. senators, and chief executives of major companies in a second-floor Homestead suite.

The biggest suite belonged to Watson, and there he felt comfortable and completely at home. Inside were two connected rooms about the same size. In one stood a bed; the other was used as a living area, furnished with chairs, tables, and a fireplace. A door off the second room led to a small patio on the roof. The bathroom, always spotless, had a tub and a white pedestal sink. Curiously, the bathroom floor was tiled in the colors and patterns of American Southwestern art.

When Watson walked into the Homestead, he would hang his hat, turn, and grin, as if the pressures and frustrations of the day had been inside that hat, and he'd brought it to the Homestead to be drained. He'd greet any customer in view, and make his way to the dining room, where he'd nod to the IBM managers but sit with customers. He'd probe the customers for complaints about IBM machines. He'd ask if the school was teaching them what they wanted to know—and if not, Watson would later bark at the education managers. When everyone tired of sitting in the dining room, Watson would meander into the living room.

Any IBMers or visitors who knew the routine scattered. Watson would spot a cluster of men (almost always men, though sometimes they were joined by the young women in Systems Service classes) and pull up a chair. He'd make a genial joke, they'd laugh, and a few stragglers would wander over to join them. When he had a nice little audience, Watson would steer the conversation to something he felt like talking about—peace, education, science, the economy, the role of business in world affairs. After a while, he'd take over, pontificating more than discussing. The people sitting there would at first seem interested, but then they'd realize Watson wasn't going to stop. They were trapped. They'd look for an opening for a graceful exit, but never find one. The clock would tick past 11 P.M. The piano playing and singing would have stopped. The chess players would have gone to bed. By midnight, Watson's audience would try to stifle yawns. On some nights, Watson would finally look at his pocket watch at 2 A.M. and announce, in an awe-shucks country manner, that he'd probably kept everyone up past their bedtimes. Watson would bound up the stairs while the rest of the guests dragged off to the bunk rooms in the wing.

The Homestead recharged Watson. He took energy from the interaction. He enjoyed the quiet escape from New York, and seeing the Country Club, factories, and schoolhouse so full of life gave him the deep satisfaction of a father watching his children succeed.

The Country Club and the Homestead endured until the 1990s, when IBM nearly collapsed. To save money and make Wall Street happy, the company contracted out the Country Club operations and ended the club's direct ties to IBM. IBM abandoned the Homestead and put it up for sale. Both buildings still stand. As of this writing, the Homestead remains vacant.

In the 1940s, Watson decided that the site of the Country Club and Homestead were the perfect place to bring the Hundred Percent Club convention—the biggest annual celebration of IBM's prosperity.[13]

As IBM grew, so did the number of salesmen meeting 100 percent of their quotas, qualifying for the Hundred Percent Club. When Watson started the club shortly after

taking over C-T-R, he promised to bring all qualifying salesmen together for several days of speeches, dinners, activities,
and entertainment—all at the company's expense. That
wasn't too difficult when the club had 20 members and they
could fit on one floor of an Atlantic City hotel. The numbers
swelled to a few hundred in the 1920s, and to more than 800
by the end of the 1930s. The conventions moved to New
York hotels such as the Waldorf-Astoria, but by 1940, the
Hundred Percenters were overwhelming those facilities.

Watson decided to bring them all to Endicott for the convention—and put them in tents. The whole idea seemed—
especially to Watson's staff—extremely far-fetched. They
would have to secure hundreds of sturdy army-style tents.
The Hundred Percenters would be there for most of a week.
The tents had to be comfortable and roomy, and they had to
hold up if a thunderstorm blew through. Watson wanted
running water and electricity at each tent, and he wanted
paved walkways so attendees wouldn't get their shoes
muddy. He ordered a stage built under a giant circus tent,
where the speeches and evening movies would take place.
Workers would have to transform a seven-acre clearing near
the Homestead into a functioning tent city.

Then IBM executives would have to convince salesmen
that they should work hard to meet quota so they could go
to Endicott and stay in a tent for a steamy week in June. The
whole concept seemed outrageous.

The preparations took more than two months, and Watson didn't make it any easier. At headquarters, he'd hold
lengthy meetings to go over every detail of the setup and
schedule, demanding perfection. He looked at and commented on the gifts that the Hundred Percenters would
receive and the badges they'd wear during the convention.
In those meetings, the executives discussed what films
would be shown, what songs would be sung, and the best
time of day to play golf. "It isn't good for men to play golf
right after lunch," Watson told Nichol in one meeting.[14]

The media and the public had already gotten hooked on the quirks of IBM and Watson, but Tent City, as it came to be called, put the fascination over the top. It could have been a disaster. It could have been dismissed by the press as an oddball stunt. Yet, against all odds, Tent City worked, the salesmen enjoyed it, and the media lapped it up. Just the sight of it was striking. Row upon row of white tents gleamed in the sunshine as men who were dressed in suits, ties, and crisp white shirts shuttled in and out of their temporary homes. Other tents housed services such as bootblacks, doctors, and portrait photography. Under another tent, the men ate their meals. Another one displayed the latest IBM products. A specially produced IBM newspaper landed at the doorway of each tent every morning, reporting on the previous day's happenings. Bands played. The air popped with the sound of attendees trying out the shooting range. Buses hauled groups out to watch the local minor league baseball team.

Nobody in the corporate world would do something so peculiar—right? It made a great story. *Life* magazine, the most popular magazine of the era, sent a team of photographers. The resulting story and several-page photo layout firmly stamped Watson's convention into the public consciousness.

Locally, residents of the region began to think of Watson in the same glowing way they thought of George F. Johnson. In the mid-1940s, the region decided to pay tribute to Watson. On an unusually cool summer evening, 5,000 cars streamed toward En-Joie Park, the golf course that Johnson built. By about 6:30 P.M., about 15,000 people—one in three area residents—filled the park and crowded in front of a 50-foot-high stage. Sixty-thousand watts of light bounced off the gowns of the singers who welcomed the throng. Opera stars Gladys Swarthout and James Melton performed classical and folk music. A slide show, projected onto a giant screen, depicted the history of IBM in Endicott. Local officials spoke about Watson's achievements as Watson listened from a dais. He sat next to Johnson, Jeannette Watson, and the two Watson sons, Tom Jr. and Arthur. The crowd cheered heartily as Watson finally walked to the podium. His voice breaking, he thanked everyone for "an overwhelming demonstration of friendship." As the local newspaper, the *Binghamton Press,* reported: "The IBM head insisted in his brief response . . . that every IBMer deserved a share in the celebration in his honor." The benevolent king won the hearts of his subjects.

❧

"Now, all you men outside engineering that are here, you understand that this is a secret meeting," Watson said. "You are not to talk about this."

Watson looked around until he got nods from all the customer service managers in the conference room on this April Fools' Day in 1941. The engineers in the room included "Army" Armstrong, now a manager of engineering, and Jimmie Johnston, who ran manufacturing engineering. They were about to experience an example of how Watson kept a longstanding monopoly from getting content and lazy.

The customer service men had written common customer complaints about IBM machines and parts on large sheets of paper and tacked them to a wall. IBM dominated its industry, controlling more than 90 percent of the electric accounting systems market. Some of IBM's practices, such as making punch cards that could run only in IBM machines, helped lock in customers. Its control of key patents helped lock out competitors. However, IBM succeeded to a great degree because it kept customers happy. Year after year, for more than two decades, the company ruled the industry because it never gave competitors an opening. To Watson, customer complaints were a weakness that a competitor might exploit. Watson would push his engineers relentlessly to make sure no such cracks appeared.

"This doesn't discourage me. This isn't serious," Watson said as he looked around at the pieces of paper from his seat. "In fact, it encourages me because I know when those things are remedied we'll save a lot of money and do a better job. That's why I like to have these meetings—to find out the worst." He admonished the engineers that they would have 90 days to fix each problem discussed in the meeting. "I don't care how many men you work, how many shifts you work," he said. "Ninety days is the limit."

Armstrong began by bringing up the topic of metal brushes, which hold cards in place inside a tabulating machine. They often wore down, then failed to hold the cards properly, causing jams. Armstrong said he was working on it.

"There is nothing to work on," Watson said crisply. "You know what change you have got to make in the material the brushes are made out of, and you've got the right material to make the brushes, and that's all there is to it."

"They are bound to wear, Mr. Watson," Armstrong said. "That's the difficulty we have."

"Then you get a different kind of metal, a different mixture, a different—whatever it is. There is nothing to work at. Is there anything else to it, Jimmie?" Watson asked, looking to Johnston.

"No," Johnston said, catering to the boss.

"Yes there is, and you know there is," Armstrong growled at Johnston.

"If your brush wears more than it should, then it isn't made of the right material," Watson said. "Isn't that the answer to that? Isn't that why it wears?"

Armstrong defended himself. "We've tried all kinds of material."

"You haven't tried the right one." Watson had no patience for excuses.

"We haven't been able to find the right one yet. We've had brush trouble for 30 years."

Those words had the effect of jabbing Watson with a hot poker—a customer complaint that hadn't been addressed in *30 years!*

"We could have corrected it 30 years ago if you had got the right kind of a chemist and analyzed this whole proposition and he told you what you needed," Watson said. "If I'm wrong, gentlemen, don't agree with me. By golly, I can't see any other answer to it.

"Try every material known to the world if necessary," Watson added cuttingly. "You could do all that in 30 years."

The meeting moved on to problems with eject drawers and feed knives—Watson wasn't quite sure what feed knives were. Armstrong mentioned contact rolls.

"What's wrong with this contact roll?" Watson asked.

"It's burning."

Watson exploded. An IBM part was catching *fire?*

"It took us two years and five months—is that the proper time to correct a thing like that?" Watson said angrily.

Of course not, the engineers agreed.

Circuit breakers, type bars that broke, springs, ribbons, hammers—they talked about every little part that gave users trouble. Watson ordered them fixed.

After nearly an hour, the engineers were limp with exhaustion. Watson wrapped up.

"Now, I'm going to leave this entirely to you to get this done," Watson said to a manager in the room. "I'm going to turn over the facilities of the Endicott plant to you. Don't sugarcoat. Give it to them in the raw."

"I won't, Mr. Watson," the manager said. "I won't pull any punches."

"When you get that done, then we'll all meet again and celebrate, boys," Watson said. "Just think how important it was to have this meeting. I guess it's the first one we've had, isn't it, of this type? It isn't going to be the last. I have learned so much. I've gotten so much encouragement. I'm very sincere when I tell you that all this encourages me. I know everything on there can be corrected in a very short time because we are going to work at it."

Watson talked about a couple of unrelated topics, then adjourned the meeting, once again reminding everyone that the conversation was to be kept confidential.[15]

Watson collected people. He loved genial contact, and he seemed to be on a mission to know as many members of the human race as possible, so he could walk down any street or wade into any crowd and find a friend. His taste in people was eclectic. He kept in touch with childhood friends. He liked to reminisce with one-time colleagues from NCR, especially the salesmen from the days when he sold cash registers in Western New York State. Watson would keep in touch with former servants, stable owners who sold him horses, and preachers from churches he'd attended.

He stretched in all directions to make new friends—some because he found them interesting; most because he found them useful. He cultivated acquaintances in the arts, politics, business, the media, European royalty, and old-money society. His basket of new friends ran into the hundreds. He actively engaged most of them, sending notes on special occasions, inviting them to lunches and events, and calling on them when he visited their cities and towns.

In business circles, Watson had reeled in impressive individuals, including General Motors President Alfred Sloan; Eddie Rickenbacher, World War I flying ace and chairman of Eastern Air Lines; oil magnate John D. Rockefeller; ketchup magnate Howard Heinz; and Kodak founder George Eastman, who once tried to convince Watson to help institute a calendar that would have 13 months of 28 days each.[16] In the arts, he was in touch with painter Anna "Grandma" Moses; opera singer Lily Pons; and writer Helen Keller.

Watson had a system: a friendship apparatus run by his five secretaries. They kept files on every acquaintance, each file jammed with every letter and telegram exchanged. The files contained notes showing dates and places of lunches and meetings. The secretaries kept a calendar of birthdays. They scanned newspapers for announcements, awards, obituaries—anything that might call for a letter, telegram, phone call, or gift. They wrote standard letters for Watson's signature. For contact that required more involvement from Watson, the secretaries coordinated with Watson using typed notes on small slips of lined paper, each detailing a certain situation. "Send a book to T. C. Campbell every few weeks from Mr. and Mrs. Watson," says one such note, referring to Thomas Campbell, who had run the IBM typewriter division. Watson, in turn, shot notes to the secretaries with orders to schedule a lunch or send flowers.

One key to the system was action. Nothing could languish. Birthday notes had to arrive on time. Special achievements had to be praised immediately.

Watson's generous pats on the back sometimes overflowed into flattering puffery. He pumped up the egos of his friends in high places, rarely failing to suggest that some monument be built to that person, or that the person should run for political office. For a man who could be so self-centered, Watson often sealed friendships by making the new friend feel bigger and better than Watson.

The friendship apparatus can be seen in two moments from two people at opposite ends of Watson's spectrum of acquaintances.

Harry Goffe and Watson had known each other growing up in Painted Post, New York. Every once in a while, Watson would invite an old friend to New York. On January 13, 1944, Watson wrote to Goffe, saying he wanted to "have you down for a luncheon and take enough time so that we can talk over many things in connection with our past relationship." Goffe was 84; Watson, 70.

The letter went off to Goffe. A carbon copy, with "luncheon" underlined in red, was shuffled to Watson's secretaries. Within three weeks, Goffe traveled to New York at IBM's expense, saw IBM's offices, and spent a long lunch with Watson. On February 6, Watson wrote again to Goffe, saying how much he had enjoyed the visit.

Two years later, Goffe died. That day, a three-by-five card landed on Watson's desk. It noted Goffe's death, said flowers were sent in the Watson name, and detailed when and where the funeral would take place.

Henry Luce founded *Time* magazine. The famous and fabulously successful Luce saw through Watson like an X-ray machine, and seemed amused by Watson's flattery. Watson wrote Luce congratulating him for an award from Italy. Luce wrote back: "I continue to be amazed at how you can keep track of the activities of your host of friends."

A few months later, Watson wrote Luce suggesting that *Time* build a Henry Luce Center, modeled on Rockefeller Center in New York. Luce wrote back: "I am overwhelmed by your suggestion that there should be a Henry Luce Center. And yet not so much by the suggestion in itself as by the fact that it is you who make it."

Not long after that, Luce received the Gold Brotherhood Award from the National Conference of Christians and Jews—a nice award, but not one that would garner much notice. Watson cabled Luce a congratulatory note. Luce, apparently feeling like Watson had a network of spies tracking his every accomplishment, wryly wrote back: "I feel that no award that comes my way is really official unless it has your endorsement."[17]

Though Watson expended a great deal of energy projecting himself outward, he was largely absent from his family's life. Watson traveled feverishly—spending time at the Homestead, scouting IBM sales offices all over the United States, and going on months-long multicity gallops through Europe. To the four children, Watson was usually more spirit than flesh. Yet he haunted their every hour, demanding they dress and behave in a manner fit for the offspring of IBM.

This man who led thousands had a difficult time connecting with his family, and yet Watson's relationship with his first-born son would become the most important of his life. The bond—and the friction—between Thomas Watson Sr. and Thomas Watson Jr. would eventually decide the fate of IBM.

(To the Tune of "Yip-I-Addy-I-Aye")

We're co-workers in IBM—all one big family.
We save materials, time, and men; increasing profits to all business when
Accurate figures and weights and time—our machines guarantee.
Oh joy! Oh what bliss! We are members of this IBM company.

—*Songs of the IBM*

9

WATSON THE SECOND

N TOM WATSON JR.'S 21ST BIRTHDAY, HIS FATHER sent him a Western Union telegram. More accurately, Watson sent a telegram to an idyllic image he had of his son.

"Your first twenty-one years have given me more happiness and satisfaction than I can express," Watson wrote. "What you have done for yourself in character building and developing a sound philosophy of life will prove to be your greatest asset in the future. I thank you sincerely for your comradeship, your honesty, your ability to resist temptation, your desire to do right, and the example you have set for your brother and sisters." Watson closed by saying that he was certain that as Tom gained success in business and civic affairs, it would "increase the happiness and usefulness of both of us."

The real Thomas Watson Jr. at 21 lacked almost everything the telegram described. Tom Jr. admitted it in his autobiography. He unabashedly described the young version of himself as an aimless playboy who had spent a lifetime getting into trouble. His grades were atrocious, and he'd bounced from one private school to another, trying to find somewhere he could succeed. He wrote that he suffered bouts of deep depression and probably was dyslexic—

neither correctly diagnosed by doctors at the time. Much of the time, Tom Jr. and Watson made each other miserable.

Yet Watson had that peculiar power to see certain things as he wanted to see them. In the telegram, as in everyday life, Watson saw Tom Jr. as he wished him to be. He never saw his son for whom he really was. Many parents probably do the same to some degree, but for Tom Jr., his father's illusory vision became both his savior and a source of ceaseless, lifelong torment.

⁓

On January 8, 1914, in Dayton, Ohio, Jeannette Watson gave birth to a boy. He was given the name Thomas John Watson Jr., after his father. She immediately started calling him Tommy.

The timing couldn't have been worse—or, perhaps, better. The senior Watson must have had trouble understanding his life at that moment. He had been convicted of criminal antitrust violations and sentenced to prison—a sentence suspended while on appeal, but still hanging over him like a piano attached to a fraying rope. A little more than a month before, he'd been forced out of NCR after 17 years with the company. Watson's one-time mentor and father figure, NCR boss Robert Patterson, had turned on him after the trial. Watson was unemployed and disoriented, and had to look for a job while still a convicted criminal. In a little more than a month, Watson would turn 40.

And there slept a baby in the house at First Street and Robert Boulevard in Dayton. The child was the delight and hope Watson desperately needed. Tommy was also the burden that made everything else more difficult for Watson to bear. Certainly, Watson didn't *always* want Tom Jr. to succeed him. In January of 1914, Watson wouldn't have wished that disaster on his son.

Within four months, Watson landed his position at C-T-R and moved the family to the New York area—at first to a hotel in Connecticut, soon after to the house in Short Hills, New Jersey. Within four years, Jeannette gave birth to three other children: first Jane, then Helen, and finally Arthur, whom everyone in the family called Dick or Dicky. Watson tunneled deeper into his never-ending, high-stress job of turning around a troubled company. Tom Jr. began his career as Watson's pride, joy, nemesis, and chief detonator.

In those early, Short Hills days, Watson worked long hours in New York, arriving home late by either commuter train or chauffeured car. He traveled often, to Endicott, New York; Washington, D.C.; and C-T-R sales offices around the country. Jeannette dealt with the precocious family with the help of one or more servants.

"Everything seems to be running along smoothly at Short Hills," one of the domestic staff wrote to Watson, who was staying at the Willard Hotel in Washington. "Tommy and Jane had breakfast this morning at the same time I had mine, and we had a fine little visit. When Jane informed Tommy that she finished her breakfast before he did, he said that it wasn't very nice to eat so fast."[1]

It could have been almost any household.

When Tommy was five, Watson took him on a trip to Dayton and led him through the scales factory that C-T-R owned. In New York, Watson would bring Tommy to the office and let him sit in during meetings, or just wander around. Watson liked showing off Tommy to his employees, and showing off his company to his young son. As Tom Jr. recalled later, the trips to the office were pretty boring—men talking intently about things a boy could never understand, cigar smell lingering on the furniture, nothing much to look at except for a few momentos and photographs on his father's desk. For entertainment, Tom would wander into a back room where tabulating machines operated, and play with the piles of confetti made when the keypunch machine punched out the tiny holes in each card.[2]

On the day before Tom Jr. was to turn seven, Watson sent a telegram to Jeannette saying he couldn't make it home just then. She was to postpone Tom's birthday party for a week. To a seven-year-old boy, postponing a birthday party is a disappointment of epic proportions.[3]

Tom Jr. began his rebellion early. By age 10, Tommy, by his own admission, was known around Short Hills as "Terrible Tommy Watson," and he strove to live up to the nickname. He had a habit of stealing petty items, like candy or a can of paint. He played pranks, like the time he put liquid from a skunk's smell glands into his school's ventilator system, forcing the principal to close the school.

The antics would ignite Watson's temper. Afraid that in a rage he might hurt his son, Watson held back and let Jeannette mete out punishment.[4] Watson Jr. maintained that his father never hit him, but Watson hurled stinging words at his son. The skunk gland incident sent Watson into a fury, as he chased after his son, roaring: "I don't have to discipline you! The *world* will discipline you, you little skunk!"[5]

Family dynamics began to solidify. Jane was seen as Watson's favorite—the firstborn girl who had her dad by the heartstrings, and knew it. As a child she started calling Watson "My Joy," instead of Father or Dad, and she called him that as long as she lived. The relationship between Jane and Watson bothered Tom Jr. all his life. Helen, caught in the middle—not the oldest, nor the oldest girl, nor the youngest—could be almost invisible to Watson. Dick was the baby, and Watson would always treat him as such. Watson paid less notice to Dick's achievements or troubles. Where Watson's explosive moments with Tom Jr. were more like arguments or confrontations, Watson could scold Dick and get no response. Where Tom sought Watson's attention through rebellion, Dick sought it by trying painfully hard to please his father—which he could never quite do.

Tom Jr. wrote in his autobiography that he never believed he was a favorite of his father's. He didn't see that the battles between them happened because Watson invested so much emotion and so much hope in his firstborn son. That investment gave great leverage to every disappointment or insurgency. It made small matters between them seem huge, and big matters seemed crushing.

The family had few rituals, thanks to Watson's travel and long hours. While the children were young, they spent many weekends at the farm that Watson bought near Old-wick, New Jersey, about 20 miles from Short Hills. Once every couple of years, Watson took the whole family along on one of his business excursions across Europe. They'd be gone for months, and the trips made for some of the happiest family moments. The children thought Watson was less stiff and more fun while traveling. Thanksgiving meant a lot to Watson. He wanted the family to be together for a groaning feast, but increasingly he invited important friends with last names such as Rockefeller and Roosevelt, which lent a greater formality to the holiday.

Otherwise, the family adhesive wore thin. Watson traveled, and sometimes took Jeannette with him. The domestic staff, including the cook and driver, looked after the children. When Watson was away, he'd often hand off Tommy to George Phillips, Watson's officious, curt secretary. It made sense. Phillips took care of so many important affairs for Watson—relationships with friends, stock purchases, dog breeding, boats, office gifts, travel arrangements, and the buying of appliances for the Short Hills house. Watson added Tom to the list. Phillips and Tom formed a bond, which began over guns. At age 12, Tom wrote to Phillips asking him to help him buy a second-hand gun. Tom had been invited to join a shooting club and wanted to be ready. Phillips bought the gun and had it in Tom's hands within five days. The two shared an interest in shooting and hunting for years.

Between Watson's absences and his skewed understanding of Tommy, Watson could not see the sadness in his boy.

265

Tom Jr. admitted hating the way he looked. He shot up and stood a head taller than other boys his age. When Tom was 13, Watson applied for a hunting license for him. He describes Tom Jr. as five feet seven inches tall, weighing 120 pounds. Tommy's eyes were a luminous blue, his hair chestnut brown. A week later, Watson reapplied for a hunting license because Tom lost the first one[6]—just the kind of irresponsible behavior that so irked Watson about his son.

Tom Jr. tried just about every sport offered at his schools. He couldn't hit a baseball. He tried playing goalie in hockey, but couldn't make the first team. He was too skinny and gangly to be much good in football, and not coordinated enough to take advantage of his height for basketball. Watson, who was just as poor an athlete, could sympathize with his son's frustrations.

In education, though, Tommy's failures prompted Watson to action. Watson got involved in his son's schooling early, and never eased up on his drive to make Tom Jr. a success.

The first of many disconcerting letters arrived in Short Hills from Neuman D. Waffl, the headmaster of Carteret Academy in Orange, New Jersey, about 12 miles from the Watson home. Tom Jr. was 13, and most of his peers had gone to prestigious boarding schools. Tom had to commute by train every day to Carteret, which he described as an "old, dingy place." Waffl reported on Tom's grades, telling Watson that his son was struggling.

"I agree with you that this report is not exactly satisfactory," Watson wrote back. "But I am very pleased that he had a passing mark in all subjects." He always clung to the positive in any report about Tom. Watson then went on to try to subtly give Waffl incentive to keep Tom from failing. "I want you to feel free to call on me for my cooperation and assistance not only in connection with my son, but in any way that you feel I can be of service to your school."[7]

Waffl would have known that Watson had a good deal of money that might be "of service" to the school.

The next summer, Watson sent Tom and Dick to a camp in Neymouth, Nova Scotia—an eternity away from Short Hills, though not so far from Camden, Maine, where the Watson family sometimes spent the summer months. Camp Aldercliff was an academic camp that was supposed to help Tom develop better study and work habits. Tom seemed to possess raw mental ability, but had no idea how to apply it.

The cheery letters from Watson to Tom at the camp ignored what was happening: Tom had fallen into one of his first severe depressions. "I was barely functioning, getting up for camp activities but going back to my bunk as often as possible," Watson Jr. wrote in his autobiography.[8] In those days, parents rarely took their children to psychiatrists. The Watsons seemingly never had a doctor evaluate young Tom's mental health. Late in his life, Tom Jr. frankly described his childhood dark episodes as depression.

After another dismal year at Carteret Academy, Watson pulled Tom out and placed him at the Morristown School in nearby Morristown, New Jersey. After one year there, Tom asked his father if he could transfer to the Hun School in Princeton, New Jersey. A lot of Hun graduates moved on to Princeton, and Tom decided that he, too, wanted to go to Princeton.

The Hun School cost $3,000 a year—more than 10 times the average household's annual income in the late 1920s. Every boy there was rich and had a car, and most liked to party. At first, Tom loved it. He finally fit in. He was rich. He owned a hot black-and-red Chrysler. He loved to party, and he was growing into his looks enough to start winning girls. Aca-demically, he was getting nowhere. His marks barely edged above passing.

At that point, exasperation would have set in for many parents. Watson never lost faith in his son, though an observer could easily have called it misplaced optimism. "I wish you were better in school, and I'm sure you do, too," Watson told Tom during one low moment. "But at some point, something will catch hold, and you are going to be a great man."

Tom remembered thinking that such an outcome was impossible.[9]

Depression set in again, darker than ever, in October 1931, when Tom was 17. Watson wrote to the Hun School that Tom had "a bad case of asthma," and would be late returning to school. On November 11, the school wrote to Watson, wondering why Tom had not yet returned. On January 9, 1932, with Tom still at home, Watson sent a telegram to the school: "Tom ill with grippe will return school soon as possible." In fact, depression was to blame for Tom's absence. The severity was crushing. Tom would lie in bed for days, eat little, and barely talk. Jeannette forced Tom to get up and go outside, thinking exercise would help. Of course, it didn't.

Lengthy depressions enveloped Tom a couple of times a year, usually for a stretch of weeks or months. If Watson knew what his son was going through, he didn't let on to the outside world. More likely, he didn't know. Medical doctors paraded through, checking out Tom, and declaring that they couldn't find anything wrong. Watson continued to send excuses to Hun. "Tom had a rather bad case of the flu which left him weak," Watson wrote after another long absence from Hun in 1933. Other times, Tom had embedded teeth that were to be pulled, or more bouts of asthma. One supposed illness after another kept him in bed.

Depression is a treatable medical problem, caused by an imbalance of chemicals in the brain. However, depressive episodes can be triggered by emotional pain or mental anguish. According to Tom Jr., a major source of anguish was his sense that the awesome weight of his father was constantly bearing down on him. That wasn't always justified, but it's not hard to understand how Tom Jr. came to feel that way.

From an early age, Tom could see that his father was important. Around the office, people snapped to attention when Watson gave an order. Other men hung Watson's picture in their offices, along with Watson's "THINK" signs. Most any boy believes his father is an icon. For Watson Jr., grown *men* thought Watson was an icon. Watson seemed so big, so powerful, that Tom felt microscopic in the presence of his father.

"I never remember, when I was growing up, Father coming right out and saying, 'I'd really like to have you follow me in this business,'" Watson Jr. wrote.[10] However, his father looked across time differently from ordinary men. Watson wasn't afraid to think ahead 30 years or a century. From the time he took charge of crumbling, inconsequential C-T-R, he believed he would turn it into a major company. Watson saved papers and meeting notes, and had photographers film his family in carefully choreographed situations, because he believed he'd become a part of history. He believed in such things when he had no reason to, just as he believed in his sickly, awkward, struggling son. When Watson looked at Tom, he looked across time, and he saw himself handing off his great company to his great son. Watson communicated those hopes to Tom, whether he ever spoke them or not. They were communicated by the trips to the office and factories, and in other actions such as outfitting his young boy in serious suits exactly like the ones Watson wore to work each day. Friends and family probably contributed, too, telling Tom that maybe he'd grow up to be like his father. When Tom was 12, Watson pulled him on stage at a convention, in front of hundreds of IBM employees.[11]

"I am happy to have one of my own sons here tonight," Watson proudly announced from the podium. "I am happy to have Tom here because his mind is centered on the IBM. His hope is that he can get a position with this company when he is old enough to work. There is nothing in the world that would please me so much, in connection with my son's future, as to have him join this business and stay with it." The message to Tom Jr. was anything but subtle.

Watson then guided his son to the podium. Tom Jr. gave what the IBM newspaper *Business Machines* called "a graceful little speech." Said Tom: "I haven't much to say. However, I do think it is wonderful to meet so many men who have been in the same business for 25 years or more." And that was it.

Tom Jr. recalled that he became convinced his father wanted him not only to join IBM, but to succeed Watson as its chief executive. The expectations that Tom Jr. perceived pressed in on him. As he saw it, his father wanted him to run IBM someday, his father was successful and imposing, and he—Tom Jr.—was an utter failure who would surely disappoint his father and ruin IBM. Tom Jr. could never escape that anxiety, and it must have driven him close to despair.

As an alternative to despair, Tom rebelled. Perhaps he could become such a failure that his father would give up on him. Tom became cynical about the grandeur of his father's plans, scoffing, for instance, when Watson changed the name from C-T-R to the expansive International Business Machines. He came to scorn the yes-men at IBM who bowed to every Watson dictate, and increasingly challenged his father, leading to heated arguments. Both father and son possessed combustible tempers, fueled by their intensifying love-hate relationship. The arguments could turn into wars. Tom Jr. wanted to be the one person Watson could not control.[12]

When Tom applied for college, his first choice was Princeton. True to form, Watson enthusiastically inserted himself into the process, going directly to meet with the dean of admissions. The dean gazed at Tom's grades, and said, "Mr. Watson, I am looking at your son's record and he is a predetermined failure."[13]

Watson would not believe it. He didn't tell Tom about the remark. Instead, Watson put Tom in his car and drove off to find a college that would accept his son. By coincidence, it turned out that Watson knew the president of Brown University from decades before, when Watson lived in Rochester. Watson got Tom into Brown, one of the best schools in the country.

~

"I hope our ways will cross before long. You always do me good," began the letter from Brown University President Clarence Barbour, who had been the minister in the church Watson had attended during his years in Rochester.

"I hear that Tom is back. His roommate, Dave Mc-Cahill, was in the office this morning and I had a good talk with him. As you know, they are living off campus with the idea that they can be more quiet in that way. The locality, 108 Waterman Street, is good.

"I hope with all my heart that Tom is going to buckle down to business and not to allow anything or anybody to be a thief of his time and strength. His business is the University work. Of course he must have a measure of recreation, but last year he let it run away with him too much. He has the makings of a big and useful man."[14] Rarely does any student have the university president watching every move, then writing reports to his father.

Watson could not leave Tom alone. He worried about his son constantly. He was determined to do everything possible to help Tom succeed and become the son Watson pictured in his mind.

Tom could not escape his father. He had entered college—a time when many sons and daughters break away from parents. However, Tom felt Watson's control everywhere, at times reading controlling behavior into his father's sincere kindnesses. Watson financed Tom's lifestyle of skiing, dating, and nightclub hopping with an allowance of $300 a month, which, during the Depression, was double what an average family brought home in a year. When Watson would visit, he'd hand Tom an extra $100 bill, and in addition Watson paid all of Tom's bills at the Brown campus store. Watson gave Tom a Cadillac convertible. He wrote Tom letters that were more like sermons about how to lead an upstanding life. He tracked Tom's erratic grades—in one semester, a C in economics, B in English, C in geology, D in history, and B in mechanical engineering. Watson checked with Barbour regularly to find out the latest about Tom's work and study habits.[15] Tom Jr. recalled that he sensed his father's presence. "I'd feel him like the keel of a boat, pulling me back upright again,"[16] he wrote in his autobiography.

Tom's mother, Jeannette, did not do these things. She was Tom's comfort zone—the person who would sympathize with him, not push him.

While at Brown, Tom found the one way he could break free of Watson's control: flying. Learning to pilot aircraft was perhaps the single most important action of Tom's life. While at Brown, he began taking lessons, and quickly found something—finally—that he could do well. His self-confidence soared, and in the air, he was liberated from his father. Watson feared airplanes and would never know or be able to influence that part of Tom's world. Piloting aircraft was never a part of Watson's vision for his son. Everything about flying felt wonderful to Tom, and he took to the air as often as possible.

Still, Tom ricocheted between resentment and love for his father. After Watson sent the telegram praising Tom Jr. on his 21st birthday, Tom wrote his father a letter:

"I shall treasure your telegram forever because I really have wanted to please you even if, at times, I didn't show it," Tom wrote. "If I have children of my own I shall do my best to follow in your footsteps as a father."

That last line is haunting. As a father many years later,

Tom Jr. would at times treat his children more harshly than anything he experienced growing up.

⚍

In 1937, Watson turned 63. He had done nothing to develop potential successors. The small group surrounding Watson at the top of IBM consisted almost entirely of men who had been at C-T-R in Watson's earliest days—Nichol, Phillips, Ogsbury, E. A. Ford, Red LaMotte, and so on. They were role players. None had the talent or savvy to run IBM. Peppered among the top ranks were a few ambitious but unproven young men. For the most part, Watson ran IBM so completely that no one talked much about succession. It must have seemed moot. The top executives assumed Watson would run IBM for the foreseeable future.

Watson didn't groom a successor because he had one in mind all along. It was, of course, his son.

On a spring day that year, as Tom Jr. approached graduation from Brown, Watson's phone rang and he heard words he'd long hoped to hear: "How do you go about getting a job at IBM?" Tom said, the question mildly spiced with sarcasm.

For the next four years, Tom grew increasingly unhappy. He went off to the IBM sales school in Endicott, and hated Endicott's dreariness. He hated the special treatment that followed him everywhere. His classmates in Endicott elected him class president. Customers agreed to see him because he was Watson's son, even if they had no intention of buying anything. The IBM newspaper *Business Machines* ran stories about his achievements. Tom hated the Watson cult—seeing his father's mottos pasted up everywhere, hearing songs about his father, the deference among IBMers to his father.

When Ruth Leach, who would become IBM's first woman vice president, first met Tom Jr., she noticed his sullen undercurrents. Tom had arrived in San Francisco with his father's entourage for the San Francisco Fair. Away from Watson's ears, she asked Tom why he carried his hat in his hand all day. "I didn't wear a hat to the train in New York," Tom told her. "When we arrived in Chicago, Mr. Nichol took me aside and bought me a homburg, probably at Dad's request, so I'd look like one of the executives— which I'm not!"[17]

Now he had a hat, but Nichol or Watson couldn't make him put it on his head.

Tom lived extremely well amid the gray of the Depression. In 1937, he filed an income tax return showing net income of $15,722.48—most of it from IBM holdings. In 1938, his net income rose to $17,686.58—an enormous sum at the time. Tom used $1,015 of it to buy a 1938 Ford Model 81-A Convertible Sedan, in maroon.

In early 1940, when Tom had just been assigned as a salesman to IBM's New York sales office, invisible hands moved large and profitable accounts into Tom Jr.'s jurisdiction. With virtually no effort, Tom became one of IBM's top salesmen and made the Hundred Percent Club by April. "I was young enough not to have had the presence to say, 'I won't have this,' " Watson told an interviewer years later.[18]

Watson sent his son a telegram on April 27 congratulating him on selling 169 percent of his quota:

"I am especially proud and happy because you have proven to yourself and others you are now a qualified IBM man not by birth or heritage but by your personal ability and knowledge of the business." Watson ended the telegram by saying he had a son "who has measured up to his father's hopes and ideals."[19] Watson never let go of the ruse. Nearly two decades later, he told a *Time* magazine reporter about Tom's first sales record, "He had to make his own records. Otherwise people might feel that he had some special help, which he did not have."[20]

Tom felt embarrassed and demeaned, he recalled decades later. Everyone at IBM knew how he became such a success.

If he had a chance at earning respect inside the company, that chance was melting away. Worse, his father's telegram seemed to mock him. His father had so little confidence in Tom that he rigged the system to Tom's advantage.

Tom wanted to get out. The war in Europe created an escape hatch. The military needed young men to fight. Tom went to his father and told him he was going to join the National Guard as a pilot. Tom then had one other important person to inform: a beautiful young model named Olive Cawley.

~

Olive met Tom on a blind date in 1939. A friend invited them both for a ski weekend in Vermont, and Olive and Tom hit it off from the moment they climbed into the friend's backseat for the seven-hour drive from New York. That drive marked the beginning of a new stage of Watson's family life—that time when children break away and a father changes into a grandfather.

Olive's high cheekbones, delicate features, and radiant smile made her a successful model, appearing on magazine covers and billboard advertisements. She grew up in an ordinary family, not of any high social rank, and had a gentle, measured nature, moving lightly through life, as if she didn't want to leave a wake. She could be just the right counterbalance to Tom's bullheadedness and volatility.

Watson welcomed Olive immediately, and she quickly came to adore him. Around Olive, Watson began to find a new part of himself. Watson's energy and his knack for generating excitement or drama made him seem magical to new members of the family, such as a daughter-in-law or, later, a young grandchild. Watson loved seeing the effect and played to it more often as he aged.

However, Olive perceived that Jeannette saw her as an interloper. Olive cut between Jeannette and her firstborn son, and Jeannette often acted coldly toward Olive.

Tom's National Guard air squadron was stationed at Fort McClellan near Anniston, Alabama. Olive still lived in New York. In November 1941, on a visit home, Tom asked Olive to marry him. She said yes, but he had to travel right back to Fort McClellan. Less than a month later, the Japanese bombed Pearl Harbor, generating fears that California might be next. Tom's squadron received orders to move to the West Coast.

"Tom contacted me and said, 'You have to come immediately,'" Olive Watson recalled. He wanted them to get married before the squadron moved. Olive fell into tears. She had no dress or hat. She wasn't ready. She rallied, though, and flew to Anniston. Watson wouldn't fly, so he and Jeannette took the train and arrived two days later. Tom asked his father to be his best man. In a rushed ceremony on the base, Olive, Tom, Jeannette, and Watson had no time for the usual wedding procession. All four walked down the aisle in a clump.

For the newlyweds' brief honeymoon, Tom had rented a brick guest house in Anniston. When Olive and Tom crossed the threshold, they found that Watson had filled the cottage with food and roses. "He went to a grocery store and put food in the house," Olive said. "I'm sure he had never been in a grocery store before."

During the first two months of marriage, Olive followed Tom to his new posting in San Bernardino, California, and then to Fort Leavenworth, Kansas. By the time they arrived in Leavenworth, Olive was pregnant. A few months after that, Tom became aide-de-camp to Major General Follett Bradley, who commanded the First Air Force. The position meant constant travel, and Tom eventually followed Bradley to Moscow, where Bradley had to untangle the problem of getting U.S.-made airplanes to Russia. Olive, getting larger with child, moved back to New York.

Watson dove into the role of caring for and spoiling Olive. In one conversation with him, Olive mentioned that she had never owned a fur coat. When Olive was eight months pregnant, she got an urgent-sounding call from Watson: Come to my office right away. "Of course, I thought I was in trouble," Olive recalled. She arrived, Watson put on his hat and took her by the arm to Bonwit Teller, one of New York's more expensive stores. He wouldn't tell her anything about what they were doing. Watson guided Olive into the store's elevator and asked the operator to stop at a specific floor. The elevator doors opened, and Watson and Olive stepped directly into the fur department.

"I let out a scream!" Olive said. "I was huge! And here was this old man and a pregnant girl. We laughed about what the sales girls must have been thinking."

Just before Christmas 1942, Tom Jr. made it to New York in time for the birth of their son. Tom stayed for the holidays, but had to join Bradley in Washington, D.C. About two months later, Olive sat at a restaurant with friends, having lunch. Watson appeared, pushing people aside as he carved through the room. He said simply, "Olive, come with me."

Watson had a car waiting. He told Olive that her baby was very sick. The child had already died, but Watson wouldn't tell her that yet. The nurse had been walking the baby in his carriage. She thought he was asleep. When she checked him, he had died, apparently from sudden infant death syndrome. Watson took Olive to her apartment, and told her there.

Watson called an IBM manager in Washington, and the man found Tom at an airfield outside of the city. The man told Tom that his baby was sick and he had to come home immediately. Tom borrowed a military plane and flew to New York. At the airport, he found Olive sitting on a wall, crying uncontrollably. Watson stood next to her, his face looking 10 years older. The instant Tom saw them, he knew the baby was dead.[21]

〜

"Dear Arthur," Watson wrote when his youngest child and only other son turned 21. Arthur had always been called Dick.

"Your fine character, good manners, sense of fairness, and desire to help others has endeared you to all who have had an opportunity of knowing you." Watson wrote in a letter. "I cannot think of anything that I would ask you to do differently if we were going through the same period again, because you have never made a major mistake, and have profited by your minor ones. I feel that I am indeed a very fortunate father."[22]

Tom Jr. didn't have a monopoly on his father's ability to distort reality. Dick held a chunk of the market, too. Dick was clownish, moody, and desperate for attention. He matched Tom for getting into trouble and stumbling through school. The brothers were separated only by their reasons for causing Watson grief. Tom did it to push back against his father's overweening presence. Dick did it because he couldn't get enough of his father's attention or approval. Whenever Watson challenged Tom, Tom's temper blew and the two fought like crazed animals. When Watson unleashed his anger on Dick, Dick would shut down and just take it, afraid that fighting back would cause him more disfavor. Dick had asthma, and when Watson scolded him, he'd sometimes get an attack and have trouble breathing.

Unlike Tom, who had inherited Watson's spiky personality, Dick could be lovable and funny—just the guy to pull Tom out of one of his black streaks, or make Jane and Helen laugh after one of Watson's tantrums. Jeannette clearly favored Dick among all four children. Dick told side-splitting jokes, could mimic any accent, and had a particular talent for yodeling, which he would do upon request.

As the years passed, Dick grew ever more unhappy. In Dick's early adult years, after Tom Jr. moved into position to take over IBM, Watson's attempts to carve out a large piece of IBM for Dick to run created a rift between Tom and Dick. Eventually, Dick's unhappiness and his sense of being a pawn in a continuous power struggle between his brother and his father were factors in his later tragic years.

Dick was born at Overlook Hospital in Summit, New Jersey, on April 23, 1919, a space of five years between him and Tom. Jane, the oldest of the two middle sisters, decided she was Dick's little guardian and caregiver, and she paid him special attention throughout his life. Dick held Tom in awe, and looked to Tom as a role model. From the time he was young, Dick seemed fragile, with his asthma and allergies. At one point the family bought an Allergirest Mattress for Dick, hoping it might help him sleep soundly.

Like Tom, Dick's grades in school fluctuated greatly. He barely passed most classes. When a teacher or subject engaged him, he'd get better-than-average marks. He loved to cause mischief or make wisecracks that would get his friends or classmates laughing, and Dick often found himself in trouble. When Dick, as a teenager, attended the Hotchkiss School in Lakeville, Connecticut, the headmaster, George van Santvoord, wrote to inform Watson that his son had just received his second vote of censure by the faculty. The censure was for a "noisy disturbance in the dormitory at 9 P.M.," the letter said. "In addition he has been warned three times by the Committee for violation of dormitory rules." One more censure, van Santvoord explained, meant Dick would be cut off from "most of the pleasures open to boys here."

Dick inherited the Watson height, growing tall quickly. His face had the oval, pointed look of Watson's features. In contrast to Tom's disheveled dress, Dick wore stylish clothes and always looked neat and crisp.

Dick got into Yale University, where he made the crew team and strained to achieve decent grades. Freshman year, he received a 65 in geology, 75 in history, 75 in English, 80 in French, and 85 in Spanish. The marks show one of Dick's strengths: He was extraordinary at picking up languages. He eventually learned French, Spanish, Italian, and German well enough to speak the languages in business settings.[23]

Watson never considered his daughters, Jane and Helen, for careers at IBM—which was ironic, because Watson proved to be one of the most progressive businessmen on the issue of women in management. Really, though, he only believed that careers were for the kind of women who would never marry, and that's not how he saw his daughters. Both daughters could have been smart, capable executives. Jane had inherited Watson's gift of magnetic charm. However, Watson skipped past them and planned for Dick's role in the company. Watson began thinking about how to give Dick a significant, high-profile role free from Tom's shadow.

Dick didn't fight the pull of IBM. On a summer break from Yale, Dick moved into the Homestead in Endicott and went to work at a milling machine in the factory—a stunning contrast to Tom's first IBM experiences in executive and sales offices. As usual, Dick told his father what he thought his father wanted to hear.

"Just a short letter to tell you how much my four days' work as an IBM employee has meant to me," Dick wrote to his father. Dick wrote about gaining prowess at milling machine No. 302, and then he poured sugar into his letter. "I could not be happier in any job any place. I have now found out why IBM is an institution which can never end. Words fail me, but I know you can understand my feelings, since all the spirit, friendliness, efficiency, etc., is entirely due to you."[24]

That same summer, Eleanor Irvine lived at the Homestead while working at the IBM school. She and Dick became friends, playing golf at the IBM Country Club and going out to movies in Endicott and Binghamton. Dick found Irvine to be a sympathetic listener, and he talked to her about his parents, Tom, IBM, and his relationship to all three. Irving's assessment after hearing all of that: "I'd say he was an unhappy member of the family," she said.[25]

The war lured Dick out of Yale. He left the school in 1941, after his third year and before completing requirements for a degree, and joined the U.S. Army. Dick eventually rose to major in the army's ordnance department—for which IBM manufactured millions of dollars' worth of ordnance during the course of the war. Dick never shook off his childlike longing for love from his family, even when stationed thousands of miles away in California or, later, the Phillipines. About two weeks before Christmas of 1945, Dick wrote to thank Jeannette for sending him a holiday package of food, including fruitcake, turkey paste, candy, crackers, and anchovies. "Thank you so much for your everlasting thoughtfulness," Dick wrote from his post in San Francisco. "I also got one from Jane and another containing a book. She is such a grand girl." He told his mother about fighting a case of strep throat, and about changing weather that was giving everyone colds. He closed by saying, "I don't know how mail is, but in case you don't hear from me until after the 25th, have a very Merry Christmas and don't think I am far away, for I shall be right in the dining room with you on Christmas Day and shall be thinking of you all and sending my best love."[26]

The army discharged Dick in 1947, and for the flash of a moment, the press made him the Watson in the headlines. Margaret Truman, unmarried daughter of President Harry Truman, chose Dick as her favorite escort. Jane Watson and Margaret Truman had become friends, and Jane introduced Margaret to Dick. Margaret Truman was more than just the president's daughter. The year of Dick's discharge—1947—Margaret made her concert debut as an opera singer, performing with the Detroit Symphony Orchestra for a nationwide radio broadcast. Two years later, she first performed at Carnegie Hall in New York and in 1950 sang on

Ed Sullivan's show *Toast of the Town*. In the second half of her life, Margaret Truman Daniel would author 20 books of fiction and nonfiction. So in those early years, when Dick and Margaret danced every dance at a function at New York's St. Regis Hotel, society pages took note.

By 1948, Watson figured out what he was going to do about his youngest son, the one who spoke four languages. Watson planned to carve off all of IBM's international operations and create an independently operating subsidiary of IBM called IBM World Trade. Dick would run it. This would be a way for Watson to bequeath his company—his life's masterpiece—to both sons without compromising Tom's position as Watson's successor. Watson didn't discuss the plan with anyone. He'd maneuver into it slowly as Dick learned—from Watson, of course—how to manage a global enterprise. The IBM insiders, including Tom, first realized what Watson was thinking in the summer of 1948, when Watson ordered Dick to join Watson on a breakneck trip through Europe—Watson's first since the war ended.

For Dick, though, the trip turned into a nightmare. He had met and fallen in love with Nancy Hemingway, from Syracuse, New York. They made plans to marry that June, and Watson's trip began immediately afterward. Watson lacked the empathy to understand that tagging along on IBM business would not be Dick's dream honeymoon. Dick could not tell his father that he wouldn't go. Watson could seem chilly toward Nancy; Olive Watson said there was an obvious and vast gap between the ways Watson treated his two daughters-in-law. Watson, Olive claimed, terrified Nancy.

Meanwhile, Watson believed he was doing his son a favor—taking him and his new wife to Europe, and launching Dick on his career as IBM's next-generation internationalist. All of the lines of misunderstanding were converging to create a miserable ordeal. Watson drove Dick hard, demanding that Dick stay at his father's side for every meeting and every function, and pulling Dick away at all other hours to instruct him on the IBM way to handle foreign businessmen and dignitaries. They arrived in a rebuilding Paris on July 22 and by the next day left for Zurich, Switzerland. Over the next two months, they cruised through Kanderseg, Switzerland; Milan, Venice, and Turin, Italy; then back north through Geneva, Paris, London, Amsterdam, Brussels and back to Paris before sailing for the United States on October 1, arriving in New York on October 6.

During the trip, resentment festered in Dick, who wanted to spend time—*alone*—with Nancy. Nancy apparently sank into gloom, wondering what kind of family she'd joined. Jeannette had also come on the trip, which meant Nancy was left in the care of her strong-headed mother-in-law.[27]

The tension increased until the relationship between Dick and Watson held the potential destructive energy of a locked catapult. Watson cut the launch cord in Stockholm, when the foursome of Dick, Nancy, Watson, and Jeannette prepared for a dinner with the king of Sweden. As they began to leave their hotel suite, Watson noticed that Nancy's dress was not floor length. Protocol dictated floor-length dresses for such occasions. Nancy said she hadn't brought one.

As Tom Jr. retold the story, Watson yelled at Nancy: "You are going to disgrace me and my family!" Nancy burst into tears. Something snapped in Dick. "Don't talk to Nancy that way," Dick yelled back. "She is my wife and has nothing to do with you." Shocked, Watson backed off and apologized.[28]

Nancy dined in her knee-length dress. The family was not disgraced. Watson probably poked at his meal feeling some hope that Dick might muster the strength and toughness to run a big chunk of IBM.

❧

The senior Watson had to get crushed by events of 1913 and 1914. The antitrust trial and conviction carved down his ego. He found himself at the mercy of societal forces greater than any single human being. He learned that a reputation can be both precious and fragile. In the aftermath of the conviction, Watson's painful split with NCR ignited his ambition to outdo John Patterson, his NCR mentor. If those events had not nearly destroyed Watson, he could never have built IBM.

The junior Watson didn't need to be destroyed. Tom needed to be discovered.

Around the time that Tom's wife, Olive, got pregnant for the first time, Tom was assigned to the First Air Force and handed a sales job. He was to sell pilots and air bases on a new invention called the Link trainer. In an uncanny coincidence, the Link trainer came right out of the same part of the world most responsible for spawning IBM: the Endicott–Johnson City–Binghamton area. Edwin Link had worked in his father's piano- and organ-building business in Binghamton. After getting his pilot's license, Link realized there had to be a safer, cheaper way to learn to fly airplanes than to do it in the air. Too many pilots crashed while learning, or crashed because they hadn't learned enough about flying in bad weather or flying when all they could see were the instruments on the cockpit panel. Link mounted a mock cockpit on a series of four bellows adapted from organ technology. The student pilot would sit in the cockpit and "fly" the airplane. Air pressure in the bellows responded to the pilot's movement of various controls. The response could mimic any type of aircraft—an aspect of the trainers adapted from player piano technology. The wrong movements at the wrong time would result in a simulated crash.

When the military needed to train large numbers of pilots in preparation for war, Link's trainers seemed like a solution. Tom gathered information on the trainers' effectiveness, and flew from base to base pitching the product. The use of Link trainers, he claimed, shot up by a factor of six.[29]

The success built up Tom's confidence—something he'd lacked in most aspects of his life. It also led to an offer to become aide-de-camp to Major General Follett Bradley, who commanded the First Air Force. After conferring with Olive, Tom took the position.

Bradley believed in Tom and complimented him in ways Watson only rarely did. Away from the influence of his father, Tom discovered who he was. In the first months under Bradley, Tom said, Bradley "showed me that I had an orderly mind and an unusual ability to focus on what was important and put it across to others." He didn't know that before.

Tom became indispensable to Bradley, and Bradley brought his young aide on the secret mission to Moscow to help deliver American-made fighter planes to the Russians. After Moscow, Bradley, with Tom in tow, took a position at the Pentagon, outside of Washington, D.C. At every stop, Tom absorbed the flow of experiences and lessons.

Some of those experiences stayed with Tom for life. One death-defying situation proved the value of grace under pressure.

Tom was flying from the United States to Russia as a copilot on a B-24 bomber, the biggest aircraft of the war. The flight path took Tom over Iran and Iraq, and into southern Russia. As the plane approached a Russian air base in Baku, the B-24 alarmed the Russian military. A squadron of Russian fighters intercepted the B-24. The fighters buzzed around Tom's plane, trying to get a good look, then dropped down as the plane began its descent. Tom, as part of his routine, left the cockpit and climbed down to the belly of the aircraft to check the nose wheel before landing.

Suddenly the Russian fighters again swooped in. Confused and anxious to land before something crazy happened, the pilot pushed the button to release the nose wheel, forgetting Tom was down there. The landing gear door swung open, and Tom tried to get out of the way. The mechanism trapped his left leg. "There I was spread-eagled over the open door with the oil fields of Baku below," Tom recalled.

Tom yelled, and a Russian navigator on board came down to see what was going on. The Russian didn't speak English, so by using sign language, Tom tried to get the Russian to hand him a nearby carbine. Tom planned to use the lightweight rifle to pry his leg loose. The Russian panicked. "The poor man thought I was going to shoot myself," Watson said. Finally, Bradley crawled down, assessed the problem, and called for a hacksaw. The Russian fighters were trying to force the plane to land. The pilot held them off for a crucial six minutes—long enough for Bradley to saw through a hinge and free Tom's leg seconds before the aircraft touched down. If the plane had landed while Tom was still stuck, the landing mechanism would have cut off his leg.[30]

Another lesson from Russia stuck in Tom's mind. As Tom recalled it, Bradley put him in charge of the aircraft crew in Russia, and gave Tom the space to manage the crew his way. Tom drove the men hard, insisted on perfection, and blistered them with petty criticism. Well into the mission, Watson told his men that they'd probably draw another assignment to Russia. The men told Tom they didn't want to work with him again—they'd take combat duty over another mission under him.

Tom realized that he was doing to them what his father had done to him. Tom had forced them to do everything his way, and failed to see the men as individuals who had different strengths, weaknesses, needs, and emotions. Tom set out to change, and to win the men's loyalty. He paid them compliments and let them perform tasks how they wanted, as long as the job got done. Weeks later, when Tom was indeed asked to lead another mission to Russia, he went to the men and asked if they'd join him. They all said yes.[31]

All of Tom's talent had hibernated inside him. Whether as a teenager, a college student, or a beginning IBMer, Tom showed no leadership ability, no particular brilliance. Educators who assessed hundreds of young men in their careers all looked at Tom and proclaimed him a human catastrophe. He couldn't control his temper. He had little self-confidence. He seemed on his way to an ignoble career of living off his trust fund and puttering around in airplanes for fun.

But the package was always there—it had to be. He couldn't have suddenly become smarter or developed charisma. Tom had lacked a purpose and a center around which to rally. He'd only known one center—his father—and one purpose—the expectation that he'd join IBM and someday run it. He fought against those every day of his life, yet found nothing to replace them. He was left adrift.

Bradley helped Tom find a center. At first it was Bradley and the air force, but gradually Tom's center became himself and his ambition. His natural, genetic charisma surfaced. Like his father, Tom was not a conventionally intelligent man, but he had dazzling clarity of thought. He could put his arms around complexity, see what was important, and throw out the rest. It was a strange kind of brilliance that allowed both the senior and junior Watson to make any mission, vision, or decision seem straightforward.

Bradley realized Tom's capabilities when Tom couldn't see them. After the war, Tom tried to decide what he was going to do. He loved flying and thrived away from his father, so Tom called the elder Watson and told him he didn't want to rejoin IBM. Instead, Tom said, he wanted to become an airline pilot or perhaps own a small aviation company.

Watson must have hung up from that call feeling defeated. He was aging. His dream of handing off his company to his sons seemed to be collapsing. But just as Watson knew the levers to pull to manipulate his executives, he knew how to manipulate his son. Confrontation would never work—it would drive Tom further away. Watson could never bring himself to plead, plus he knew Tom would never be happy if he joined IBM out of guilt. Watson decided to deromanticize Tom's thoughts about an aviation career. He sent Nichol, his most trusted man, on a full-throttle mission to make Tom squarely face his options. Nichol contacted the president of United Air Lines, Pat Patterson, who knew Watson from business settings. Tom soon got a letter from Patterson saying, "Come see me." Nichol dredged up a seaplane maker that Tom might want to buy. Nichol wouldn't let up. He kept pushing one possibility after another in front of Tom. "Nichol's eagerness to find me something outside IBM made me wonder what I was passing up, which was probably the effect Dad intended," Watson Jr. wrote.[32]

Confused, Tom felt that he needed to talk to Bradley. They hadn't seen each other in a year. Tom and Olive invited Bradley to dinner at their apartment in Washington, and Tom picked up his guest at the Pentagon. On the drive to the apartment, Bradley said: "Tom, what are you going to do when the war is over?"

Tom told Bradley: I'm going to be a pilot with United Air Lines.

"Really?" Bradley said. "But I always thought that you would go back and run the IBM company."

In that moment, Tom realized he'd always recoiled from IBM because he was afraid he would fail there. He never believed he could meet his father's expectations. Tom told Bradley he'd never considered running IBM.

"I just thought you would go back and run IBM," Bradley repeated.

There in the car with Bradley, the sun setting on a spring day, Tom asked the question that had gnawed at him all his life.

"General Bradley," he said, "do you think I could run IBM?"

Bradley spoke two words that completed Tom's transformation. He said: "Of course."[33]

~≈~

One of Watson's last two great decisions might, in fact, have been among his first decisions while at C-T-R. Then he made the decision to make Tom his successor over and over again for 30 years, rethinking and refining it as the situation changed. Still, the decision didn't coalesce into solid reality until the day after Tom's dinner with General Bradley.

The phone on Watson's desk rang. Tom's voice, traveling over the lines from Washington, crackled from the receiver.

"I'd like to come up on a workday and meet the people there," Tom said, "because, to be honest with you, I may be coming back to IBM if you will have me."

Working hard to make an understatement, Watson said: "I'd be delighted, son."[34]

During the war, IBM became a different kind of company. It more than doubled in size, transforming into a vast, sprawling, complicated enterprise—a challenge for Watson to effectively manage.

During the war, Tom became a different kind of man. Watson again got lucky. This new and improved Tom Watson Jr. showed up at exactly the right moment. Otherwise, Watson might have lost control of IBM, crippling what he'd built.

Watson was thrilled and relieved that Tom returned. Then he fought his son for power every moment of the next decade.

THE IBM SLOGAN

Who are we? Who are we?
The international family.
We are T. J. Watson men.
We represent the IBM.
Are we right? Well, I should smile!
We've been right for a very long while.

—Songs of the IBM

10

WATSON'S WAR

RDINARY PEOPLE IN ALL PARTS OF THE UNITED States were often fascinated by the famous president of IBM. When they thought about Watson, it was usually with respect and perhaps admiration. But overexposure wears thin in America, and in the 1940s Watson and his visibility agitated an increasing number of people.

"It is fascinating to note that your president, the poor, ridiculous old blatherskite, Thomas J. Watson, had the acumen to discover as early as 1940 that a Hitler decoration . . . was not generally considered an honor," wrote Fred C. Kelly of Peninsula, Ohio, in one of a number of letters he sent to IBM headquarters. "I am wondering, by the way, why in the interest of decent public relations you wiser heads in the corporation do not contrive to overcome his mania for personal publicity and keep his picture from appearing in the newspapers."[1]

Watson approached 70 years old. He had no intention of backing away from his celebrity. He had more to do. He had a plan as big as the moon. And he became very impatient with anything that got in the way.

❧

"Gentlemen, I am sorry to have to open my talk with you this morning on this line that I'm going to open it," Watson said, "but I only know one way to deal with men and that is right face to face and right to the front."

Watson was mad—the kind of anger that wells up from a deep emotional wound. He stood inside IBM's New York sales office, looking into the eyes of a small group of salesmen and sales managers based there. This was not at headquarters, in a boardroom full of high-level executives that Watson wantonly pushed around. The men staring back were the employees he loved most—salesmen. Watson always felt that he was one of them. But the group before him had betrayed him. Watson experienced few instances at IBM that made him so unhappy.

"I received this telegram at my home," Watson said. He pulled out the sheet of paper and began reading.

The writer referred to a problem that had already been agitating Watson. After the United States joined the war effort, the government's National Emergency Proclamation forced IBM to lease new or available machines only to *priorities*—the term used inside IBM for companies that contributed to war production. At the same time, IBM cut back on the manufacture of new machines so it could devote factory space and workers to building guns, ammunition, and other devices for the military. The combination meant that everything IBM made had a predetermined customer, either the military or a company designated as a priority. Many companies that wanted IBM products could not get them. Salesmen didn't really have anything to sell.

Watson built his career on selling. It was what he did best and enjoyed most. His fondest memories recalled harsh days in Upstate New York, learning how to close deals for NCR cash registers. The war took selling away from him. "He had no new markets to conquer," observed Ruth Leach, who worked by Watson's side during that time.

"Made tense by this change, he would blow his top at the slightest provocation."[2]

Watson felt all the worse because the situation also threatened his salesmen. They were left with little to do, and they had little control over their earnings. A small percentage of IBM salesmen were lucky enough to work a territory rich in priorities or military customers. They made a lot of money because a salesman earned commission on any sales made in his territory, regardless of how the sales happened. Most of the other salesmen saw their earnings plummet because they had no priorities or military customers.

Watson was determined to maintain his sales force. He didn't want to lay off any salesmen, nor lose them to more lucrative opportunities. All of that was weighing heavily on Watson when the telegram arrived.

" 'Ninety-nine percent of New York force are frozen tight because they cannot get priorities,' " Watson quoted from the telegram. " 'This places hardship on them as they never participated in boom commissions on defense orders. Having faith in your pledge of fair treatment . . . to immediately inaugurate more equitable sales plan to prevent serious financial dislocation. Regards, George Allman.' "

Watson paused and gazed around the room.

"Is there a George Allman in the sales organization here?" he asked, indignation dripping from every word. "I know there isn't. It is spelled A-l-l-m-a-n. He is kind of a tricky fellow."

The telegram was written by a handful of anonymous, disgruntled salesmen, signed with the made-up name derived from "all man."

"All I have to say is that I feel very sorry in my heart for the man who wrote it," Watson said to those gathered. "It is a little disappointment to feel that we have got a man in the IBM organization that hasn't got the guts to sign his name—who hasn't got the guts to come into the open when he has anything to say about anybody, anywhere, anytime. It is amazing to me."

A stillness saturated the room.

"Furthermore, it has been stated that practically every man in this organization was looking for another job," Watson said. "If that is true, gentlemen, I will go right out and start this morning to help you look for them. And every deserving, loyal man of good character will get a fine recommendation from me, personally."

Watson let out his injured feelings, laying on guilt like a disappointed father.

"Have you men forgotten what happened during the Depression?" he said. "Have you men forgotten that the IBM Company is the only company in the world who took care of all its salesmen and added more during the Depression? Has any man in this organization ever been left in want? Has any man in front of me this morning ever been turned down when he had sickness or trouble in his family and asked for aid?"

Watson veered into stories about those early lessons in hard work from his first mentor, NCR's John Range. No one interrupted. He circled back to the matter at hand.

"You understand, we are not anxious to lose any good salesman if he has the interest of this company at heart, if he is loyal," Watson said. "That is number one. If he is not loyal to the cause that we represent, we don't want him in this organization, regardless of how much business he can sell. Now, that goes, because the policies of IBM are built on character and loyalty—not to me, I am just an individual. Loyalty to this company, to the ten thousand stockholders who finance it. And any man who hasn't got IBM loyalty in his heart should go someplace else and get a job."

He had been talking for half an hour. The anger was beginning to drain from him. As usual, when Watson's anger ebbed, regret flowed into the evacuated spaces inside him.

"You gentlemen may think that I'm a little bit angry this morning," he said.

A little bit? He was obviously extremely angry.

"I am not, not the least bit." Watson said. "But my loyalty to this company, my interest in all of the loyal, deserving employees in this company, is just absorbing everything that is in me. When I get on that subject, I give out everything I've got, and if I speak loudly and I speak rapidly, that doesn't mean that there is any anger within me at all. Not at all. It just means that I am interested."

What a strange rationalization. The salesmen must have felt confused.

"Understand, gentlemen, I don't take exception to a group of salesmen sitting around and talking and finding fault with the sales manager and the president of the company and so forth, because that is a pastime occasionally for salesmen," Watson said. "If I were with you, I would be doing it, too. I've been a salesman. I know all about it.

"At the present time, it would be impossible for me to do anything for George Allman, as he signs himself, because at the moment I don't know who he is," Watson said. "If betting were a part of the policy of IBM, I would be willing to give good, long odds that I will know, and I am not going to ask about it either. I'm not going to make any inquiry. But that is going to come to me just as sure, I believe, as I am standing here in front of you, because so far in my career it has never failed.

"Personally, I would rather not know. Some of you men may know. If you do, try and help this fellow. He needs help. His mind isn't working right. If anybody knows, go to him and try and straighten him out. That I would like to have done."

For the next 10 minutes, Watson assured the salesmen that he would look out for them, and he promised they'd be in position to make more money than ever after the war.

The meeting concluded after a couple of the New York sales managers submissively pledged their loyalty to IBM.

Watson intensely disliked the role of running a company's operations during wartime. He hated the restrictions. He hated the de-emphasis on sales and marketing. He hated making weapons in the factories he so prized. The situation wore down Watson's already-thin line between rationality and anger.

But he loved his company, his salesmen, his factories, and his job as a leader. Instead of letting the war defeat him, Watson decided to use the war as a means to an end. He saw how he could use war contracts as a slingshot to double or triple the size of IBM in a phenomenally short time— an expansion almost entirely paid for by money from the government. He formulated an intricate, farsighted plan. It's difficult to tell how many pieces of the plan Watson intended, and how many could be attributed to the luck that followed Watson everywhere. Either way, he fit the pieces together in an impressive feat of management.

Carrying out the plan was the second of Watson's final two great decisions.

Of course, it wouldn't be much of a Watson plan if it didn't also risk the company's collapse.

⁓

In the spring of 1940, the Nazi army marched across Denmark and Norway, seizing both countries. In June, Germany took Paris, and Italy joined the war on Hitler's side. In early July, the German Luftwaffe started bombing ports along Britain's coast—an action that within a month would escalate into Germany's full-throttle bombing of London.

The United States, comforted by the ocean between it and Europe, remained uncertain about entering the war. President Roosevelt began finding ways to help the Allies without committing troops. The Lend-Lease Act allowed Great Britain to borrow U.S.-made ships, tanks, and weapons.

Congress approved the draft, and the U.S. military rapidly ballooned from 188,000 men at the end of 1939 to more than 1 million men one year later and five million the year after that. To support the Allies and U.S. military, the Roosevelt administration set in motion a massive conversion of U.S. industry, turning its production from cars, washing machines, and stockings to the products of war.

On July 8, 1940, newspapers around the country ran stories about a theatrical announcement made by Watson. The headline in the *Binghamton Press* read: "IBM Offers Its Full Facilities for the War Effort."

Most major American manufacturing companies—General Electric, General Motors, DuPont, Goodyear, RCA—had begun converting portions of their factories to war production, usually without much fanfare. Watson, though, never saw much sense in doing something quietly, especially when it was rich with public relations possibilities.

Watson called in the press and said that he would essentially allow the U.S. government to commandeer IBM. "The International Business Machines Corporation has offered its full manufacturing facilities to the Federal Government for National Defense purposes," Watson stated. IBM "is prepared to change over at short notice to the manufacture of essential war materials." To head off criticism that he only wanted to profit from the war, Watson said he'd freeze his salary at 1939 levels. He'd also limit profit margins to 1.5 percent, and all of the profits would be invested in a fund for widows and orphans of IBM employees killed or injured in the war. IBM would break even on all war production.

Many of the news stories that appeared lauded Watson for his patriotism and bold leadership in the fight against Nazi evil—and, generally, didn't note that he'd returned his Hitler medal only a month earlier.

As with most of Watson's words and actions, nothing was as simple as it seemed. No doubt Watson wanted to use

IBM to help defeat the Nazis. Hitler's actions in Europe convinced Watson, along with most of the rest of America, that Germany had to be stopped. Beyond that, Watson now had a personal grudge against the Führer: Hitler had lied to him when they met in 1937, made him look like a fool, and left Watson's "World peace through world trade" campaign in ruins. When Watson talked about the war, he often aimed his venom straight at the Nazi leadership.

"When you boil this war proposition down to the last analysis," Watson told students in the IBM school, "you are going to find that there are very, very few people who are responsible for it. I believe, gentlemen, sincerely, that God almighty is not going to allow a few people to ruin this wonderful world."

When Watson announced that he'd yield IBM to the government, he probably didn't yet envision the whole of his plan. That kind of foresight seems impossible. However, Watson knew he could use war production to achieve much more than just the defeat of the Nazis.

The pieces of the plan began with the idea that IBM could get bigger by winning large-scale war contracts. In 1940, U.S. companies assumed that they would continue to manufacture their usual products in existing factories, and in addition build war products in new factories or in renovated old ones. The companies would hire thousands of new workers for the new production lines, and military contracts would guarantee that the plants would stay busy and profitable.

Likewise, IBM didn't intend to alter its existing factories. It would build or buy new plants for war production. If IBM aggressively sought war contracts, it could boost its factory space and number of factory workers with little short-term risk.

Most of the other companies, though, correctly assumed that at some point the war would end and the contracts would dry up. The companies would then close factories and shrink back to a more sustainable size. Bethlehem Steel grew during the war from 100,000 workers to 300,000, but always planned to shrink back to 100,000. The much smaller Carnegie Illinois Steel planned to cut 18,000 jobs after the war.

Watson, though, decided he would not shrink IBM. First of all, Watson considered employees to be members of the IBM family. If IBM hired people to build weapons, he would not fire them. More important, if IBM could maintain its wartime size, it would come out of the war a much bigger company.

The risk of not shrinking ran as high as Watson's Depression-era gamble. If IBM remained twice its previous size, it would have to sell twice as many products as before the war. Otherwise, the cost of owning idle factories and paying idle workers would implode IBM.

Any responsible chief executive in 1940 knew that selling twice as much immediately after the war was an unattainable goal. Following previous wars, economic analysts noted, the U.S. economy plunged into a recession, followed sometime later by a boom. Economists believed the same would happen after this war. Even IBM's internal planning documents projected a postwar economic decline.

Watson knew that he would have to double the demand for new IBM products in an economy that everyone expected to plummet. Watson liked to mix business with a dash of insanity.

Piece by piece, Watson developed a strategy to pull this off. He'd start by drastically cutting production of commercial data processing machines. If the war escalated, Watson figured, demand would escalate for weapons, munitions, and other war products. IBM would build new factories for most war production, but as military work surpassed the capacity of new plants, IBM could fill up Endicott and other factories that had been building punch card machines. "It is clearly advantageous to avoid building any machine the construction of which can reasonably be postponed," said a 1942 planning document. "Both prudence and patriotism, therefore, dictate the IBM policy of reducing construction . . . to the lowest point at which the necessities of our customers can be satisfied."[3]

The symbiosis was elegant. Building more war products instead of peacetime machines was good for the country, and doing so allowed IBM to curtail supply and expand its manufacturing capability at the same time, which is as good as losing weight while shoveling down desserts.

There's more to the way the plan worked. Watson anticipated a problem that could have hobbled his maneuvers. The military and government used thousands of IBM machines during the war. The machines kept track of millions of soldiers, paychecks, supplies, airplanes, ships, guns, and more. It was IBM machines that also calculated gun trajectories and broke enemy codes.

IBM never sold its machines—it rented them. When a customer returned a machine in peacetime, IBM normally renovated it and put it back into circulation. This had to be done to keep revenues up. If a machine wasn't resurrected, the rental income from that machine would end, sucking money out of the company even as IBM made money by renting new machines. If IBM didn't keep machines in circulation, the company wouldn't be able to grow as fast.

During the war, IBM rented thousands of machines to the military and government. When the war ended, the military and government were going to return those thousands of machines all at once. IBM would have to recirculate them or watch the company's revenue dive. But the machines would cause a flash flood of IBM products on the market.

That meant Watson would have to double the demand for new IBM products *on top of* the demand that could be met by recirculating the returned machines—again, in an economy that everyone expected to plummet.

Watson cooked up a way to deal with those thousands of returned machines. IBM would use them to open new, lower-end markets. Watson told his engineers to figure out how to take a returned machine and lower its performance. In effect, the engineers were to break perfectly good machines. Then IBM could rent the hobbled machines to smaller companies, a market that IBM had never attacked, at lower prices. Salesmen could then convince big companies to rent new IBM machines, rather than those old clunkers that, apparently, got worn down during the war. IBM could also sell the geared-down machines to European companies, which would be hunting for bargains as they restarted in the Continent's ruined economy.

If it all worked, IBM would disperse the flood of returned machines while grabbing the lead in two largely untapped markets—smaller-size companies and Europe.

Watson's wartime plan affected IBM's workforce, too. Watson learned from George F. Johnson the value of good employee relations. High pay, progressive policies, and benefits such as the country club and paid vacations bred loyalty and kept unions completely out of IBM. During the war, IBM made instant loyalists out of almost every new hire. IBM hired salesmen who had been laid off from other companies and put them into factories. The company made trained factory workers out of artists, store clerks, and teachers. He hired hundreds of women who had never worked on a factory floor. He got the hiring process down to a science. He could send a few well-trained, experienced IBMers out to Poughkeepsie or some other location. They'd hire 2,000 people, drill them in IBM values and skills, and turn them into company loyalists in a few weeks.

One particular IBM policy won the hearts of the company's employees. In the early 1940s, hundreds of employees left to join the military. Watson announced that all departing IBM servicemen would continue to receive about

25 percent of their pay during their tours of duty, and Watson guaranteed they would get IBM jobs when they returned home. Though Watson's promise boosted employee loyalty, it also added yet another degree of difficulty to Watson's gamble. When the war ended, 4,000 employees would return from service. IBM's postwar business would have to become brisk enough to absorb them, on top of everything else.

Overall, Watson's plan laid down an all-or-nothing bet on the future—a more complicated bet than the chance he took during the Depression. A deep or lengthy postwar recession would weaken demand for IBM products and leave the company's new factories and workers idle. The financial burden could ruin IBM. Against the odds and conventional wisdom, Watson gambled that a vastly larger IBM could plow through a postwar economic lull and emerge as a powerful, unstoppable giant when the world's economies rebounded.

One remarkable note about that: Watson never anticipated the immediate postwar boom that was to come. He never realized that the economy would take care of IBM's surplusses.

The gamble scared Watson—perhaps for the first time, Watson wasn't completely confident that he'd succeed. Watson seemed always on edge during this period. In meetings, he demanded more from his executives than ever, and he exploded at them when they didn't deliver. He talked about "after the war" constantly—on long car rides to Endicott, at dinners, in the middle of discussions about art or advertising, and always with his executive team.

Watson never wavered, though. He had no backup plan.

No one questioned his decisions. Watson's top executives were weak yes-men. The board of directors voted yes on anything Watson wanted. Major stockholders weren't about to second-guess the man who'd made them rich. So IBM charged ahead, undaunted, into the war.

The plan emerged in parts. In 1940, Watson wasn't yet thinking that IBM would produce war products in existing factories. Watson loved his factories in Endicott. He had a hard time imagining them making weapons. Maybe Ford or General Motors could turn a car-making assembly line into a tank-making line, but to Watson converting a punch-card machine line to a gun line seemed sacriligous.

In the fall of 1940, Watson began keeping his pledge to turn over IBM to the government. Watson called his inner circle to his office, and they took their places around the dark wood table. Nichol, Charles Ogsbury, and Phillips came in, as did Charley Kirk, along with four other executives. The military had asked IBM to make 100 guns a month as its first job. The job would require about 300 workers, the executives estimated.

Watson set the rules immediately. "Mr. Watson said that we could not make a gun in our present factory," say notes from that meeting. He mentioned a seven-and-one-half-acre plot that IBM owned in Dayton. "We might build up a munitions plant out there, keeping all except the engineering end away from Endicott," say the notes, which paraphrase Watson.

The group discussed building a factory in Owego, New York, about 30 miles west of Endicott. An executive mentioned putting up a separate building in Endicott.

"Mr. Watson said . . . he did not want to get our business mixed up with the gun business." According to the notes, Watson stated that he considered organizing a small subsidiary company for the manufacture of guns.

Americans didn't yet anticipate the scale of the war. That came a year later, when the Japanese bombed Pearl Harbor. In late 1940, Watson thought military contracts could be contained in a tidy little subsidiary.

In a few months, Watson found his solution for the

gun-making factory. IBM bought 215 acres on the Hudson River in Poughkeepsie, New York. On it sat two small food processing buildings belonging to R.U. Delapenha and Company.[4] In March 1941, Watson created a subsidiary, the Munitions Manufacturing Company, to handle all military work. One year later, two 140,000-square-foot factories opened, and 250 employees began turning out guns and aircraft cannons.

The government paid IBM $3,065,000 to build the factories and guaranteed it would buy $13,490,000 worth of cannons.[5] Watson had begun using the war to cheaply and quickly expand. In 1940, IBM employed 12,656 people. By 1943, it would employ 21,251.

Of all the possible calendar appointment books that might befit a company president, Watson used a black hardcover book labeled, *The Real Estate Board of New York Inc. Diary & Manual*. It wasn't a leather-bound calendar sporting IBM's logo, nor a calendar bought from a store. Year after year, Watson's male secretaries jotted his schedule into a handout from the New York Real Estate Board, which stuffed the first third of the clunky calendars with directories of real estate agents and page after page of tiny print describing New York's zoning laws.

Watson's 1940 calendar tracked his movements through the year in the scratchy handwriting of various male secretaries. It tells a story about Watson's restless way of working—an important part of his success and a reason age and ill health eventually eroded his ability to manage.

On the first page of Watson's calendar, the entry says that he took a train from New York to Endicott on Friday, January 5, staying over the weekend and returning on Tuesday, January 9.

The next two months, Watson stayed in New York. On

Wednesday, March 6, he again took a train to Endicott, returning the next night.

Two days later, March 9, Watson boarded a train for a trip to visit IBM sales offices and customers in Mississippi, Louisiana, Arkansas, and Texas. Jeannette went with him. They returned two weeks later, on March 31—a Sunday.

Watson spent the following workweek anchored in New York. Here's what he did the week of April 1, 1940:

Monday.   Watson arrived at his office in IBM's headquarters building, 590 Madison Avenue, at 10 A.M. and immediately conferred with Nichol, Charles Ogsbury, and Phillips, then spent the day in a series of meetings in the building.

Tuesday.   Watson came in at 10:15 A.M., working straight through until 7 P.M., almost entirely in meetings.

Wednesday.   He arrived at 10:45 A.M. and disappeared from IBM for the day at 1:45 P.M. The entry doesn't say where he went.

Thursday.   He arrived at 11:40 A.M. Watson believed that thinking—simply thinking—was more important than getting to work on time. "Any time you people have the urge to think at home, just stay there until you get through thinking," he said in one meeting.[6] Because Watson arose early each morning, he must have stayed home thinking. Curiously, this is one place where Watson and the ongoing culture of IBM diverge. In the decades after Watson's death, IBM expected workers to start the day early and work long, late hours. But on this day in 1940, after arriving at 11:40, Watson left at 12:15 for a lunch meeting with the director of the Federal Reserve Bank of New York. He got back at 3:30, and left for the day at 6:40 P.M.

Friday. Watson came in at 10:15 A.M. and, the calendar says, "called for Mr. Nichol." Watson went to lunch at 2:20, ate quickly, and at 2:45 conferred in his office with Nichol, Ogsbury, Phillips, and Red LaMotte. It doesn't say when Watson left.

Watson sometimes worked on Saturdays, but not this one, April 6.

On Sunday, April 7, he boarded a train for Washington to attend an event at the Corcoran Art Museum, returning to New York on Monday morning. The next day, Watson left by train for Endicott—about a five-hour trip—and returned that night on a sleeper car.

The fidgety Watson made another run to Endicott two weeks later, hustling back to New York for the company's annual meeting on April 30.

During the first few days of May 1940, Watson hosted the thousands of IBM employees at IBM Day at the World's Fair. The calendar doesn't mention anything about Watson's drive to Port Jervis, New York, to visit the train wreck and comfort the injured.

May 20, Watson left for the West Coast, where he'd attend San Francisco's version of the World's Fair. That's where he met and hired Ruth Leach. Watson's family tagged along for the trip. The train took four days to cross the country.

In June, Watson had lunch with Lily Pons in Norwich, Connecticut. It was on a Sunday. She was the opera star whom Watson adored. There was no mention of whether Jeannette was also invited to lunch.

Watson's calendar left plenty of open time in June for the boss's favorite event: IBM's Hundred Percent Club convention. He'd spend a week in Endicott among IBM salesmen in Tent City. Few things in life made Watson happier. He left New York on Sunday, June 23, returning on Friday.

In the summer, the Watsons alternately stayed at their

place on East 75th Street in New York and an imposing house that Watson bought in New Canaan, Connecticut. Watson's secretary always wrote on the calendar which home they were in during a week.

Watson again took the four-day train ride to San Francisco, leaving July 26, returning to New York August 10.

August brought another trip to Endicott.

September 9 was a big day—his daughter Helen's wedding in New York. Later in September, Watson traveled by car to Endicott, which was unusual.

He made five trips to Endicott between October 8 and December 6.

The family celebrated Christmas in New York.

New Year's Eve found them in Montreal, Canada, where Watson closed out a year in which he turned 66, made a splash at the World's Fair, grabbed headlines with his pledge to put the company at the disposal of the government, and won the ire of all of Germany by returning the Führer's medal.

Events of 1940 kept Watson in the United States. In previous years he'd almost always traveled to Europe at least once, manically bouncing through five or six cities before heading home. In 1940, Watson had no chance to visit Berlin, Paris, London, Milan, or any of the other European cities he loved, because war was destroying them.

On the evening of February 23, 1942, nearly every person in the United States joined friends or family members around a radio. On the tables and floors of households across the country, listeners spread out world maps, opened atlases, or propped up globes. The newspapers had been instructing them to do just that in preparation for President Roosevelt's speech, which was about to travel over the airwaves from the White House.

The familiar voice flowed through millions of radio

speakers as the president took on the role of teacher, explaining the war that was engulfing the world.

"This war is a new kind of war," Roosevelt said. "It is different from all other wars of the past, not only in its methods and weapons, but also in its geography. It is warfare in terms of every continent, every island, every sea, every air lane in the world."

Sitting at his desk, gesturing toward a map no one in the audience could see, Roosevelt directed his listeners' eyes to each battle zone—Japan, China, Northern Africa, Russia, Europe, England, the Atlantic, the Pacific. He described the strategic importance of each place on the map. He frankly told the public what the United States had to do to win, not hesitating to deliver frightening news. Roosevelt asked for the unwavering support of the American people, and notably asked for sacrifices from American industry.

"With few exceptions," Roosevelt said into the bank of microphones on his desk in Washington, "labor, capital, and farming realize that this is no time either to make undue profits or to gain special advantages, one over the other. We are working longer hours. We are coming to realize that one extra plane or extra tank or extra gun or extra ship completed tomorrow may, in a few months, turn the tide on some distant battlefield. It may make the difference between life and death for some of our fighting men."

By the end of his speech, Roosevelt made certain everyone understood: U.S. industry was now a full participant in a world war to save democracy.

Manufacturing companies of all kinds were already pumping out war material alongside their other products. As the fighting escalated in 1942 and 1943, war production overran the manufacture of nearly everything else.

At IBM, too, the war effort was overtaking the company. Watson jettisoned the idea of a military subsidiary. Some IBM factories continued to build punch card machines, but the military or government absorbed 85 percent of them.

Plants in Rochester, New York, and Washington, D.C., switched to making ordnance. Even in Endicott, IBM retooled major sections of factories for war production. The company feverishly built and expanded factories in Pough-keepsie—mostly at government expense. Total factory space doubled from 1940 to 1942, and IBM had not stopped building.

When Watson and his executives first met to talk about that initial 100-gun order, few of the men around the table even knew what such a gun looked like, and none of them knew how to make one. By 1943, IBM was manufacturing three-inch tank guns, bomb fuses, bomb sights, fire control instruments for Navy guns, 20-millimeter cannon, and carbine rifles. IBM also made parts for other companies' war products.

The United States could not have successfully conducted the war without IBM's punch card machines. The machines transformed from civilian to military products, and IBM supplied 90 percent of the machines used by the military. They clanked away in the headquarters of the Army's Chief Signal Officer, generating codes that the enemy could not break. After Pearl Harbor, an IBM installation churned through the night to compute and sort the number of troops and amount of equipment immediately available to the U.S. military. As the Army grew to 5,400,000 men, it needed exponentially more IBM machines to keep track of the troops. In one example, tabulators and sorters mechanically matched a punch card noting a casualty with a corresponding punch card containing that individual's next of kin. The promptness and accuracy of casualty notifications greatly improved. The wife of a serviceman was far less likely to get a telegram saying her husband was dead, when in fact he was not.[7]

At IBM in early 1942, the company was well into leveraging war production to get big fast. For Watson, though, implementing this plan presented a personal problem. More of his time and energy were being sucked up by a part of the business he disliked.

For Watson, IBM *was* his life. Family, friends, leisure, civic duties, dogs, laughter—they were elements of Watson's IBM life. Watson woke up early and thought about IBM, and he stayed up late talking about IBM. He enjoyed his role as president of IBM more than anything else. When he attended a party, dinner, or opera, he did so as president of IBM. At family dinners, he was more IBM President than Father, always preparing two sons to join the business. In 1940, as Watson's calendar showed, Watson didn't take what most people would call a vacation all year, which was typical of most years. However, he took two lengthy trips to San Francisco, one with his family. Surely Watson didn't work during the four days and nights he spent on the train, cut off from communicating with the rest of the world. For long stretches, he would have read books, laughed with his children, chatted with fellow passengers, and watched the scenery—but he'd have done all of it as president of IBM, never as just a man named Tom Watson. That's the way he wanted to live. So if the job of running IBM turned sour, Watson's life turned dreadfully sour.

He didn't like running factories that made weapons. He didn't like operating on the basis of government contracts instead of the laws of the marketplace. He hated having nothing to sell. But he wanted to use the war to expand, and that necessarily meant that the war production side of IBM became an ever greater part of his job—for the duration of the war.

What could Watson do? Fred Nichol, who had been Watson's chief aide and IBM's de facto second in command, had suffered what Watson described as a "physical breakdown," and was taking a few months off to recuperate. Nichol, in his mid-50s, would not be able to handle additional assignments. Next in line were Phillips and Ogsbury, who acted more like superassistants than managers. Watson must have concluded that they weren't up to running IBM's war production; otherwise, he would have handed the job to one of them.

IBM employed a lot of smart and competent executives. But the top of IBM had been clogged by Watson and his pals for decades. If an ambitious and talented manager climbed IBM's ladder and then bumped against that immovable clump, that man would measure his options and, perhaps, leave. He'd join a company that would give him a shot at the top.

Watson had to reach down into the company to find some young fireball who had the raw talent, if not yet the experience, to run a huge piece of IBM. Watson found Charley Kirk. Kirk looked like a football lineman and had the supercharged exuberance of a nightclub comedian. He turned 38 in 1942, and stood just under five feet, eleven inches tall, with a solid, broad body that always looked slightly overweight. His chestnut hair receded from his forehead, his long nose jutted straight out, and his cleft chin scooped like a snowplow. He wore thin-wire glasses, talked and laughed loudly, and thundered through life like a rhinoceros through the underbrush. Kirk was blessed with a contagious sense of humor that made people want to be around him. He played piano whenever possible, and loved to gather a group to sing popular songs as he played and sang along. Kirk could work hard and long, and learn quickly. When evenings rolled around, he would revel in a rich dinner and drink a good deal of wine. That last trait Watson either didn't know about or chose to ignore.[8]

Kirk was born in the town of Bucyrus, Ohio, and he joined IBM in 1927 as a salesman in Cleveland. He climbed the sales organization, and 10 years later—1937—was named manager of the IBM sales office in St. Louis, Missouri.

After three years in St. Louis, Kirk jumped to the manufacturing side of IBM, taking a job as executive assistant in

Endicott. One year later, he was in charge of the Endicott factories. A year after that, 1942, Watson called Kirk, brought him to New York headquarters, gave him the title of executive vice president and a salary of $120,000 per year, put him on the board of directors, and assigned him to run all of IBM's war production.

Kirk did the job exceptionally well. He made the production line for the 20-millimeter guns so efficient, IBM delivered them at half the price quoted in the contract—and sent hundreds of thousands of dollars back to the government.[9] Within eight months, Kirk eliminated $2 million in costs.[10] All the while, Kirk's dynamism and humor kept morale high and helped him win friends and allies throughout IBM.

Within months, Watson got hooked on Kirk. Watson enjoyed the younger man, trusted him, and handed him increasing responsibility. Watson hastily turned Kirk into his number two, and Kirk swept away all of the unpleasant pieces of Watson's job, leaving Watson to plan and prepare IBM for the looming postwar challenge of doubling sales.

Underneath the ongoing work of running IBM, Kirk's arrival put some heat under a simmering power struggle for IBM's future. Though Kirk made Watson happy, the new star grated on Tom Watson Jr., who in 1943 still served in the military. Tom realized that if his father died, Kirk would take over IBM. Within two more years, Tom Jr. would come to detest Kirk.

As it turned out, Tom Jr. didn't have to worry about Kirk. Years later, one of the strangest twists in IBM history took care of that.

⤲

Twenty-one men crowded into a conference room at IBM headquarters on a Friday morning in June 1943. Some of the most important men in the company, particularly in engineering, sat around the table. They included Nichol and Phillips, superinventor James Bryce, and IBM's two best engineering managers, "Army" Armstrong and John McPherson.

"What we are after here is to get some action on new machines," Watson stated, opening the meeting. "We have got 103 projects in the laboratory but they are not coming out, and we're all hoping and praying that this war might end tomorrow morning. When it does end, if IBM has not got a lot of new things to present, why, [IBM is] just going to be behind the times, because everybody else will have them."

During the war, Watson drove the engineers like no other group inside IBM. The engineers held the ultimate key to the success of Watson's grand plan. Their inventions for the military could win IBM more war contracts—and of course, help the Allies win the war. Watson also expected the engineers to simultaneously invent for postwar commercial markets. If IBM was going to rake in more than twice the revenue it earned before the war, the sales force needed new products that would excite customers and drive up demand for information machines.

Over and over, Watson told IBM's engineers that the war changed the pace of everything. "It isn't safe to figure on a shorter period than five years from the time you conceive an idea until you have the product on the market," he told them. "This war has taught us that you don't have to figure in terms of years on a new device. It has brought it down to terms of months."[11] Executives of the early 2000s aren't the first to feel business cycles quickening.

Watson frequently gathered top engineers for planning and brainstorming meetings. He wanted to know what to expect out of the labs, and he would push and cajole the engineers, or belittle them if necessary—whatever it took to keep up the pressure for inventions.

"One of the typewriter companies has a complete new electrical typewriter made entirely of plastics, and I have talked my head off about plastics," Watson said. "Yes, we had a plastics man up at the laboratory. You remember how many times you told me that, Mr. Armstrong? Did you ever make anything out of plastics?"

"We have plenty of parts," Armstrong said defensively.

"What machines are made of plastics?" Watson said.

"None."

"Did you ever try to make a machine out of plastics?" Watson growled.

"Yes, sir," Armstrong answered.

Watson addressed the group.

"Do not mistake me, men. I'm just full of this because I can't keep it inside me, because it's our job to do this. I can't feel we're making progress when I find—I know who has a machine, and if they can have one machine made out of plastics, we ought to have 500, with our crowd. We've got the best crowd of engineers and inventors in the world for our type of business. There is nothing that can touch it."

Watson said he wanted to use this meeting to decide on the five most important research projects underway, and then commit to getting them made into finished products.

"What are your five jobs?" Watson said to McPherson.

McPherson first named the wheel printer—a politically smart choice, because it was a Watson favorite. The wheel printer would cut in half the time it took for an electronic accounting machine to print its results. Next, McPherson named a new device to more efficiently punch cards, a couple of machines for small-business customers, and a new kind of time recorder.

Watson disagreed. He said the machines for smaller companies should rank second on the list. McPherson immediately acquiesced, but asserted the importance of the punch device, which would cut the time needed to punch the correct holes into cards. "We can improve all existing jobs and say immediately that all jobs can go further, because we can punch more economically," McPherson said.

Watson menacingly turned on McPherson. "Now, let's all just stop right on that. We've known that right along, haven't we?" For years, the engineers had talked about improving the punch.

"It has been a question of deciding how we could make a better punch," said McPherson.

"No," sneered Watson, "it has been a question of deciding to start it."

The meeting rolled on, and the list changed as Watson or the engineers mentioned other projects. Watson seemed unable to pull out of a sour mood, but that changed when an engineer mentioned the Radiotype.

In the early 1930s, Watson's acquaintances at Columbia University told him about Walter Lemmon and his little company, Radio Industries Corporation. Lemmon was researching ways to connect two electric typewriters by shortwave radio, so a message typed on one would get typed automatically on the other typewriter miles away.

Watson already was thinking about ways to send information over long distances. IBM engineers had been working on a project that would use telephone lines to transmit the sequence of holes on a punch card to an automatic punch device in another location. Lemmon's work caught Watson's attention. Watson called Radio Industries' lab in New York, and asked Lemmon for a demonstration. After seeing the prototype, Watson convinced Lemmon and his associates to dissolve their company and join IBM, promising that IBM would fund all the research necessary to create a marketable product.[12]

In 1941, Lemmon presented a working model. Bolted onto a desk were an electric typewriter wired to a shortwave radio and a metal box that housed a unit that could punch holes onto a tape. The unit worked something like a ticker tape machine, but it perforated a paper tape instead of printing on it. When a Radiotype operator typed a message, each keystroke sent pulses to the tape-punching unit, which translated the pulses into holes on the tape. The tape was then fed into a shortwave radio, which transmitted the sequence of holes much as it could transmit Morse code. On the other end, it worked backward—the radio punched a tape, and the tape was fed into a reader that told the electric typewriter which keys to activate.

The Radiotype was hard to use, easy to jam, and made lots of mistakes, but nothing like it existed. The army installed Radiotypes in record-keeping offices around the world, allowing the military to quickly send routine information to remote areas. A lieutenant colonel called the Radiotype "one of the most impressive developments" of all the information products created for the war.[13]

Watson felt that he discovered Lemmon and brought him into IBM, so Watson rarely missed a chance to brag about the Radiotype. In the engineering meeting on that June day, Watson predicted that the Radiotype would someday eclipse IBM's mainstay accounting machines. Nichol primed the boss by saying that the Radiotype increased the speed of communications "300 percent over anything else ever known in warfare."

"Stop for a moment," Watson said, "and imagine somebody else coming along with something that will increase the speed of what [information] machines do by 300 percent. You fellows would all be in my office with tears in your eyes. That is something. Now, we just take that in our stride. We've got to get excited about that one."

Watson continued: "I dare not start on what I see as possibilities for the future. My horizon for that machine goes so far out, I don't dare to stop to think about it."[14]

Although the military loved the Radiotype, IBM never made it work for the commercial market. Like a lot of CEOs, Watson had some product visions that were on target and some that whizzed off in the wrong direction. To him, though, the important thing was to never quit trying.

                          ✑

The engineering managers needed to hire more engineers to meet Watson's demands. Few, if any, could be found. Most young men were fighting a war. Watson suggested that women could learn engineering. McPherson said he'd tried taking women—girls, as the men called them—from the drafting department and training them in engineering, but the women had only modest success.

"Don't you think it would be better to select girls who had some training in college along that line?" Watson asked.

"I believe they have been looking for people in these trips through the colleges along that line," said McPherson.

"I don't think so," Watson countered.

"Miss van Vechten started at [Stevens Institute of Technology in New Jersey], if you remember," said Roy Stephens, an executive from the accounting machines division. "They put in a special course over there, and she got in touch with the people."

"But where are the girls we got from Stevens?" Watson asked.

"That I don't know," said Roy Stephens.

"I would like to have Mr. Beattie and Mr. Page (two other executives in the room) go to Stevens and get hold of the head of the Placement Bureau and find out if they have some girls there who have been taking the engineering course," Watson said.

"Yes, sir! I will do that," Beattie said with playful enthusiasm.

"And Rutgers," Watson said, apparently not laughing. "They have a very good engineering course down there. And Princeton—John, you might . . ."

"There are no girls there," McPherson interjected.

Laughs blurted out all around. Princeton University enrolled only men. "In fact, there is no *college* at the moment—they're all in the army."

"I think they have some girls at Rutgers," said another executive.

"I forgot Princeton and some others are so far behind the times that they have no girls," Watson said flatly. "Has anybody else anything to say on the subject?"

No one did. Desperate as they were, IBM's male engineers never pursued the hiring of women engineers with conviction. Companies around the world found themselves short of male engineers during the war. If Watson had pushed his point more strongly, IBM could have gathered woman engineering talent overlooked by nearly every business. Watson had clearly seen the potential, but then missed this chance to grab an important strategic advantage.

⌘

On March 13, 1943, a letter from Frank Gannett, president of Gannett Newspapers, landed on Watson's desk. The letter, marked "Personal and Confidential" across the top, opened by saying: "Interests that would be objectionable to you are again active in an effort to buy the *Binghamton Press*."

Gannett started his company in 1906, when he bought a half-interest in the *Elmira Gazette* in Elmira, New York. In 1918, he bought two Rochester newspapers, consolidated them, and moved headquarters to that city. Over the next 35 years, Gannett continued to buy newspapers around the Northeast United States, creating one of the first newspaper chains.

Gannett and Watson met while Watson ran the NCR office in Rochester, and they stayed in contact after Watson left for Dayton. A rabid Republican, Gannett could never comprehend how Watson, as a businessman, could support Roosevelt's New Deal. But Gannett continued to invite his old friend to parties and dinners, and Watson continued to go. When Gannett saw a chance to exploit alleged mutual interests in IBM's home region, he grabbed it.

"It is rather difficult to get you on the phone, so I suggest when it is convenient for you, that you call me on Main 2241 during the day or Hillside 2194 during the evening," Gannett wrote. "I am rather concerned about this situation, and have a plan that may interest you."

The *Binghamton Press* had a colorful past. It was started at the turn of the century by Willis Sharpe Kilmer, who made a fortune selling a patent medicine called Swamp Root. He also owned racehorses, including the famous Exterminator, winner of the 1918 Kentucky Derby on 30-to-1 odds. In the early 1940s, after Kilmer's death, Kilmer's estate wanted to sell the newspaper and his vast Binghamton real estate. Possible deals surfaced and faded. There's no telling what party Gannett considered hostile to Watson. Perhaps none really were. However, Gannett found the situation to be a convenient reason for pursuing the Binghamton newspaper with Watson's help. There seems to be no indication of whether Watson helped financially or politically, or just lent his good wishes. Watson didn't need to be overly concerned about the region's media. The other major newspaper, the *Binghamton Sun,* was exceptionally friendly to IBM. Watson and the *Sun*'s president and publisher, William Hill, called each other "Tom" and "Billy," respectively. When Hill's mother died in 1944, Watson sent Hill a "certificate of honorary membership in the International Business Machines Corporation."[15]

Gannett got what he wanted. The deal closed on May 27, 1943. The Kilmer estate had asked $1.5 million for the *Press* and the Kilmer real estate. Cornell University agreed to buy the real estate for $400,000. Gannett got the paper for $1.1 million. On June 21, Gannett wrote a triumphant letter to Watson, saying why he was glad he bought the *Press.*

"First, it will prevent others who would not be quite so acceptable from getting control of this property. I think you know the facts in the case," Gannett wrote, conspiratorially. He noted that he was "especially happy [to] have a deep interest in Binghamton. I hope we may see each other soon, and that this deal will keep us more closely in touch with each other."[16]

By June 1943, Watson's friends ran the most powerful newspapers in IBM's most important location. At least in Endicott, Watson effectively silenced one more potential critic.

⬥

In early 1944, the Glenn Miller Band's peppy swing coerced smiles out of war-weary Americans at home, Bing Crosby sang for troops in London, and Betty Grable posters hung on walls and in lockers from North Africa to the Philippines. Allied armies made progress at the edges of the war zone, landing in Italy and taking the Marshall Islands from Japan in the Pacific. People began to allow themselves to think about an end to the war.

So Watson pushed harder.

In March 1944, Watson traveled to a lab in New Jersey, just outside of New York. He sat down with McPherson, Bryce, and three other engineers. Watson turned to Bryce, and ordered him to assign his best engineer to figure out how to "gear down" the machines that the government and military would return after the war. The high-speed, top-of-the-line models were to go back out to customers operating at one-half or even one-tenth of their original speed. The machines would not be any different, other than some internal adjustments. Watson wanted the lab to run break-down tests so IBM could calculate the lowest amount it could charge for rental and service on these recycled machines, and still make a profit.

IBM was going to market the old machines to smaller

businesses that had never before been able to afford an IBM installation. "They will start with the low-speed machine," Watson said to the engineers, "and as their business increases, perhaps in five years, they will go on to higher speeds until they reach the point where they will be using our regular machines, the same as our regular customers."

In theory, an IBM salesman could sell one of these new customers on a faster machine, and an IBM serviceman could take out the slower machine, change the internal settings so it worked faster, and reinstall the same machine. That probably never literally happened, but a slow machine could have been returned to IBM by one small business, retooled, then rented to a bigger business as a higher-speed model.

"We will be utilizing the machines that everybody has been figuring on scrapping," Watson said in the meeting. "We'll not only be saving money, but we'll be increasing our business. If you will just start figuring it out on that basis, you will soon see how this business will be trebled. We'll be able to cut the rental on our machines in half and still make more money for our stockholders."[17]

It was a practical decision of murky integrity. Even a CEO devoted to a puritanical image can sometimes make such choices.

President Roosevelt died on April 12, 1945, and Harry Truman was sworn in as president. On May 8, the war in Europe ended. On August 6, the United States dropped an atomic bomb on Hiroshima, Japan. On September 2, aboard the U.S. battleship *Missouri,* Japan surrendered. World War II was over, and all of Watson's plans had to work.

IBM finished the war with two and one-half times the factory space the company owned in 1940. For about a year, employment shuffled—a few thousand women factory

323

workers left jobs they'd taken during the war, and about 4,000 servicemen returned to their old IBM jobs. IBM ended up employing about 22,000 people, up from just under 13,000 in 1940.

In meetings with engineers, salesmen, and factory workers, Watson repeated his vow to fill all of the factory space—two and a half times more than IBM had in 1940—and avoid laying off any employees. "Now that means getting two and a half times as much business as we had before the war," Watson said.[18]

Watson complained that he'd been carrying too much of a management load and announced that Kirk would run all of IBM's operations, not just the war production. Watson would focus on whipping up the sales force, driving the engineers, and tending to IBM's culture. Notes from a meeting stated: "Mr. Watson said to Mr. Kirk that in his judgment one of the first and most important things he should do is to get back . . . the IBM spirit that used to be present."[19]

Defense work drained from IBM factories as the government cut back the military as quickly as it could. Of 12 million American servicemen in uniform when the war ended, all but 3 million would return to civilian life within a year. A year after that, only 1 million would be left in the service.

Watson's sons came home from war, and Watson assigned Tom Jr. to be Kirk's assistant. Dick went back to Yale to finish college.

In the first months after the war, the United States veered toward the grim recession predicted by economists and corporate planners. Most companies severely cut their workforces, and almost 3 million people were left unemployed. Prices for consumer goods, so scarce during the war, shot higher. IBM salesmen worried they'd never make their quotas in such a market.

Once again, Watson's guardian angel appeared, and proved him prescient. The U.S. economy roared back to life as consumers rushed to get products that had disappeared during the war. Millions of returning servicemen needed houses, so millions of houses were built. Those new homes needed millions more refrigerators, couches, carpets, and everything else. Companies cranked out cars, refrigerators, stockings, wire hangers, and Coca-Cola.

The companies suddenly busy making all those products needed tools, paper, desks, and delivery trucks. To keep track of their businesses, the companies also needed electric accounting or tabulating machines, and they lined up at IBM's door.

When demand exploded, IBM was ready to take advantage of it. It had acres of modern, efficient, newly built factories. It had a trained, cohesive, loyal workforce. It had new products designed by the engineers during the lull in commercial business during the war. Also, it had a hungry worldwide sales force motivated to make up for years of idleness and lost income.

IBM brought in $138 million in revenue in 1945, when war production ran at full tilt. In 1946, as the economy wavered before taking off, revenue dipped to $116 million. In 1947, IBM's commercial business soared, and the company pulled in $139 million—almost exactly two and one-half times the revenue of 1940.

Only one part of Watson's grand plan went awry. He didn't realize that by fathering a new super-IBM, he was setting himself up for his own obsolescence.

⤚

(To the Tune of "Where Do We Go from Here, Boys?")

We punch the cards and sort them by our electric machines,
Which then compute and print results—so marvelous it seems.
This international system saves you time and money every day.
Investigate and verify the truth of all we say.

—*Songs of the IBM*

11

OLD MAN, NEW ELECTRONIC AGE

HE SCRAPPY FARMBOY WHO GREW UP THINKING that Elmira was a worldly place often tried to do what he thought a wealthy president of a major industrial company ought to do. As a wealthy president of a major industrial company, Watson believed he ought to collect exceptional and expensive pieces of art. Watson began buying paintings as an executive at C-T-R. As his wealth and fame increased, Watson enthusiastically bought art for himself and made IBM into a patron of the arts. The art world generally dismissed Watson's tastes as bland and pedestrian, and then gladly took his and IBM's money.

Watson displayed his art in his office and in his New York and New Canaan homes. An art tour of the New Canaan house would have told a visitor a lot about Watson's taste—and about Watson.

In the foyer and front hall of the enormous house hung portraits of Watson's children, a landscape by the relatively unknown D. A. Teed, and a dark and tempestuous seascape by one of the most critically esteemed artists of the time, Henry Mattson. Watson didn't like popular art. The Mattson and its prominent position might have been a nod to IBM, which sponsored Mattson's work. In effect, Watson devoted the home's entranceway to images of his progeny: his children and IBM.

329

In the drawing room, two paintings dominated. One was a four-foot by three-foot portrait of Jeannette Watson, the woman who made Watson a husband and father and acted as a counterweight to his temper. The room's other huge painting—four feet by three and one-half feet—fought with Jeannette's somber, stiff likeness for control of the room. Called *Arabian Horseman,* by Adolf Schreyer, the bright painting huffed with masculinity and the dramatic action of a lone horseman on a broad desert. A second, smaller Schreyer painting—*Horse with Rider Seated on Ground*—teamed with the first to give the more flagrant works an advantage over Mrs. Watson. The other eight paintings depicted landscapes, including a dark and moody winter landscape by François Cachoud. All in all, the collection in the room reflected Watson's bold, stormy emotions, and Jeannette's moderating effect on those emotions.

The living room art kept to an entirely different theme. The 13 paintings hanging on the walls were all elegant, beautiful landscapes, including George Inness' *Edge of the Woods,* J. Francis Murphy's *Landscape,* and Bruce Crane's *Russet Fields.* Most of the works belonged to a turn-of-the-century movement called Tonalism, a style of landscape painting emphasizing evening or winter scenery in subdued colors, often conveying the majesty of nature. It was a style considered hostile to industrialism and progress—ironic in the Watson household. Tonalist paintings were also considered feminine, which seemed to echo Watson's feminine side.[1]

Except for the Mattson, all of the art on the first floor was created in the late 1800s. Watson assembled an impressive collection, but not one that a company president of 1945 would have been expected to buy. The art reflected the tastes of a company president of 1900 or 1915. That, again, said something about Watson as he crossed into his seventies. As the war ended and the world changed dramatically, Watson's core remained in a previous era.

Watson did not possess great vision for how a new technology would play out in the market. He was wrong about the Radiotype. He was wrong about xerography. Chester Carlson brought his new invention before Watson and offered to sell it to IBM. Watson couldn't figure out why IBM would want to get into the business of paper copiers. Carlson went away, and founded Xerox. Four decades later, long after Watson was gone, IBM would try to get into the photocopier market—an ultimately futile effort.

New technology—much of it developed or improved for military use during the war—poured into the market in the late 1940s. Among the developments were nylon, the Polaroid instant-film camera, and Leo Fender's electric guitar. Television was still a curiosity, and Watson could not grasp the product's business model. Watson considered making TV sets in a partnership with General Electric. Why would IBM, which rented expensive machines to businesses, make a product that would be *sold* to consumers? It wouldn't. Watson proposed renting TV sets to homeowners, perhaps through electric power companies, which would profit from the increased demand for electricity. The arrangement would have been much like leasing punch card machines to companies and making big profits on the sale of punch cards. It was television as only IBM could see it.[2] IBM never got into the business.

Electronics at first fooled Watson, too. He knew about electronic technology well before he knew what it meant— or knew that electronics would threaten his company. His understanding evolved in steps, some of them embarrassing. Like anyone who wishes that something weren't true, Watson would not easily accept that electronics would make punch card machines obsolete.

To his credit, once he understood, Watson chased the new technology. Watson myths portray him as stubbornly rejecting electronics, but the stories are untrue or out of context. Tom Watson Jr., who eventually led IBM's charge into electronic computers, said of his father: "Electronics was the only major issue on which we didn't fight."[3]

Electronics was a fuzzy word around World War II. At first, it applied to calculating machines that worked using electromechanical relays, which could do computations quite a bit faster than the gears and wheels inside a punch card accounting machine. But relays were a transitional technology. Later, electronics referred to a computing machine based on vacuum tubes. Such tubes dramatically increased the speed of information processing.

Lee de Forest invented vacuum tubes in 1906. The tubes were basically a light bulb with a third element, a triode, which could amplify or switch a flow of electrons. In the 1930s, the amplifying trait had tremendous impact because it made possible radio broadcasting and home receivers. Through the decade, no one figured out how to take advantage of the tubes' ability to operate as a switch—to repeatedly turn on and off in a fraction of second. No one realized that millions of lightning-fast combinations of on and off could be made to represent numbers and make calculations—the basic insight behind every modern computer.

In 1939, John Atanasoff, a professor at Iowa State College, built the first computer to use binary, on-and-off switches to make calculations. However, his switches were electromechanical. A physical switch had to literally flick back and forth to turn on and off, taking much longer than a similar switch in a vacuum tube. Atanasoff's invention went largely unnoticed, though today he is considered the father of the modern computer.

That same year, Watson's research lab first briefed him on a way that vacuum tubes might apply to IBM. Jim Bryce, who ran the labs, sent Watson a description of ongoing research projects. Vacuum tubes came up in item number three.

Bryce told Watson that the lab was investigating "the development of computing devices which do not employ the usual adding wheels, but instead use electronic effects and employ tubes similar to those used in radio work." Bryce informed Watson that with tubes, "it will be possible to compute *thousands* of items per second." The emphasis is Bryce's. He added that the technology "appears to look very promising"—but only suggests that it would be appropriate for work that required "extreme speed," such as scientific calculations.

Through Watson's eyes in 1939, vacuum tube electronics was intriguing but distant. Watson had no reason to think customers would want to process data thousands of times faster. Customers seemed satisfied with the pace of IBM's electromechanical machines. The machines often awed potential buyers. IBM offered a system that worked—punch cards zipping through clattering machines that could add, subtract, multiply, sort, and print results.

Because Watson built IBM on punch card machines, every pathway in his brain somehow led back to punch card machines. The technology hadn't been challenged in Watson's 25 years of running the company. Punch card machines weren't to him an interim technology in the broader realm of data processing—they *were* the broader realm, as if punch card machines would go on forever, while interim technologies like 80-column cards, plastics, and electronics would come and go on the punch card timeline.

Watson challenged IBM's engineers to improve the punch card technology that existed. As a practical businessman, he focused on profitable improvements. Make the machines more reliable, and IBM servicemen would make fewer service calls, saving money. Make them a little faster, and salesmen could pitch current customers to upgrade. But don't make the machines too much faster, or the rest of IBM's product line would seem obsolete. High-speed electronics didn't have a place in that universe.

IBM's stumble toward electronics began when Watson decided to court the favor of Harvard University. IBM and Columbia University had long enjoyed a solid relationship, which began when IBM helped Ben Wood build test scoring machines in the 1920s. IBM sent machines to Columbia's astronomy lab and worked with scientists such as Wallace Eckert. Watson was asked to join Columbia's governing board. Now Watson, always aiming for the top, wanted IBM to develop a similarly close relationship with the nation's most elite school, Harvard. Watson sent his dutiful executive, John Phillips, to Harvard's campus in Cambridge, Massachusetts, to meet with deans and faculty.

At Harvard, Howard Aiken, an extraordinarily brash young researcher who had written groundbreaking papers about high-speed calculating machines, joined Phillips and faculty members at a dinner. Around the school, Aiken was considered arrogant and difficult. The school's dean had been known to say that the only way to respond to Aiken's table pounding was to pound the table right back at him.

Catching Phillips's attention, Aiken said that he could build an experimental supercalculating machine out of IBM accounting machine parts—with "a certain amount of additional work and wiring." The machine would far exceed the size and speed of any existing calculating machine. Harvard had previously turned down Aiken's proposal, in part because of its great cost. Phillips relayed Aiken's ideas on to Watson, who saw an opening.

Watson didn't believe Aiken's work would lead to anything useful, but funding the project would advance IBM's relationship with Harvard. IBM would pay for Aiken's machine, which IBM workers would construct in Endicott according to Aiken's design. The machine would then be trucked to Harvard, where it could be studied and used for scientific calculations. Watson approved an initial donation of $15,000, and work started in 1939.

Watson didn't fund it as a hedge against future

technology. It was a vehicle for joining IBM with Harvard through research that might benefit both.

Aiken's design included no vacuum tubes, and it couldn't even be called electronic. It truly was a giant IBM punch card machine with some clever twists that tied them together to solve complex mathematical equations. Watson and Bryce assigned Clair Lake, the respected old-timer of IBM's engineers, to work with Aiken, trusting that Lake would look after IBM's patent interests. For Watson, the project then faded into the background.

In the first years of World War II, IBM continued to fund Aiken's work, which crawled forward in Endicott. However, the war altered IBM's research priorities. Watson ordered his engineers to work on much-needed war-related products first, and commercial or experimental products when time allowed. To keep the engineers focused, Watson pared commercial research to a list of five projects that would have immediate implications for accounting machines. Electronics never made the list, despite pleas from the engineers.

"Electronics research should go on regardless of the projects we are rushing to current completion," John McPherson, head of engineering, told Watson in one meeting. "We must attempt to use vacuum tube circuits in business machines."

Watson replied that it wasn't one of the five most important projects.

"I want to put electronics in a class by itself because I think it's that important," McPherson said.

"Can you have something ready in six months that we can go out in the field with?" Watson asked.

"No."

"Well, then, it isn't of first importance."[4]

Watson heard occasional reports about the work on Aiken's Harvard project. He'd stop in and see the machine on his trips to Endicott. In early 1943, Aiken and the IBM workers finished the machine, dubbed the Automatic Sequence Controlled Calculator Mark I, abbreviated to ASCC/Mark I, and referred to inside IBM as simply the Mark I. IBM had pumped in $500,000, hundreds of hours of IBM employees' time, and valuable floor space in Endicott—and still no one at IBM, including Watson, could see any practical use for the machine.

However, Watson realized the public was increasingly fascinated by "thinking machines," and that reporters and photographers would rush to see one. Watson put a high value on anything that spread IBM's name and boosted its reputation. Ever mindful of image, Watson wanted the Mark I dressed up. It was ugly—like a collision of naked punch card machines with parts sticking out every which way. To make the Mark I photogenic, Watson hired Norman Bel Geddes, who had created gems of art-deco design for everything from cocktail shakers to the Metropolitan Opera building. When Bel Geddes finished, the Mark I looked like nothing before it. The machine stood 8 feet high and stretched 51 feet long. At one end, hundreds of knobs covered a panel the size of a garage door. Exposed in the middle were neat rows of 72 *storage counter relays,* which could be removed or plugged in to program the Mark I. Another panel, more than 10 feet wide, sported sleek knobs and plugs—those were the *interpolators.* On a shelf on the far end sat an assortment of input and output devices, including two typewriters, a card feeder, and a card punch. The whole machine was bordered by Bel Geddes's trademark curvy, smooth metal skin. To observers, the Mark I seemed like a visitor from a future age.[5]

The Mark I solved its first problem in January 1943, and for nearly a year remained in Endicott as engineers ran it through tests and Aiken wrestled with IBM for credit and patents. Watson would not publicly unveil the machine until the issues with Aiken were resolved and the Mark I was moved to Harvard.[6]

While Aiken tested, another ping about electronics hit Watson—this time about a project at the University of Pennsylvania, called the Electronic Numerical Integrator and Computer (ENIAC). He learned about ENIAC in a straightforward way. The two designers, John Presper Eckert and John Mauchly, contacted IBM asking for help. They had asked the same of RCA and AT&T's Bell Laboratories, and were getting money from the U.S. Army. IBM agreed only to design a custom-made card-reading device that would load numbers into ENIAC.[7] The access allowed IBM engineers doing the work to gather intelligence about the machine.

Eckert and Mauchly proposed to use 18,000 vacuum tubes as switches, linking them so they could solve an equation. Other than peripherals such as the card reader, ENIAC would have no moving parts. Mauchly's proposal stated that if an electromechanical machine could solve a particular equation in 15 to 30 minutes, ENIAC could do it in 100 seconds.

Watson had no reason to get anxious about ENIAC. Hardly anyone thought it would work. The university turned down the ENIAC proposal once, then during the war grudgingly gave permission to Eckert and Mauchly when the army showed interest. The Army, though, by Mauchly's admission, funded ENIAC only out of desperation to find some technological advantage in the war. The chief scientist at RCA proclaimed that 18,000 tubes could never work together. Nothing about ENIAC pushed any buttons that said to Watson: Emergency! Do something quick!

Instead, Watson prepared to announce the Mark I. In mid-1944, the machine had finally been set up at Harvard. On Sunday, August 6, 1944, Watson and Jeannette arrived by train at the Boston station. Outside, low clouds were dumping an all-day, shoe-soaking rain. Watson disembarked inside the station and looked around for a greeting party from Harvard. In a situation like this, a group of important people always met Watson at the train station and ceremoniously welcomed him. This time, the only person awaiting the Watsons was IBM's Boston branch manager, Frank McCabe—a lone figure carrying an umbrella. Instead of a limousine from Harvard, McCabe's Chevrolet would take the Watsons to their hotel.

Jeannette struggled to climb into the backseat. McCabe and Watson folded themselves into the Chevy and closed the car doors. Watson seethed, but didn't lash out at McCabe, an innocent bystander in the Harvard snub. Then McCabe handed Watson that day's newspaper. Watson looked at it and his eyes flashed. The Mark I was on the front page, a day ahead of the ceremony, and a day before the news was supposed to be out. McCabe apparently informed Watson that all the newspapers in Boston put the Mark I on their front pages, and all the reporters gave Aiken all the credit, because that's what Aiken and Harvard told them.

"Automatic Brain for Harvard" trumpeted the *Boston Post*. The subheadline read: "Navy Man Inventor of World's Greatest Calculator." IBM was mentioned once in the story, and not identified as a coinventor or backer. The Mark I got the publicity that Watson desired, but none of it flowed to IBM. Aiken and Harvard had issued a press release without consulting IBM, and the release portrayed Aiken as the sole inventor.[8]

No one on earth would have wanted to be McCabe at that moment. A Watson rage could blow the windows out of a Chevy. Watson ranted, cursing Aiken from his car seat, until McCabe pulled up to Boston's Copley Hotel—probably in a sweat. Stomping to his room, Watson telephoned his hosts and ripped into them. He told them he refused to attend the ceremony scheduled for the next day. Aiken and a Harvard dean sped to the Copley to apologize and ask Watson to reconsider. "You can't put IBM on as a postscript!"

Watson snarled at Aiken. "I think about IBM just as you Harvard fellows do about your university!"[9]

When Watson calmed down, he agreed to speak as planned at the dedication, and deal with Harvard later. He charmed his way through the luncheon at 12:30 and the ceremony at 2:30, then boarded the train for New York. For weeks after, Harvard officials sent Watson letters of explanation and apology. Watson fired back terse responses. "Your letter clearly indicates to me that you are not familiar with the invention and development of the IBM Automatic Sequence Controlled Calculator," said one three-sentence letter.[10]

In those first days after the Mark I debacle, Watson vowed to show Harvard and the rest of the world that IBM could build an electronic computer without Aiken's help. Watson met with Jim Bryce and Clair Lake, and ordered them to build a computer that would make Aiken's current and future machines look like child's toys.

IBM got into electronics as an act of vengeance.

⤳

When World War II ended in 1945, Watson was 71 years old. IBM factory workers, salesmen, and managers referred to him as "the Old Man" when talking about him. Of course, using the term in Watson's presence would've meant career suicide.

When Watson looked in the mirror, he could see an aged man of faltering health carrying an overwhelming workload. IBM grew two and one-half times in five years, yet Watson didn't restructure the company to spread out decision making. He clung to his godlike management style, running a sprawling global corporation the same way he had run feisty little C-T-R. Everything that happened at IBM still flowed through Watson. The company builder didn't know how to metamorphose into a professional chief executive.

Even if Watson could have stayed young and healthy, he would have sagged under the growing load of IBM's demands. As the years passed, though, one or another of Watson's parts broke down, and illnesses lingered. Watson's life of sleep-deprived nights, gallons of coffee, heart-thumping tantrums, rich business dinners, and stressful decisions were exacting their toll. The increasing complexity of the company ran counter to Watson's decreasing energy to manage it. IBM was getting away from its builder.

The issue of succession clanged mercilessly in the back of his mind. A growing awareness of death heightened his sense of urgency. His closest contemporaries passed away in the 1940s. In 1942, Watson lost Sam Hastings, the Dayton scale man who had helped Watson stabilize C-T-R, and Harry Evans, the funny writer of IBM songs. Watson's old friend and advisor, Walter Cool, died in 1945. That same year took Watson's North Star, President Roosevelt. In the late 1940s, Watson saw the passing of George F. Johnson, the shoe magnate who greatly influenced Watson, and A. Ward Ford, who brought Watson to C-T-R and remained a friend and board member. All those losses made Watson starkly realize the limits of his time running IBM. He wanted to leave leadership of the company to his two sons. Watson needed to prepare them, and set up the mechanisms that would ensure they came to power. Watson's age meant he'd have to construct shortcuts to speed his sons' climb.

Watson had to handle the growing load of management issues without Fred Nichol. Worn out and increasingly ill, Nichol went on a leave of absence in late 1944 to try to improve his health. Tom Watson Jr. believed that the stress of working for Watson finally got to Nichol, leading to a nervous breakdown.[11] Watson lost his most reliable executive, who was also a friend, confidante, proxy, and butler. Watson tried to coax Nichol back, writing to Nichol about the plan to use Kirk to lighten the management load.

"When you do get back," Watson wrote, "you and I must figure out a way in which we can do our jobs in IBM without the strain that we have worked under in the past years."[12] Nichol never returned to IBM, fighting health problems for three years before sending Watson a melancholy letter of resignation in 1947.

Watson's health on occasion kept him out of the office for a week or more. In December 1944, Aiken noted that he and a contingent from Harvard arrived at IBM and found Watson out sick. Watson sometimes sent word to headquarters that he was suffering from a bad cold or stomach ache, and instructed senior executives to come to his New York home for important meetings.[13] He suffered from chronic heartburn and an ulcer, complaining at times of discomfort or pain in his gut, downing bicarbonate of soda, and burping when he thought no one was around. Watson rarely consented to see a doctor. As the years marched on, Watson's ailments kept him out longer. "I have just recovered from a bout with the shingles," Watson wrote to a friend. "I had a very mild case and it was not at any time serious; but I do say that it was very disagreeable to live with, and I would not recommend the malady to anybody. I was laid up at home a little over a month, but I am glad to say I am now feeling fine again."[14]

In his 70s, Watson for the first time needed and wanted less of a relentless pace. At headquarters, Watson rarely arrived before 10 A.M., and his last meeting would rarely begin after 4 P.M. After lunch on many days, he'd duck into an anteroom attached to his office, lie on the couch, pull a blanket over himself, and nap for an hour. Still, he'd often pack a day with 10 meetings plus a business lunch. Watson could yet hurtle across Europe like a shooting star, as he showed in 1948 on his two-month spree through a dozen cities. Yet unlike previous years, Watson took long vacations to rejuvenate. In 1945, 1946, 1948 and 1949, he spent a month in either Palm Beach or Del Ray Beach in Florida. During those vacations, Watson kept his business schedule empty.[15]

As Watson sometimes struggled in the years right after the war, IBM raced ahead and kept growing because of Watson's greatest creation: the IBM culture. The culture told lower-level managers and employees how to act even if Watson didn't send down timely instructions. The culture's adhesive preserved loyalty even if the leader faltered, or the company seemed to make a wrong turn. Employees didn't want to leave this family if something went wrong. Instead, they wanted to stay and work to make it better. The culture bought Watson a margin of error.

Outside of IBM, one other aspect of Watson's life fought for his attention and energy: grandchildren. Watson enjoyed his grandchildren more than almost anything before. While Watson's children remember him as a stern and demanding father, his grandchildren remember him as magical. The first Watson grandchild, Thomas Watson Buckner, arrived in August 1941, the son of Watson's daughter Helen and her husband, Walker Gentry Buckner. By 1946, Helen had two more, and Tom and Olive Watson added two. Eventually Watson had 15 grandchildren. A different shade of his personality came out around them. After a lifetime of walking into rooms where people feared him, Watson could walk in on the grandchildren, and they would joyously jump up to greet him. The youngest ones called him Gaga; the others called him Grandfather. Watson saved a birthday card from little Jeannette, in which she wrote in a child's script: "I wish I were with you so I could kiss you eighty times I love you so much, and I hope I see you soon."

Watson worked hard to win the adoration of his grandchildren. At times, that meant whisking one or two of them off to shopping sprees at New York's FAO Schwartz toy store, or taking the boys sailing, or bringing the girls dresses from Paris. He sent them crisp $5 bills as a surprise. At other times, Watson entertained his grandchildren using skills not apparent to his business colleagues. He could roll his tongue around in a way that made a false tooth pop out. And he could crack walnuts in his hand.[16]

~

Tom Watson Jr. left the army at the end of 1945, and rejoined IBM on the first business day of 1946. He walked into Watson's office that morning, expecting to begin learning about managing IBM from his father. Instead, Watson informed Tom Jr. that he'd work as Charley Kirk's assistant. "I'm sure I shook Kirk's hand and said how glad I was, but I was so surprised that I don't remember doing it," Watson Jr. recalled.[17] If Tom Jr. thought he had a bloodline right to the throne, the assignment to Kirk told him otherwise. Watson wanted his son to run IBM, but the message from father to son was: You'll step up when you're ready, and I'll step down when I'm ready.

Kirk enthusiastically coached his new assistant, pulling a chair next to his desk and showing Tom Jr. everything he did. Kirk and Tom attended meetings together and visited Endicott together. Tom appreciated Kirk's openness, but found more reasons to dislike him, even while so many others at IBM found Kirk charming and smart. Just the fact that Kirk was so well liked bothered Tom. Kirk had obviously won a place in the heart of IBM—a place Tom felt belonged to him.[18]

Three months into Tom Jr.'s apprenticeship, Kirk decided to go see the ENIAC at the University of Pennsylvania. Eckert and Mauchly finished the ENIAC just as the war ended in 1945. None of IBM's top executives had gone for a close look. Watson showed no interest. So on a gray March day on the school's campus in 1946, Kirk and Tom Jr. walked into a room made tropically hot by 18,000 lit vacuum tubes. Eckert, cocky and impetuous, explained how ENIAC worked, and then described how electronic computers were going to replace electromechanical machines like IBM's. Tom Jr. and Kirk, two relatively young men who might have been open to new ideas, shrugged their shoulders and decided that Eckert was a dreamer. They both dismissed ENIAC as too costly and unreliable—how could a business do critical work if tubes keep burning out and shutting down the machine?

A few weeks later, Watson took Kirk and Tom Jr. to one of IBM's labs. Neither of them knew much about the activities that had blossomed out of Watson's desire to avenge Aiken's slight.

When Watson returned from the Mark I ceremonies and ordered Jim Bryce and Clair Lake to build an Aiken-beating supercalculator, the two engineers sank in their chairs, knowing that it couldn't be done without breakthroughs in the lab. Bryce, in an impressive bit of tap dancing, suggested that instead of taking a long time to build a supercalculator, IBM could quickly build a simpler calculating machine based on vacuum tubes—and then IBM would be first on the market with a production-model electronic calculator. It wouldn't outperform Aiken's machines, but it would be a public relations coup, and provide a stepping-stone to building an Aiken-smashing electronic supercalculator.[19] Watson bought into Bryce's plan.

During the war, when Watson shut down the lab's research on electronics, a passionate young engineer named Halsey Dickinson continued to work on vacuum tube electronics in his basement at home. After Watson's order to beat Aiken, Bryce assigned Dickinson to build that first electronic calculator.

In mid-1945, after Kirk and Tom Jr. sniffed at the ENIAC, Watson took the boys to see Dickinson's working prototype. Dickinson had linked a high-speed punch card machine to a black metal box about four feet tall. Tom Watson Jr. asked what the box was doing. One of the engineers told him it was multiplying using radio tubes. The engineers explained that it could multiply 10 times faster than the punch card machine. In fact, the box spent nine-tenths of its time waiting for the punch card mechanism to catch up. For some reason, while Tom Jr. failed to see any good in the gigantic ENIAC, Dickinson's electronic black box excited him. "That impressed me as though somebody had hit me on the head with a hammer," Tom Watson Jr. recalled. That moment marked Tom Jr.'s awakening to electronics and its potential role in IBM products.[20]

In Tom Jr.'s memory, he immediately told his father that IBM should put Dickinson's device on the market, and "that is how IBM got into electronics." In reality, Watson and Bryce from the beginning set a goal of making an electronic calculator that *could* be produced and sold *if* anyone wanted to buy one. At the National Business Show in New York in September 1946, IBM unveiled the IBM 603 Electronic Multiplier—the first production electronic calculator. It contained 300 vacuum tubes, as opposed to ENIAC's 18,000. It had no storage, so it couldn't handle complex equations. It couldn't divide. It couldn't do much more than multiply two 6-digit numbers read from a punch card, but it could do that multiplication 10 times faster than anything else on the market. To IBM's astonishment, customers liked the 603 and placed orders for it. Somewhat embarrassed about the 603's limitations, Watson cut off production at 100, and the engineers built a more refined, versatile follow-up, the IBM 604 Electronic Calculating Punch. It used 1,400 tubes and could be programmed for simple equations. Over the next 10 years, IBM would build and lease 5,600 of the 604 machines. No one at IBM had predicted such success. For the first time, Watson got the message: *Customers will buy electronic products.*

In fact, if Watson had absorbed the message earlier, he might have taken a different attitude into a meeting with Eckert and Mauchly in mid-1946, just months after Kirk and Tom Jr. saw the ENIAC. Eckert and Mauchly had resigned from the University of Pennsylvania because of a dispute over who owned the ENIAC patents. The duo lost their financial backing and place to work. They called on Watson in his office, and Watson offered to bring Eckert and Mauchly into IBM and let them start a computing laboratory. Eckert and Mauchly, however, considered themselves a business and wanted to sell the business to IBM and then join the company. Otherwise, they'd build their own company. Watson said no to the deal, and rushed them out the door. Once Eckert and Mauchly left, Watson turned to Jim Birkenstock, who had recently been named general sales manager, and expressed relief that he didn't buy out the ENIAC partners. "This guy Mauchly wears these loud socks," Watson commented. "I wouldn't want him in my business anyway."[21]

❦

"Have you read this article?" Watson said.

Watson shoved a newspaper clipping across his desk toward Frank Hamilton, one of IBM's top engineers. Tom Watson Jr. had just walked into his father's office, and he found Watson's face in a scowl and Hamilton looking pensive. Watson had cut the news story out of the August 25, 1947, New York *Herald Tribune*. The headline read: "Two Electronic 'Brains' Will Be Set Up by U.S." The story reported that the National Bureau of Standards, an agency in the U.S. government, planned to set up and fund two separate laboratories for building two "ultra-high-speed electronic computing machines, said to be faster and better than any previous device." Most troubling to Watson was the information in the seventh paragraph: Private companies would build the machines in cooperation with the agency. The story mentioned two companies. One was a large company, Raytheon Corporation. The other was Electronic Control Company, started by Eckert and Mauchly. The way Watson saw it, the U.S. government was funding competition for IBM. Jim Bryce had already pointed out to Watson that before the war, only IBM could muster the resources to develop new kinds of calculating machines and put them on the market. But after the war, the government and military concluded that America must hold onto its lead in technology—and so they began throwing money into computing projects at companies and universities. The British government was doing the same in the United Kingdom. The field of electronic computing popped with activity—much of it outside of IBM.

IBM could still claim a lead. The company's engineers built on their successes with the 603 and 604 electronic machines, and drove on toward Watson's main objective: to build the world's most powerful supercalculator, and blow past Howard Aiken. Watson recruited Wallace Eckert (no relation to ENIAC's J. Presper Eckert) from Columbia University and put him in charge of the supercalculator project. Eckert's team finished assembling the machine in Endicott in the summer of 1947.

IBM spent $950,000 to develop the machine, named the Selective Sequence Electronic Calculator (SSEC). The SSEC could compute more than 250 times faster than Aiken's Mark I. It was the first computing machine that could be programmed with software. The ENIAC, for instance, could only be programmed by manually rearranging plugs on a plugboard.

Still, the SSEC was not a real electronic computer. The engineers had concocted a hybrid of electronics and old punch card machines. Information was stored on punch cards, not on a new and more efficient invention: magnetic tape. Only the programming resided on tape. Watson could not or would not see the enormous advantages of tape for data, such as the storage space it would save, and the way it could shoot the data into a machine at great speed. As Watson often pointed out, magnetic tape could accidentally get erased. Punch cards held information on a tangible medium.

347

Why would IBM's customers want to risk losing the information on a tape? The IBM engineers dared not construct a machine that didn't rely on punch cards.

However, up-and-coming competitors were building all-electronic machines, using tape to store data. Watson's concern about such rivals led to this day's meeting with Hamilton, who acted as chief engineer on the SSEC project.

Hamilton looked at Watson's newspaper clippings, and told Watson the story was similar to others about the government funding development of electronic calculators that could be sold for $50,000 each.

"If they can build a machine for $50,000, where do we come in?" Watson asked.

"That's not an overall machine," Hamilton replied. Those machines, he said, were simple machines designed to do a single, narrow task.

"Don't you think we ought to get out a calculator that will do a specific job?" Watson said. "Something that will be available to all universities? Now, I understand these fellows who built the ENIAC machine are being backed by insurance companies to build something for them."

That was true, Hamilton told Watson. In addition to any government funding, Eckert and Mauchly's Electronic Control Company was backed in part by insurance companies.

"What I would like to find out now is just what the insurance companies need, and then we should go ahead and produce a machine to do the job for them," Watson said.

"You know, Mr. Kirk and Mr. Douglas went over to Prudential and talked to the men there. We have a set of their specifications," Hamilton said.

"Then why don't we build a machine to meet their specifications?"

"I think we intend to do something on that."

"We can't think and intend when other insurance companies are backing this outfit to build machines," Watson shot back. "We can't afford just to think about it and intend to. What is the quickest way to go ahead and build a machine to meet their specifications in the very shortest possible time?"

Well, Hamilton said, the engineers can start by looking over Prudential's specs.

"If we can't build it, let's drop out. If we can do it, let's do it at a price those other fellows can't meet," Watson said, getting roiled. "It's an indictment against IBM to have these two fellows backed by those insurance companies."

Watson told Hamilton to pull together Bryce and other key people for a meeting. "We will see whether we can do it," Watson said, "and then do it."

Hamilton tried for a more cordial tone. "I hear you and Mrs. Watson stopped in to see the machine downstairs," he said, referring to the SSEC.

"About that machine, I am worried about the dust. We should not have exposed all of that equipment to dust. We should have covered those machines and sealed it up."

"We did do that," Hamilton said.

"I saw the whole thing," Watson said. "The dust could get right into it. I think it's terrible."

"I've been watching it," Hamilton said, getting defensive and probably thinking that Watson didn't know what he was talking about. "I've been down every week," Hamilton added.

"You should have been there every minute the men were working on it," Watson barked. "Never mind what instructions you had from other people. You should have been there every day and all day. It was just left to a lot of workers and electricians to do as they please. Now, when is it going to be fully completed and ready to start up and test?"

"We're going to start testing the end of this week," Hamilton said.

Satisfied with the answer, Watson dropped the subject of dust. But he ordered Hamilton to draw up a plan for a computer to meet Prudential's specs.

Until 1947, the development of electronic computing had been pushed by inventors and by the engineers at IBM. That elite group created technology for technology's sake— and for prestige and public relations. Few if any customers stood at the other end begging for the machines. The technologists built solutions to problems that didn't yet exist.

By the time of his meeting with Hamilton, Watson sensed growing evidence of a pull from customers for electronic computing. He first saw it in the success of the 604. Then Prudential, which knew nothing about designing computers, drew up specifications for a computer that it wanted. Insurance companies surrendered entire floors of office buildings to the storage of millions of IBM punch cards, and they needed a better solution.

At 73 years old, Watson started grasping the potential for electronic computing. Yet he still saw electronics as a new, additional business, not as something that would supersede punch card machines—and definitely not something that would sweep aside punch cards. Watson understood that IBM had to move into computers, but his decisions on the matter remained conservative. In decades past, Watson had bet the company three times, and won. Maybe a younger Watson would have bet the company again, putting it all on electronics. The 73-year-old Watson, though, was tired, overburdened, and concerned about his legacy. On this one, he'd move more deliberately. Watson needed his son to push electronics on IBM, and for that to happen, Charley Kirk had to suffer his peculiar death.

⬦

Tom Watson Jr.'s animosity toward Charley Kirk fouled the atmosphere at the highest levels of IBM. Tom Jr. regarded Kirk as an interloper—a wedge driven into the Watson family. The younger Watson was supposed to be Kirk's assistant, but he doggedly tried to upstage Kirk and win his father's approval. Kirk responded by zealously trying to please Watson, sometimes overreacting to an order. For example, if Watson told Kirk to look into some manager's poor performance, Kirk might immediately fire the man.

Watson felt torn by the competition. He wanted his son to perform well and eventually run IBM, but Watson needed Kirk to help him manage the company. Tom Jr. was the future; Kirk, the present.

In the spring of 1947, Tom Watson Jr. lost patience. He marched into his father's office and laid out the arithmetic: Kirk was nine years older than him, so if Kirk remained next in line for the presidency of IBM, Tom Jr. would have to work for Kirk for 22 years before Kirk retired. Then the younger Watson would run the company for only eight or nine years. Tom told his father he was not looking forward to hating his boss for the next 22 years.

"Look, Dad, Kirk is here," Tom said. "I can get along with all the other people you've hired, but not Kirk." Tom told his father he quit. They argued, and Tom stormed out of Watson's office and out of the building.[22]

Late that night, at Tom Jr.'s house in Greenwich, Connecticut, Watson and his son talked again. Tom Jr. recalled Watson saying, "You just can't do this to me. You can't quit."[23]

Tom insisted he couldn't work for Kirk. He forced his father to decide: him or me.

Watson chose to stall for time. He would send Tom Jr. and Kirk together to Europe, where they'd both attend an International Chamber of Commerce meeting in Switzerland, and then tour IBM facilities across the continent. Tom Jr. recalled that Watson told him to "take Mr. Kirk to Europe. Introduce him to the managers there, and I'll think of something."[24] Watson knew how much Tom despised Kirk, though, so he wouldn't have nonchalantly suggested they go overseas together. Watson was wilier than that. He must have hoped that during an extended trip away from the day-to-day pressures of headquarters, Tom and Kirk might find a way to work together.

If he were forced to decide, Watson wouldn't let the situation crumple his dream of handing IBM to Tom. While Kirk and Tom were away, Watson could think about a way to ease Kirk aside if necessary.

Tom Jr., Kirk, and their wives sailed for Europe in May 1947. Despite weeks together on the ship, on trains, in hotels, and at dinners, nothing eased the hostility that Tom felt for Kirk. At one point, Tom admitted, they nearly came to blows during an argument about a side trip in France. That same night—June 16—Kirk, Tom, their wives, and a small support staff arrived at their destination in Lyons, France. They checked into the Carlton Hotel, and that evening attended a dinner put on by IBM France managers.

Kirk ate what was described as a hearty meal. He drank about four glasses of wine, judging by the blood alcohol levels found later.[25] Toward the end of the dinner, Kirk felt violent pains in his chest and stomach, excused himself from the table, and vomited, apparently in the men's restroom. Kirk and his wife left the dinner and returned to the Carlton, where they called a doctor. Kirk kept vomiting. The doctor, Dr. Buffard, listened to Kirk's heart and reported the noises were normal, though a bit muffled. Kirk had "an abnormal painful sensitivity" on the left side of his chest, the doctor found. He gave Kirk some painkilling drugs and told him to try to sleep.

At 4 A.M., Kirk's wife called the doctor back. Kirk's heart had gone into spasms. Kirk's secretary ran down the hall of the Carlton and pounded on Tom Jr.'s door, saying that Kirk was very sick. Tom and Olive pulled on bathrobes and rushed to Kirk's room, where they found Kirk lying unconscious on the bed. Before Dr. Buffard could get back to the room, Kirk died. He was 43 years old.

Olive tried to comfort Kirk's wife, who had been at

Kirk's bedside. His daughters, 15 and 9, had stayed behind with Kirk's mother in the Endicott area.[26]

In New York, where the time was six hours behind France, Watson got a late-night phone call from Tom, who told him of Kirk's death. Watson became emotional—some accounts say he wept. His thoughts must have ricocheted in every direction. He lost a colleague and friend, and the executive he relied on most. At the same time, however, providence solved Watson's awkward problem. Kirk was out of Tom Jr.'s way. Watson must have felt guilty that the solution came at the cost of Kirk's life.

Watson also apparently thought the convenience of Kirk's death could raise suspicions. Kirk had been a vigorous workhorse, putting in 18-hour days, yet never seeming to tire. He was young and, as far as anyone knew, healthy. In the quiet of night, in a small French city, in a hotel where both Kirk and Tom Jr. were staying, Kirk suddenly died. To be clear: There's no indication that anyone in France or the United States accused Tom Jr. of wrongdoing. Watson and Tom Jr. asked for an autopsy, just to sweep away any doubts. Indeed, the report concluded Kirk suffered a massive heart attack.

Watson ordered a glorious funeral in Endicott. On July 2, about 400 of Kirk's family and close friends crowded into the Homestead. A large portrait of Kirk hung in the main dining room, and the IBM Glee Cub and Chorus sang. More than 3,000 other mourners assembled at the IBM Country Club, down the hill from the Homestead. Loudspeakers were set up so anyone in or near the Country Club could hear the eulogies and prayers, which continued for two and one-half hours. Watson did not speak—a rarity at an IBM event. He and Tom Jr. were among the pallbearers.

Once Kirk was laid to rest, his death handed Watson a new problem: In Watson's eyes, Tom Jr. was not ready. Tom was 33 years old, confident, aggressive, ambitious, and far smarter than his schoolboy struggles would ever suggest. But Watson felt that Tom didn't yet have the experience to jump into Kirk's executive vice president role, much less control IBM. So for the interim, Watson named jowly old George Phillips to Kirk's job. Phillips wouldn't actually *do* Kirk's job—despite his lofty position at IBM, Phillips was never much more than Watson's supersecretary and yes-man. Watson and Tom Jr. took on most of the work that had been delegated to Kirk.

Every manager at IBM knew Phillips was only a short-term buffer. They understood that Tom Watson Jr. would be IBM's next leader. IBM rustled with the sound of loyalties shifting.

❧

Old Man Watson didn't know much about how to build an electronic computer. In 1947, though, Watson was the only person on earth who knew how to *sell* an electronic computer.

The engineers finished testing the SSEC in late 1947, when Watson made a decision that forever altered the public perception of computers and linked IBM's name to the new generation of information machines. He told the engineers to disassemble the SSEC and set it up in the ground-floor lobby of IBM's 590 Madison Avenue headquarters. The lobby was open to the public, and its large external windows allowed a view of the SSEC for the multitudes cramming the sidewalks on Madison and 57th Street. As part of putting the SSEC in front of the public, IBM announced that scientists could run problems through the SSEC for free, while commercial enterprises would pay $300 per hour, which was the cost of operating the machine. The point was to keep the SSEC running, so anyone who looked in would see that it worked.

Watson told IBM designers to make sure the SSEC looked sleek and impressive, just as Watson had wanted the

Mark I stylized. The spectacle of the SSEC defined the public's image of a computer for decades. Kept dust-free behind glass panels, reels of electronic tape ticked like clocks, punches stamped out cards and whizzed them into hoppers, and thousands of tiny lights flashed on and off in no discernable pattern. Operators standing at desk-size consoles in the center of the room fed the SSEC information on cards and watched the results print out.

Pedestrians stopped to gawk and gave the SSEC the nickname "Poppy." The *New Yorker* magazine published a cover story on the SSEC and its public display. The machine influenced Hollywood, most famously as the model for the computer in the 1957 movie *Desk Set,* featuring Katherine Hepburn and Spencer Tracy. Before the SSEC, most people thought of computers as fascinating but incomprehensible laboratory experiments. Watson took the computer out of the lab and sold it to the public. As a public relations strategy, it worked brilliantly and more than made up for the Aiken fiasco.

As Watson publicized computers in the late 1940s, he supposedly made one of the most boneheaded statements in the history of computers. Toward the end of the twentieth century, it became widely circulated that Watson said there would only ever be a market for five computers. Such a statement might have reflected his sentiments around the time of the Mark I, but by 1945, when Watson entertained the possibility of hiring Eckert and Mauchly, he believed that computers would at least be bought by science laboratories around the world. That would add up to many more than five computer sales. No evidence exists that Watson made the remark about five computers. It's not in any of his surviving speeches, nor in any stories about IBM in major magazines and newspapers. He says nothing like it in surviving meeting notes or letters.[27]

There are a number of theories concerning the statement and how it became attached to Watson. One involves a

1953 speech by Tom Watson Jr., who said that in the 1940s, IBM developed a plan for an electronic computer it considered building, and it anticipated that IBM would get five orders for the machine. Instead, IBM got 18 orders, Tom Jr. told the audience. Another theory: In the late 1930s, when Howard Aiken began work on the Mark I, Aiken told colleagues and reporters that only one supercalculator would ever be built. "He could not conceive of there being enough work for more than one such giant," *Popular Science* magazine reported.[28] Aiken revised his forecast while working on the Mark I with IBM, saying 5 or 10 might be built, according to Aiken contemporaries. That prediction by Aiken could have been mistakenly attributed to Watson, or perhaps Watson repeated Aiken's prediction.

It's equally possible that someone in recent decades fabricated Watson's most famous quote, and it spread because it seemed such a potent example of misreading a technological shift.

⌇

The major shift in information technology from electro-mechanical to electronic unfolded at exactly the right time for IBM. Once again, Watson either got lucky or pounced on an opportunity, or both.

As the new technology emerged, Watson "gave" the initiative in electronics to his son. Simultaneously, Tom Jr.—young, impetuous, and daring—latched onto electronics and evangelized it inside IBM. He saw it as a way to make his mark.

Father and son never discussed any agreement concerning electronics. Both simply acted—Tom Jr. ran ahead, and Watson stood aside and let him go. Yet this unspoken and perhaps unconscious mutual agreement meant a great deal to IBM's ability to survive the transition from Watson, who molded IBM in his image and ran the company for more than 30 years, to Tom Watson Jr. Electronics allowed Tom

Jr. to *not* be his father. Because Tom Jr. rode in on a new technological era, no one expected him to be a clone of his father. In fact, most IBMers hoped Tom Jr. would be his own man with his own agenda.

Though they didn't fight about electronics, Tom Jr. felt he had to fight for his position. The faster IBM moved into electronics, the more Watson felt he was being shoved out the door, and the more he battled against that impression. He often used the phrase, "I'm not ready to be cast in bronze yet."

When in the same room, Watson and Tom Jr. were like two open containers of gasoline. Tom's wife, Olive, remembered how she'd anxiously wait for that one little spark that would set off a blast of harsh words, insults, yelling, and dramatic exits.[29] Tom Jr.'s autobiography recounts battle after battle. On many occasions, they fought late at night, when Tom Jr. stayed at the Watson's East 75th Street house instead of commuting back to his home in Greenwich, Connecticut. "He'd get livid," Tom Jr. recalled. "His jowls would shake. All the old family tensions would come boiling out, and I'd let him have it with everything I had." One time, Tom Jr. ran out of his father's office after a fight, burst into another executive's office, threw himself on the man's divan, and sobbed as the befuddled executive watched.[30]

What did they fight about? Often, it was more about power than the issue at hand. Tom Jr. would make a decision, Watson would question it, and the missiles would start flying.

Other times, they clashed about change. One spark concerned business conduct. In meetings, Tom sometimes yelled at other executives, "Shut your mouth," or, "If that's your best argument, keep it to yourself."[31] Watson would reprimand Tom Jr. about the break with IBM's civility. Watson shredded a lot of executives in a lot of meetings, but never so crudely. Tom Jr. wanted to be addressed as Tom, not Mr. Watson. For decades, everyone at IBM called each other Mister or Miss, even when angry. Tom Jr.'s breech of IBM protocol annoyed Watson.

The two battled about changing attitudes toward debt. Watson felt that debt was dangerous. Tom Jr. believed that it was a necessity for IBM's tremendous growth. IBM's business model created a unique problem in boomtimes. IBM leased out all of its machines. If an IBM salesman convinced a new customer to lease an IBM machine, IBM had to spend money up front to make the machine. Instead of selling the finished product and quickly making back the money plus a profit, IBM made money in increments, over time. In a growing economy, IBM factories would run all-out, spending ever more money on raw materials, parts, and labor to make lots of costly machines. IBM would take out loans to pay those costs, knowing it could repay the loans month by month with the rental fees that flowed back in. The more IBM got orders for new machines, the more it had to borrow.

In the postwar boom, IBM salesmen had success like they had never known before. Orders stacked up. The factories fell behind until customers couldn't get some machines for a year or more. By 1949, IBM's debt hit $85 million—the largest corporate debt in the United States.[32] Watson, in his old-fashioned way, resisted borrowing more. "I cannot get that $85 million out of my mind," he said in one meeting. "It's there all the time. It's something which can't be laughed off. Every one of us must think about it all the time."

Tom Jr. told his father that the company had to borrow, or tell the salesmen to stop selling, or cut the number of salesmen that IBM employed. Watson was appalled. Never would he reign in hard-working salesmen. The Watson men argued until Watson relented and allowed IBM to borrow significantly more money.

Watson and Tom Jr. argued ferociously about the engineering lab. Watson, always proud of the lab, believed it was the best in the world. Tom Jr. saw it falling behind in electronics. The SSEC, impressive as it was, ran into a technological dead end. It had been built by Watson's aging compatriots in the lab: Wallace Eckert, Clair Lake, Jim Bryce, and John McPherson. Although those engineers believed in the power of electronics, they had been building punch card machines for Watson for decades. They were mechanical engineers, "monkey-wrench engineers," as Tom Jr. caustically called them. With the SSEC, they tried to marry the mechanical with the electronic, but it meant the electronic components could operate no faster than the mechanical parts—a serious design flaw. Customers wanted the speed and efficiency of electronics and magnetic tape. The press frequently reported on the start of new computer projects. Universities such as the Massachusetts Institute of Technology pumped out a new generation of engineers seeped in electronics—and they were getting hired by other companies, not IBM. The lab had to stop revolving around punch cards, Tom Jr. told his father, and had to attack electronics.

Eventually, Watson gave Tom Jr. approval to appoint a new director of engineering: Wally McDowell, an MIT graduate and electronics specialist. Tom Jr. assigned McDowell to hire hundreds of electronics engineers, transforming the lab from the bottom up.

Tom Jr. challenged his father more as he gained power, and he gained that power by bringing allies into IBM's highest positions. Watson's men had all gone except for faithful old Phillips. Kirk was the last of the real Watson executives—the doggedly loyal men (and, occasionally, women) who worked primarily to please Watson and do his bidding. Tom Jr. latched onto a new generation of talented managers more willing to think independently. Among them were financial wizard Al Williams, who helped Tom Jr. win arguments about debt. Other key allies were vice president of sales Red LaMotte, and punch card division sales manager Vin Learson.

Tom Jr. found a loyalist in Birkenstock, who Kirk had plucked out of a St. Louis sales office and brought to headquarters. When Kirk died, Birkenstock was running Future Demands, a toothless department assigned to research customer desires and advise management of coming trends in the industry. Because he'd been devoted to Kirk, Birkenstock expected Tom Jr. to run him out of headquarters. Instead, Tom Jr. gave Birkenstock a chance, and Birkenstock used his Future Demands findings to hound Tom Jr. to move faster on electronics. In later years, Tom said that no one did more to push IBM into electronics than Birkenstock.[33]

The young allies helped Tom Jr. grab electronics and run with it. As the U.S. military assessed a possible conflict in Korea, it wanted powerful new computers to help it design guided missile trajectories, study atomic energy, and develop jet engines. Birkenstock, Tom Jr., and Cuthbert Hurd, who ran the IBM department that sold systems to science labs, saw a way to get Watson to approve IBM's boldest move yet into electronic computing. Every computer had been a one-of-a-kind, hand-built laboratory product, designed to do specifically what the customer requested. The military asked for three or four different computers, each devoted to a specific task. Birkenstock and Hurd proposed designing a general-purpose computer that could be reproduced over and over in a factory, then programmed to handle almost any task. They knew that if they could do this for the military, they'd wind up with a computer they could sell commercially. Tom Jr. backed the idea and took it to his father, calling the machine the Defense Calculator.[34] "We called it that because we knew Watson would be in favor of anything military," Birkenstock recalled. "But it evolved. It wasn't a plan with Tom to go around the Old Man."[35]

Watson approved the project. In a quick round of customer research, Birkenstock and Hurd found 11 buyers for the machine. Birkenstock pushed to skip the test phase and rush from the final design into production, committing to building 20 Defense Calculators. In what seemed like a blink, IBM leapt from cautious steps toward electronic computing to plunging into radical risks.

The risks paid off. The Defense Calculator turned into the IBM 701, the first successful line of general-purpose computers. All of IBM knew that the initiative came from Tom Jr. and his team.

"I think Dad decided the electronics opportunity should be mine," Watson Jr. recalled. "And the Defense Calculator was the first big risk he let me take as an executive."[36]

⇔

The events around Tom Jr.'s move into power and IBM's jump into electronics proved crucial for everything IBM became after that. It raises intriguing "what if" questions.

What if Tom Watson Jr. never existed?

Kirk's death in 1947 would have left a terrible void between Watson and the next level of executives, who were talented but nowhere near ready to lead IBM. Watson's absolute rule squashed the development of successors. Watson would have reabsorbed almost all of Kirk's job, and felt it necessary to continue running the company as long as possible.

In all likelihood, that would have spelled disaster for IBM. First, fast-growing IBM couldn't have been governed by Watson, with his spider-and-web management style. Decisions would have taken longer and longer. Problems would have gone unsolved. Like Napoléon trying to hold together his empire, Watson would have watched helplessly as IBM frayed at the edges, lost marketing and technological battles, and slowly crumbled inward.

Second, IBM would have come late to electronics—perhaps too late. Watson understood the importance of the technology, but he probably would have remained cautious.

361

Watson's greatest technological gaffe wasn't misjudging vacuum tubes and computing speed—it was misjudging magnetic tape and storage. Even while accepting electronic computing, he held onto punch cards as the best means of data storage, and that would have left IBM behind. "The Old Man's insistence on saving the punch card would've killed them," says Peter Drucker, the management specialist and Watson acquaintance.

If Tom Watson Jr. hadn't been there, the lab would not have aggressively stocked up on electronics experts. Birkenstock would not have found a sympathetic ear. The Defense Calculator would never have been built. Remington Rand's UNIVAC, which arrived in 1951, would have captured the computer market and stolen IBM's customers.

The traits in Watson that were so crucial to building IBM probably would have conspired to weaken or wreck the company. As IBM got big and Watson got old, his management style and seat-of-the-pants business instincts worked against him. As the symbol of IBM, he projected the image of an old man from a previous era trying to compete in the young and fast-moving field of computers. If Tom Jr. hadn't been born, IBM might have withered.

What if Kirk had lived?

When Kirk and Tom Jr. returned from Europe, Watson would have faced one of the most precarious decisions of his career. If he left Kirk in place, Tom Jr. would have quit. Kirk might have been an effective chief executive, but he showed few signs of being a bold, creative leader. He probably would have been too conservative about electronics, although Birkenstock might have convinced Kirk to move more quickly. Kirk's biggest burden would have been his ties to Watson. Kirk carried out Watson's orders and became a dutiful extension of the Old Man. He wouldn't have had the distinct break from Watson that helped Tom Jr. succeed. Employees, customers, and investors would have expected Kirk to be IBM's second Watson, not its first Kirk. IBM under Kirk probably would have endured, but as something less than what it became under Tom Jr.

Watson might have pushed Kirk aside, banishing him to run an IBM outpost or to a powerless job away from head-quarters—perhaps even demanding Kirk's resignation. That decision might have shaken the loyalty of IBM executives, who would wonder about Watson's professed loyalty to good IBM employees. Dispensing with Kirk also might have hurt Tom Jr.'s ability to so quickly gain allies. Key executives might have seen Tom Jr. as conniving and power hungry. In the long run, though, Tom Jr. probably would have gained control, and run the second generation of IBM much as he did.

All in all, the planets lined up perfectly for Watson. By genetic happenstance, Watson sired a son blessed with exceptional leadership talent. Then fate, though cruel to Kirk's family, took Kirk at precisely the right moment for IBM.

The wild card in both "what if" questions is IBM's culture—one of the most powerful corporate cultures ever crafted. By the late 1940s, the culture was a living, regenerating entity, like millions of individual cells, each one containing the DNA that tells it what to do and how to work with the other cells in the organism. Because of the culture, IBM might have survived the kind of leadership void that would instantly kill most other companies. Eventually, the culture might have raised up a leader who could rejuvenate the company.

Actually, that's exactly what the culture did nearly 40 years after Watson's death, when IBM faced a leadership crisis that could have ravaged the company. The IBM board, its largest shareholders, and its next-tier executives together found exactly the right new chief executive, Lou Gerstner, who rallied the company. The messy process seemed at the time to be driven by individual actions and unrelated steps. However, it happened because everyone involved was guided by the values and the strength of Watson's culture.

❦

Late in the evening on Sunday, July 10, 1949, a chauffer-driven Chrysler glided around the circular driveway in front of the Homestead in Endicott, stopping next to the door. Watson, 75 years old, climbed out with more effort than he once did. He paused and looked through the darkness in the direction of the paved parking lot about 100 yards away. His ear picked up the sounds of hammers hitting nails and workmen talking. The annual Hundred Percent Club convention was to open the next morning. Many of the 1,221 members of that year's club had already unpacked and stretched out in their white canvas temporary homes in Tent City, just up the hillside. Under a massive white circus tent covering the entire parking lot, dozens of workmen finished assembling the stage and testing microphones. In the morning all of those Hundred Percenters would tramp down the hillside and gather under the big top to hear the day's speakers and award presentations.

A barrel full of problems had crowded around Watson during his five-hour ride from New York. Management problems, decisions about electronics, the development of Tom Jr., the communist Iron Curtain threatening IBM's international business—any of those topics could have elbowed in and called for Watson's attention. But once at the Homestead, as soon as the local IBM man opened the Chrysler's door for the chief executive, Watson heard the Hundred Percent Club celebration coming together. The Old Man felt lighter, younger, more energetic. He wanted to go see. Come on, let's go over there, he said to his escort.

Watson waded into the activity, dressed in his heavy, somber suit, a bowler resting on his head. He said hello to everyone he met, dispersing kind words about the work being done.

Until he saw the stage. The workers had pretty much finished building it, and now a handful of carpenters touched up details. Watson stared at the stage, finally saying that it seemed a bit small. No, said one of the foremen, it's the right size. Watson said that it didn't look that way—it looked smaller than what he'd requested. He wanted it measured. A tape measure rolled out, and the stage was indeed a few feet too narrow, front to back. Watson turned dark.

"I want it the right size by 8 A.M.," he said.[37]

So many important decisions hung over Watson, and now he had to face this—a temporary stage built a few feet too narrow.

The construction bosses knew better than to tell Watson it couldn't be fixed in time. They called in every carpenter in the area and offered to pay just about anything if they'd come work through the night.

In the morning, Watson returned to the same spot in the clearing, accompanied by Tom Cawley, a popular writer on the staff of the *Binghamton Press*. The carpenters finished the stage to Watson's specifications, and Watson beamed.

"I wish you could have seen these fellows last night," Watson told Cawley, who wrote about the exchange. Watson clenched both wrinkly, age-spotted fists and smacked one down on the other, like a hammer hitting a nail. "They didn't hammer nails like this," he said, banging his fists slowly. "They hit nails like this!" He rapidly hit his fists together. "I wish that people who sit around New York dinner parties and say men don't work hard anymore could see these carpenters."[38]

The carpenters probably didn't feel so glorious. They had probably groused all night about what a nut Watson was. If no one inside IBM could see it, the carpenters could: The stage ordeal smacked of a narcissistic dictator who'd lost touch with the real world. Watson neared the point of turning into a parody of himself.

In fact, Watson was too self-centered to see that the whole concept of his Hundred Percent outdoor revival was getting ridiculous. He forced thousands of employees, many fresh from war, to sweat through their suits on hot, muggy nights while listening to endless empty speeches. The footlights on the stage drew swarms of bugs, which got into the ears, hair, and clothing of the audience—and sometimes into the mouths of speakers at the podium. The regimentation and discomfort irked those who had their fill of army life. After a long week, at last came the grand finale, which featured a wall of fireworks spelling out "THINK."[39]

Think about what? A lot of the younger Hundred Percenters probably thought: This is IBM's idea of a reward?

❧

Glory, glory Hallelujah!
All the nations are our users.
Every business man a booster
Of IBM machines.

—*Songs of the IBM*

12

WORLD
CONQUEST

S WATSON REACHED THE AGE OF 76, THE SKIN JUST under his eyes sagged like pants pockets filled with change. His drooping jowls hung from each side of his jawbone like bunting. His neck had acquired the turkey look, and when he tilted his head down, the excess skin bunched up and overflowed from his collar. Gravity, though, had no effect on the hard bone of Watson's prominent chin. As the rest of his face slumped, his chin stayed defiantly in its place, and the contrast made that chin look pointier and longer than ever.

Watson's appearance, once so dynamic, now made everyone who saw him think: Wow, he's gotten old. Beyond appearances, Watson's energy flagged, and he sometimes fumbled for words. His ulcers pained him constantly. Yet Watson stubbornly refused to give in to old age. He kept a schedule that at times bordered on manic. As an example of his pace during these years, this was what Watson did on January 23, 1950:[1]

~ *9:20 A.M.* Watson arrived at his office.
~ *9:22 to 9:45 A.M.* Watson met with his son Dick about IBM's budding World Trade division—a meeting that ticked off Tom Jr. because he felt that his father and

369

brother were becoming closer, while Tom and his father battled more often.

~ *9:45 to 9:52 A.M.* Watson took a phone call from an IBM executive in Madrid, Spain.

~ *9:52 A.M. to 12:10 P.M.* After the call, Watson fit in seven meetings before lunch. The longest ran 37 minutes; the shortest, 5 minutes.

~ *12:10 to 1:12 P.M.* Watson ate lunch in his office with Phillips and Joseph Keenan, a retired federal judge who from 1946 to 1948 had been chief prosecutor for the International Military Tribunal for the Far East, which prosecuted Japanese war crimes. Watson had hired Keenan to help IBM negotiate with the U.S. Department of Justice, which had launched an antitrust investigation of IBM. The meeting, like Watson's earlier meeting with Dick, annoyed Tom Jr., who thought Keenan was "a wormy guy" doing a terrible job in the negotiations.[2]

~ *1:12 to 4:45 P.M.* During the rest of the afternoon, Watson whisked through 12 meetings in his office, the last one ending at 4:45 P.M. He mostly met with IBM executives, including Al Williams and Ruth Leach. One of the afternoon meetings, though, had more to do with sentiment than business. Watson called in Warren Hoar, the son of Harry Hoar, who had been Watson's chauffer for 22 years before World War II. Out of gratitude for his chauffeur's allegiance, Watson gave Warren a sales job at IBM a couple of years before. In his office that day, Watson handed Warren a $1,000 check to send to his father, who was having financial difficulties.[3]

~ *4:45 to 5:10 P.M.* "Mr. Watson went out," the calendar entry says, though it doesn't say where he went.

~ *5:10 to 5:54 P.M.* Watson came back to meet with Phillips and another executive in the boardroom. The meeting ended at 5:54. After that, Watson went home.

Over the rest of 1950, he similarly crammed meetings into his days at headquarters while fitting in a number of remarkable events and foreign excursions. Here are some examples from the rest of 1950:

~ *January 26.* Watson and Jeannette sailed for South America. Over the next two and one-half months, they visited IBM offices in Brazil, Argentina, Chile, Ecuador, Colombia, and Panama. In Chile, Watson lunched with the country's president, Gonzalez Videla, known for imposing a state of siege as he tried to rid Chile of communists. In Rio de Janeiro, Watson hosted the Latin American Hundred Percent Club Convention, attended by 49 Hundred Percenters. His last stop was a visit to the Panama Canal.[4]

~ *April 11.* Two days after returning from South America, Watson was back in his office at IBM, working through a packed schedule. He paused midday to walk over to the Waldorf-Astoria Hotel's barbershop to get his hair cut.

~ *April 12.* Watson and Jeannette drove to the Roosevelt home in Hyde Park, New York, for a memorial service for Franklin Roosevelt, followed by lunch with Eleanor Roosevelt.

~ *April 19.* Watson got to see Chilean President Videla again, this time in New York. Watson attended a black-tie dinner in honor of Videla. At the dinner, Watson chatted with *Time* magazine founder Henry Luce.

~ *April 28.* Watson, Tom Jr., Dick, and Tom Jr.'s son, Thomas Watson III, boarded a train to Indiana, where they spent time at Shadeland Farms. In September 1939, Watson bought 2,712 acres in Benton County, on the northwest edge of Indiana, for $200,000. He deeded the property to his four children, and set out to accumulate as much land around the farm as possible. He first purchased the farm because he liked to think he was a gentleman farmer, and indeed Shadeland functioned as a working farm under a hired manager while Watson sat in New York reading *Your Farm* and *Successful Farming*—magazines to which he subscribed. By 1950, a year after the Soviet Union tested its first atomic bomb, Watson was finding additional comfort in owning the farm, believing his family could escape there in the event of a nuclear strike against major U.S. cities.[5]

~ *June 1.* Watson sailed for Europe. He stayed three months, and visited nearly every European capital. While in Scotland, Watson picked a site for a new IBM factory.

~ *A week after Watson's return to the United States.* Watson, Jeannette, Tom Jr., and Phillips hosted a dinner for 41 at the Homestead in Endicott, in honor of Margaret Truman.

For the rest of 1950, Watson stayed around New York and New Canaan, and eased up on his schedule. In the remaining years of his life, he could never again keep such a pace. The Old Man truly was becoming an old man.

❧

On Scotland's west coast is the port city of Greenock, known for hundreds of years for its whiskey, and as the birthplace of steam engine inventor James Watt. In July 1950, Greenock's recently appointed Town Clerk, Jack Liddell, took a call from the region's Minister of Parliament, Hector McNeil. Liddell listened as McNeil said he was going to bring to Greenock some American businessmen who were interested in building a factory in or near the town. McNeil wanted Liddell to give the visitors a good lunch in a restaurant called The Tontine. McNeil added one special instruction: "For God's sake, don't offer them anything to drink."[6]

The next week, McNeil arrived in Greenock, accompanied by eight impeccably dressed Americans. McNeil introduced Liddell to Watson, Dick Watson, Phillips, and the five other IBM men. Liddell had never heard of any of them, and barely knew about IBM. The IBM group and Liddell talked a while, then Liddell gave each visitor a packet of information on potential factory sites. The men then broke into small groups and found seats in the waiting cars. Liddell drove the lead car. Squeezed inside were Watson, McNeil, and a local official.

The caravan drove to the first site, an idle 16-acre manufacturing area called the old Cairds Yard. Watson immediately disliked it. They left without getting out of their cars. At the next site—10 acres at Dunrod at Inverkip—the group walked around for 45 minutes before Watson turned it down. The men sifted back into the cars and started out for a third site.

While on a country road along the way, Watson suddenly asked Liddell to slow down. Watson gazed out the window at a hillside and valley warmed by a bright sun. Watson asked Liddell for the name of the farm, and Liddell told him it was called Spango. Watson took in the scene for about two minutes, then gave Liddell the okay to speed up and go on to the next site.

The Spango valley must have reminded Watson of Endicott, which sat in a similarly scenic valley. When the day ended, Watson asked Liddell to show him Spango's location on a map. As Liddell recalled: "He studied the map for a few minutes, spoke to two of his colleagues, and then said, 'We will build our factory at Spango. It will be the valley of opportunity.' "

The choice delighted and baffled Liddell and McNeil. They'd never considered it for a factory. Watson was making the decision despite having no information about the property. He'd only looked at it out a car window for two minutes. The *Greenock Telegraph* interviewed Watson that day, and reported: "Mr. Watson said he could already visualize a great factory erected there."

Watson didn't care to know any more about his chosen site. To him, the deal was done. He left the same day, ordering two of the IBM men to stay behind and negotiate the purchase.

Watson's seat-of-the-pants impulse created difficulties. IBM had to convince Scottish officials to rezone Spango so it could be developed into an industrial site. Spango's roads and its water, sewer, and electrical services were never meant to support a factory. The purchase threw real estate prices in the region into chaos. Competing Scottish authorities fought over whether to force IBM to move elsewhere. IBM had difficulty finding suitable locals to hire—Watson hadn't asked any questions about the area's workforce. After more than two years of uncertainty and toil, IBM finally broke ground.

The episode in Greenock exposed Watson's growing liability to IBM. He made the decision as if he were an entrepreneur racing to build a company, gambling on his intuition because that was the company's best asset. He acted as if he were picking a site for a small outpost that would employ a few dozen people and stay invisible to politicians and power brokers. Watson behaved the only way he knew—the way he ran his company during its years as a limber, fast-growing phenomenon.

By 1950, however, IBM was a worldwide, world-famous corporation—among the biggest in the United States. Watson was choosing a site for a factory that would splash into the region with all the subtlety of a meteor hitting a swimming pool. He was making a decision that would involve millions of dollars and hundreds of jobs. Watson ignored all of that in Greenock. Watson still had the power to do anything he wanted at IBM, and he used it, which was his greatest management sin at this stage of his life. He continued to impose his will on IBM, but it was time for the company to be run in the more professional, systematic way of a modern corporation.

Eventually, the younger managers made it work out. On July 26, 1954, Dick Watson hosted the dedication of the factory, taking a tour of the bright, clean factory while a Scotsman in a kilt blew the bagpipes nearby. The two-story factory building stood in a dip between two vibrantly green hills, a short drive from the port at Greenock and the old city built around the waterfront. Dick Watson brought a message from his 80-year-old father: "Mrs. Watson joins me in extending our warm regards and kindest wishes to every member of the IBM family in the United Kingdom, our good neighbors whose friendship we deeply appreciate." The Spango factory began turning out IBM typewriters, card punches, card readers, and high-speed sorters. More than 50 years later, IBM began the process of pulling out of the site. In the interim, the factory had tripled in size and the country lane, where Watson first saw the valley for two minutes, had been paved into a four-lane highway.

On stationery from his IBM office in New York, Dick Watson, the youngest of Watson's four children, handwrote a letter to his parents:

"To have a father and mother as devoted, generous, kind, and understanding as you two is a blessing that is rare and almost hard to believe," he wrote. Dick then explained his reason for gushing: "Your generous gifts, including your help in getting our home, the life insurance, the furniture (sofas, chairs, rugs), the paintings (particularly the Corot, as well as the Innes), are completely overwhelming to us. I'm sure there isn't a house in New Canaan or its surroundings that has such beautiful contents."[7]

Dick Watson posed a problem for his father and for IBM: He never grew up. He was the baby of the family, five years younger than Tom Jr., and had always been treated that way. Watson and especially Jeannette coddled him, as they did when they furnished the house Dick and his wife bought in New Canaan. It's not as if Dick was just starting out in life—he was 33 years old and an officer of IBM. He moved into the same small Connecticut town where his parents spent half the year. Tom Jr. lived 10 miles down the road in Greenwich.

Compared with Tom Jr.'s corrosiveness, Dick at his best possessed far more charm, grace, and humor. But while Tom inherited the Watson headstrong gene, though, Dick was pliable and weak. Tom Jr. built self-confidence by defying his father. Dick spent his life trying to please his father, and often failed, leaving Dick's confidence in a constant state of red alert. Dick fell apart under duress, either sinking into quiet despondency or, at the other extreme, exploding into rages so wild, they made Watson and Tom Jr. seem stoic by comparison. Writing in the mid-1960s, with access to people who had worked for Dick, author William Rodgers recounted the observations of one group of secretaries and executives who had recently endured a Dick Watson tirade:

" 'The guy just goes off his rocker,' one of those present said. There were other reports of hurled objects and uncontrolled rage. Yet within a day or so, meeting one of the men he had castigated, Dick would throw an arm around him and conduct himself as a warmhearted friend. It was [Old Man] Watson all over again, with the exception that Dick's technique and style did not always restore a man's lost dignity."[8]

Ironically, considering Watson's aversion to liquor, Dick often relied on alcohol to hide from his unhappiness. Decades later, Tom Jr.'s wife Olive Watson recalled Dick with a sense of tragedy. "He was not a strong person. He was [Jeannette's] favorite. He was a lot of fun, but he couldn't control his drinking. He was a naughty boy. [His father] was always disappointed in him. Stories would reach him about Dick drinking too much."

As a conclusion about Dick's life, Olive Watson added: "It's just sad. Very sad."[9]

Watson apparently had no confidence that Dick could fight his way up through IBM to become Tom Jr.'s equal. Watson wanted to leave IBM to both his sons. He wanted Dick to help Tom Jr. run IBM, and become the next chief executive when Tom Jr. retired. By the late 1940s, Watson could see that Tom Jr. had the talent and strength to fulfill the first part of the dream. Dick, however, would have to be helped.

In an ingenious maneuver, Watson formed IBM World Trade for Dick. Instead of making Dick climb IBM's ladder, Watson made a new ladder, and put Dick at the top of it. Watson carved IBM's international business off of the domestic business and put it into a semiautonomous subsidiary, which he called IBM World Trade. It gave Dick a shot at building a reputation as IBM's internationalist. To the executives at the top of IBM, including Tom Jr., World Trade's primary purpose was transparent.

Creating World Trade made some business sense. IBM had conducted business internationally since Watson took charge, and both domestic and international operations had always reported to Watson. After the war, Europe and Japan rebuilt and the world economy roared to life, amplifying global demand for punch card machines. IBM, in its desperation to more than double its sales so it wouldn't have to shrink back to prewar size, fanned out to capture that demand. In the late 1940s, IBM's international business grew faster than the domestic business. Such international growth came with unique problems, such as dealing with dozens of languages, currencies, customs, and trade barriers. A specialized organization might better handle globalization.

Watson organized World Trade in 1949 and put Dick in charge, routing Dick around his brother by having World Trade report directly to Watson.

Watson ran smack into the law of unintended consequences. By trying to solve the Dick problem, he created a new family problem. Tom Jr. resented Watson's efforts to help Dick. When Watson first told Tom Jr. of the World Trade plan, Tom countered the rationale, growling, "If you do this, you'll live to regret it."[10] A week later, Watson, Tom Jr., and Dick met in Watson's office to discuss the plan. Tom Jr. again argued against it. Watson stood and yelled, "What are you trying to do, prevent your brother from having an opportunity?"[11] Tom Jr. felt it was a cheap shot, delivered in Dick's presence. The meeting opened a fault line between the brothers. Watson suspected Tom Jr. wanted to undermine Dick, and in response, Watson increasingly spent time working with Dick to ensure World Trade's success.

Whenever the three of them met, Tom Jr. and Watson argued. Dick, intimidated by both, usually kept to himself. Once, when all three were at New York's Metropolitan Club discussing World Trade, Tom Jr. ranted and cursed at Watson and Dick, drawing the attention of onlookers. Years later, Tom Jr. found a note that his father wrote but never sent following the incident. In effect, the note, addressed to Tom Jr., said: If you can't work with Dick, you're fired.[12]

In 1950, Watson plunged into establishing World Trade—it's why he subjected himself to two lengthy trips abroad at age 76. Dick accompanied Watson to Europe, but not to South America. As he hopscotched around two continents, Watson set up two key mechanisms for World Trade. The first had already been put in motion: selling the banged-up machines returned by the U.S. military to European companies reemerging after the war. The second mechanism: Every overseas office would be managed and staffed by natives. A Frenchman would run IBM France and employ other Frenchmen, who in turn would sell to French managers of French companies. The combination of local management and the stability of an American corporate giant proved irresistible in the war's aftermath. IBM filled World Trade with some of the most talented businessmen in Europe.

World Trade took off, growing so quickly that some observers believed World Trade would come to eclipse the domestic business. By 1953, World Trade employed 15,000 people, making it about half the size of IBM in the United States. The success of World Trade established Dick at IBM, and Watson must have felt triumphant. One way or another, he would leave IBM to both his sons. Either IBM would stay in two pieces, with Dick running the international half and Tom Jr. running the domestic half, or the two Watson boys would run all of IBM together.

Watson, however, hadn't changed Dick—the Old Man only manufactured Dick's prominence. Certainly, Dick was smart and capable, and contributed to World Trade's success, but Watson stood behind the scenes, pulling levers. Dick proved time and again in his IBM career that he had difficulty managing and motivating people. His temper alienated employees, and he would blame others instead of taking charge. He couldn't stand up to either Watson or Tom Jr. Birkenstock recalled a disagreement between Tom Jr. and Dick about whether a machine invented by IBM United Kingdom should be developed by World Trade or domestic. "Tom goes into his brother's office and takes me along," said Birkenstock, who at the time oversaw IBM's patents. "He and his brother have an argument. Tom says, 'This is not right. It's Birkenstock's responsibility. I want you to lay off.' Dick blamed *me*." Dick found it easier to put the onus on Birkenstock instead of on Tom Jr.

Peter Drucker knew both Watson brothers. "If Dick hadn't been the son of the boss, he would've been a division general manager, at best," he said.

⟳

Watson was addicted to flattery. He lived with a flattery habit for decades. Nichol built a career by staying at

Watson's elbow with a ready supply of adulation. The IBM culture—in effect, the Watson cult—revolved around Watson worship that was both flagrant (Watson's photo hanging in every office and factory) and subtle (managers mimicking his style of dress). Watson wasn't selfish about praise. He generously passed it around, preferring that his friends and colleagues imbibe along with him. However, nobody could seek out and drink in more adulation than Watson, and do it without a hint of embarrassment.

Watson drew strength from the flattery. It helped him feel sure of himself when he took bold risks. It gave him a sense of self-importance, which was a great help in the early days, when he acted as if he and IBM were important when, in fact, they weren't.

The habit was also a great weakness. It sucked critical thinking out of the company and allowed Watson to think he was always right. When Tom Jr. rejoined the company in the late 1940s, he felt his father's desire for exaltation— and IBM's ability to deliver it—had reached a point of absurdity.

The older Watson got, the more he gave into the addiction. He encouraged a series of 75th-birthday tribute luncheons in 1949, and laudatory dinners celebrating the 40th anniversary of C-T-R (dating to the merger of the three companies) in 1951. At each event, a series of respected speakers would congratulate Watson not only for his business acumen, but for his treatment of employees, his model citizenship, and his quest for world peace. At the Hundred Percent Club conventions, Watson spent days among hundreds of people who constantly thanked, complimented, and all but bowed to him.

Watson became particularly susceptible to three kinds of flattery:

1. Who's Who *entries*. *Who's Who* was a canon of supposedly important people, listing each person's

accomplishments, titles, awards, honorary chairman-
ships, trusteeships, and lay memberships of societies
and foundations. In the early 1950s, Watson was
notable for having the longest *Who's Who* entry, claiming connections to hundreds of organizations. For the
vast majority of them, Watson did nothing except
donate some money, lend his prestige, or speak at a
dinner. He was a member or patron of, for example, the
Peruvian American Association, the Japan Society, Jewish War Veterans of the United States, Camp Fire Girls,
and the Honorable Order of Kentucky Colonels, even
though Watson definitely was not Peruvian, Japanese,
Jewish, a war veteran, a Camp Fire Girl, or a Kentucky
colonel. In 1950, Watson claimed to be a member of
both the Republican party and the Democratic National Committee. To be fair, Watson also served as a
high-ranking member or leader of some organizations
that mattered to him, including the Boy Scouts of
America, the Metropolitan Museum of Art, and the
Metropolitan Opera Association. Over the course of his
career, Watson was made a member of organizations
promoting chess, golf, light opera, guns, sailing, acting,
polo, and beagle breeding—even though Watson spent
little time on leisure activities. Perhaps the most ironic
listing was Watson's honorable membership on the
Council for Moderation. It was one of his shortest
tenures: He lasted one year, 1935.

2. *Honorary degrees.*   Watson's formal education stopped
at his graduation from the Elmira School of Commerce.
Recognition from important universities seemed to help
Watson feel less inferior about his education. Watson
collected 31 honorary degrees from universities including Rutgers, LaFayette College, Colgate, Syracuse,
Georgetown, and Grenoble University in Paris.[13]

3. *Medals.*   Watson loved pomp and ceremony. He loved
the feeling of importance that came from an audience

with a national leader. Most of all, he imagined himself an international statesman—the Franklin D. Roosevelt of business, the purveyor of "World peace through world trade," the creator of a great global corporation. A medal and its award ceremony packaged up all of those Watson loves. He sought them out and raked them in. The medals all had the usual regal names: Grand Officer of the Ducal Order of the Crown of Oak from Luxembourg; Officer of National Order of Merit, Ecuador; Grand Officer Bernardo O'Higgins Order of Merit, Chile; Chevelier of the Legion of Honor, France. Of course, this predilection played a role in Watson's acceptance of the Nazi medal. By the time he was done, Watson collected more than 40 decorations from 29 countries.

Watson led a public life, and he and IBM never shied from crowing about his awards, degrees, and decorations. As they piled up, Watson appeared to be a vain old man clawing for recognition. In 1952, hard-bitten national columnist Westbrook Pegler skewered Watson's vanity. "I wish I had a movie, with sound, of Mr. Watson pawing over his souvenirs at his home in New Canaan and telling some poor, trapped, and helpless guest the details of each badge, garter, and button," Pegler wrote. "[A friend] encountered old Tom Watson one night at a gridiron or some such hassle and, knowing his weakness, asked: 'Tom, what about that Grand Cross of the Order of Minnie the Moocher of Madagascar? That come through yet?' 'No, not yet,' Mr. Watson replied. 'But they're working on it.' "[14]

In 1951, the top level of IBM looked like this:

~ *Watson—chairman and chief executive*. He spent most of his time on the domestic punch card machine business and on World Trade, while maintaining responsibility for IBM's overall direction and strategy.

~ *George Phillips—president.* The aging Phillips had little direct responsibility. Watson used Phillips as an emissary and assistant, and Phillips helped watch and temper Tom Jr., who officially reported to Phillips.

~ *Tom Watson Jr.—executive vice president.* He led the company's embryonic electronics effort and ran much of IBM's day-to-day business. In more modern times, his title would have been chief operating officer.

~ *Al Williams—vice president and treasurer.* He was the equivalent of today's chief financial officer. Williams had also become Tom Jr.'s de facto right-hand man, and the two often worked as a team to run IBM's operations. Young and cracker-jack smart, Williams could quickly absorb a situation and make decisions. He seemed to be one of the few people at IBM who truly won Tom Jr.'s respect.

~ *Red LaMotte—vice president.* LaMotte was the equivalent of a vice president of marketing with the additional job of running IBM's vast sales organization. He often worked as a third member of the Tom Jr.–Al Williams team, but he was quite a bit older. LaMotte had been on hand when Watson broke ground on the engineering lab in 1933.

~ *Dick Watson—vice president,* in charge of World Trade, reporting directly to Watson.

Watson needed and wanted Phillips by his side. Phillips was the last of the old crew—the only person left who would remember what Watson remembered about the early days. Watson trusted Phillips to take care of Tom Jr. when Tom was a boy, and he could trust him to do the same once Tom Jr. worked in an executive office.

Tom Jr. liked Phillips but did not respect him. To Tom Jr., Phillips was his father's spy and yes-man. In the spring of 1951, Watson, working in his office, looked up to see Tom Jr. angrily stomping into the room, barking about Phillips reversing decisions. After Phillips and Tom Jr. agreed on something, Tom alleged, Phillips would talk to Watson and do as Watson wished.[15]

Watson must have expected that Tom Jr. would grow tired of answering to Phillips. Instead of clicking into fighting mode and blasting back at his son, Watson calmly asked Tom Jr. to wait in a small room next to the office. Watson called in Phillips and talked with him about a change in the arrangement at the top of IBM. Phillips, of course, agreed, and they both asked Tom to rejoin them.[16]

"We've decided to make you president," Watson said.

Tom Jr. stood speechless.

"What's the matter? Don't you want the job?" Watson said, obviously enjoying his son's disorientation.

Tom Jr. had imagined that his father would make him president with a more satisfying formal gesture ceremoniously telling him about the promotion. This improvised promotion left Tom feeling hurt and disappointed. Tom Jr. later told *Time* magazine, "I was completely disarmed."[17] Watson had a knack for lifting up and undermining his son at the same time.

Arrangements for the title changes took months. On January 15, 1952, Watson announced that Tom Jr. was named IBM's president. Phillips would take the new title of vice chairman. The announcement didn't say so, but Phillips would continue to function as he always had, by Watson's side. Watson retained his titles of chief executive and chairman.

The division of power at IBM was murkier than ever. In many ways, Tom Jr. and his team led IBM, yet Watson retained ultimate power. The new and the old overlapped, producing a fog that would slow decisions and confuse managers.

The day after making the announcement, Watson left for an eight-week vacation in Del Ray Beach, Florida. Six days after Watson named Tom Jr. president, the U.S. Department of Justice filed a multicount, wide-ranging antitrust suit against IBM. Clearly, if IBM were to fight the suit and lose, Watson would go down in history as an unrepentant monopolist, and the government could break up the company. Watson's worst nightmare from four decades before had come back to haunt his last years, and Watson was mad.

⪥

Watson knew lots of lawyers—some were old friends, some were on IBM's board, others did legal work for IBM. Those lawyers were all members of big law firms in major cities. They were the kind of lawyers who wore tailored suits and worked in spacious, posh offices decorated with oriental carpets and mahogany furniture.

Lawyers at the Justice Department in Washington, D.C., led a different life. They worked for the government and got unimpressive paychecks. They bought clothes off the rack and squeezed into undersized, low-budget offices where bare floors and metal desks amplified the sharp sounds of typewriters clicking and papers rustling. Harsh lighting made the offices feel as synthetic and unwelcoming as a hospital operating room. H. Graham Morison, the Truman administration's assistant attorney general and head of the Justice Department's antitrust division, worked in one such office. And that's where he was in 1952 when the men from IBM came to call.

Morison stood to greet his guests, shaking hands with Watson and Tom Jr. and inviting them to sit down. But Morison did not welcome them, did not like them, and did not like their tactics. Morison recalled: "[Watson] had a hundred and sixteen people—everybody I had known since childhood—call me at night and say, 'Don't bring this suit against IBM. Mr. Watson is an aged man. It will kill him and so forth.' "[18] Morison was annoyed.

"Of course, he had been a robber baron," Morison said. "He had been violating the antitrust laws and getting away with it for years, and I was as gentle with him as possible because of his age."

Tom Jr. had carried in a set of diagrams. One of them showed a pyramid defining IBM's market as the entire range of business calculations. The bottom third was labeled "Pencils and Ledger-Books"; the middle third was "Adding Machines, Posting Machines, Bank-Teller Machines"; and at the top was "Punch-Card Machines." By defining the market so broadly, IBM could claim that it only did about 16 percent of the accounting work in the United States.[19]

"They had a presentation they put up on my desk," Morison said, "all prepared by, I guess, a public relations outfit, the words hand-painted. They'd turn a page, we've done this, and done that, and this and that, and I kept my mouth shut and listened to it all very politely."

In his Tennessee lilt, Morison then sternly laid out some of the Justice Department's complaints. By making machines that only worked using IBM punch cards, IBM prevented others from making and selling cards, and forced customers to buy cards from IBM. By controlling or buying patents, IBM killed off potential competitors. By leasing machines, IBM blocked the development of a secondary market in used IBM machines, parts, and service.

"On the facts, IBM really deserves a criminal suit," Morison said to Watson, using words—*criminal suit*—that would have hit Watson like shrapnel. They flung Watson back to his criminal antitrust conviction at NCR. Instead, though, Morison had filed a civil suit, which could not result in jail sentences.

"Oh, this can't happen," Watson said, as Morison recalled.

"I will not dismiss the suit or accept a consent decree as offered by your lawyers," Morison replied.

In Morison's words, here's what Watson did next: "He wept and finally went out."

It seems implausible. Did Watson actually cry in Morison's office? Watson was 78 years old and as tough and cagey as anyone in business. His eyes sometimes welled up on sentimental occasions, like when a few thousand people would turn out in Endicott to pay him tribute. Those tears, however, were endearing. Crying in the assistant attorney general's office would have been embarrassing.

Then again, Watson had reason to break down. He'd built IBM as a way to rise above his past—his childhood poverty, his break with Patterson, and above all, his criminal conviction for antitrust violations in the early 1900s at NCR. The Presbyterian morality seared into IBM's culture was Watson's way to bury the damage to his reputation with the certainty of a dozen coats of paint over a dirty wall.

As Watson saw it, the government's suit threatened to undo his 38 years of work. If that thought washed over Watson as Morison insisted the government would not drop the suit, Watson might indeed have wept.

~

Tom Jr. thought the antitrust suit might be just what IBM needed.

From the moment Watson took charge of C-T-R in 1914, two sides of Watson tugged at each other. Picture them as two figures, one perched on each shoulder, like the proverbial angel and devil. The first was Watson the Businessman. At NCR, that side of Watson learned about the advantages of a near-monopoly. It was the kind of business he understood and knew how to manage. If the opportunity presented itself, Watson would naturally drift toward monopolist tactics. On the other shoulder, though, was Watson the Chastened. That part of Watson learned from the antitrust conviction that America doesn't like monopolists, and learned that ignoring such a reality can lead to ruin. As Watson's angel and devil whispered in his ears, he continually tried to create a monopoly while at the same time working to preempt any appearance of trying to create a monopoly.

That mode of operation began within months of Watson taking the job at C-T-R in 1914. Although tabulating machines could barely be called an industry at the time, Watson recognized that C-T-R's Tabulating Machine Company division had virtually no competition. Only the Powers Accounting Machine Company maintained a toehold in the business, and C-T-R's broad patent coverage prevented Powers from making better tabulating machines that could effectively compete against C-T-R's machines. If nothing changed, Powers would wither and die. So Watson paid a visit to Powers and offered to license C-T-R patents for a fee of 25 percent of revenue from Powers's equipment sales. Powers had no choice but to accept. After that, in meetings and lectures throughout his career, Watson described the gesture as magnanimous, saying it proved that he welcomed competition. Powers, however, probably didn't think Watson was so generous. The deal automatically saddled Powers with 25 percent higher costs per machine than C-T-R. To add insult to the burden, Powers would pay those fees back to C-T-R—*plus,* Watson excluded some key tabulating machine patents from the deal, leaving Powers with a technical as well as financial handicap. It was as if Watson agreed to let an opponent stay in a footrace with him, as long as the opponent ran backward and carried an anvil.

Despite the deal, or maybe because of it, Powers nearly collapsed in 1922. By then, tabulating machines were becoming a good-sized industry, and a monopoly might have drawn scrutiny by government antitrust lawyers. Sensing the need to keep Powers alive, Watson cut Powers's licensing fee in half—so Powers had to run with only half an anvil. Powers stayed alive long enough to be bought by Remington Rand in 1927, which is how James Rand came to be Watson's principal opponent.[20]

During the 1930s, as IBM flourished while competitors around the world clung to life, Watson accumulated patents as a way to build higher walls around his 90 percent market share. With IBM lab chief Jim Bryce's help, Watson did that in three ways: (1) Internally, he built IBM's research lab in Endicott and increased spending on research and product development. (2) Then he and Bryce hired key engineers away from struggling competitors. (3) Finally, IBM bought existing patents, wringing bargains out of companies that needed the money to survive the Depression. Watson always felt his patent strategy was merely good business sense, never seeing it as a monopolistic tactic. In the 1952 antitrust suit, the government opposed IBM's patent grab. As Morison said to Watson during their meeting: "The record shows and you cannot deny, I use a bad word to shorten a long discussion—you *stole* the French Bull patent."[21] IBM cut a favorable deal for patents held by France's Machines Bull, which became yet another information machine company that IBM crushed in the marketplace.

Watson's monopolist devil stepped over the line in 1931, when IBM and Remington Rand entered into an agreement to lease and not sell tabulating machines and sorters. In 1932, the government filed a complaint against both companies. In 1934, before the case came to trial, the companies canceled the agreement.

World War II put antitrust concerns aside for a while, but after the war the Justice Department started investigating IBM's practices. Around 1950, as the investigation rolled along and Justice moved toward filing a meaty antitrust suit, Watson grew angry, believing that he had done more than necessary to stay within the law. He ranted: "The patents on our ordinary machines expired so many years ago that anyone could have gone ahead and built up a line."[22] He placed full-page newspaper ads designed to defend IBM's position.

One of Watson's oldest friends—lawyer John Hayward—tried to convince Watson that "no matter how clean may be the record of a company's conduct," current interpretations of the Sherman Antitrust Act concluded that the company could be sued for antitrust simply because the company possessed monopoly power. In other words, Hayward argued to Watson, an antitrust action wouldn't necessarily be a condemnation of Watson. In fact, it might be considered a sign of Watson's enormous success. Watson never accepted the argument.[23]

Tom Jr. tried to persuade his father to settle with the Justice Department. Tom Jr. saw that all of the government's charges concerned IBM's past and current products—tabulating machines and punch cards. The government wanted IBM to loosen its hold on that market, not on the broader information processing market, and not on the computer market, which at the time had a flowering of competitors. A settlement would call for IBM to license more of its punch card machine patents to other companies, sell machines as well as lease them, and stop requiring customers to buy cards solely from IBM. Though such changes would have been difficult for IBM to implement, Tom Jr. believed that they would have been mild compared with the dangers of fighting a drawn-out antitrust suit in court.[24]

Tom Jr. had other reasons—unspoken in front of his father—to settle and move on. In 1952, nearly all of IBM's revenue came from leasing punch card systems and selling punch cards. Despite the excitement about electronics, IBM remained an electromechanical company. As long as the old machines remained such a lucrative, protected business, IBM would be reluctant to leap into the next age, where competition and uncertainty lurked. If IBM could sign a consent decree that didn't cripple the company but did make the punch card machine business look vulnerable, Tom Jr. could more easily move IBM forward.

During the government's investigation, IBM hired lawyer Robert Patterson (no relation to Watson's old NCR boss) to help the company maneuver through Washington. Patterson was a former secretary of war who had moved into private practice. In a last desperate measure, Tom Jr. asked Patterson to try to convince Watson to settle. As much as Watson respected Patterson, he again refused. To Watson, settling meant admitting guilt. Watson never admitted guilt or signed a decree in the NCR case, and he wouldn't now. Watson was absolutely certain that he was an honorable man, and he could not bear the thought of even one person clucking, "See? I knew Watson was always a shady character. He's guilty now, and I bet he was always guilty, all the way back to that NCR business." Nothing would persuade Watson to change his mind.

On Tuesday, January 22, 1952, a front-page story in the *New York Times* was headlined: "Trust Suit Charges IBM Monopolizes Tabulating Field." The Justice Department had filed its civil antitrust suit, charging IBM with unlawful restraint of trade and monopolizing the tabulating machine industry. One of the charges accused IBM of buying patent rights in other fields of office technology—*not* tabulating machines—so IBM could retaliate against a company that threatened to enter the tabulating machine industry.[25] Newspapers quoted Watson saying the charges were unfounded and that he intended to fight the suit in court.

The following day, Robert Patterson was on a commercial flight from Buffalo, New York, to the airport in Newark, New Jersey, when the plane crashed into an Elizabeth, New Jersey, neighborhood. Patterson and 23 others were killed. The news shook Watson, who was superstitious enough to believe the event was an omen.

Two weeks later, Watson addressed IBM employees on the front page of the company's in-house newspaper,

391

Business Machines. "By now you have learned that the Department of Justice has filed a complaint against IBM alleging that it is a monopoly," the message began. "IBM has adhered to the highest standard of conformance to all laws and business ethics. We have never employed any measures to eliminate or restrain competition. We reject as unfounded any construction of our business conduct as in violation of the anti-trust laws, and intend to vindicate our position in the courts."[26]

The message was signed by Watson, but not by Tom Jr.

The November 1952 election of Dwight Eisenhower as president added to the illusion that Watson always seemed to be in the middle of everything.

President Roosevelt's death in 1945 had stranded Watson with no great man in his life—no man, that is, who Watson could look up to. Watson couldn't muster admiration for Harry Truman. The president was too shrill and unrefined for Watson, and Truman in his first term attained his office through an act of God, Roosevelt's death, not because he'd earned it by winning an election. Watson remained cordial to the Truman administration, but kept his distance.

Soon after World War II, Watson met Eisenhower, and they immediately liked each other. Watson believed that Eisenhower, as the commander of Allied forces in the war, earned every ounce of the respect and love showered on him. No one alive had done more for the United States and democracy. Further, almost everyone assumed that Eisenhower would achieve further greatness in private or public life, and probably would one day become president. For all of those reasons, Watson wanted to be in Eisenhower's orbit—or pull Eisenhower into his.

Eisenhower was predisposed to like Watson. The general particularly admired businessmen who started with nothing and made a fortune building large, successful companies. To him, such a person perfectly represented the American way of life, which Eisenhower valued dearly and had given his all to protect.

Soon after they first met, Watson asked Eisenhower to speak at the Metropolitan Museum of Art. Eisenhower gave the speech on April 2, 1946. By that time, Watson had become enmeshed in the search for a new president of Columbia University. Watson served on the Columbia Board of Trustees. The school's long-time president, Nicholas Murray Butler, was 85 years old and infirm. By force of personality, Watson dominated the Board of Trustees, and decided Columbia should find a superpresident to succeed Butler. Watson wanted someone who would lift Columbia's profile and lure the money and talent to challenge Harvard as the nation's elite university. Perhaps a dash of a lingering grudge over Aiken spiced up Watson's action.

As he often did, Watson shot for the top. Who would be the most super of any possible superpresident for Columbia? The answer, in the postwar euphoria, was Eisenhower.

The odds of getting Eisenhower to take the job as Columbia's president were about the same as the odds of getting Yankees star Joe DiMaggio, who retired in 1951, to coach a high school baseball team. Eisenhower could have done anything after the war. Companies offered him CEO jobs and seats on boards. Publishers asked him to write a book. Both political parties tried to convince him to run for president.

As usual, Watson ignored the odds and charged ahead with a full tank of optimism. After the speech at the Metropolitan Museum, Watson asked Eisenhower to be Columbia's president. Eisenhower, baffled about why Watson thought he could run a university, said no, and added that military obligations prevented him from taking another position for about two more years.

Watson worked at the relationship. Four days after the Met speech, Watson invited Eisenhower to a cocktail party held by old friends of the late Theodore Roosevelt.[27] About a year later, Watson again asked Eisenhower to consider the presidency of Columbia. Watson laid out reasons Eisenhower should take the job. By strengthening a major U.S. university, Watson said, Eisenhower would help produce the men and women who would best continue the American success story. Also, by taking such an apolitical job, Eisenhower could stop the speculation about which party he'd join and whether he'd run for president in 1948. Eisenhower fervently did not want to enter the presidential race at that time. Finally, Watson said Eisenhower would get a high salary but have few duties.

Eisenhower again said no.

A month later, Watson learned that Eisenhower was to speak at West Point, about 40 miles up the Hudson River from Manhattan. Watson drove there and asked again, this time saying he needed an answer in three weeks. During that period, Eisenhower conferred with Truman and with his brother Milton Eisenhower, who was president of Pennsylvania State University. Truman probably stifled a smile as he gave Eisenhower his blessing, knowing the job would remove Eisenhower from the presidential race that Truman hoped to win. Milton, familiar with the job of university president, recommended taking the position. Finally, Eisenhower said yes.[28]

Watson lived up to his reputation as an extraordinary salesman, selling Eisenhower on an unlikely first move following the Allied victory. On June 27, 1947, Watson wrote Eisenhower saying that the trustees unanimously accepted Eisenhower as Columbia's president. Eisenhower would begin the job once he was released from military duties a year later, in June 1948. In the interim, Watson sought to strengthen his link with Eisenhower. "When it is possible for you to do so, Jeannette and I would like to have you and

Mrs. Eisenhower come to our country home in New Canaan, Connecticut, over a weekend, when we can have some people who are interested in you and Columbia University meet you," Watson wrote. Because Eisenhower would need to find a place to live, Watson offered to play real estate agent: "We also will have some houses for you to look over at that time."[29]

Soon after, the political intrigue began. Newspaper columnists wrote that Watson was preparing Eisenhower to run for president—and the press and politicians speculated that the Columbia position was a ruse to give Eisenhower some breathing room before the campaign began.

Business leaders have often aided presidential candidates, but rarely has a single business personality been depicted as such a kingmaker. In the 1890s, Ohio business baron Marcus Alonzo Hanna essentially created William McKinley and thrust him into the presidency. Hanna owned a bank, a newspaper, an opera house, and was a dealer in iron mines and shipping. He groomed McKinley and led the campaign of 1896 as chairman of the Republican National Committee. In the twentieth century, individual businessmen played lesser roles, generally helping presidential candidates by donating money and using their positions to influence others. That political columnists and pundits paid such attention to Watson attests to Watson's extraordinary profile among business leaders. Mixed with the great expectations placed on Eisenhower, a Watson-Eisenhower connection fed a wildfire of intrigue. Perhaps the same level of gossip would be generated today if Microsoft Chairman Bill Gates suddenly befriended war hero Colin Powell just before a presidential election.

Watson issued at least two statements to the press denying the rumors and declaring that he was not backing Eisenhower for the presidency. Through 1947, Watson and Eisenhower grew closer, inviting each other to dinners and overnight stays. They addressed their letters to "Tom" and "Ike." In November 1947, well-known columnist Drew Pearson wrote that Watson was hosting "a very significant private dinner at the Waldorf-Astoria tomorrow night to launch Eisenhower for president." The story was untrue. The next day, Eisenhower wrote Watson: "It was odd that after your exhortations to me on Saturday to 'have nothing to do with this political business,' you should be accused by a Sunday night commentator of holding a dinner somewhere to promote my active participation in politics, and I hope you can take all this stuff with a grin."[30]

Eisenhower, who still had not joined a political party, tried to stop the rumors by announcing in January 1948, that he would not accept any nomination for president. Relieved, Watson told Eisenhower that the general would now "be able to take a vacation, and wherever you go it will be without any possible misunderstanding of where you stand politically."[31]

It didn't work. The rumors continued. Political activists pushed on with "Draft Eisenhower" campaigns. Letters begging Watson to convince the general to run piled up on Watson's desk at IBM. In June, newspapers reported that Watson and Eisenhower met with prominent Republicans at the home of CBS President William Paley. Paley denied it.

Columbia installed Eisenhower as its president in October 1948, slightly later than anticipated. In November, Americans elected Truman as their president, while Eisenhower stayed out of the process.

Two years later, Eisenhower left Columbia when Truman appointed him Supreme Allied Commander of the newly formed North Atlantic Treaty Organization, formed primarily to stop the spread of Soviet communism. Eisenhower stepped back into public duty.

A warm friendship between Watson and Eisenhower continued into 1952, when Eisenhower decided to seek the nomination for president as a Republican. Watson was sucked into politics and pestered by the media for inside information about Eisenhower, but Watson tried to remove himself from the central swirl of the campaign. As a Democrat, a social liberal, and a fervent New Deal supporter, Watson would not publicly support a Republican candidate. Yet the Republican candidate was a personal friend and colleague, and Watson felt he'd played an important role in Eisenhower's transition from military general to civilian leader. Watson was stuck in the middle.

"As you know, I have been taking a rest out in New Canaan," Watson wrote Eisenhower on July 17, 1952, "which gave me an opportunity to follow the [Republican political] convention from beginning to end on television. I had a set put in my bedroom so that I could get the reports night and day." Watson heartily congratulated Eisenhower, but didn't explicitly say he would support or vote for him.[32]

Four months later, Watson must have watched the presidential election returns with similar fascination. It's hard to believe Watson would not have stared at the screen, pulling for his friend. Eisenhower won. Watson attended the inauguration as Eisenhower's guest. Once in office, Eisenhower gave Watson a private address for personal correspondence and invited Watson and Jeannette to a formal White House dinner. Eisenhower, though, never offered to end the government's antitrust suit against IBM, and Watson apparently never asked.

⋘

On election day in 1952, at almost the same instant Watson learned that Eisenhower would go to the White House, IBM suffered the most humiliating public relations defeat of Watson's career. Watching the returns on television that night in 1952, Watson witnessed Remington Rand's Universal Automatic Computer (UNIVAC) computer snatching from IBM the perceived leadership of the computer industry.

IBM had always raced against itself. Competitors didn't drive the company to change and grow, because for almost all of its history, IBM essentially had no competitors. From the mid-1920s to 1950, IBM controlled 80 to 90 percent of the market in its core business of information processing machines. The company changed and grew primarily because of challenges generated internally, by Watson. We'll beat the Depression! We won't shrink after the war! Rarely did a new product, technology, or company steal a dollar from IBM and spur management to repel a challenge.

That began to change in 1950. IBM found itself in a race against capable outsiders in the nascent computer industry. The experience was like that of a tiger raised in a zoo and let loose in the wild, where it discovers that dinner doesn't land at its feet at the same time every evening. Computers were the new wilds of information processing, and IBM could not win by just showing up.

For Tom Watson Jr., an alarm about IBM's position went off when Red Lamotte caught up to him at an airport, and told him that the U.S. Census Bureau had agreed to buy two UNIVAC computers to replace IBM punch card machines. Tom Jr. and his father took it as a personal affront, kicking IBM right in its heritage. The Census Bureau had been IBM's customer since Herman Hollerith first wrenched together his invention in 1880.

The bad news kept coming. An IBM executive reported to Watson that 14 U.S. organizations were developing computers, all backed in some way by the government. The Cold War scared the Truman administration into pumping money into technology in hopes of maintaining an advantage over the Soviets. In June 1950, North Korean troops charged into South Korea in a surprise attack, starting the Korean War, which prompted the United States to shovel more war-related money into computer projects. Some of that money went to university labs; some went to sprouting companies with names such as Engineering Research Associates; and some went to Eckert and Mauchly, who were building the UNIVAC, the first machine to actually scare

IBM. Watson had been increasingly nervous about growing competition in computers, and then the UNIVAC rose up and bit him.

After creating the ENIAC, Eckert and Mauchly barely scraped together enough money and government contracts to continue their work as an independent company, which at its peak employed about 140 people. In early 1950, Remington Rand founder James Rand invited Eckert and Mauchly to his home in Florida, and took them for a luxury cruise on his yacht. For decades, Remington Rand had been fighting for IBM's scraps—the lone viable competitor in punch card machines, perpetually a frustrated and distant second even when it offered more innovative technology than IBM. In computers, Rand saw an opening. On his yacht, he cut a deal to buy out Eckert and Mauchly. The duo would join Remington Rand and get the money they needed to build the UNIVAC and bring it to market.

In the summer of 1950, Eckert and Mauchly began testing the UNIVAC in their Philadelphia lab, a cramped room made so hot by the machine's 5,000 tubes that engineers worked in their underwear. That first machine was destined for the Census Bureau, which took possession of its UNIVAC in March 1951. By the end of the year, Eckert and Mauchly's group built two more UNIVACs and had orders for another three, vaulting Remington Rand into the lead in computers.[33]

Watson and Tom Jr. suddenly found themselves in an unaccustomed position: looking at James Rand's backside. They responded by lighting rockets under IBM's engineers. IBM labs were working on three major computer projects. The first of these projects, the Defense Calculator, championed by Tom Jr., took priority as it evolved into the IBM 701 commercial computer. A second project, in a comparatively earlier stage of development, was the Tape Processing Machine (TPM). Engineers had just begun experimenting with a third computer, which would store information on a magnetic drum instead of tape or punch cards. Tom Jr., clearly running IBM's electronics effort, convinced Watson that IBM should pull resources from the TPM and the drum computer and throw everything behind the 701.

Tom Jr. then called on IBM's culture to adapt to a new reality: Speed to market had become paramount. In the past, Watson spurred IBM engineers to finish projects faster, but time had never been a principal factor in product development. As news of the UNIVAC spread, customers started calling Watson and asking when he was going to offer a machine like the UNIVAC. IBM salesmen reported that customers were thinking about defecting. IBM engineers no longer had the time to meticulously design, construct, and test a new machine. Factory managers, who had always put regimented efficiency first, would have to improvise now, designing the world's first computer assembly line before seeing the computer it would manufacture. In an eerie echo through time, IBM faced almost the same set of challenges in the 1980s and 1990s, when the technology industry shifted from the centralized computing of IBM's mainframes to the distributed computing of personal computers. Product cycles shortened, customers questioned IBM's ability to respond, and IBM had to change or suffer the consequences.

In 1950, the UNIVAC provided the motivation to change. IBMers, so dedicated to their company and the Watsons, felt their pride was at stake—and possibly an important part of IBM's future. The culture responded in a surge of esprit de corps. (A similar response helped save the 1990s IBM.) The burgeoning 701 design team couldn't wait for the space it needed inside IBM, so it started work on the third floor of a tie factory, then moved to an empty supermarket building. "Tar leaked down from the roof on hot days," said Clarence Frizzell, one of the project managers. "We had to scrape it off the drawings to keep working."[34]

Engineers got stuck trying to figure out a conventional

way to make something called a vacuum switch on the machine's tape drive. One engineer went to a store and bought rubber pants made for babies, and his group cut out pieces and used them for the switches. The 701 team threw aside budgets and schedules, previously a fact of life in the labs. "Maybe that's why we did things so fast," said Jerrier Haddad, a managing engineer on the 701. "We didn't have schedules to slow us down."

The 701 spirit spread to the Poughkeepsie factories, which would make the computer. The general manager, Smith Holmans, assigned the task of designing the assembly line to one of his talented subordinates, Richard Whalen. As Holmans handed Whalen the job, he said: "It's the first one (computer assembly line) in the world. I can't tell you how to do it. But customers will be coming to visit us, so you've got to make it look like we know how to build computers."

Tom Jr. spent every Monday morning with the design team and drove the 701 forward. As the team coalesced, it increasingly seemed like the new IBM—Tom Jr.'s IBM. Watson stayed in the background, focusing on World Trade and the business of punch card machines—which was, after all, still the money-making engine inside IBM.

In a little less than two years, the team developed and began building the enormously complex 701, which featured a number of breakthroughs in design. By election day on November 4, 1952, IBM was about two months away from finishing the first production model and shipping it to the IBM headquarters lobby. The plan was to unveil the 701 there, amid Watson-style hoopla. But IBM was about two months too late to avoid public humiliation by the UNIVAC.

Over the summer, a Remington Rand executive thought that the UNIVAC might be able to take an early sampling of votes on election day, run it through equations derived from patterns in past elections, and predict the result before all the votes were counted. Nothing like it had been done before. The company approached CBS about the possibility of using UNIVAC predictions in its election day coverage. Sig Mickelson, then director of news for CBS, recalled that the UNIVAC executive told the network that the company "could give us a machine that would predict election returns. I knew enough to know that wasn't true, but I knew it would be possible to speed up the analysis of the returns."[35] CBS news anchor Walter Cronkite thought it would at least be entertaining, though he recalled that the Remington Rand people admonished him to stop calling the machine an electric brain. CBS agreed to take a chance on UNIVAC.

The computer was too unwieldy to set up in the CBS studios in New York, and the heat from the tubes would have roasted the anchors and crew. So CBS set up a fake computer in the studio. It was basically a panel embedded with blinking Christmas lights and a teletype machine that could relay information from the real UNIVAC, which remained in Eckert and Mauchly's Philadelphia lab. Mathematician Max Woodbury, a former Eckert and Mauchly colleague from the University of Pennsylvania, worked out the probability equations and programmed the computer.

On the evening of November 4, CBS reporter Charles Collingwood and a camera crew set up in front of the UNIVAC in Philadelphia. Eckert and Woodbury stood ready to explain the machine's workings. Cronkite sat in the New York studio next to the fake panel, and told a nationwide audience about his electronic guest star, calling it, despite Remington Rand's admonition, a "marvelous electronic brain." Cronkite cut to Collingwood, who introduced the actual UNIVAC. For millions of Americans, it marked the first time that they'd seen a computer.

It was, also, doubtlessly the first time Watson saw a UNIVAC. He had never traveled to a UNIVAC installation, and there would have been no way IBM engineers could have acquired a UNIVAC to examine. On election eve, Watson was at home, and he felt a deep, personal interest in whether Eisenhower became president. Even if Watson started out watching NBC's election coverage, unaware of the UNIVAC on CBS, within moments of Cronkite's introduction some friend, relative, or IBM executive would have dialed Watson's phone number to excitedly tell him to tune into CBS.

As the first polls closed, programmers started feeding UNIVAC early returns from New York, Pennsylvania, Massachusetts, Ohio, Illinois, Minnesota, Texas, and California. Preelection surveys had predicted a close race between Eisenhower and his Democratic opponent, Adlai Stevenson. About 8:30 P.M., off-camera in the Philadelphia lab, UNIVAC typed out on its printer: "It's awfully early, but I'll go out on a limb. UNIVAC predicts . . ." It tapped out its projection: Eisenhower would win in a landslide, getting 438 electoral votes to Stevenson's 93. "The chances are now 00 to 1 in favor of the election of Eisenhower," UNIVAC typed, running into trouble because the computer's programmers only allowed for two digits. The actual projection was 100 to 1 in favor of Eisenhower.[36]

Behind the scenes, CBS scoffed at UNIVAC. Considering the polls, CBS thought that Eisenhower couldn't possibly win by that much. CBS's Mickelson decided not to use those numbers. Woodbury, the UNIVAC programmer, rushed to run a new set of numbers through the machine, this time giving Eisenhower 8-to-7 odds of winning. At 9:15 P.M., Cronkite and Collingwood reported those figures on-air. In the meantime, Woodbury found that he'd made a mistake in the second set of calculations. When he corrected the mistake, UNIVAC again spit out 100-to-1 odds for Eisenhower.

Late in the evening, as real election results came in, the astonished CBS team realized that the UNIVAC had been correct. Eisenhower won 442 electoral votes to Stevenson's 89. UNIVAC's 8:30 P.M. prediction had been off by less than 1 percent. CBS decided to confess. Collingwood came back on the air and told millions of people—company executives, farmers, writers, waitresses, teachers, politicians—of UNI-VAC's phenomenal feat. That report seared UNIVAC into the minds of Americans. The machine's accurate prediction made newspaper front pages and kindled conversations at bars, dinner tables, and office water coolers. The word *UNIVAC* entered the vernacular, and at a time when *computer* had yet to become an accepted term, *UNIVAC* transformed into the word that referred generally to those blinking electronic brains. When IBM introduced its first computer, people often called it IBM's UNIVAC—an insult unlike any that IBM had ever endured before.

Watching the UNIVAC's exploits live on television, Watson was savvy enough to immediately understand the damage to IBM's reputation. The general public and IBM's customers saw Remington Rand's UNIVAC as the new leader in the information industry.

The moment "shook Watson badly and caused tremors throughout the IBM organization," wrote author William Rodgers. "The whole episode, said one of the IBM men involved, 'frightened the pee out of the old man, who was convinced he had lost his grip.' "[37]

⋙

(To the Tune of "Marching Through Georgia")

International is our name—it well befits our line.
Serving in all nations—we're known in every clime.
Just watch us grow from year to year until the end of time.
Our IBM corporation.

—*Songs of the IBM*

13

THE
MAVERICK
AND HIS
HUMANITY

S O MUCH BECAME SO DIFFERENT IN 1953. JOSEPH Stalin died after brutishly running the Soviet Union since 1924, the year Watson renamed C-T-R as International Business Machines. Senator Joseph McCarthy whipped up paranoia about communism inside the United States. A cease-fire treaty in Korea set America free from the pain of either a depression or war for the first time in almost 25 years. A Republican, Dwight Eisenhower, sat in the White House for the first time in 21 years. In the nation's living rooms, television passed the tipping point when Lucille Ball gave birth to her real son, Desi Arnaz Jr., on the same day as her fictional Lucy Ricardo gave birth to Little Ricky on *I Love Lucy*. No single event had ever been shared by more people at exactly the same moment. In the nation's bedrooms, new attitudes stirred, brought into the open by the debut of *Playboy* magazine, which featured a nude Marilyn Monroe sprawled on its cover. Only in sports did the status quo march on. The two most dominant franchises in sports history won their respective championships once again: the New York Yankees beat the Brooklyn Dodgers in baseball's World Series, and the Montreal Canadians defeated the Boston Bruins in hockey's Stanley Cup.

At IBM, the excitement, the glamour, and the best people veered toward electronics and away from the punch card business. Every day, a few more tablespoons of the company's leadership drained from Watson into his son. New ideas—Tom Jr.'s ideas—percolated through IBM. Watson had long valued loyalty, devotion, and conformity. Tom Jr. valued imagination, professionalism, and individualism. Tom Jr. wanted more "wild ducks," as he called them—people who broke formation and took chances. The new ideas appealed to a high-flying postwar generation of workers who balked at blindly following orders and dressing alike. They didn't want to sing IBM songs—they wanted to *swing* to Rosemary Clooney and chuckle over Dean Martin's *That's Amore.*

IBM had been growing at an almost unimaginable rate. Before the war, Watson knew every corner of the company, presided over every major event, and approved every significant promotion. A decade later, no one person could possibly comprehend IBM. In 1953, revenue hit $497 million, more than triple IBM's revenue just five years earlier, and more than eight times the revenue of 1941. IBM employed 46,170 people in 1953, nearly doubling the number of employees in five years. Young technology companies sometimes grow that fast, but IBM grew at that pace 40 years after Flint's merger created C-T-R in 1911. IBM in the 1950s was adding on the equivalent of a company the size of IBM in 1930 *every year.*

It was no longer Watson's world. The stage around him was filling with new scenery, new props, and new players acting out a new plot—yet Watson refused to leave the scene. Though great company builders often have trouble letting go of their creations, few have so overstayed their effectiveness. Some, such as Sam Walton of Wal-Mart, groomed successors and handed off vibrant companies. Others, such as Walt Disney, died before that critical point arrived. Watson wasn't prepared to bow out, and he had a lot of life left in him. So he held tight onto his position atop IBM. The younger IBM executives viewed him alternately as a curmudgeon, an inspiration, a nuisance, and an anachronism. Watson told the same simple stories over and over in meetings. There was the one about John Range teaching him perseverance while selling cash registers in Upstate New York. There was the one, trotted out at nearly every meeting about the antitrust suit, about cutting Powers's patent fees in half. There was the one about his father saying, "Never spend a dollar of your company's money that you would not spend if it were your own money," which he repeated in nearly every discussion about debt. IBM's young executives, pressed for time as they tried to deal with the multiplying issues of a hypergrowth company, often cringed when the Old Man joined their meeting.[1] Watson was becoming like an old war hero who still wore his uniform around the house and tried to get his family to fall in at reveille.

On the morning of April 7, 1953, the doors of IBM's headquarters building opened to allow the first public viewing of the IBM 701, the general-purpose computer that would go head-to-head against the UNIVAC. The raw-looking machinery of the SSEC had been hauled out of the lobby and replaced by the elegant 701, showcased in a new setting of soft-finished aluminum walls and recessed lighting. Unlike any computer before, the 701 was housed in a collection of cabinets, each roughly the size of a refrigerator. To move previous computers—IBM's and those from other companies—from one location to another, engineers had to break the machine down and then build it again at the next site. The 701's modular concept, which customers loved, would let IBM representatives wheel each piece through a regular-size door, plug the cabinets together, and get the computer working in a fraction of the time necessary to set up a UNIVAC. To make that point, IBM spread out the 701's components in the lobby display, arranging the pieces like furniture. One wall of the display was left open for pedestrian gawkers. For official visitors, a conference room hung overhead on a balcony enclosed by sloping plate glass—"a vantage point for observing operations and discussing computations," IBM stated in a press release.[2]

For the official unveiling, Watson demonstrated IBM's clout by drawing 150 of the nation's elite scientists and businessmen, including guest of honor Robert Oppenheimer, who led the Manhattan Project as it developed the world's first atomic bomb. Although Oppenheimer no longer worked on weapons, his appearance created a stir. The government had set off an atomic bomb test in the Nevada desert just the day before. Watson addressed the scientists, lauding them for their accomplishments. He noted: "Now that we have the machines, they are of no value until scientists put them to use."[3] He frequently returned to a similar theme in many of his speeches, emphasizing that electronic calculating machines were not brains. "It annoys me when they speak about the electrical brain," Watson said in one speech. "There isn't any such thing and never will be. These machines play a small part and are assistants to the scientists who are trying to get the answers quickly. The only benefit of the machines is time, and time is important."[4] Uncomfortable with the stardom of computing machines, Watson tried to remind everyone that the machines were only tools. In Watson's old IBM, machines were never the stars. People were. Or rather, he was.

A CBS news crew showed up to report a story on the 701 dedication. When it aired, commentator Don Hollenbeck began by saying: "This is the latest of the mechanical brains devised by International Business Machines."[5] Despite Watson's unease, TV made the 701 a star and gave it a brain.

Watson and Tom Jr. continued a bitter struggle for power in both their relationship and IBM. Their struggle escalated into one particularly disturbing encounter. Watson and Tom Jr. were thrashing each other in an argument in Watson's office, and Tom Jr. walked out, angrily saying he had a plane to catch. Watson called for his limousine and raced after his son, catching up to him on the airport tarmac. In front of a group of people, Watson reached for Tom Jr.'s arm, and Tom Jr. snapped: "God damn you, old man! Can't you ever leave me alone?" He turned his back on his father and climbed the steps to the airplane door.[6] As Tom Jr. recalled, the incident deeply wounded both father and son. Yet their fights continued.

On June 26, 1953, two months after the 701 introduction, Watson boarded the S.S. *United States,* bound for Europe on a two-month mission for IBM World Trade. This time, Dick didn't join him. The trip was pure Watson. He and his entourage raced around the continent by first-class rail, living in luxury and coating their every move with a shellac of pageantry. Watson laid a wreath at Lafayette's tomb in France; stayed as a guest at the Royal Palace at Soestdijk, the Netherlands; and entertained IBM employees in seven countries. He triumphantly tramped all around West Germany, from which he had been banished forever by Hitler. Watson gave the dead and defeated Führer one last kick by meeting with the U.S.-friendly leader of West Germany, Chancellor Konrad Adenauer, in the nation's new capital of Bonn. Watson sailed for home on September 1.

During that trip, thoughts about his place in the world must have lined up and clicked into position. Watson's son and the other young executives were proving they had the talent and knowledge to run IBM. Under them, the company had taken on a life of its own. IBM's culture, personality, and desire for greatness carried Watson's genetic code and value system, but IBM showed that it could change and grow apart from Watson's direct supervision. Watson finally must have realized that perhaps IBM *should* live apart from him. Tom Jr. and IBM could probably adapt to the times in ways that eluded a near-octogenarian.

The Old Man turned 79 in 1953. Ulcers churned his insides. Friends and peers had died. Nichol was very ill.

Watson must have visualized the potential tragedy of living his last moments at war with his firstborn son.

Watson's mind also would have been full of fresh thoughts about his European trip. He liked going to elegant dinners where he was the guest of honor and the subject of endless adoring speeches. He liked the role of international industrialist, received by heads of state and led on tours of overseas factories where employees greeted him as a hero. He liked building up World Trade with Dick, who acceded to his father instead of challenging him.

After returning from Europe, Watson seemed to add up his frustrations, his joys, and his health, and he decided to let go. He wouldn't retire. That was out of the question. Separating himself from IBM would be like a fish choosing to flip onto dry land. However, Watson would separate himself from the heat of daily decision making and unload his duties. Then, he could get involved only in what he chose. He seemed to look forward to that. In his new-found time, Watson could travel to branch offices, see Eisenhower in the White House, sit at the head table at high-society banquets, and generally hang around and be deified. Watson essentially decided to create a constitutional monarchy at IBM. Watson would be the beloved, ceremonial emperor. Tom Jr. would be the prime minister, doing all the hard work.

The change was apparent in Watson's date book. After the 1953 European trip, his schedule began to empty out of business meetings and events. The change came through in the memoirs of Tom Jr., who recalled that his father became more of a mentor than a hard-driving boss and father. The two fought less often and less viciously.[7]

Watson had always enjoyed commemorating significant dates, and the timing of his decision to let go corresponded perfectly to two such dates. The following year, 1954, would mark the 40th anniversary of Watson's arrival at C-T-R, and it would be Watson's 80th birthday. Over the course of 1953 and 1954, Watson attended dozens of tribute dinners and luncheons that celebrated the anniversary and his birthday. Events were held by family, friends, IBM divisions, charitable and artistic organizations, and ambassadors from countries around the world. The most baroque occasions included 50-pound cakes, live bands, celebrity speakers, and extravagant gifts ranging from portraits of Watson to gold-plated figurines. Watson soaked up the accolades wearing a warm grin, and concluded each occasion by stepping to the podium and saying, like a humble country boy, that all he did was set down a few simple principles. He owed the rest of his success, he would say, to the IBM family.

≈

If Watson needed proof that IBM would endure without him, he got it in the electronics wars. Consider IBM's position in 1953. The UNIVAC had beaten IBM to the market by more than a year and was stealing IBM customers, starting with the U.S. Census Bureau. Thanks to the election night exposure, UNIVAC had become synonymous with computers, leaving IBM wincing as people referred to the IBM 701 as IBM's UNIVAC.

Remington Rand had nothing to lose in promoting the UNIVAC over its old punch card systems, which never captured more than a small fraction of the market. The company never had to measure its steps in computing to avoid cannibalizing existing businesses. IBM, though, had a huge legacy business to protect. In 1953, IBM brought in $497 million in revenue, and only $14 million of it came from electronic machines, mainly the 604 electronic calculator. The rest of the revenue came from punch card systems, punch cards, computing services (performing batches of computing tasks for other companies for a fee), and time recorders (a shrinking part of IBM). While some of IBM's big customers clamored for the speed of computers, the majority wanted the reliability and lower cost of punch card systems. Although Tom Jr. believed that IBM had to become a computer company, a good deal of the company's resources and attention had to flow to the old money-making part of the business.

IBM at the time was caught in a wrenching management transition. Watson was the only IBM chief executive whom anyone who worked at the company had ever known. He was stepping back, to be succeeded by his son, a relatively untested young man. The slow-motion transfer of power created confusion over who was really running the place.

Meanwhile, the U.S. government seemingly lined up against IBM. The military funded computer projects that might compete against IBM, and the antitrust suit ate up IBM executives' time and froze decisions that might have an impact on the case.

Still, despite the handicaps and uncertainty about leadership, IBM vanquished the most serious competition it faced to that point. How?

First, IBM got a lot of help from Remington Rand. James Rand didn't share Watson's singularity of purpose. Watson concentrated on information machines for business. Rand shot off in a number of directions at once, creating a conglomerate that made products such as electric shavers and industrial television systems, along with punch card machines and computers. The structure dispersed Remington Rand's strengths. For instance, Remington Rand had a vast sales organization, but a shaver salesman couldn't effectively sell UNIVACs, or vice versa. The company had to manufacture so many different kinds of products, it never developed the manufacturing efficiencies and expertise to match IBM, which could concentrate on only a few kinds of products. Remington Rand couldn't make even a limited number of UNIVACs quickly enough to satisfy demand. As UNIVAC delivery dates stretched farther out, IBM had an opportunity to bust in and offer to deliver a computer sooner. It's a classic business lesson in the pitfalls of a lack of focus.

The differences in the organizations became clear when IBM and Remington Rand competed to win a contract to build a massive computing system for air defense. The decision makers chose IBM. "In the IBM organization we observed a much higher degree of purposefulness, integration, and esprit de corps than we found in the Remington Rand organization," wrote MIT's Jay Forrester, who guided the project for the military.[8] Forrester noted that he was discouraged by a lack of cooperation between UNIVAC's designers and the factories that would make the machines.

Once IBM swang into action in computing, Remington Rand must have felt like it walked into a cannonade. IBM's lavish spending—following Tom Jr.'s order—to lure hundreds of electronics engineers paid off in technological improvements and rapid development of new product lines. Less than a year after IBM announced the 701 as its antidote to the UNIVAC, IBM announced the 702, a direct descendant of the Tape Processing Machine that the labs worked on in parallel to the 701. About the same time, the company began selling the 650, a smaller electronic calculating machine based on the Magnetic Drum Calculator that had also been progressing through the lab. The 650 rented for $3,250 a month, one-quarter the cost of leasing a 701. Instead of relying on punch cards or magnetic tape, the 650 stored information on a low-cost, low-maintenance magnetic drum—an innovation out of IBM's labs.

Remington Rand had no answer to the 702 or the 650. By itself, the 702 vaulted IBM ahead of the UNIVAC in technical quality. The type of vacuum tubes that IBM used, licensed from a British company, processed information twice as fast as the UNIVAC tubes and were more reliable. IBM's magnetic tape system solved problems that made UNIVAC's tape system a maintenance nightmare.[9]

Ultimately, though, IBM didn't beat Remington Rand with technology; rather, IBM won with that powerful Watson legacy: salesmanship. Computer historian Stan Augarten pinpointed the difference between the companies' approach to selling:[10]

> When a team of IBM salesmen called on a customer, they worked hard to show how the installation of an IBM computer would get the payroll out faster, keep better track of sales, boost efficiency, and save money.
>
> When a group of UNIVAC salesmen visited a client, however, they tended to harp on technological matters—mercury delay lines, decimal versus binary computation—that went right over the heads of their customers, who were chiefly interested in the answer to one question: What will a computer do for me?

Remington Rand wasn't uniquely clueless—technology companies make the same mistake today.

In 1955, IBM blew past Remington Rand in the computer market. IBM had 193 computing machines on order, whereas Remington Rand had orders for 65.[11] From that point on, the gap widened, and newcomers to computing—including RCA, Raytheon, and, in a twist of fate, NCR—never challenged IBM's lead.

IBM's victory was made complete when the March 28, 1955, issue of *Time* magazine landed on newsstands. Tom Jr. gazed out from the front cover, his hair graying and the corners of his eyes etched with wrinkles. Behind him was a drawing of a computer, made lifelike with facial features and arms. The headline: "IBM's Thomas Watson Jr.: Clink, Clank, Think." Inside, the lengthy story described the wonders of computers: "In just twelve machine-hours, the brain will do 1,200 cost reports that normally take 1,800 man-hours." All of the photos are of the Watsons or IBM, and almost all of the text is about IBM. The story was a milepost in the public's understanding of computers, and after the story IBM replaced UNIVAC as the recognized leader in what laymen still called "electronic brains" or "electric brains."

Watson had nothing to do with IBM's impressive response to the UNIVAC. He stood back and let Tom Jr. handle it. If Tom Jr.—39 years old in 1953—made leadership mistakes while chasing the UNIVAC, the self-motivation and cohesiveness embedded in IBM's culture kept the effort on track. Watson's babies had grown up—both Tom Jr. and IBM.

~

A heartwarming photograph in that *Time* magazine article showed Tom Jr. with his wife and five children. Taken outdoors, four of the children (Tom III, Jeannette, Olive, and Lucinda) climb on a web of ropes strung between two trees. The youngest, Susan, sits on the shoulders of Tom Jr., who is wearing a suit and tie. Tom Jr.'s wife, Olive, stands a few feet away from him, flashing a glamorous smile. They appeared to be a happy, admirable family of the 1950s. They weren't.

On professional levels, Watson's children led exceptionally good lives. Tom Jr., in his later years, would become one of the most successful chief executives in history. Dick would eventually become U.S. ambassador to France.

On a personal and emotional level, though, Watson's family developed deep problems. When Tom, Dick, Jane, and Helen were children, their father put IBM first, traveled incessantly, threw temper tantrums when home, and delivered stern lectures rather than warm hugs. His behavior affected all of his children, but none more than Tom Jr.

That perfect-looking family in the *Time* photo suffered at the hands of a depressive, volatile Tom Jr., who had a frightening temper and a willingness to wound those he loved most. Olive Watson didn't stand up to her husband,

and she and the children lived in fear of a Tom Jr. blowup.

Tom Jr. confesses regret for his behavior in his memoirs. He wrote about coming home from IBM, "carrying my frustration home with me, where my wife and children would bear the brunt."[12] Small household disturbances, such as an argument between two of the kids, would set him off, yelling and being disturbingly mean. In the wake of his tantrums, Tom Jr. would fall into a depressive state, sometimes crying as he emotionally crumbled. "Those were the blackest moments of my adult life," Tom Jr. wrote.[13] Often Dick was the only person who could pull Tom Jr. out of one of his emotional pits. Dick would drive over, talk with his brother, and soon get him to laugh.

Tom Jr. didn't write about how his father reacted to the strife inside his family. Watson must have known about it, and probably had seen it in action. Perhaps in his waning years, Watson recognized the damage that he'd passed down from one generation to the next. It's a sin not uncommon among successful businessmen who put their work first and leave a wake of family troubles. However, in Watson's ever-present optimism about his son, he might not have seen the damage at all. Watson could have died oblivious to his failure to his family.

For some unknown reason, one day in 1954 Watson emptied his pockets and put the contents in a file. There they remain, stored in IBM's corporate archives. Like anyone's personal affects, they are intimate scraps of life and personality. Among the items saved:

~ An envelope with his handwriting on the back: "Get list of all who wrote letters on my 80th birthday and write them on their birthdays." He no doubt intended to give that order to one of his secretaries. This is Watson as people collector—the friend of thousands.

~ A cartoon of a woman standing in a bathroom looking at two towels, one monogrammed "His" and the other "Think." He had a sense of humor, and he loved that he'd created a bit of American culture.

~ A scrap of paper on which he scribbled: "Our big machines on television great adv." The last word is an abbreviated form of *advertising*. Another scrap read: "Phone murphy re report to stockholders." He left no clue about Murphy's identity.

~ A schedule for a Friday typed on an unpunched punch card. It's how he often carried his day's schedule, and he always stayed busy.

~ A business card of Fernando Lobo, the Brazilian ambassador. Watson liked being an internationalist.

Watson also saved items from his desk, which was typically piled with mail, memos, newspaper clippings, and other odds and ends. Some of those items:

~ A daily calendar, with one small page for each day. On each page was the date, a biblical lesson, a prayer, and a hymn. Watson had been moderately religious all his life, attending church and giving considerable money to Presbyterian churches in New York, his one-time home of Rochester, New York, and his boyhood home in Painted Post, New York.

~ A handful of clippings of stories that discuss whether the THINK slogan is at cross-purposes with making machines that think—a popular topic of the day. Again, Watson would have loved that his company stirred public discourse.

~ A brochure for Fruitainer Products: "Delicious food products in edible containers," such as marmalade in a "natural fruit shell." Everybody likes a novelty, even the wealthy and powerful.

419

~ Numbers from the most recent quarterly financial report, typed on an unpunched punch card.
~ Notes for an upcoming speech in which he planned to defend the United Nations—still reaching for a role beyond business.
~ A completed crossword puzzle.[14]

On November 16, 1955, Watson met in his office with Red LaMotte and three other executives, and began talking about an idea: He wanted to build a structure, something like the Eiffel Tower, as a monument to IBM. It would be built in New York, and rise 100 feet higher than the Empire State Building, which was then the tallest building in the world. The notes from the meeting read: "He (Watson) sees tremendous amounts of dignified advertising in IBM's having such a structure."[15] There is no more flagrant sign of Watson's sense of his own grandeur.

It's easy to imagine LaMotte and his colleagues gathering in one of their offices after the meeting, closing the door, and either worrying that Watson might actually do it, or laughing until their eyes watered.

Fred Nichol, Watson's closest male companion for more than 40 years, died on October 27, 1955. Physically, Watson appeared as if he'd soon join his friend in the hereafter. Watson's churning, painful gastrointestinal system made eating unpleasant, and Watson was losing weight quickly— about 10 pounds off of a body that had never looked overweight. On his face, discolored patches splotched the skin, and his cheeks caved in because of the weight loss.

Watson learned that his longtime friend Frank Gannett, the 78-year-old newspaper magnate, had fallen at his home and suffered a severe spinal injury. Watson sent him a book,

The Big Four: The Story of Huntington, Stanford, Hopkins and Crocker, and of the Building of the Central Pacific, Oscar Lewis's depiction of early years of the railroad industry. Watson's favorite gift to a friend now was either *The Big Four* or an IBM electric typewriter.

Most days, Watson went to the office. He sometimes packed his schedule like he used to, though more often he sat through a couple of meetings, talked with Tom Jr., received a dignitary or visiting Boy Scout troop, then went home by 2 P.M. He wrote memos to Tom Jr. and Dick, making specific suggestions at times, and other times broadly laying out his business philosophy.

Free from the headache of big decisions, Watson poked around in minutia. At one point, he inserted himself into a sales crisis in Miami. This episode briefly rejuvenated the old salesman—the "world's greatest salesman," as the media labeled him. A Miami bank wanted to defect from IBM and buy a competitor's system. Watson joined the Miami sales office's effort to retain the account. "This experience has stirred my imagination and has extended and broadened my vision," Watson wrote to Tom Jr. "I am determined to try to do more to help and develop new things for the future."[16]

One issue still burned hot inside Watson: the antitrust suit. Ever since the suit was filed in January 1952, negotiations between the Justice Department and IBM had plodded along. Watson couldn't separate the best interests of IBM from his visceral need to scrub his name clean of any taint of antitrust. Whereas Tom Jr. met with Justice lawyers to talk about terms of a settlement, Watson refused to change his mind. In meeting after meeting, Watson repeated his stance. He would not settle. Settling was an admission of guilt, and IBM had done nothing wrong. He'd fight the suit to the finish. When IBM was exonerated in court, Watson believed the government would owe IBM a public apology.

A court battle probably would have been disastrous for IBM. The company had not behaved badly, but it had acted aggressively. In a competitive market, IBM's actions might have been considered good business. For monopolies, the courts held, such actions were an abuse of power. The government had been winning big antitrust suits. The atmosphere around antitrust echoed the early 1900s, when the trust busters won a string of cases, including the one against NCR. If IBM took the suit to court, it probably would have lost, and Justice would have been able to impose harsh terms on IBM, perhaps breaking up the company.

The opposing views of Watson and Tom Jr. scraped against each other like tectonic plates. The inevitable earthquake hit IBM on a morning in late-1955. Watson arrived in his office at about 9:30. Tom Jr. was getting ready to leave. A number of accounts of the conversation exist, all of them slightly different. It started when Watson asked his son where he was going. Tom Jr. replied that he was going to the Federal Courthouse to talk to the government lawyers and the judge about the antitrust case.

Watson blew up. "You're totally incompetent to do that!" Watson screamed. The two blasted each other in a ferocious argument about antitrust—and, underneath, about Watson hanging onto power. Finally, Tom Jr. said: "Either tell me you want me to go [to the meeting], and I'll leave, or tell me you don't and I'll call and cancel."

"No, you go. But don't make any decisions!" Watson growled.[17]

Tom Jr. recalled taking the elevator downstairs, walking through the lobby, and getting in a company car that was waiting for him. According to other accounts, Tom Jr. stepped out of IBM headquarters and stood on the New York sidewalk unsure of what to do. He walked a while, trying to think and stop shaking, considered the possibility of quitting IBM, and then he hailed a taxi and directed the driver to take him to the courthouse.

While sitting at a conference table with the lawyers and judge, one of Watson's secretaries ducked into the room and handed Tom Jr. a slip of paper. It read:

100%
Confidence
Appreciation
Admiration
Love
Dad

There, in front of the judge, Tom Jr.'s eyes welled with tears.

On January 25, 1956, IBM signed a consent decree, settling the case. IBM would have to change some practices, offering machines for sale as well as lease. It would have to allow others into the punch card business and to license patents. However, Tom Jr. correctly recognized that the terms would not damage IBM, and signing the settlement allowed IBM to unleash its forces on the computer market.

On February 10, Watson left for a month in Florida. On February 26, he sent a letter from Florida to Phillips at IBM. Watson instructed Phillips to ask the board of directors to eliminate Watson's salary and cut his profit sharing in half. Watson also threw his support behind Tom Jr.'s consent decree, writing that the executives must "see that everyone in our sales organization measures up 100% to the terms."[18] Reading between the lines, the letter was essentially setting up his resignation.

⁂

In Florida, Watson's vitality evaporated. It might seem melodramatic to link Watson's ebbing physical life to his fading role at IBM, but nonetheless, that link seems real. The two played off each other in a spiral. As his health worsened, Watson backed further away from IBM. The company, though, was his habitat. Leaving it left him disoriented and sapped his energy, which whittled away his health. Then in turn, he gave up more of IBM, and so on. Sometimes, the inexplicable happens. Thomas Jefferson and John Adams, bonded to each other and to the birth of the United States, died of old age on the same day, July 4, 1826, hundreds of miles apart, precisely 50 years after they both signed the Declaration of Independence. Watson was IBM, and IBM was Watson. Separated, Watson could not exist.

After returning from Florida at the end of March, 1956, Watson rarely went into the office.

On April 11, according to his date book, "Mr. Watson went to [the] doctor for tests."[19]

On April 24, Watson attended the annual stockholders' meeting in the Grand Ballroom of the Hotel Commodore in New York. Two days later, Watson and Jeannette hosted a dinner at his East 75th Street home in honor of the visiting Prince Franz Joseph of Liechtenstein.

On May 8, Watson arrived at IBM at 10:08 A.M. He called Tom Jr. into his office, and graciously asked his eldest son to take over as IBM's chief executive. There was no struggle or hurt feelings, like when Watson offered to make Tom Jr. president. There was no overdone ceremony—no bands playing, no opening of curtains on a wall-size portrait. Tom Jr. said the moment had "a great sense of dignity, which meant a lot to me because it was the first promotion I ever got from him without a fight."[20]

Watson would remain chairman; Phillips, vice chairman. A photographer captured Watson and his son in the moment. They stand in front of a book case in Watson's office, shaking hands tentatively, gripping each other's fingers rather than clasping palm-to-palm. Watson, at 82, looks ancient, and he stares intently into Tom Jr.'s eyes, as if to say, "I can't believe I'm doing this. I'm handing you my life. Don't screw it up." Tom Jr., handsome as a Hollywood version of a CEO, stares back calmly, his eyes reassuringly saying, "Trust me, Dad. I won't let you down."

On May 10, a *New York Times* editorial thanked Watson for investing in research labs and giving the world products that could tame information and use it to make life better. "We have all benefited from his faith in science in technology," the *Times* said.[21]

Over the next several days, congratulatory telegrams and letters from the business elite streamed into Watson's office.

"What a privilege you have enjoyed in turning over to your son, the executive direction of your great company," wrote C. K. "King" Woodbridge, chairman of Dictaphone.[22]

"No small part of that satisfaction must rest in being able to pass active direction into such capable and experienced hands as those of your son," wrote Kingsbury Nickerson, president of The First National Bank of Jersey City.[23]

"So you have handed the reins over to Tom Watson Jr.!" wrote Merrill "Babe" Meigs, vice president of publishing company The Hearst Corporation. Looking at that same photograph of Tom Jr. and Watson shaking hands, Meigs said that Tom Jr.'s "strong features softened by a whimsical smile are a sure indication that he has everything it takes to carry on with wisdom, ability, and understanding."[24]

The letters came saturated with envy. In handing off IBM to a talented son, Watson pulled off a company builder's fantasy.

⁓

On May 18, 1956, Watson and Jeannette took the train to Endicott to attend the Watson Trophy Dinner, the annual event to hand out trophies for IBM sports events. When they arrived in Endicott at 9:30 P.M., a date book entry said, "Mr. and Mrs. Watson retired at once." The next day, Jeannette attended a luncheon without Watson, who, the entry noted, was "slightly indisposed," which probably meant he napped. Watson rallied to attend and speak at the dinner, then go to a reception at the Homestead that began at 10:45 P.M. The following morning, Sunday, May 20, Watson boarded the train for New York. As it rolled out at 10:07 A.M., Watson took his last look back at a place he dearly loved.

Tuesday, May 22, Watson showed up at his office at 10:42 A.M. At 10:49, he met with Tom Jr. for 16 minutes.

For the next 21 minutes, he got a haircut and a manicure in the office.

At 11:38, he met with the IBM board of directors for 40 minutes.

The day's next entry, covering 12:18 P.M. to 1:10, said Watson was in the anteroom next to his office. That's where he took naps.

At 1:10 P.M., Watson arrived for a luncheon at the St. Regis Hotel, a few blocks from IBM headquarters. Tom Jr. acted as host, and most of IBM's directors and top officers joined him to honor his father. Fifty minutes later, Watson went home. It was the Old Man's last real day at work. Six days later, he came in for two brief World Trade meetings in the morning, then gathered his hat and walked out of his office door, forever leaving behind his old wooden desk, the French furniture, the heavy draperies, and the THINK signs that had surrounded him for years. Watson took the elevator down to the lobby, where he walked past the new display of IBM's latest commercial computer, the 702. On Tom Jr.'s orders, workers had ripped up the oriental rugs and dark wood that had been in the lobby since the 1930s, and installed a modern decor that included bright white floors, crimson walls, metallic desks, and a sleek, simple "702" on the wall above the computer housing.

After passing the 702, Watson exited the lobby and slid into a car waiting to take him to his home in New Canaan, Connecticut.

The Old Man left behind a company that surged with youth and spirit. The exuberance fed off of Tom Jr.'s investments in electronics research and the leadership of a new generation of daring executives. IBM tore into the budding computer industry. The company was a month away from unveiling Semi-Automatic Ground Environment (SAGE)—the massive military project that IBM had won over Remington Rand. SAGE was to analyze radar signals to guard the skies against Soviet aircraft and missiles. It was by far the biggest, most complicated, and most reliable computer system yet built. IBM prepared to roll out another thrilling new product that June: the IBM 305 Random Access Memory Accounting Machine (RAMAC). The RAMAC 305 was based on IBM's Disk Storage Unit, a breakthrough that allowed data to be stored on rotating disks, which were cheaper and more efficient than the magnetic drums. Overall, IBM employed 72,504 people in 1956, more than double the number of employees five years earlier. Its 1956 revenue would hit $892 million, more than double the revenue of four years before. Like a dad teaching his child to ride a bicycle, Watson ran alongside and steadied IBM for the previous decade or so. Once he let go, IBM sped away on its own, going faster with each confident pump of the pedals.

No longer needed, Watson grew weak. His gastrointestinal system began shutting down. Scar tissue from years of ulcers had slowly closed off the outlet from his stomach to the small intestines. Watson felt constant nausea, making it difficult to eat. If he did eat, the food would not get through to be absorbed into his body. He lost weight until he looked skeletal. A year or so before, Watson's doctor told him that surgery could repair the opening and prolong his life, but Watson refused. He'd never had surgery, and he couldn't bear the thought of it now. In effect, Watson decided it was time to die.

He stayed in the New Canaan house, and family and friends visited regularly. He talked at length with each of his four children, trying to establish a final peace. On Sunday, June 17, Watson's 82-year-old heart began failing. His doctor sent an ambulance to pick him up in New Canaan and take him to Roosevelt Hospital in New York. The next day, Jeannette, Watson's children (Tom Jr., Dick, Jane, and Helen), and their spouses milled around in the hallway outside his room. One or two at a time went in to sit with Watson and talk to him. "I'll never forget how white he was," Olive Watson remembered. The family members told Watson about the "get well" telegrams they were receiving from around the world, including one from President Eisenhower. Watson seemed to hear, but he could not respond.

The following day, Tuesday, June 19, 1956, Watson's breathing grew labored. As the family watched, his heart stopped, his lungs settled one last time, and he gently died.

⌇

The funeral at Brick Presbyterian Church on Park Avenue in New York began at 11 A.M. on June 21. Hundreds of IBM employees packed into every corner. They were joined by business leaders, politicians, diplomats, and celebrities from opera and the theater. In all, about 1,200 people jammed the church, straining to see the casket covered in a blanket of dark red roses.

The minister, Paul Austin Wolfe, delivered the eulogy. He and Watson had become friends. When Watson could, he and Jeannette had attended Brick Presbyterian. In one passage in the eulogy, Wolfe came as close as anybody to explaining Watson's success. "He had a singleness of mind," Wolfe said. "He saw things simply. It was because of that simplicity in seeing through a problem that he could make wise decisions. In a confused world, he never lost his sense of values."[25]

After the funeral, a hearse carried Watson north through upper Manhattan, along the Hudson River to Sleepy Hollow Cemetery near Tarrytown, New York. On a hill looking down to the water, Watson was buried next to his first grandchild, the baby that Tom Jr. and Olive lost.

IBM offices and factories around the world remained closed for the day, a silent tribute to the man who created all of those jobs in all of those communities. Newspapers and television stations retold his story. The *New York Times* wrote: "To a great extent, the International Business Machines Corporation is a reflection of the character of the man who gave it its name and who led it to a position of eminence." The Watson family received a torrent of telegrams from employees, friends, business figures, and world leaders. President Dwight Eisenhower issued a statement to the media. It read: "In the passing of Thomas J. Watson, the nation has lost a truly fine American—an industrialist who was first of all a great citizen and a great humanitarian. I have lost a good friend, whose counsel was always marked by a deep-seated concern for people. Mrs. Eisenhower and I join with the many thousands of his friends in many countries in extending our heartfelt sympathy to Mrs. Watson and her family."

In the 1930s and 1940s, Watson was one of the highest-paid business leaders in America—famous in the 1930s for being "the thousand-dollar-a-day man." Watson's fortunes peaked at about $100 million. During his last years, he gave millions of dollars to organizations such as New York's Metropolitan Museum, educational foundations, and universities. At his death, Watson willed $1 million to various charities and $200,000 to the Boy Scouts. He left from $1,000 to $5,000 to 42 staff members, secretaries, former secretaries, receptionists, and elevator operators. The rest went to Jeannette and the four children. As of August 1956, the Watson family's IBM holdings were worth about $80 million.[26]

Watson made a lot of other people rich, too. In his obituary, the *New York Times* pointed out that if an investor had purchased 100 shares of C-T-R stock the day Watson joined the company in 1914, the price would have come to $2,750. If the investor held onto the shares for 42 years, in 1956 those 100 shares, with stock splits, would have been worth $2,164,000. Plus, the investor would have collected $209,000 in dividends over the years. Watson would have smirked if he'd seen those figures—public proof that he won the match against his boyhood poverty and his early business failures.[27]

On the other side of the continent, the *San Francisco Chronicle* praised Watson in an editorial that today seems prescient, considering that in the 1980s the San Francisco Bay Area surpassed IBM to become the global hub of the technology industry.

"He will be remembered by posterity, we think, not for his ability to sell but for having made possible the age of automation into which the world seems now to be entering," the *Chronicle*'s editors wrote. "Denizens of that brave and accurate and button-pushing age will doubtless revere Thomas J. Watson precisely as inhabitants of the present automotive age revere Henry Ford."[28]

That was something Watson strove for: a place in history.

In the end, he earned a place more majestic than even he—the ultimate optimist—ever imagined. Watson built a great American institution. He changed the way executives ran their companies. He led the march into an entirely new epoch called the Information Age. The *Chronicle* was right: Watson's name belongs next to the likes of Henry Ford, John D. Rockefeller, Andrew Carnegie, and later businessmen such as Bill Gates and Walt Disney. They are the select few who used business to change society and life around the world.

❧

IBM employees had a chance to see Watson one last time—on film. Early in 1956, Watson hired a film crew to come to his house in Manhattan and shoot footage for an end-of-year message to be shown to all IBM employees.

In the stiffly staged film, four male IBM executives arrive at the door, as if dropping in to say hi and bask in the Old Man's wisdom. Watson and Jeannette greet the men, and guide them into a formal-looking room. Logs burn in the fireplace in the background. Watson sits in a high-back leather chair that looks too big for his withering body. The executives take places on a couch. Jeannette sits in a chair to the side. The camera pans the guests' pasted-on grins. The men barely move, as if they're afraid to make even the faintest rustling sound. The film cuts to a camera framing Watson, who leans forward and begins speaking in a hoarse voice. He gestures with knotty hands.

He talks about his principles of business and IBM's four constituencies: customers, employees, stockholders, and the community. We must take good care of our customers, Watson says, so they can be profitable and buy more IBM products. Plus, we must be good to our employees and compensate them to encourage them. "By taking care of those two, that will take care of the third one, stockholders," he says.

If customers are happy and employees work hard, Watson says, profits will come naturally and the stock price will rise.

As for the fourth constituency, communities, Watson tells the camera that a company must put in more than it takes out.

Before the film ends, Watson can't resist trotting out "The Man Proposition"—the presentation he gave to C-T-R employees in 1914. He had used it hundreds of times in meetings and speeches, always believing it was as insightful as a great Shakespearean riff. On-camera, Watson lays out his theory exactly as he did in 1914: Sales*man*, *man*ager, factory *man*, service *man*—all are based on the word *man*, Watson says. Titles are just titles, he continues, but people—individuals—are the heart of a business. Watson takes a long time telling us this, halting often to clear his throat. Finally, he makes his point, saying: "After all, it's the manpower that does it."

The moment, preserved in black and white, is haunting. From the grave, or maybe from the heavens, this tycoon who gave the world machines that could do the work of clerks, who mass-produced thinking machines, who built *electronic brains*—reminds us to rely on our humanity.

⚮

EVER ONWARD

There's a feeling everywhere of bigger things in store,
Of new horizons coming into view.
Our aim is clear: to make each year exceed the one before,
Staying in the lead in everything we do.
The will to win is built right in,
It will not be denied,
And we will go ahead we know by working side by side.
Ever onward, ever onward,
That's the spirit that has brought us fame.
We're big but bigger we will be.
We can't fail for all can see
That to serve humanity has been our aim.

—*Songs of the IBM*

432

14

GENERATIONS
AFTER

HOMAS JOHN WATSON SR. LIVED A GREAT AMERICAN life. He started out poor, built a grand company, made millions of dollars, and changed the world.

He did so despite magnificent flaws. His temper was at times inexcusable. Work consumed his life. He raised a family that flew apart after his death, and his sons fought demons such as depression and alcohol abuse. As he achieved greater success, he became more vain, and in his last years his desire for praise reached absurd proportions.

Watson's strengths, though, were extreme. He was blessed with that rare charisma that inspires followers to actually *love* their leader. He had unshakable faith in himself, a trait that allowed him to take tremendous business risks. For all his vanity, Watson lived for the company. He embodied it. Every ounce of his personal ambition was inseparable from his ambition for IBM. They became great business successes together.

Of course, Watson had luck by the boatload.

Watson built one of the most successful and admired companies of the twentieth century. His legacy, though, goes well beyond IBM. Three contributions stand out:

1. *He turned information into an industry.* Tabulating machines and computers would have been invented and

sold without Watson, by the likes of Powers and Remington Rand. However, Watson made it a business. He
figured out how to sell information processing to companies, universities, the government, and the military.
IBM achieved critical mass early, giving it the momentum and cash to invest in sustained research and development. The company's near-monopoly made IBM a de
facto standard, which made it safe for businesses and
institutions to buy IBM products. A customer knew
IBM wasn't a one-hit wonder, and the corporate decision maker felt the security of knowing lots of other
concerns were using IBM. The IBM standard also
allowed information to be shared among a company's
divisions or across an industry. Because IBM existed,
information processing coalesced into an industry and
had a far-reaching impact sooner than if a dozen little
companies had fought it out in the marketplace.

2. *Watson discovered the power of corporate culture.*
Before Watson, a company's culture just happened,
or didn't happen. It wasn't something management
purposefully grew and tended, studied and analyzed.
Watson created a powerful, well-defined culture, and
constantly looked for ways to reinforce it. He built the
IBM school, instituted the Hundred Percent Club, put
on events such as IBM Day at the World's Fair, and both
talked about and personified the culture. He imple-
mented radical ideas about respect for employees at all
levels, and management's duty to those they supervise.
The core of IBM—its ultimate economic engine—was
not information machines; rather, it was its culture.

Watson ran an information company by chance. He
inherited the tabulating machine when he took the
C-T-R job. Watson was not a technologist at heart. He
was a salesman. If Watson had built a company with a
similar culture around another product, he probably
still would have been a major business success.

3. *Watson was the first celebrity CEO.* In the early 1900s, the American public liked to read and talk about the nation's wealthiest industrialists. People knew the names of John D. Rockefeller, J. P. Morgan, and Henry Ford. However, those men became famous because of what they accomplished, not who they were, and they didn't court personal publicity. Watson, though, became a celebrity when his company was still a pipsqueak. He worked at becoming famous. His "THINK" slogan entered popular culture. During much of his time at IBM, Watson was more famous than his company. Publicity about Watson, in fact, contributed greatly to the success of IBM.

As the twentieth century turned into the twenty-first century, celebrity CEOs popped up like dandelions. Among them have been Bill Gates of Microsoft, Jack Welch of General Electric, and Chrysler's Lee Iacocca. The most direct descendent of Watson-style celebrity might be Larry Ellison of Oracle, which develops and sells corporate database software. Ellison is known as one of the nation's richest people, he's known for his quirky personality, and he runs a company that sells technology that most people never touch. Ellison is far more famous than Oracle. The spirit of Watson lives on.

How did Watson change the world? Management expert Peter Drucker saw it firsthand. "Again and again I have been laughed at in Japan when I talk about Japan's management embodying Japanese values," Drucker noted. " 'Don't you realize,' my Japanese friends asked, 'that we are simply adapting what IBM has done all along?' And when I ask how come, they always say, 'When we started to rebuild Japan in the 1950s, we looked around for the most successful company we could find. It's IBM, isn't it?' "[1] Reverberations from Watson helped shape the entire Japanese postwar economy. Not coincidentally, IBM and Japan

437

both ran into trouble in the 1990s when global business models shifted, making Watson-style management and paternalism obsolete. IBM found a leader, Lou Gerstner, who could keep IBM's core values while making changes necessary to compete in modern times. Japan still hasn't found the leader, or the will, to do the same.

❧

Here's what happened after Watson's death to some of those who most affected his life:

George Phillips. Stayed on as IBM's vice chairman until the end of 1956, and then retired. Phillips died in 1964.

Al Williams. Became Tom Jr.'s indispensable second in command, rising to president of IBM. He retired at 55, in 1966, for golf and warm weather in Florida. Williams died on December 30, 1982.

James Rand. A year before Watson died, Rand merged Remington Rand with another electronics company, Sperry, to form Sperry Rand. Rand turned 70 in 1956, but continued at the company. He took the title of vice chairman after the merger, and remained in charge of the UNIVAC division, which lost computer market share to IBM year after year. Rand finally retired in 1959. At the time, UNIVAC held onto about 10 percent of the electronic computer market, and IBM had 70 percent. In 1973, Sperry Rand lost a court battle over its claim to own the patent broadly covering all computers. Lawyers for two Sperry Rand competitors, Honeywell and Control Data, convinced the court that Iowa's John Atanasoff invented the computer, and UNIVAC inventors Eckert and Mauchly used Atanasoff's ideas after seeing Atanasoff's machine. The Sperry Rand patent claim was invalidated. The company struggled for a decade, then merged with computer company Burroughs in 1986 to form Unisys. In 2002, Unisys was a technology company with $6 billion in sales—one-fourteenth of IBM's sales that year.

Jeannette Watson.   Soon after her husband's death, she sold their house on East 75th Street, but kept the New Canaan home. IBM gave her Watson's board seat, which she relinquished in 1959. Jeannette died on February 10, 1966, at 82 years old. Two weeks later, IBM honored her with a special memorial edition of *IBM News,* a twice-monthly internal publication. The main headline showed where IBM placed her in its history: "Wife of IBM Founder Shared in Company Development." The story stated: "The uphill struggles to make IBM one of the world's leading enterprises were shared by Mrs. Watson. Her husband often deferred to her judgment. Frequently, when he had taken work home to mull over, he would turn to her for an opinion." To long-time IBMers, Jeannette lives on as a mythical first lady of IBM.

Dick Watson.   The life of Watson's youngest child fell apart over the next two decades. At Watson's death, Dick ran IBM World Trade, which operated quite independently from IBM headquarters. In the late 1950s, Tom Jr. brought his brother into the corporate mainstream, making him the head of engineering and manufacturing. In 1964, Tom Jr. put Dick in charge of the development of IBM's bet-the-company project, the System/360 computer. As the 360 ran into trouble, Tom Jr. and Dick clashed, and Tom Jr. demoted his brother. Furious and broken, Dick looked for a way out of IBM. He left in 1970 when President Nixon appointed him to be Ambassador to France.

Dick continued to struggle with alcohol problems. In 1972, while serving as ambassador, Dick allegedly drank heavily on a transatlantic flight and groped a flight attendant. Investigative columnist Jack Anderson wrote a graphic account of the incident, and it was published in newspapers worldwide. On Nixon's infamous White House tapes, released after the Watergate scandal, Nixon is heard telling aides why he wasn't bothered by Dick's behavior. "Look, people get drunk," Nixon said. "People chase girls. And the point is, it's a hell of a lot better for them to get drunk than to take drugs. It's better to chase girls than boys. Now that's my position and let's stop this crap."[2]

Nixon never asked for Dick Watson's resignation. Dick quit the post when Congress began an investigation of the incident. Two years later, at the age of 55 and in poor health, Dick Watson died after falling down the marble stairs of his New Canaan home.

≈

Only a few days after Watson's funeral, a writer for *Fortune* magazine, Robert Sheehan, met Tom Jr. at IBM headquarters. Tom Jr. decided to keep his own office on the 16th floor, and not move into his father's on the 17th. Sheehan found a man trying to gather his strength. Suddenly the solitary helmsman at IBM, Tom Jr., age 42, felt scared and lonely. He'd relied on his father in more ways than he cared to admit. He had an intimidating job to do.

"IBM had grown so big so fast that it is inadequately organized and perhaps inadequately staffed for the billion-dollar company it may soon become," Sheehan wrote. "It still bears some of the psychological scars of the long-time one-man rule."[3]

Tom Jr. knew IBM had to change. His task was not to assume his father's powers, but to disperse those powers, he told Sheehan that day.

In late 1956, Tom Jr. took 100 of IBM's top people to a retreat in Williamsburg, Virginia. They were not to leave until they'd reorganized IBM into a corporate structure befitting the 1950s and IBM's size. Tom Jr. and the executives split IBM into six autonomous divisions, plus World Trade, and named an executive to run each unit. At the top, CEO Tom Jr. would only see the biggest decisions. The job once done almost entirely by Watson was scattered among at least 13 people.

For the next 15 years, Tom Watson Jr. guided IBM through the most spectacular growth period in business history. During that time, IBM created more wealth for its shareholders than any previous company. IBM passed $1 billion in revenue in 1957, bringing in $1.2 billion for the year. In 1967—10 years later—IBM's revenue was nearly five times greater: $5.3 billion. In another six years, the company would double its revenue again, to $11 billion.

In 1957, IBM employed 83,588 people. Ten years later, it employed 221,866.

In the 1960s, IBM developed the landmark System/360 computer line. After Tom Jr. replaced his brother Dick with Vin Learson, Learson saw the project through. The 360 opened the door to scalable computing—the idea that a company could buy a small computer system and keep adding onto it as the business grew. Companies loved it, and the 360 fired up yet more growth for IBM. For the next 20 years, IBM utterly dominated the information industry.

Tom Jr. "virtually wrote the book on managing fast, sustained, hugely profitable growth," wrote *Fortune* in 1999, as it named Tom Jr. one of the greatest businessmen of the twentieth century. "A tough boss, he helped set the high-stress tone of executive life in the 1950s and '60s."[4]

Although he was highly effective, Tom Jr. managed by using contention, fits of rage, and massive amounts of compensation for top performers. He spread more fear among subordinates than his father ever did. In the words of a number of people who knew him, Tom Jr. was "not a nice man."

In November 1970, at the age of 55, Tom Jr. suffered a heart attack. The following June, he retired from IBM. In 1979, President Jimmy Carter made Tom Jr. the U.S. Ambassador to the Soviet Union. He left the post in 1981, and he and Olive returned to Greenwich.

IBM didn't pause after Tom Jr. left. The momentum from the Watson dynasty hurled the company forward. The IBM culture had become a machine, its thousands of employees coordinated by common values, working together to move the company in one direction—toward domination of the American corporate landscape. Two of Tom Watson Jr.'s hand-picked men—Vin Learson and Frank Cary—managed IBM into the 1980s. When Tom Jr. quit in 1970, IBM was raking in $7.5 billion in annual revenue and employing 269,291 people all over the world. Ten years later, IBM had more than tripled in size—in 1980 it brought in $26.2 billion in revenue and had 341,279 employees.

Through most of the 1980s, no company inspired more awe. IBM seemed incapable of being slowed. *Fortune* magazine perennially named IBM as America's most admired company. Corporations and governments worldwide utterly depended on IBM's gargantuan mainframe computers. IBM was bigger than its next five competitors combined, and like Snow White and the Seven Dwarfs, the computer industry became known as IBM and the BUNCH—Burroughs, UNIVAC, NCR, Control Data, and Honeywell. The culture that Watson built rolled on.

Eventually, though, the culture lost its way. The next two CEOs—John Opel and John Akers—had known Tom Watson Jr. but never worked in his inner circle. (No other Watson family members joined IBM's management, and none now have any significant role at the company—not even as a board member.) Opel joined the company in 1949 as a sales rep in Jefferson City, Missouri. By the time he moved into management, Thomas Watson Sr. no longer ran IBM. Akers joined IBM in 1960, four years after Watson died.

Under Opel and Akers, the company suffered from acute cautiousness, excessive bureaucracy, and flawed moves, such as an ill-fated attempt to get into the photocopier business and the purchase of an interest in telephone equipment company Rolm, which IBM sold seven years later. Opel and Akers simply did not have Watson coursing through their veins. They both were supersmart, charming, clever executives, but they had too little of Watson's devotion to customers, his competitive hunger, and his willingness to bet big. Absent those characteristics, the CEOs lost Watson's ability to internally jazz employees' competitive juices—so important to a company that usually faced weak competition in the marketplace. Without tending from the top, the culture of Watson eroded.

Pieces of the culture got bastardized. A tangible example is the old IBM dress code of suits and white shirts. IBMers came to believe that wearing formal business suits—a tradition started by Watson—was essential to IBM. They forgot *why* Watson favored formal dress: So his salesmen would fit in with the bank presidents and company comptrollers on whom they were calling. In the 1990s, when businesspeople increasingly adopted more casual dress, IBM representatives often stood out and looked hopelessly old-fashioned in their suits. The real IBM culture—Watson's culture—would have dictated that IBMers dress like their customers. In his first year of running IBM, Gerstner struck down the formal dress code to howls from IBM traditionalists. Gerstner was more right about the IBM culture than were thousands of long-time IBM employees.

In the 1980s, arrogance ran through the halls of IBM while divisions pulled in diffuse directions. Management concentrated on maintaining what IBM had, rather than constantly grasping for more. When the personal computer era arrived, it distributed computing power to individuals and threatened IBM's centralized computing model. The company's lethargic reaction resulted in customers believing that IBM was too big and too set in its ways to respond to changes in technology. Many began looking elsewhere for information systems.

If Watson of the 1930s or Tom Jr. of the 1960s had been in charge of the IBM of the 1980s, the company might have made an all-or-nothing bet on distributed computing. The tech landscape that gave openings to Microsoft, Intel, and Apple Computer might have been very different.

As it was, IBM nearly unraveled under Akers. From a high of $68.9 billion in revenue in 1990, sales figures began to slip and profits crumpled. IBM lost $2.8 billion in 1991; $5 billion in 1992, and $8.1 billion in 1993.

That's when IBM turned to Gerstner. He had been chief executive of a food and tobacco company, RJR Nabisco, and previously was an executive at American Express and consulting company McKinsey. Perhaps IBM's board of directors realized that Watson no longer resided inside the heart of IBM, and they'd have to find him somewhere else. Or maybe the board only thought it was searching for an effective CEO who also happened to be available to take the offer. Either way, the choice of Gerstner proved fateful. After coming aboard in 1993 and taking time to understand why IBM had faltered, Gerstner decided that IBM had to be reminded that it was IBM—Thomas Watson Sr.'s International Business Machines. Gerstner had to manage a lot of meaty and difficult steps, but they all came back to realigning IBM with its greatest strength: its culture. "I came to see, in my time at IBM, that culture isn't just one aspect of the game—it is the game," Gerstner wrote in his book, *Who*

Says Elephants Can't Dance? "In the end, an organization is nothing more than the collective capacity of its people to create value."[5]

One morning, soon after Gerstner took the CEO position, he walked out of his house to go to work. A car and driver were waiting for him, just as a car and driver had for years picked him up to take him to his offices at RJR Nabisco and American Express. "I went to sit down and realized there was somebody sitting in the other seat," Gerstner said in an interview at IBM headquarters. There, in the back seat, sat Tom Watson Jr. In an odd, almost cosmic coincidence, Gerstner lived right next door to Olive and Tom Jr. in Greenwich, Connecticut. The Watson house stood on the waterfront; Gerstner's was one house up a tiny road. Gerstner had lived there well before joining IBM, yet the proximity had nothing to do with Gerstner getting the job. Imagine the odds of them being neighbors! "He asked if he could please ride to work with me," Gerstner said.

As Gerstner got over his surprise and climbed into the car, Tom Jr. let loose that he was angry about what had happened to "my company." He urged Gerstner to tear the place up and move quickly. Gerstner recalled that Tom Jr. emphasized "the need he had seen over and over again to take bold action." Tom Jr. prodded and encouraged Gerstner, but he did not attempt to tell the new CEO what he should do or how he should do it.

"I was sitting there thinking, 'This is really a special moment.' " Gerstner recalled.[6]

In a sense, Tom Watson Jr. in that moment closed the link between the great IBM of the past and the possibility of reviving that greatness for the future. It was almost as if Watson Jr. rode in the car so he could hand Gerstner the keys to the Watson culture.

On December 31, 1993, Tom Watson Jr. died at age 79 from complications following a stroke. IBM under Gerstner lived on and returned to profitability, though not to its one-time dominance. At the end of 2002, Gerstner retired from a much healthier IBM. The next CEO, Sam Palmisano, is a career-long IBMer. He has a reputation as a world-class salesman. At the time of this writing, he just proclaimed that his goal is to make IBM great again. Interestingly, Palmisano's appearance, actions, and attitude seem reminiscent of Charley Kirk, once one of Watson's favorites. Watson would probably approve, seeing the business blood lines running from IBM's past out into its future.

SELECTED BIBLIOGRAPHY

Ambrose, Stephen E. *Eisenhower*. Norwalk, CN: Easton Press, 1987.

Amonette, Ruth Leach. *Among Equals*. Berkeley, CA: Creative Arts Book Company, 1999.

Austrian, Geoffrey D. *Herman Hollerith: Forgotten Giant of Information Processing*. New York: Columbia University Press, 1982.

Belden, Thomas Graham, and Marva Robins Belden. *The Lengthening Shadow: The Life of Thomas J. Watson*. Boston: Little, Brown and Company, 1962.

Black, Edwin. *IBM and the Holocaust*. New York: Crown Publishers, 2001

Campbell-Kelly, Martin, and William Aspray. *Computer: A History of the Information Machine*. New York: BasicBooks, 1996.

Ceruzzi, Paul E. *A History of Modern Computing*. Cambridge, MA: The MIT Press, 1998.

Cohen, I. Bernard. *Howard Aiken: Portrait of a Computer Pioneer*. Cambridge, MA: The MIT Press, 1999.

Conover, Charlotte Reeve. *Builders in New Fields*. New York: GP Putnam's Sons, 1939.

Cortada, James W. *Before the Computer: IBM, NCR, Burroughs, & Remington Rand & the Industry They Created 1865–1956*. Princeton, NJ: Princeton University Press, 1993.

Crowther, Samuel. *John H. Patterson: Pioneer in Industrial Welfare*. Garden City, NY: Doubleday Page & Co., 1923.

DeLamarter, Richard Thomas. *Big Blue: IBM's Use and Abuse of Power*. New York: Dodd, Mead & Co., 1986.

Drucker, Peter F. *Adventures of a Bystander*. New York: John Wiley & Sons, 1998.

Drucker, Peter F. *The Ecological Vision.* New Brunswick, NJ: Transaction Publishers, 1993.

Flint, Charles R. *Memories of an Active Life: Men, and Ships, and Sealing Wax.* New York: G.P. Putnam's Sons, 1923.

Goodwin, Doris Kearns. *No Ordinary Time: Franklin and Eleanor Roosevelt: The Home Front in World War II.* New York: Simon & Schuster, 1994.

Inglis, William. *George F. Johnson and His Industrial Democracy.* New York: Huntington Press, 1935.

McCartney, Scott. *ENIAC: The Triumphs and Tragedies of the World's First Computer.* New York: Walker, 1999.

Morgan, Ted. *FDR: A Biography.* New York: Simon & Schuster, 1985.

Pugh, Emerson W. *Building IBM.* Cambridge, MA: The MIT Press, 1995.

Rodgers, William. *Think: A Biography of the Watsons and IBM.* New York: Stein and Day, 1969.

Smith, Gerald R. *The Valley of Opportunity.* Norfolk, VA: The Donning Co., 1988.

Sobel, Robert. *I.B.M.: Colossus in Transition.* New York: Times Books, 1981.

Sobel, Robert. *Thomas Watson Sr.: IBM and the Computer Revolution.* Washington, DC: BeardBooks, 2000.

Sonnenfeld, Jeffrey. *Hero's Farewell: What Happens When CEOs Retire.* New York: Oxford University Press, 1988.

Truman, Margaret. *Harry S. Truman.* New York: William Morrow & Co., 1972.

Watson Jr., Thomas J., and Peter Petre. *Father Son & Co.: My Life at IBM and Beyond.* New York: Bantam Books, 1990.

Watson, Thomas J. *Human Relations.* New York: International Business Machines, 1949.

Watson, Thomas J. *Men-Minutes-Money.* New York: International Business Machines, 1934.

NOTES

PROLOGUE
1. Dialogue is from verbatim meeting transcripts: July 15, 1943, at the Endicott labs; July 19, 1943, in Watson's office. IBM Archives.

CHAPTER 1
1. Photos and items from the Montgomery County Historical Society in Dayton, Ohio.
2. Thomas Graham Belden and Marva Robins Belden, *The Lengthening Shadow*, Little, Brown and Co., 1962.
3. Records from NCR archives.
4. Ditzler to Watson, September 7, 1907. NCR archives.
5. NCR sales figures from James W. Cortada, *Before the Computer: IBM, NCR, Burroughs, & Remington Rand & the Industry They Created 1865–1956*, Princeton University Press, 1993.
6. Photographs in the NCR Archives show various scenes of executive exercise.
7. Samuel Crowther, *John H. Patterson: Pioneer in Industrial Welfare*, Doubleday Page & Co., 1923.
8. Engineering meeting transcript, June 18, 1943. IBM Archives.
9. Watson Homestead, East Campbell, New York.
10. Quote from May 12, 1942, meeting notes. IBM Archives.
11. July 22, 1931, letter from Chalmers to Watson. IBM Archives.
12. The book is held at the Dayton Public Library in Dayton, Ohio.
13. February 7, 1949, speech at the Breakers Hotel, Palm Beach, Florida. IBM Archives.
14. Contemporary accounts from the *Dayton Daily News* and *Dayton Journal*.
15. Interview with Peter Drucker at his home in Claremont, California, March 7, 2001.
16. Belden and Belden, *Lengthening Shadow*, p. 73.
17. The *Sun* newspaper, New York, March 27, 1913.
18. *Dayton Daily News* book of historical articles, held by the Dayton Public Library.

19. *NCR Weekly.*
20. Jennie Parsons, "Prisoners of the Flood," *McClure's Magazine,* July 1913.
21. Telegrams courtesy Montgomery County Historical Society. I've added punctuation and capitalization to some of the messages to make them easier to read. Telegrams typically had neither.
22. *Detroit News,* March 29, 1913.
23. NCR Archives.
24. March 25, 1935, letter from Cool to Watson. IBM Archives.
25. September 8, 1914, letter from Watson to Deeds and September 12, 1914, reply from Deeds. IBM Archives.
26. December 15, 1933, letter from Deeds to Watson. IBM Archives.

CHAPTER 2
1. Charles R. Flint, *Memories of an Active Life: Men, and Ships, and Sealing Wax,* G.P. Putnam's Sons, 1923.
2. October 26, 1917, telegram to Watson from A. M. Kittredge. "Charles R. Flint invited to Dayton by Orville Wright. Arrives Saturday morning twenty-seventh Pennsylvania Railroad at nine twenty-three a.m. Appreciate it if you would make reservation Miami Hotel. If convenient meet him at train."
3. Flint to George W. Todd, April 25, 1916. IBM Archives.
4. Thomas Watson Jr. and Peter Petre, *Father, Son & Co.: My Life at IBM and Beyond,* Bantam Books, 1990.
5. August 5, 1914, letter from Watson to Kittredge. IBM Archives.
6. December 5, 1916, Watson to Kittredge. IBM Archives.
7. December 5, 1916, Watson to Kittredge. IBM Archives.
8. Figures from IBM.
9. *Think* magazine, T. J. Watson Memorial Issue, 1956.
10. Interview with Robert Schumann, grandson of A. Ward Ford. Ford's obituary in the *Binghamton Press* called him "one of the men instrumental in obtaining the services of Thomas J. Watson."
11. Geoffrey D. Austrian, *Herman Hollerith: Forgotten Giant of Information Processing,* Columbia University Press, 1982, p. 324.
12. Ibid., p. 325.
13. Otto Braitmayer to J. E. Braitmayer, June 9, 1926. IBM Archives.

14. Watson to Hollerith, December 11, 1917. IBM Archives.
15. Fairchild to Watson: May 3, 1919; January 4, 1921; January 1, 1919. IBM Archives.
16. Watson to Fairchild, December 21, 1917. IBM Archives.
17. Austrian, *Herman Hollerith*, p. 333.
18. Transcript of Tabulating Machine conference, December 7, 1914. IBM Archives.
19. Text of Watson speech at ITR in Endicott, New York, January 15, 1915. IBM Archives.
20. March 13, 1915, exchange. IBM Archives.

CHAPTER 3

1. Watson apparently instructed Nichol to write a word-for-word account of the conversation between Nichol and Houston. The document, dated April 1, 1915, is in the IBM Archives.
2. Thomas J. Watson, *Human Relations: A Collection of Excerpts from Talks and Articles,* published by IBM, 1949, p. 367.
3. Austrian, *Herman Hollerith*, p. 337.
4. Memo from Braitmayer to Watson, February 22, 1918. IBM Archives.
5. Otto Braitmayer to Joe Braitmayer, December 28, 1926. IBM Archives.
6. Speech at a dinner honoring Ford, October 30, 1929. From the book *Men-Minutes-Money: A Collection of Excerpts from Talks and Messages Delivered and Written at Various Times,* by Thomas J. Watson, published by IBM in 1934.
7. "International Business Machines," *Fortune,* January 1940.
8. Letter from Nichol to Watson, December 19, 1951. IBM Archives.
9. Nichol to Watson, December 22, 1941. IBM Archives.
10. Watson to Nichol, February 26, 1918. IBM Archives.
11. Adair Nichol to Watson, October 1955. IBM Archives.
12. Spahr to Watson and Hastings, March 7, 1921. IBM Archives.
13. Watson to Spahr, March 3, 1922. IBM Archives.
14. Federal regulation of securities didn't come until the Securities Act of 1933. Thanks to Professor Eugene White at Rutgers University for background on stock exchanges in 1914.
15. In a document dated November 18, 1937 (IBM Archives), Watson discloses an incident from years after the stock incident. Watson met a Wall Street trader while on a train ride, and once

the trader found out who Watson was, the trader said that he'd helped the Ogsbury and Fairchild group back in 1914. Watson had generally known about the stock scheme, but the trader filled in and confirmed details, which Watson believed were true. Ogsbury continued to deny any involvement. I could find no documents that showed Fairchild mentioning the scheme at all.

16. Ogsbury to Watson, circa 1937. IBM Archives.
17. Watson to Ogsbury, November 24, 1937. IBM Archives.
18. Ogsbury to Watson, April 26, 1929. IBM Archives.
19. Transcripts of two meetings on December 18, 1916. IBM Archives.
20. "Memorandum RE Door Lock for Discussion with Mr. Rogers," undated. IBM Archives.
21. Transcript of December 14, 1916, meeting in Watson's office. IBM Archives.
22. January 15, 1917, speech at the Convention of The Tabulating Machine Company. There exists both a transcript and a film of the speech. IBM Archives.
23. January 27, 1921, meeting at the Hotel Miami in Dayton, Ohio. IBM Archives.
24. Transcript of a December 18, 1917, meeting in Watson's office. IBM Archives.
25. Letter to Watson from architect Benjamin White, who was hired to plan the renovations. IBM Archives.
26. Interview with Olive Watson, April 2000.
27. Films from this period are held in the IBM Archives.
28. Watson Jr. and Petre, *Father, Son & Co.*, p. 4.
29. On December 15, 1922, Watson wrote to White Star St. Bernards Kennels in Long Branch, New Jersey, inquiring about the Newfoundland puppies.
30. Belden and Belden, *Lengthening Shadow*, p. 60.
31. Chamberlain to Watson, April 12, 1918. IBM Archives.
32. Watson Jr. and Petre, *Father, Son & Co.*, p. 20.
33. Letter from Watson to John Hayward, March 4, 1919. IBM Archives.
34. Bill for fire fighting services from the city of Summit, New Jersey, dated February 26, 1919. Watson had to pay $84.
35. Typewritten document dated March 10, 1919. IBM Archives.

36. Watson to Fairchild, March 13, 1919. IBM Archives.
37. Transcript of meeting April 9, 1917. IBM Archives.
38. IBM figures.
39. James W. Cortada, *Before the Computer: IBM, NCR, Burroughs, and Remington Rand and the Industry They Created,* Princeton University Press, 1993, pp. 80–81.
40. Ibid., p. 82.
41. C-T-R's early engineering work is discussed in a number of places in the books *Building IBM* by Emerson W. Pugh, Massachusetts Institute of Technology, 1995; and Cortada's *Before the Computer.*
42. Ford to Watson, July 1, 1926. IBM Archives.
43. Speech at the Watson Trophy dinner in Endicott, New York, October 26, 1940.
44. Address to the Second C-T-R Executive School, held at the Buckwood Inn, Shawnee-on-Delaware, Pennsylvania, September 20–25, 1920.
45. Meeting notes, May 20, 1921. IBM Archives.
46. January 27, 1921, executive meeting at the Hotel Miami in Dayton, Ohio. IBM Archives.
47. November 13, 1922, meeting in Dayton, Ohio. IBM Archives.
48. November 8, 1922, meeting in Watson's office. IBM Archives.
49. Furlong to Watson, February 16, 1924. IBM Archives.

CHAPTER 4
1. Taken from Watson's copy of the form. It's not dated, but is probably from 1931 or 1932.
2. Flint to Phillips, October 20, 1925. IBM Archives.
3. Watson memo, June 30, 1920. IBM Archives.
4. Notes from an engineering and development meeting, IBM boardroom, September 22, 1925. IBM Archives.
5. Bryce to Watson, September 2, 1924. IBM Archives.
6. Lab report dated June 30, 1928. IBM Archives.
7. L. Fles & Co., an Amsterdam-based agent for IBM, to Tabulating Machine Company, September 15, 1924. IBM Archives.
8. Braitmayer to Lake, October 22, 1927. IBM Archives.
9. My cousin, Beth Sullivan, and her husband, Eric, collect and sell old Binghamton-area postcards and similar artifacts. Thanks to them, I had a pile of period Endicott-Johnson postcards for

visual reference, and a wonderful little 1919 company booklet that includes photographs of every building that E-J owned.

10. George W. Johnson to Walter Lyon, June 27, 1940. IBM Archives.
11. May 8, 1933, speech to a class in Endicott. Watson, *Men-Minutes-Money,* p. 817.
12. William Inglis, *George F. Johnson and His Industrial Democracy,* Huntington Press, 1935, p. 43.
13. *New York Herald,* magazine section, February 11, 1917.
14. Inglis, *George F. Johnson,* p. 294.
15. Johnson to Watson, September 9, 1931. IBM Archives.
16. Anderson to Watson, February 3, 1923. IBM Archives.
17. Johnson to Watson, April 23, 1937. IBM Archives.
18. Johnson to Watson, April 17, 1936. IBM Archives.
19. Watson to Johnson, November 30, 1936. IBM Archives.
20. Johnson to Watson, April 23, 1937. IBM Archives.
21. Minutes of meeting, September 20, 1928. IBM Archives.
22. Belden and Belden, *Lengthening Shadow,* p. 145.
23. *Saturday Evening Post,* May 24, 1941. Story by Gerald Breckenridge.
24. Watson to Winfred Green of Califon, New Jersey, June 3, 1927. IBM Archives.
25. Tuttle to Watson, January 9, 1933. IBM Archives.
26. The 1927 will is at the IBM Archives.
27. December 22, 1927, receipt. IBM Archives.
28. Document from Watson files, May 29, 1928. IBM Archives.
29. From *Songs of the IBM,* 1929 edition.
30. *New York Times,* October 30, 1929.
31. *Business Machines,* November 30, 1929.
32. *New York Times,* October 30, 1929.
33. *Binghamton Press,* October 30, 1929.

CHAPTER 5
1. Notes from meeting November 18, 1929. IBM Archives.
2. Interview with Bob Novak, Endicott, New York.
3. Interview with Eleanor Irvine. She had at times gone into a women's room at an event and found Jeannette Watson there, prone.
4. Interview with Eleanor Irvine.
5. Watson Jr. and Petre, *Father, Son & Co.,* p. 20.

6. William Rodgers, *Think: A Biography of the Watsons and IBM*, Stein and Day, 1969, p. 145.
7. Ibid., p. 21.
8. The hand-scribbled note was found in Watson's file at the IBM Archives.
9. Interview with Peter Drucker, December 2000.
10. "Victors in Adversity" by Lee C. Cresswill, *Magazine of Wall Street*, 1931.
11. Speech over the public address system in the Endicott factory, January 8, 1940.
12. To a great extent, the IBM lab and school still look like they did in the 1930s. Thanks to IBM Endicott for the tours.
13. Belden and Belden, *The Lengthening Shadow*, p. 162.
14. LaMotte to Watson, April 17, 1931. IBM Archives.
15. Phillips to Watson, August 4, 1932. IBM Archives.
16. Interview with Jim Birkenstock at his Florida home in 2001. He sat in a guest room next to the swimming pool, his hair and mustache stark white and his eyes a glittering blue. He recalled events from 60 years before with clarity and detail.
17. The executive who vomited told this to Birkenstock, who related it to me.
18. Lee Olwell wrote "The Genesis of Think" for the *New York Evening Journal* while he was publisher of the newspaper.
19. Note from the 1932–1933 "General Correspondence" folder in the Watson collection. IBM Archives.
20. Address to a class at the IBM school in Endicott, October 30, 1929.
21. Watson to Hansen, May 31, 1935. IBM Archives.
22. Yacht receipts, descriptions, and instructions are in the "Recreation" file in the Watson collection at the IBM Archives.
23. Rodgers, *Think*, p. 136; Matthew T. Downey, *Ben D. Wood: Educational Reformer*, 1965, pp. 49–51.
24. Ibid., p. 137.
25. Meeting notes, December 16, 1936. IBM Archives.
26. Hale to Phillips, circa 1928. IBM Archives.
27. Hale to Phillips, February 3, 1928. IBM Archives.
28. Hale to Phillips, 1938. IBM Archives.
29. Watson issued the bonus order in a memo dated December 24, 1935.
30. Watson Jr. and Petre, *Father, Son & Co.*, p. 46.

CHAPTER 6

1. van Vechten to Watson, March 24, 1935. IBM Archives.
2. Waters to van Vechten, March 27, 1935. IBM Archives.
3. van Vechten papers at IBM archives; and Ruth Leach Amonette, *Among Equals,* Creative Arts Book Co., 1999.
4. van Vechten to her parents. IBM archives.
5. This side of Watson was described by Eleanor Irvine and Olive Watson in interviews, runs through van Vechten's papers, and is evident in Amonette's memoirs.
6. Phillips to Braitmayer, September 27, 1934. IBM Archives. Appalling as the policy seems to later generations, women at IBM at the time generally accepted it with little resentment. To them, in fact, IBM offered women more opportunity than most companies. IBM's marriage policy wasn't completely out of step with contemporary attitudes toward working women. The media, for instance, never mentioned the marriage rule in a critical way.
7. Interview with Eleanor Irvine.
8. Leach Amonette, *Among Equals,* p. 14.
9. Leach Amonette, *Among Equals,* p. 23.
10. Reader's Digest Association, *Our Glorious Century,* 1994.
11. Roosevelt to Watson, August 25, 1932. IBM Archives.
12. Watson does not appear in any of these biographies of Roosevelt: Doris Kearns Goodwin, *No Ordinary Time,* Simon & Schuster, New York, 1994; Frank Freidel, *Franklin D. Roosevelt: A Rendezvous with Destiny,* Little, Brown & Company, Boston, 1991; Kenneth S. Davis, *FDR: Into the Storm 1937 to 1940,* Random House, New York, 1993; Ted Morgan, *FDR: A Biography,* Simon & Schuster, New York, 1985.
13. *New York Times,* July 1, 1937. The *Times,* like many newspapers, ran the wedding story on the front page. Inside it printed the long guest list of American royalty. Watson's name did not appear.
14. Watson to Roosevelt, June 19, 1936. IBM Archives.
15. Western Union telegram from the White House to Watson, June 23, 1936. IBM Archives.
16. Roosevelt to Watson, from Hyde Park, New York, August 27, 1938. IBM Archives. The original was framed and hung in IBM CEO Louis Gerstner's office in January 1995.
17. Address at a National Recovery Act pledge card meeting at IBM headquarters, September 7, 1933.

18. Belden and Belden, *Lengthening Shadow*, pp. 185–186.
19. Watson to Cool, November 18, 1939. IBM Archives.
20. Letters between Watson and Lippincott, 1934. IBM Archives.
21. Watson to Erford Gorton, September 2, 1939. IBM Archives.
22. Gorton to Watson, August 28, 1934. IBM Archives.
23. Watson to Gorton, September 20, 1934. IBM Archives.
24. Watson note to Phillips, November 1943. IBM Archives.
25. Hyatt to Watson, March 9, 1945. IBM Archives.
26. Interviews with Olive Watson, Lucinda Watson.
27. Watson Jr. and Petre, *Father, Son & Co.*, p. 152.
28. Leach Amonette, *Among Equals*, p. 76.
29. Leach Amonette, *Among Equals*, p. 117.
30. Lucinda Watson interview.
31. Memos dated December 3, 1936; January 17, 1938; February 16, 1938. All in Phillips's file in the IBM Archives.
32. Titus to Watson, January 2, 1939. IBM Archives.
33. Titus report, April 3, 1933. IBM Archives.
34. Titus files. IBM Archives.
35. Watson to Nichol, January 19, 1939. IBM Archives.
36. From interviews with Birkenstock and from Birkenstock's memoir, published in the January-March 2000 issue of *IEEE Annals of the History of Computing*.
37. Watson Jr. and Petre, *Father, Son & Co.*, p. 79.
38. Leach Amonette, *Among Equals*, p. 132.
39. This section comes from a remarkable verbatim account of a March 24, 1941, meeting at IBM headquarters at 590 Madison Avenue. Watson probably wanted the document saved because it documented his management philosophy. IBM Archives.

CHAPTER 7
1. Belden and Belden, *Lengthening Shadow*, p. 191.
2. "German Administration of American Companies: 1940–1945," Dr. Greg Bradsher, National Archives and Records Administration.
3. Pugh, *Building IBM*, p. 18; Edwin Black, *IBM and the Holocaust*, Crown Publishers, 2001, pp. 43–44. Black cites a June 18, 1943, "Declaration to the IBM Advisory Committee" by Willy Heidinger.
4. Watson Jr.'s words in Watson Jr. and Petre, *Father, Son & Co.*, p. 54.

5. From Watson Jr. and Petre, *Father, Son & Co.*, p. 54; Policy Review no. 106, Hoover Institution; Walther Kiaulehn, *Berlin: Destiny of a World City,* 1958.
6. *The New York Times,* June 29, 30, July 1, 1937.
7. A copy of Shacht's speech resides in the IBM Archives.
8. In a January 31, 1938, address to IBM stockholders, Watson refers to "visiting thirteen countries last year." He would have visited them all in one trip. He began in London, traveled to Berlin, then on to the 11 other nations.
9. "Ford and GM Scrutinized for Alleged Nazi Collaboration," *The Washington Post,* November 30, 1998.
10. Watson to Schacht, August 18, 1937. IBM Archives.
11. Letter from J. C. Milner in Geneva, Switzerland, August 4, 1938, addressed to J. T. Wilson, manager of IBM's foreign division in New York and copied to Phillips.
12. A series of 1934 letters from Heidinger to IBM, deposited at the Elmer Holmes Bobst Library at New York University, New York.
13. IBM lawyer Harrison K. Chauncey to J. C. Milner of IBM Geneva, July 14, 1938. Bobst Library, NYU.
14. Unsigned IBM internal memo of March 10, 1941, and other documents around that time, held at the Bobst Library, NYU.
15. December 2, 1941, Phillips to Hull. Bobst Library, NYU.
16. Milner in Geneva to Wilson in New York, August 4, 1938.
17. Watson to May, April 8, 1938. IBM Archives.
18. May to Watson, November 28, 1938. IBM Archives.
19. Watson to May, December 9, 1938. IBM Archives.
20. Watson to Hitler, November 25, 1938.
21. Memos and letters from this period in the Bobst Library, NYU.
22. Zerwick to Watson, June 4, 1940. IBM Archives.
23. Cohen to Watson, April 26, 1940. IBM Archives.
24. Quoted letters and telegrams from the IBM Archives.
25. Chudnow to Watson, June 17, 1940. IBM Archives.

CHAPTER 8
1. Meeting notes, June 5, 1940. IBM Archives.
2. Gerald Breckenridge, "Salesman No. 1," *The Saturday Evening Post,* May 24, 1941.
3. Many picture books and Web sites contributed to my images of the World's Fair, but my perspective was aided tremendously by

computer scientist David Gelernter's book, *1939: The Lost World of the Fair,* The Free Press, 1995.

4. IBM films and videos of IBM Day. IBM Archives.
5. IBM films and videos of the IBM Day banquet. IBM Archives
6. Watson Jr. and Petre, *Father, Son & Co.,* pp. 84–85.
7. *New York Times,* May 14, 1940.
8. Account of the train wreck derived from Watson Jr. and Petre, *Father, Son & Co.;* IBM's *Business Machines* in-house publication; and contemporary news stories and personal accounts on file at the Broome County Historical Society, Binghamton, New York.
9. Interview with Peter Drucker.
10. Although Watson, chastened by antitrust, remained a stickler about complying with laws and regulations, he rarely missed a chance to interpret a law or regulation as he saw fit. Therefore, in his view, just about any big company could be classified as part of the war effort. Companies that produced steel, lumber, oil, or any raw material played a part, as did banks, insurance companies, and Wall Street firms, which war-related businesses needed to keep running. Food distributors, paper companies, railroads—they were needed. IBM might have a hard time trying to justify supplying a candy maker or distillery.
11. Robert Novak interview.
12. From an address at the Watson Trophy Dinner at the IBM Country Club, April 27, 1940.
13. Accounts of the sights, scene, and typical activities at the Homestead and Country Club come from published accounts, personal interviews, and on-site visits to IBM Endicott.
14. July 3, 1941, meeting in Watson's office. IBM Archives.
15. Transcription of meeting at IBM headquarters, April 1, 1941. IBM Archives.
16. Letter from George Eastman to Watson, May 26, 1927. IBM Archives.
17. Letters between Watson and Luce, 1950s. IBM Archives.

CHAPTER 9
1. Letter dated July 10, 1918, to Watson, but no signature or sender's name. IBM Archives.
2. Watson Jr. and Petre, *Father, Son & Co.,* pp. 27–28.
3. January 7, 1921, telegram from Watson. IBM Archives.

4. Watson Jr. and Petre, *Father, Son & Co.*, p. 5.
5. Ibid., p. 7.
6. The two hunting license applications are in the IBM Archives.
7. Watson to Waffl, October 24, 1927. IBM Archives.
8. Watson Jr. and Petre, *Father, Son & Co.*, p. 31.
9. Ibid., p. 34.
10. Ibid., p. 26.
11. "Clink Clank Think," *Time*, March 28, 1955.
12. This section, in addition to Watson Jr.'s own words in *Father, Son & Co.*, is based on interviews with members of the Watson family, and with outside observers such as Peter Drucker and James Birkenstock.
13. Watson Jr. and Petre, *Father, Son & Co.*, p. 37.
14. Barbour to Watson, October 9, 1934. IBM Archives.
15. From Watson Jr. and Petre, *Father, Son & Co.*, p. 42; and the Watson Jr. file in the IBM Archives.
16. Watson Jr. and Petre, *Father, Son & Co.*, p. 49.
17. Leach Amonette, *Among Equals*, p. 14.
18. Jeffrey Sonnenfeld, *The Hero's Farewell: What Happens When CEOs Retire*, Oxford University Press, 1988, p. 153.
19. Watson to Watson Jr., April 27, 1939. IBM Archives.
20. "Clink Clank Think," *Time*, March 28, 1955.
21. The section on Olive is woven from interviews with Olive Watson and other family members, and from Watson Jr.'s autobiography, *Father, Son & Co.*
22. Watson to Arthur Watson, April 23, 1940. IBM Archives.
23. Arthur Watson's grades are in his file in the IBM Archives.
24. Arthur Watson to Watson, undated but apparently from the summer of 1939. IBM Archives.
25. Interview with Eleanor Irvine, September 2000.
26. Arthur Watson to Jeannette Watson, December 10, 1945. IBM Archives.
27. Interviews with Olive Watson contributed to this section.
28. Watson Jr. and Petre, *Father, Son & Co.*, p. 177.
29. It seems that Tom Watson Jr. missed an opportunity he should have seen. He'd become enthusiastic about the Link trainers. They were built only a few miles from IBM's Endicott factories. It became obvious by 1950 that computers would be used to control Link flight simulators. However, Watson Jr. didn't see the potential for IBM—he neither bought Link's company nor

pushed IBM into simulators. Link's business grew to provide trainers for every major airline, the military, and eventually NASA, which used Link machines to train astronauts. Edwin Link sold his company to General Precision Equipment Corporation of New York in 1954. The company has since had numerous owners, and it still makes simulators. Edwin Link died in 1981 in Binghamton, New York. Resource: The Edwin Link papers at Binghamton Public Library, and other published material.

30. "New York Close-Up" column in the *New York Times,* August 30, 1950; Watson Jr. and Petre, *Father, Son & Co.,* p. 101.

31. Watson Jr. and Petre, *Father, Son & Co.,* pp. 106–109.

32. Ibid., p. 127.

33. From Sonnenfeld, *The Hero's Farewell,* p. 153. Sonnenfeld interviewed Watson Jr. before he died and quoted him directly telling the story of the conversation with Bradley. The conversation is recounted much the same way in Watson Jr. and Petre, *Father, Son & Co.,* p. 127; Belden and Belden, *Lengthening Shadow,* p. 224.

34. Watson Jr. and Petre, *Father, Son & Co.,* p. 128; Sonnenfeld, *The Hero's Farewell,* p. 153.

CHAPTER 10

1. Fred C. Kelly to Kirk, dated May 26 with no year. Because of its relation to his other notes, this one is probably from 1940 or 1941.

2. Leach Amonette, *Among Equals,* p. 56.

3. Internal report, "Effect of Cessation of Hostilities Upon IBM Operations," dated January 29, 1942. IBM Archives.

4. Pugh, *Building IBM,* p. 90.

5. From an IBM document titled "From the Beginning of Defense to Pearl Harbor," undated. IBM Archives.

6. June 7, 1944, meeting in boardroom. IBM Archives.

7. "The Use of Machine Records by the Army," an address by Lt. Col. Carl G. Allen at the Command and General Staff School, Fort Leavenworth, Kansas, on November 21, 1945.

8. Description of Kirk compiled from many sources: interviews, published accounts, newspaper stories, and the autopsy report following his death in 1947.

9. Figures quoted by Watson at a meeting in Watson's office on January 11, 1944. IBM Archives.

10. Watson commented about the $2 million savings in a meeting in 1951. Other than the year, the document is undated. IBM Archives.
11. This paragraph from a May 7, 1943, meeting in Watson's office. The same phrasing comes up in other engineering meetings during the war. IBM Archives.
12. The beginnings of the Radiotype are best described in Pugh's book, *Building IBM*, p. 94.
13. "The Use of Machine Records by the Army," an address by Lt. Col. Carl G. Allen at the Command and General Staff School, Fort Leavenworth, Kansas, on November 21, 1945.
14. All quotes in this section are from notes from an engineering meeting at the 590 Madison Avenue headquarters, June 18, 1943. IBM Archives.
15. Telegram from Watson to Hill, 1944. IBM Archives.
16. Gannett letters to Watson are in IBM's Archives. Other information about the sale are from Gannett Corporation's company history and histories of Binghamton.
17. Quotes from notes from an engineering meeting at the East Orange, New Jersey, laboratory, March 7, 1944.
18. Engineering conference, November 4, 1944. IBM Archives.
19. Meeting in Watson's office, August 14, 1945. IBM Archives.

CHAPTER 11
1. For analysis of the paintings, I thank Abraham Dijkstra, author of art history books and professor of literature at the University of California—San Diego.
2. "Salient Features of a Conversation with Mr. T. J. Watson," dated May 6, 1944. IBM Archives.
3. Watson Jr. and Petre, *Father, Son & Co.*, p. 205.
4. June 18, 1943, meeting notes, as cited in Pugh, *Building IBM*, p. 119.
5. Descriptions of the Mark I and the sequence of events are well documented. Particularly helpful were Martin Campbell-Kelly and William Aspray, *Computer: A History of the Information Machine*; I. Bernard Cohen, *Howard Aiken: Portrait of a Computer Pioneer*; James W. Cortada, *The Computer in the United States: From Laboratory to Market, 1930 to 1980*. Those publications informed most of the book's depictions of developments in computers. For historical background, I also had help

462

from Gordon Bell of The Computer Museum at Moffett Field in the San Francisco Bay Area, and Paul Ceruzzi of the Smithsonian Institution, Washington, D.C.

6. Cohen, *Howard Aiken,* p. 103.

7. Scott McCartney, *ENIAC: The Triumphs and Tragedies of the World's First Computer,* Walker, 1999, pp. 140–145.

8. Cohen, *Howard Aiken,* pp. 123–124.

9. Belden and Belden, *Lengthening Shadow,* p. 260.

10. Watson to Harold Westergaard, dean of Harvard's Graduate School of Engineering, August 28, 1944. It is a response to Westergaard's letter to Watson dated August 12, 1944.

11. Watson Jr. and Petre, *Father, Son & Co.,* p. 130.

12. Watson to Nichol, August 17, 1945. IBM Archives.

13. Leach Amonette, *Among Equals,* p. 132.

14. Watson to Gilbert Hodges, staff executive of the *Wall Street Journal,* March 13, 1951. IBM Archives.

15. From Watson's date books, 1945 to 1949. IBM Archives.

16. Interview with Jeannette K. Watson.

17. Watson Jr. and Petre, *Father, Son & Co.,* p. 131.

18. Ibid., p. 132.

19. Pugh, *Building IBM,* pp. 123–126; Campbell-Kelly and Aspray, *Computer,* pp. 113–114.

20. Watson Jr. and Petre, *Father, Son & Co.,* pp. 136–137.

21. Interview with James Birkenstock.

22. Watson Jr. and Petre, *Father, Son & Co.,* p. 143. Much of the story of Tom Watson Jr. threatening to quit because of Kirk comes from Watson Jr.'s autobiography, cross-referenced with interviews and references in documents from the IBM Archives and Rodgers's book *Think.*

23. Watson Jr. and Petre, *Father, Son & Co.,* p. 144.

24. Ibid., p. 144.

25. Details of Kirk's death are found in the translation of an autopsy conducted on Kirk. The translation is dated October 1, 1947. Kirk had blood alcohol levels that would qualify for driving while intoxicated in most of the United States in 2002.

26. These and other details were found in *Binghamton Press* stories from June 17, 1947, to July 2, 1947.

27. A number of times each year, someone calls the IBM Archives and asks to confirm Watson's comment about a market for only five computers. None of the Archives staff, past or present, has

been able to find anything to substantiate the quote. I've found the Archives staff to be diligent no matter what question is asked, so I don't think they're not trying.

28. *Popular Science,* October 1944, "Robot Mathematician Knows All the Answers, A Story about the Mark I."
29. Interview with Olive Watson.
30. Both fights—the one at Watson's house and the one where Tom Jr. cried in the executive's office, are in Watson Jr. and Petre, *Father, Son & Co.,* p. 212.
31. Rodgers, *Think,* p. 225.
32. October 27, 1949, meeting notes. Watson discusses the debt and delivery lag time. IBM Archives.
33. Watson Jr. and Petre, *Father, Son & Co.,* p. 196.
34. Ibid., p. 204; Pugh, *Building IBM,* pp. 167–168.
35. Interview with Birkenstock.
36. Watson Jr. and Petre, *Father, Son & Co.,* p. 205.
37. Interview with Bob Novak, who was at the scene.
38. *Binghamton Press,* July 9, 1949, and July 11, 1949.
39. Leach Amonette, *Among Equals,* pp. 174–175.

CHAPTER 12
1. All entries are from Watson's 1950 datebook. IBM Archives.
2. Watson Jr. and Petre, *Father, Son & Co.,* p. 219.
3. Entry in Watson's date book, plus a letter from Watson, addressed to Harry Hoar and dated January 23, 1950. Watson gave the letter and check to Warren Hoar at the meeting. IBM Archives.
4. "Summary—South American Trip," 1950 but otherwise undated. IBM Archives.
5. Numerous letters and documents about the farm, including a 1940 map of property lines in the area and the farm's profit and loss statements. IBM Archives.
6. Jack Liddell wrote this account in Greenock in 1984. It subsequently was quoted, substantiated, and put in context in a manuscript written in 1999 by Greenock resident Tom Stevenson, who was hired at Greenock's IBM plant soon after it began operating. Local IBM officials edited Stevenson's manuscript and published it in a booklet about IBM Greenock. In 2001, Stevenson read a piece I'd written about Watson for *USA*

Today, and he generously sent me his original manuscript, the IBM booklet, and a letter explaining the origins of both.

7. Dick Watson to Watson, April 6, 1952. IBM Archives.
8. Rodgers, *Think,* p. 264.
9. Interview with Olive Watson.
10. Watson Jr. and Petre, *Father, Son & Co.,* p. 178.
11. Ibid., pp. 178–179.
12. Ibid., p. 180.
13. *Think* magazine, Watson memorial issue, July-September 1956.
14. Westbrook Pegler column from 1952, distributed by King Features Syndicate. Found in the archives of the *Binghamton Press.*
15. Watson Jr. and Petre, *Father, Son & Co.,* p. 220.
16. Ibid., pp. 220–221.
17. *Time* cover story, March 28, 1955.
18. Morison's recollections are all from an "Oral History Interview" conducted for the Harry S. Truman Library on August 10, 1972.
19. Watson Jr. and Petre, *Father, Son & Co.,* p. 217. Watson Jr. refers to a meeting with Attorney General Thomas Clark, who was Morison's superior. Watson and his son might have met with Morison and Clark on separate occasions.
20. Document "Notes taken in Mr. Watson's office," January 5, 1956. IBM Archives. Also, *Unisys History Newsletter,* May 2000.
21. Morison "Oral History Interview," Harry S. Truman Library.
22. "Notes taken in Mr. Watson's office," January 5, 1956. IBM Archives.
23. "When Does a Corporation 'Monopolize' Under the Sherman Anti Trust-Law?" written by John Hayward and sent to Watson. It is undated but must be from the mid-1950s. Hayward seemingly argued the point to Watson many times over the years.
24. Watson Jr. and Petre, *Father, Son & Co.,* p. 219.
25. *New York Times,* January 22, 1952. Also, because the case never went to court, the charge of buying patents for retaliation was never proven. IBM denied the accusation.
26. *Business Machines,* January 29, 1952.
27. Watson to Eisenhower, April 6, 1946. IBM Archives.
28. There are many accounts of Watson wooing Eisenhower to the Columbia presidency. One of the best is in Stephen E.

Ambrose's *Eisenhower, Volume One, Solider, General of the Army, President-Elect, 1890–1952*.

29. Watson to Eisenhower, June 27, 1947. IBM Archives.
30. Eisenhower to Watson, November 17, 1947. IBM Archives.
31. Watson to Eisenhower, January 24, 1948. IBM Archives.
32. Watson to Eisenhower, July 17, 1952. IBM Archives.
33. Campbell-Kelly and Aspray, *Computer: A History of the Information Machine,* p. 121.
34. *Think* magazine, April 22, 1973.
35. CNN.com, *Univac Predicts Winner of 1952 Election,* April 30, 1999.
36. Campbell-Kelly and Aspray, *Computer,* pp. 122–123; CNN.com, April 30, 1999; McCartney, *ENIAC,* p. 95.
37. Rodgers, *Think,* p. 199.

CHAPTER 13

1. In an interview, Jim Birkenstock recalled his attitude toward Watson, which was shared by other young IBM executives: "Watson should have retired in 1939, when he was 65."
2. IBM press release, March 27, 1953.
3. *IBM Record,* April 1953. IBM Archives.
4. "Notes taken during the visit of Dr. Lee DeForest to the Calculator on Thursday, April 10, 1952." IBM Archives.
5. *IBM Record,* April 1953. Hollenbeck erred by calling the 701 "mechanical."
6. Watson Jr. and Petre, *Father, Son & Co.,* pp. 223–224.
7. Ibid., p. 267.
8. Pugh, *Building IBM,* p. 208.
9. Campbell-Kelly and Aspray, *Computer,* p. 126.
10. Stan Augarten, *Bit by Bit: An Illustrated History of Computers,* Houghton Mifflin Company, Boston, 1984.
11. Campbell-Kelly and Aspray, *Computer,* p. 127.
12. Watson Jr. and Petre, *Father, Son & Co.,* p. 223.
13. Ibid., p. 315.
14. All are from scraps found in a folder at the IBM Archives.
15. Meeting notes, November 16, 1955. IBM Archives.
16. Watson to Watson Jr., March 3, 1955. IBM Archives.
17. The quotes are from Watson Jr. and Petre, *Father, Son & Co.,* p. 271. Two other accounts are in Rodgers, *Think,* p. 227; and Belden and Belden, *Lengthening Shadow,* p. 311. All three

accounts describe the six-line note from Watson exactly the same.

18. Watson to Phillips, February 26, 1956. IBM Archives.
19. Dates and entries are from Watson's 1956 date book. IBM Archives.
20. Watson Jr. and Petre, *Father, Son & Co.,* p. 271.
21. *New York Times,* May 10, 1956.
22. Woodbridge to Watson, May 9, 1956. IBM Archives.
23. Nickerson to Watson, May 10, 1956. IBM Archives.
24. Meigs to Watson, May 29, 1956. IBM Archives.
25. As reported in *Fortune* magazine, September 1956.
26. *Fortune,* September 1956.
27. *New York Times,* June 20, 1956.
28. *San Francisco Chronicle,* June 20, 1956.

CHAPTER 14
1. Peter F. Drucker, *The Ecological Vision,* Transaction Publishers, 1993, pp. 47–58.
2. Nixon tapes, March 14, 1972.
3. *Fortune,* September 1956.
4. *Fortune,* November 22, 1999.
5. Louis V. Gerstner Jr., *Who Says Elephants Can't Dance?: Inside IBM's Historic Turnaround,* Harper Business, 2002, p. 182.
6. Interview with Lou Gerstner at IBM headquarters, October 29, 2002.

INDEX

GAYLORD S